EDINBURGH'S TRANSPORT

First Published, 1964

© D. L. G. HUNTER, 1964

ERRATA
The Publishers and Author regret the following and crave readers' indulgence.
Page 293 Line 3. For pages 297/8 read 298, 299 and 300.
Page 357 Half way down. 152 ASF 364 (New 1935) read New 1937.
Page 363 Under O Leyland Lioness. No. 2. was SY 3388 and not SY 338 as stated.
Page 377 15 lines down, Daimler SC 7889 was Number 748 and not 148 as stated.

Edinburgh's Transport

by

D. L. G. HUNTER
M.I.Mech.E., M.Inst.T.

Printed and Published by
THE ADVERTISER PRESS LIMITED, HUDDERSFIELD, YORKSHIRE

STEAM-HAULED BUS OF 1870 run between Edinburgh and Leith

CONTENTS

5

ILLUSTRATIONS

PREFACE

Of all the public services in any community transport has generally attracted people's interest more than other services since the individual user is inevitably more closely identified with its operations. It is surely fitting that its history should be recorded, the more especially since the pattern of transport in our lives is now so rapidly changing. It is hoped that the story will interest the general reader who knows Scotland's capital and its surroundings, as well as the specialist who is interested in the subject as such and for whom some of the considerable detail is necessarily given.

No excuse is made for the extended treatment given to the tramways and buses where this has been possible, for little on these has appeared in print before. On the other hand the literature of railways is prolific and so the student of road transport history has long been at a disadvantage.

Some readers may have preferred the adoption of the now usual code for describing bus body types, but it was felt that this was not suitable for the many types of twenty five years ago, so different from today.

Much of the information regarding the cable tramways appeared in your author's article in the "Journal of Transport History" for May 1954 to which invaluable publication due acknowledgement must be made.

The material has been gathered from contemporary sources, principally the files of "The Scotsman" and "The Leith Burghs Pilot", but also from the predecessors of "The Passenger Transport

Journal" and "The Transport World" and in some cases the "Edinburgh Evening News", to all of which acknowledgement is due; also the minutes of Edinburgh Town Council, of Leith Town Council and the Edinburgh Transport Department's annual reports. These sources have necessarily been supplemented by the author's copious notes, many old documents and time-tables and much information gathered from a host of individuals over many years.

This history could not have been written without the help which has been given by very many people, and in now expressing grateful thanks to those mentioned it is hoped that anyone inadvertently omitted will exercise forgiveness. Thanks are especially due to the following: The present and past staff of Edinburgh Corporation Transport including Messrs. W. M. Little, T. Gray, T. Glass, J. Henderson, J. Thomson, D. K. Francis, the late R. Shaw, the late E. O. Catford, and many others, inspectors, drivers, conductors and staff at Shrubhill works, whose names it would be impracticable to list.

James Amos, former Chairman, and the present and past staff of Scottish Omnibuses Ltd. including Messrs. R. Mackenzie, R. Beveridge, T. Kinley, J. Clark, the late A. Bracken, the late R. Harrison, and several drivers and others.

Others who must be specially mentioned are : Mr. R. M. Hogg of the British Transport Commission Historical Records at Waterloo Place, Mr. Gordon of the City's Archives Department, Mr. D. Macrae of the Motor Taxation Office, Mr. C. H. A. Collyns of the South Scotland Electricity Board, and Messrs. J. Blair, W. Cheyne, J. Coutts, T. Findlater, G. E. Langmuir, J. Lindores, N. Main, D. Munro, W. L. Russell, J. R. Williamson.

Also the staff of the Central and Leith branches of Edinburgh Public Libraries for their labours in getting out the many large volumes required, and Messrs. Thomas Murray and Company Limited for the loan of their record file of Murray's Edinburgh Diaries and to Mr. C. R. Clinker for his help in reading and editing the original manuscript.

Mention must also be made of the illustrations, for while acknowledgment is gladly given where the photographer is known, use has been made of a considerable number of interesting old photographs the origin of which could not be traced. For their anonymous use only apology can be offered, and it is hoped that anyone thus overlooked will appreciate the regard placed in their works by its inclusion in this book. A number of blocks have kindly been lent by the individuals and organisations shown, and in addition Scottish Omnibuses Ltd. have been generous in providing the blocks for most of the illustrations of their vehicles and also certain others. The plates of the E.C.T. and S.M.T. tickets are from the fine Reinohl collection at the Institute of Transport where facilities were kindly provided. The end paper has been borrowed from "Speed" for which thanks are due to Edinburgh Corporation Transport.

The dust cover is a reproduction of a drawing by Robin Paterson and kindly loaned by I. Cormack.

In conclusion production of the book has been made possible by the kind co-operation of Ian Cormack of the Scottish Tramway Museum Society and G. Halstead of the publishers, to both of whom thanks are also due.

D. L. G. HUNTER

INTRODUCTION

A hundred years or so ago public travelling facilities in and around Edinburgh were mainly provided by horse-drawn omnibuses and coaches which rattled over the cobbled streets of the town and along the dusty roads of the surrounding districts. Some of these vehicles were old stage coaches, or in the summer time "brakes". The latter was a vehicle with rows of benches, and no sides, access being usually gained by a ladder.

Omnibuses ran from the Tron to the Shore at Leith every five minutes, and from Dean Terrace, Stockbridge to Minto Street, Newington every half-hour. From the East end of Princes Street omnibuses ran to Granton in connection with the ferry steamers; and there was also a less frequent service to Morningside.

One could travel further afield by coach. Ratho, West Linton, Innerleithen, and Earlston were served daily, while more frequent journeys were made to Penicuik, Lasswade, and Dalkeith. Two operators each provided an hourly service to Portobello, and there were connections also between Dalkeith and Portobello and Musselburgh.

Of course it must be realised that even these latter were quite separate towns, and the districts we regard as suburbs of the City today, such as Colinton, Corstorphine, Liberton, or Granton, were then little villages right out in the country. A week at some such resort was a fine summer holiday to those who could afford it. This leads to the difficulty of defining the limits of the area with which our survey should deal. While it is intended to concentrate on the City and immediately surrounding districts, it will be necessary, especially in the light of modern facilities, to allude to places a good deal further away. Though a hard and fast line cannot be drawn, a radius of about twenty miles south of the Forth may serve as a guide.

Except for the short journeys the railways provided the more usual means of conveyance. The main lines as we now know them were in use and even the local services were competitive. From

11

Canal Street station, at what is now the Waverley Market, trains went by rope down the tunnel to Scotland Street station, from where locomotives took them to Bonnington and Leith, — the erstwhile North Leith station at the Citadel, — every fifteen minutes. Several of them carried a portion which was detached at Scotland Street to proceed by locomotive to Trinity and Granton, where passengers and goods were ferried to Fife. The Musselburgh branch was served seven times a day from the General Station, — later to be known as Waverley when it was reconstructed. From the tiny station of South Leith, which can still be seen at Tower Street, trains ran to Portobello, connecting with the main line. This had been a part of the Leith branch of the old Edinburgh and Dalkeith Railway, perhaps better known locally as the "Innocent Railway".* The main line of the latter from St. Leonards station, and its Fisherrow branch had already been superseded for passenger traffic by the new North British line from the General Station through Portobello to Niddrie.

The opening in May 1868 of the new line through Abbeyhill to Trinity and Bonnington brought the closure of the Scotland Street tunnel route, the North Leith and Granton trains then taking the new route to and from the Waverley station and calling at intermediate stations at Abbeyhill, (opened February 1869), and Leith Walk. The Caledonian had the branch from Slateford to Granton but this did not have any passenger service. The North British company were also operating branch line trains to South Queensferry via Kirkliston, Dalmeny and New Halls; to Macmerry, serving Smeaton, Ormiston, and Winton; to Dalkeith; and to Polton serving Broomieknowe, and Lasswade. Looking a little further afield, there were also the Peebles, Dolphinton, North Berwick, and Haddington branches. The Peebles branch had stations at Bonnyrigg, Hawthornden, (as far as which the line was double), Rosslynlee, Pomathorn, Leadburn, and Eddleston. The Dolphinton branch from Leadburn served Lamancha, Macbiehill, and Broomlee which was the station for West Linton. Dirleton station, about a mile from the village, was on the North Berwick branch from Drem, while there was no intermediate station on the Haddington branch from Longniddry. A ferry to Fife ran from New Hall Pier on the South Queensferry branch. Excepting North Leith, Granton, and Musselburgh, all the North British branches were single line.

* The origin of the name is found in Robert Chambers' essay (in Vol. 1 of Select Writings of Robert Chambers; Edinburgh 1847) wherein he says a friend of his "calls it The Innocent Railway, as being so peculiar for its indestructive character, and also with some reference to the simplicity of its style of management". The essay is well worth reading. It is not true that no one was ever hurt on this railway.

The North British main line stations were at Portobello, Joppa, New Hailes, Inveresk, Prestonpans, Longniddry, Drem, East Fortune, East-Linton, and Dunbar to the East: Millerhill, Eskbank, Dalhousie, Gorebridge, Fushiebridge, Tynehead, Heriot, Fountainhall, Stow, Bowland, and Galashiels to the South: Haymarket, Corstorphine, Gogar, Ratho, Winchburgh, and Linlithgow, also Drumshoreland for Broxburn, Uphall, Livington, and Bathgate to the West. The Caledonian served stations at Slateford, Kingsknowe, Currie, Ravelrig, and Mid-Calder. The latter station in fact lies between the villages of Kirknewton and East-Calder; and Prestonpans, Corstorphine, Uphall, and Livingston station were all a considerable distance from their respective villages.

It is perhaps not out of place to mention that in the summer seasons steamers sailed from Granton to Alloa and Stirling, and from Leith to Aberdour in Fife. The former were transferred to Leith also in 1870. These steamer facilities were more in the nature of excursions and so hardly form part of our survey. Nevertheless they increased in scope considerably in the seventies and eighties and did provide a useful link to Aberdour, Burntisland, Kirkcaldy, etc. at very cheap rates. Several firms were involved, some using tug boats, but well appointed paddle vessels regularly ran the important trips. M. P. Galloway, of Leith, which later, with railway interests, became the Galloway Saloon Steam Packet Co. was probably the best known concern. The opening of the pier at Portobello in 1871 gave the trade a fillip. At Leith the West Pier was the usual starting point though some used the Shore on the Inner Harbour. Sunday sailings were popular and occupied the attentions of the Sabbath Alliance whose protests were made in many quarters.

New ideas on transport have often been developed in the Edinburgh area. Some of the earliest colliery wagonways were to be found in the adjacent coalfields, and Leith was the scene of some of the earliest experiments with steam coaches. There was a revival of interest in the latter in the late sixties.

R. W. Thomson, a Stonehaven man who travelled abroad and then settled in Edinburgh, practising as a civil engineer, had been designing light traction engines which were built for him by Messrs. Tennant and Co. at their Bowershall works. These machines of six horsepower and weighing under six tons had indiarubber tyres and were being successfully used in 1870 to haul substantial loads to the docks and elsewhere. To comply with the law, a boy had to run ahead bearing a red flag and Mr. Thomson was in trouble for failing to fulfil this requirement on occasion. An omnibus proprietor, Mr. A. Ritchie, thought this machine might be an improvement on his horse buses between Edinburgh and Leith, and he had a passenger carrying trailer built by Messrs. Drew and Burnet. This rather cumbersome vehicle was carried on a single axle, and seated 21 passengers inside. 44 passengers could be carried on top and were protected, — in some measure, — by an awning. When the outfit had been tried with success, Mr. Ritchie was prevailed upon to run it on the Portobello route instead, and this service started on 2 June 1870, the vehicle rejoicing in the name of "New Favourite".

Another Leith engineer, Andrew Nairn, had also produced a somewhat similar traction engine, a three-wheeler of eight horsepower with hemp tyres, and he was now at work on an omnibus incorporating his engine. This vehicle also ran on three wheels and had a three-cylinder engine and a "Field" type boiler. It weighed seven tons and carried eighteen passengers inside and 32 on top. It appears to have been intended to call it the "Edinburgh" though contemporary reports refer to "Pioneer". This machine was however either rebuilt or replaced by a ten ton "Pioneer" in 1871, and was hired by a bus proprietor named Johnston, who, after running some demonstration trips put it to regular public service on the Portobello route on 2 June of that year charging 4d inside and 3d. outside. It ran twelve trips a day for four months, till one day it caught fire. It was thereafter purchased by a David Charters who restarted a half-hourly service to Portobello in October 1871.

Another steam bus appeared in 1872, designed by Leonard J. Todd of Leith. This was a four-wheeled machine seating 20 inside and 50 on top, and in this case an awning was provided. It seems to have been an improvement on "Pioneer" and bearing the name "Edinburgh", was operated between the West End and Bernard Street, with $\frac{1}{2}$d. "outside" fare stages.

While these steam omnibuses were fairly successful, the roads were still unsatisfactory for such vehicles and they did not survive. The legal necessity for a boy to run in front with a red flag was an impediment too. So the public were still dependent on the horse-bus services provided by a number of proprietors. John Croall was probably the biggest operator, but others were Robert Aitken, A Ritchie, George Hall, T. Johnston, David Adamson who joined forces with Mr. Atkinson, and Messrs. Carse and Co. Regular services were running between High Street and Leith every twelve minutes; Newington and Haymarket every hour; West

End and Leith every seven minutes; Newington and Stockbridge every half-hour; and a circular route from Princes Street via Newington and Morningside every hour. The vehicles running on these routes were painted respectively yellow, orange, green, blue, and red. Croall also ran to Portobello and Musselburgh; to Dalkeith; and to Lasswade. A Mr. Elliot also ran a coach to Musselburgh. Ratho, and Queensferry for Dunfermline in Fife were served also. Competition was keen at this time and led to the introduction of three-horse teams instead of two. A new route was started in March 1869 from the Mound to Bonnington and Newhaven, every hour. George Hall was the original proprietor but the route seems to have been taken over by Croall and Atkinson. The routes, stances, timetables, and number displayed on the vehicles were fixed by the Magistrates under a Provisional Order of 1867. Conductors were required to display on their coat the number of their bus. There were twenty buses plying between Edinburgh and Leith, but in May 1870 the various proprietors agreed to a measure of regulation among themselves. Two buses were taken off the Morningside circular route, and one each from the Newington — Leith, Newington — Haymarket, and Newington — Stockbridge routes. There were no more cut fares; 3d. inside and 2d. outside was standardised.

From 16 May 1870 therefore the services provided were as follows : West End to Leith every six minutes run by Croall, Carse, Adamson, and Ritchie with buses Nos. 1 to 9 and 26. High Street to Leith each hour and at 12, 30, 42, and 54 minutes past each hour, run by Croall, and Carse with buses Nos. 11, 13, 14, 15, and 31. Princes Street, Grange, Morningside circle every hour, run by Croall with No. 17 clockwise and No. 18 anti-clockwise. Register to Morningside Asylum every hour run by Atkinson's No. 19. Stockbridge to Newington, run by Croall, Atkinson, and Adamson, with buses Nos. 16, 22, and 24. Mound to Newhaven, every hour by Croall, and Atkinson, with Nos. 29 and 23. High Street to Newhaven, every hour, by Croall's No. 27. Haymarket to Lauder Road, every half-hour, by Croall, and Atkinson, with Nos. 20 and 32. Haymarket and Duncan Street, every hour, by Adamson's No. 33. In several cases operators exchanged routes with one another on alternate weeks. Ritchie sought to run a bus from Waverley to Strathearn Road in December 1870 but permission was not granted. It is of interest to note that the services did not start till about 9.0 or 10.0 a.m.; the workman could not afford bus fares and generally lived near his work if he could.

However an important new development was afoot. In the 1860s there had been some experiments in other parts of the country with street tramways, and in 1870 "An Act to facilitate the construction and to regulate the working of Tramways" was passed. This act was a landmark in transport history, and empowered local authorities, or with the latter's consent, other persons or companies, to obtain Provisional Orders from the Board of Trade authorising the construction of tramways. Various rules and regulations were laid down concerning the construction and other matters, and the Orders had to be confirmed by Act of Parliament. An important point was that a local authority having constructed or acquired a tramway, were not to operate it, but could with the consent of the Board of Trade, lease to any person the right of using it.

Edinburgh should not lag in this new system of course, and so the press, while appreciating the improvements the horse-bus proprietors had made, and also the steam buses already mentioned, urged the formation of a company to provide a tramway system. So let us now proceed to the development of passenger travel in and around the City after 1870, it its various forms.

I

THE HORSE TRAMS AND BUSES

Two groups of promotors put up tramway bills in 1870. The first, styled the Edinburgh and Leith Tramways was handled by Messrs. H. & A. Inglis, W.S. and sought powers of incorporation and to lay down and work the following tramways: 1. From Donaldson's Hospital west gate to the east end of Waterloo Place; 2. Post Office to Powburn, Newington; 3. West End to Jordanburn, Morningside; 4. Post Office to Foot of Leith Walk; 5. Foot of Leith Walk to Bernard Street; 6 Foot of Leith Walk via North Junction Street to the Chain Pier at Newhaven; 7. St. Andrew Street to Picardy Place; 8. Hanover Street, Heriot Row, Howe Street to Stockbridge and Comely Bank; 9. Church Lane, Newbattle Terrace, Whitehouse Terrace and Grange Loan to Salisbury Place. Triangular junctions were proposed at the Post Office, St. Andrew Street, and Hanover Street. All the routes were to be double line except the portion through Newhaven from the Whale Brae to the Chain Pier.

The other concern, the Edinburgh Street Tramways, was in the hands of Messrs. Lindsay and Paterson, W.S. and Thomas Bouch, the engineer of the first Tay Bridge, was connected with it. This scheme seemed to find more favour and the Edinburgh and Leith Tramways promotors, in the interests of an agreed scheme arranged to drop their bill. Edinburgh and Leith town councils both supported the scheme, but when the former learned that the North British Railway were not opposing the bill because they believed they would be able to use the system for goods traffic, they quickly insisted on a protective clause. The Sabbath Alliance likewise secured some protection regarding Sunday traffic. Agreement being thus reached the bill was passed unopposed.

The Edinburgh Street Tramways Company was thus incorporated on 29 June 1871 by the Edinburgh Tramways Act 1871, which authorised the company to construct the following tramways "to be worked by animal power only" in Edinburgh, Leith, and Portobello:

1. Haymarket to Portobello, (Bellfield Lane).
2. Register House to Bernard Street, Leith.
3. St. Andrew Street to Picardy Place.
4. Frederick Street to Stockbridge, (Kerr Street).
5. from Royal Circus via Great King Street, Pitt Street, Golden-acre, Trinity Road, Trinity Crescent, Stanley Road, Newhaven Road, Ferry Road, and Junction Street to Foot of Leith Walk. Also a loop along East Trinity Road to Stanley Road with triangular junctions at each end.
6. Post Office to Powburn, Newington.
7. West End to Churchhill.
8. from Churchhill via Clinton Road, Hope Terrace, Kilgraston Road, and Grange Road to Salisbury Place.
9. from Earl Grey Street, Tollcross via Lauriston Place and Chambers Street (then being made) to South Bridge.
10. Haymarket to Coltbridge (Railway bridge).

There were to be triangular junctions also at the Post Office, St. Andrew Street and Frederick Street. The section from the Foot of Leith Walk to Charlotte Street, Leith was single line with one passing loop, otherwise double lines were proposed, but crossovers were to be provided in the narrow streets.

The capital of the Company was £300,000 and the works were to be completed within three years. Other clauses laid down the gauge to be 4ft. 8½in.; Fares not to exceed 1d. per mile, though 3d. could be the minimum fare until three years after the opening when the Board of Trade could reduce this to 2d. Two workmen's cars were to be run on each route with ½d. per mile fares and 1d. minimum; and there were to be no Sunday services without the local authorities' consent. Attached to the Act were Schedules of agreement with the local authorities which gave them power to regulate the traffic in the same manner as they did the omnibus traffic. Under one of these agreements Edinburgh Corporation undertook to widen the North Bridge within two years and the Company were to pay £2500 towards the cost of this work. The Haymarket to Leith, Newington, and Morningside sections were to be constructed immediately and the remainder as soon as possible. The Chairman of the Company was Dr. Alex. Wood, and D. W. Paterson the Secretary. Some compensation was paid to some of the omnibus proprietors.

The Company's Engineer was John Macrae, and the con-struction of the lines was let to a contractor named James Gowans (later Sir) who proceeded rapidly with wrought iron rails weighing 52 lbs. per yard laid on longitudinal timbers which in turn rested on a concrete bed and were tied to gauge by wrought iron tie-bars.

On Monday 6 November 1871 the first section, from Bernard Street to Haymarket, was opened to traffic without ceremony. Throughout most of the day a six minute service was provided between Leith and the West End with alternate cars proceeding on to Haymarket. Although the loop via York Place and St. Andrew Street was also completed this was not used at that time, the cars proceeding by Leith Street and the Post Office with the aid of an extra pair of trace horses up the hill. Ten cars, apparently of German manufacture, were operated, the horses being provided under contract by John Croall. The horses were adorned with bells on their necks and the drivers had a whistle with which to warn other traffic. The fare from the Register House to either terminus was 2d. inside and 1d. outside. The whole journey cost 3d. inside and 2d. outside.

The service quickly proved very popular and by the end of the year most of the omnibuses on the route had succumbed: only three were left. Croall had withdrawn theirs from the route immediately. The branch from the Foot of Leith Walk to Junction Bridge was now laid and cars commenced to use it about the middle of January 1872. There was no intimation of this and the public were now beginning to have doubts about the management. It appears that the service was looked after by an Inspector and that the "management" was in the hands of D. W. Paterson, the Secretary. The cars were heavy and therefore slow, and the service unreliable. The press, especially in Leith, voiced complaint of the lack of experienced men to direct the Company's operations. The level of the rails was causing difficulty in some places and the St. Andrew Street — York Place curve had to be relaid. Even the oil used in the lamps had a bad smell!

In April 1872 the Company advertised the service as follows : Between Bernard Street and Haymarket via Leith Street every 16 minutes; Between Junction Bridge and Haymarket via Leith Street every 16 minutes; From Bernard Street to St. Andrew Street via York Place and returning via Leith Street every 8 minutes.

But from 1 May this was altered to a five minutes service between Leith and Haymarket via Leith Street, most of the cars running to Bernard Street. The York Place line thus dropped out of use again.

Gowans the contractor had started on the Newington line at the end of January 1872 and this was nearly finished by the spring, when objection was raised that the North Bridge, — still un-widened, — was too narrow for a double line, and interdict was threatened. This was overcome however and the line was completed and advertised to be opened on Saturday 25 May 1872. This had to be cancelled and the new service actually started on 29 May.

Four cars provided a ten minutes service from the Post Office to Duncan Street, it being announced that they would continue on to the foot of Minto Street and back to the Duncan Street stance if time permitted, which proved to be the case. The fare was 2d. inside and 1d. outside. 3d. inside transfer tickets could also be bought.

Another complaint arose over the narrowness of the top of Leith Street, and from 10 June the street was closed and the cars diverted to the York Place loop for a fortnight or so while adjustments were made. Similar complaints were made in respect of the Grange route, then under construction. This route was opened as far as the top of Marchmont Road on 6 July, alternate cars being diverted from the Newington line thus giving a twenty minutes service. At the same time the Newington cars made Mayfield Loan their terminus and returned back to Salisbury Place "wrong line."

The Board of Trade also raised complaint regarding the level of the rails, and improvements were applied in the construction of the Morningside section, including clasp plates instead of bolts and nuts to secure the rails to the sleepers. Later, Gowans introduced a new rail, 21ft. long with a wide bottom resting on soleplates direct on the concrete bed, the wooden sleepers being eliminated.

With the opening of the new line from the West End by Churchhill to the Grange Road on 11 November, the Company revised their services, announcing that sixteen "light and commodious cars" had been added to their stock. A ten minutes service was now provided over three routes: Bernard Street and Haymarket; Leith and Powburn; and the Princes Street — Churchhill — Grange — Bridges circle. The cars carried coloured destination boards, and coloured lights at night, respectively red; green and red; and green. Some cars ran to Junction Bridge instead of to Bernard Street. New 2d. inside and 1d. outside fares were given between Post Office and Grange; Salisbury Place and Churchhill; Churchhill and West End; Tollcross and Post Office; while 3d. inside and 2d. outside applied between Post Office and Churchhill. A ride right round the circular route cost 6d. inside and 4d. outside.

While the superior comfort of the cars was generally admitted the service that the system offered was a growing disappointment. There were other complaints. The car wheels were unguarded and thought to be dangerous: They ran too close to the pavement in some places: The horses were overworked; etc. There were a number of accidents, some fatal; and many Court cases on charges of furious driving; of obstruction both by and to trams; of overcrowding; touting; bad timekeeping, and other things. Furious riding of trace horses also came before the Court, and the omnibus crews did not escape either. Town Councillors and Baillies who were alleged to be tramway shareholders were accused of putting their own interests first. The rails in Princes Street were laid well to the North side and many wanted them relaid nearer the other side so that carriages had room to reach the shops. The parking and waiting problem was with us then! Mechanical power, such as steam engines, was suggested in place of the poor horses. The city authorities urged the Company to put the earlier tracks in order in compliance with the Board of Trade complaint.

Thus encouraged, the omnibus proprietors had drifted back and proclaimed a 1d. fare inside or out between Register House and Newington, and a "fast bus" every ten minutes from Hope Park to Leith cutting the tram's journey time by ten minutes. The Edinburgh and Leith General Omnibus Co. (Ltd.) was formed on 23 October 1872 to take over Adamson's business (five buses and sixty horses) and buy new buses, and to run extended services beyond the City. The Hope Park terminus was extended to Duncan Street. The Edinburgh and Leith General Omnibus Co. had Nos. 22, 26, 28, 30, and 34 on the route, and Atkinson had a share with Nos. 20, 23, and 24. Croall's Stockbridge bus now ran from Waterloo Place every fifteen minutes, but Atkinson still ran half-hourly from Duncan Street now using his No. 19. From 21 April 1873 the Edinburgh and Leith General Omnibus Co. put on new Nos. 1 and 2 giving a half-hour service from West End to Leith, but in August concentrated their seven new buses on the Newington to Leith route. The crews were resplendent in scarlet coats and caps. So for a while, up till the summer of 1873, the buses enjoyed something of a "come-back", but in the end they had to give up.

Late in November 1872 the Company gave notice of their intention to promote a Parliamentary bill the next year. The main provisions of this bill were : An extension of time, limited to one year, for the construction of the Portobello route; the Stockbridge route; the route through Trinity and Newhaven to Leith except for the part in Ferry Road between Junction Bridge and Newhaven Road; and the route from Tollcross to Chambers Street: Power to make additional crossings, sidings, and connections: Authority to use other than animal power provided the local authority agreed : and authority to buy and run omnibuses. Many regarded the extension of time as an attempt to abandon the construction of the aforementioned routes. While this found favour in some quarters, particularly in Leith and Trinity, the Edinburgh Town Council eventually decided to oppose the bill, although the Company offered to withdraw the provision for "other than animal power". The provision for additional sidings and connections worried many citizens for it was recalled that railway companies wanted to use the tramway tracks to gain access to various parts of the town, and the sight of a railway wagon being pulled along Princes Street, —even by a horse—was unthinkable. It should be remembered that at that time many of the railway facilities to Leith had not been constructed, and the Caledonian Company was at a disadvantage in the keen competitive conditions of the times. A Committee of Owners and Occupiers of Property on the Tramway Lines in the City of Edinburgh was appointed at a public meeting and took steps to oppose the bill. Charles Jenner was chairman.

Nevertheless the Edinburgh Street Tramways Act 1873 was passed on 5 August, though the provision for additional sidings and connections had been struck out, as also were the clause to use other than animal power, and authority to buy and run omnibuses. Parliament added three new clauses. The routes were to be laid with a single track if the local authority or road authority so decided. The latter also had power to approach the Board of Trade if they found a line to be dangerous, and the Board of Trade could, after enquiry, call for alterations, including altering to a single track if necessary, though the local authority or road authority were to meet the cost of such alterations. A penalty of £50 per day up to a total of 5% on the total estimated cost of their schemes, viz. £156,220 was to be imposed in the event of non-completion of the works unless arising from accident etc. Both the Company and the opposition expressed themselves as satisfied! The threat of goods traffic was removed. This was common enough elsewhere in the country but the nearest approach to it in Edinburgh was the temporary sand car in 1937.

Meanwhile construction inwards to Haymarket of the Coltbridge extension was commenced in February 1873 and opened about the beginning of June, the route being covered by a sparse service between Coltbridge and Powburn. It was proposed to start work on the Ferry Road and Newhaven route in April but this appears to have been deferred on account of the opposition to a double line. Leith Town Council tried to persuade the Company to arrange a bus service instead, but in October the Company agreed, — in accordance with their new Act, — to lay this route as a single line with passing loops.

On 23 April 1873 a trial was made with a spring wire guard before and between the wheels of the cars, but this was not very successful. On the other hand an increase in the diameter of the cars' wheels from 2ft. 6in. to 3ft. 6in. proved beneficial as might be expected. A few months later, Henry Shiels, the Company's Carriage Superintendent, evolved a more successful life guard, although apparently of similar pattern.

Accidents continued to occur however, and it appears there was difficulty in winding on the brakes in emergency. A sprag

22

could be dropped to prevent a run-back, and a similar arrangement fitted with a pneumatic cushion was proposed as an emergency brake. The effectiveness of the brakes as such was also in question, as there was sometimes difficulty in controlling a car, e.g. on Leith Street. There was a particularly nasty occurrence on 24 September 1873, when one of the last cars at night overcame brakes and horses descending the hill. The horses tried to get clear and fell near the Theatre Royal. The harness gave way and left them aside, the car, No. 20, careering on down Leith Walk unchecked until it crashed into the back of a preceding car at Shrubhill, resulting in a number of injuries.

The overworked horses still aroused indignation, and the Company too, was not very happy about the position and their contract with Croalls who kept increasing their charges. According to D. K. Clark* the type of animal used was not suited to the arduous duty. So the following year, 1874, the Company terminated Croall's contract and acquired the horses at a valuation of only £28 each, thereafter providing the horses themselves. During the following two years the stud was replaced by sturdier beasts, and a rota was arranged whereby they worked a few months on the heavier sections and then had a spell on the easier parts of the system where they recovered their strength. This was an improvement, but even so the system was probably the most difficult in the country to work. In 1876 the horses could average only 5.8 miles per day and the average cost was 7¾d. per mile. But the "powers that be" had rejected "other than animal power".

In July 1873 alterations to the tracks at the foot of Constitution Street were carried out and the cars turned short at Charlotte Street for a few days. In October a proposal to provide loop sidings for waiting cars at the Waverley Market and at Haymarket was rejected. Then on 8 November a new timetable and fare schedule was introduced. Details are lacking but "The Scotsman" indicated the fare changes were "towards an increase". Both Edinburgh and Leith Town Councils protested and the Company agreed from 12 November to reintroduce the 2d. inside and 1d. outside fare between "Waterloo Place" and Bernard Street or Junction Bridge. From the Foot of Leith Walk to either of the termini was 1d. outside or in. Discount tickets were withdrawn. Then on 25 December 1873 the Register House to Bernard Street or Junction Bridge became 2d. both outside and in, but two cars either way at 5.10 p.m. and 6.10 p.m. were announced to carry workmen outside for 1d.

Work was now proceeding on the Ferry Road and Newhaven line and this was opened in January 1874, cars running from the

* "Tramways; Their Construction and Working," Second Edition, 1894.

new terminus at the west end of Stanley Road every half-hour to St. Andrew Street via York Place and returning via Leith Street. After turning into Ferry Road the extension was single line with three passing loops in Ferry Road and another three in Newhaven Road. A short siding curved southwards into Craighall Road at the terminus. There was a facing crossover east of Junction Bridge. A new timetable commencing 17 January 1874 shows four cars on this service, four on the Bernard Street — Newington line, eight on Bernard Street — Haymarket, three on Coltbridge — Powburn, and six each way round the Morningside circle. In the summer of 1874 two cars were run between Coltbridge and Newhaven via York Place. The Stanley Road cars were extended to the West End in the summer of 1875.

Early in 1874 after considerable discussion, and resulting from some influential instigation as to the desirability thereof in the interests of the animals, the Corporation concluded that it had power to license drivers and trace boys, and this measure of control was put into effect.

The widening of the North Bridge under the agreement between the Corporation and the Company scheduled to the 1871 Act had also been started on 11 November 1873, but the stipulated two year period for its completion had, of course, already expired. A further Act was therefore called for, and in this the Company obtained important changes in its commitments.

Passed on 30 June 1874, The Edinburgh Tramways Act, 1874, provided a three years extension of time for the widening of the North Bridge by the Corporation. On completion of the work the Company were to lift their tracks and lay a single line in the middle of the roadway. They were also empowered to construct the Portobello route as a single line. It also allowed the Company to abandon the construction of the routes from Frederick Street to Stockbridge, and through Trinity to Stanley Road, and also the Tollcross to South Bridge route. The Company however were required to pay the Edinburgh Road Trust within twelve months sums totalling £3000, to be applied to causewaying the sides of streets in which tracks were laid. They were further bound, when required by the local authority, to arrange for a "good and sufficient conveyance by means of omnibuses" between Princes Street and Stockbridge, and between the Royal Institution (at the Mound) in Princes Street and such point in Trinity as the local authority of Leith may fix. A minimum fifteen minutes service was stipulated for the former, and on the latter a twenty minutes service between 9.00 a.m. and 9.00 p.m. from June to September and a half-hourly service between 9.00 a.m. and 8.00 p.m. for the rest of the year. The Company were accordingly empowered to buy horses and buses for this purpose. A fare not exceeding 2d. per mile for first class passengers was authorised on these routes, and on "any tramway routes worked in connexion therewith", but the through bus and car fare between Stockbridge and Newington was not to exceed 3d. first class and 2d. second class. The words "any tramway routes worked in connexion therewith" were soon to give rise to great trouble.

Horse-hauled tramcars were clearly impracticable on these steep North side routes and the buses plying between Stockbridge and the Register House and the Mound and Trinity continued to run. The Trinity terminus was at Stanley Road. This service appears to have been provided on behalf of the Company by Croall.

Construction of the Portobello route was commenced at Bellfield Lane terminus in October 1874, and in accordance with the provisions of the 1874 Act, was made a single line with passing loops.

A small car shed and stables were built at Rosefield Place, not far from the Portobello terminus. The service from Waterloo Place was opened on 12 May 1875, but did not immediately crush the omnibuses running on this route. This now completed the Company's system as then authorised, and amounted to 13⅜ miles.

In 1874 the Company again enjoyed a monopoly on Leith Walk, and at this period adopted a most uncompromising attitude towards the public. The most serious complaint arose over their action in charging inside passengers 3d. from Bernard Street to the Post Office. In November 1874 Leith Town Council decided to test the matter in Court as the distance was less than two miles. On instructions therefore, Leith's Town's Officer, Alex. Torbain, made the journey and sued the Company for the penny overcharge. The case was heard in the Sheriff Court on 4 December when the Company argued that by Section 4 of their 1874 Act they were empowered to charge up to 2d. per mile for first class passengers, i.e. inside, on their Stockbridge and Trinity buses "and on any tramway routes worked in connexion therewith", and claimed that their whole tramway system was "in connexion therewith"! The Sheriff gave his decision in favour of the plaintiff and the Company appealed to the Court of Session. This would take some time, so a notice was displayed in the cars stating that until the final decision was given the fare was 3d. inside. Many passengers refused to pay and several had their names and addresses taken. It seems conductors accepted two pennies but if change was required retained 3d. The Leith folk complained the fare was now the same as it had been on the buses: Where was the promised advantage? On the other hand passengers who sought to pay only one penny for short journeys, — under one mile, — were successfully sued by the Company for their 2d. minimum fare.

In November 1875 Lord Shand also decided against the Company in the Court of Session, whereupon the Company appealed to the House of Lords. There was of course a further long delay and meanwhile the Company continued to be awkward with passengers. When some residents in Ferry Road asked the correct fare to Fort Street Mr. Paterson referred them to the time-tables displayed on the cars. On pointing out that the information was not there given, Mr. Paterson wrote to say he had no more information to offer! The Workmen's cars had apparently been dropped after only a few weeks operation and now both Edinburgh and Leith Town Councils had to prod the Company into running them again. They had already had to insist on the Company meeting its obligations regarding the frequency of the Trinity bus service.

The inconvenience of the single line scheme for the North Bridge had now become apparent, and an amending act was passed on 19 July 1875, the Edinburgh Tramways Act 1875, which permitted the double line to remain except between the Tron Church and the south end of the actual bridge.

In 1876 the Company promoted a Bill to extend their Porto-bello route to Musselburgh terminating at Pinkie Dykes, and to enable them to work the route with mechanical or other than animal power. There had already been another proposal for a roadside steam tramway from Portobello, through Musselburgh, Tranent, and Haddington to East Linton. The House of Lords had not heard the Company's fares case yet, but as the tide seemed to be against them the Company sought to make sure of their increased fare by including a clause in this new Bill authorising a 3d. fare between Edinburgh and Leith.

The Musselburgh people supported the Bill wholeheartedly and Portobello Town Council's support was also secured in return for certain financial agreements. Edinburgh and Leith, on the other hand, strongly opposed it on account of the fares clause. When the Bill came before the Parliamentary Committee it was found that it did not comply with Standing Orders in respect of the extension. The Company endeavoured to have the other parts of the Bill considered, but with Edinburgh and Leith opposition, the Committee decided otherwise and the Bill had to be dropped.

The fares appeal was at last heard by the House of Lords on 2 and 3 July 1877. It was dismissed with costs, Lord Chancellor Cairns expressing himself as "unfavourably impressed" and re-ferring to the Company's arguments as "audacious" and "un-founded". So the matter was settled, and the Company apparently realised it would be better to adopt a more public-spirited policy.

Reverting for a moment to the rolling-stock, an open "toast-rack" car was introduced in the summer of 1876 and proved popular on the Portobello route. It is reputed to have had twenty rows of seats for six, totalling 120 passengers! Two more new cars by the Starbuck Company of Birkenhead also took the rails in 1877. These seated 16 inside and 22 outside instead of the usual 18 inside and 16 outside, and had an improved stairway to the top deck. The lamps were outside so the oil smell would be avoided! More of these larger cars were added to the fleet in the next few years.

Trials with a kind of portable cash register were made on various routes in April 1878. This locally devised apparatus was in the form of a box carried by the conductor. The passenger inserted his pennies which were then recorded on a dial, at the same time sounding a bell. Nevertheless rolls of tickets showing the fare value and the car number were adopted.

In 1879 the earlier tracks were calling for reconstruction and considerable expenditure was incurred by this work. 106 lbs. per yard steel rails were used. On the other hand the running costs had been reduced by over 3d. per car mile by reason of the better arrangements for horsing. So in September 1879 the Company introduced a new fare scale which included several penny "outside" fares and other reductions.

In 1880 the Company put forward a big scheme of expansion, including the doubling of the Portobello route which was doing well in the summer. A lengthy Bill was promoted which on 11 August 1881 became the Edinburgh Street Tramways Act 1881. The following new routes were authorised, and all were duly constructed: 1. From Haymarket to Ardmillan Terrace; double line to near Caledonian Road, thereafter single line with a passing loop at the railway bridge. 2. A single line continuation from Ardmillan Terrace by a new private road — what is now Harrison Road, — into Polwarth Terrace with a passing loop at the railway bridge. 3. A single line from the end of Polwarth Terrace at Colinton Road joining the latter line in Polwarth Terrace. 4. A single line continuation of this inwards to join the Morningside line in Home Street with passing loops on the town side of the trailing junction with the line from Ardmillan, near Merchiston Avenue, and at Upper Gilmore Place. 5. From Home Street via Lauriston Place, George IV Bridge and High Street to join the Newington line in North Bridge. Between Portland Place and the curve into Forrest Road this was single with passing loops at Lauriston Street and at Graham Street. The rest was double. 6. A double line connection into the Lauriston Place route from Earl Grey Street. 7. A double line connection between Shandwick Place and Lothian Road thus forming a triangular junction at the West End. 8. A double line branch from Junction Bridge to the foot of North Junction Street. 9. A branch from the foot of Leith Walk to Restalrig Road. This was single with passing loops at Easter Road and at Lindsay Place. No. 10 covered the doubling of the Portobello route from Waterloo Place to the Figgate Burn, with removal of the old passing loops, and a re-alignment at Jock's Lodge. A proposal for an extension to Musselburgh was dropped.

There were 37 Sections in the Act and five Schedules. These covered the usual financial and technical details and interests of other parties. The tramways were to be used for passenger traffic only, though small parcels could be carried if the local authority agreed to such use. Passenger's luggage was to be accepted. Two years were allowed for the completion of the new works except for the Ardmillan — Polwarth line in which case the period was three years. Section 34 was however important, for by it the Company at last secured general power to acquire build and operate omnibuses. They were of course subject to the licensing conditions of the Magistrates, including stances.

Meanwhile in 1881 important changes in the Company's personel took place. D. W. Paterson, the Secretary resigned and Dr. Wood took his place being in turn succeeded in the chair by Thomas Hill. Dr. Wood was also appointed General Manager and the Company's office moved to 54 North Bridge. There were further changes. Early in 1883 James Clifton Robinson became General Manager. He had been in at the very beginning of tramways, having as a youngster from Birkenhead joined G. F. Train twenty years earlier. He did not remain long in Edinburgh however, departing early in the following year for the Highgate Hill Cable Tramway in London. Later he was to take a leading part in the London United Tramways system, and received a knighthood.

We must now deal with an interesting phase regarding haulage. It will be remembered that by their Act the Company were to work their tramways by animal power only. This stipulation also applied to most tramway companies elsewhere, but experiments were taking place with steam power. Such experimental journeys of course, could not be used for public traffic.

The Edinburgh Street Tramways Company were interested in the idea and a 12 h.p. steam tramway engine made by Henry Hughes of Loughborough was put on the Portobello line. On 9 September, 1876 it journeyed about a mile before a condenser fault halted it. On 13 September the Board of Trade Inspector visited some additional passing loops which had been constructed on this route and he was given a demonstration of the engine, which continued to run trial trips daily before breakfast time for the next week. It then departed to show its paces on the Vale of Clyde

Tramways, returning to Edinburgh in April 1877, when a further week's trials were run between Portobello and Waterloo Place and along Princes Street to the West End, culminating on 28 April with a large official party aboard, they being also entertained to a champagne lunch in Portobello's Royal Hotel. Passing horses seem to have given it a mixed reception and although otherwise apparently considered very satisfactory the authorities do not seem to have been persuaded to agree to its regular use. Another machine described as a steam car arrived at Leith from Greenock in December 1877 and was put on the rails at Junction Bridge. This engine was then tried out on the Ferry Road line.

At this time there was a proposal to build a new bridge across the Harbour at Leith and continue the Bernard Street line via Commercial Street and North Junction Street and so form a circular route to the foot of Leith Walk which could be operated at a penny fare with steam engines. Leith Town Council were not at all in favour and the matter was dropped.

Yet another engine ran a trial on the Portobello line on 2 July 1880. This machine was said to be made by Messrs. Duncan and Wilson of Liverpool.

However in 1879, in the Tramways Orders Confirmation Act (11 August 1879) power was given to the Board of Trade to license the public use of steam engines on a tramway as an experiment notwithstanding an "animal power only" clause in a company's Act and provided the local authorities responsible for two-thirds of the route approved. Such licences were valid for a year if not revoked, and could be renewed for a second year. So in 1881 the Edinburgh Street Tramways Company persuaded the Corporation to let them have a real trial on the Portobello line. Portobello Town Council were receptive to the idea.

A Kitson steam tramway engine was therefore obtained and after a trial run on 12 April, which the Board of Trade Inspector found satisfactory, commenced regular service hauling an ordinary car between Waterloo Place and Portobello on 23 April 1881. Its working seems to have been moderately successful and in March 1882 a second similar engine was obtained and put to work on the route. These Kitson engines were small four-wheeled machines, the boiler etc. being enclosed in a casing resembling a small tramcar body. The 2ft. 4½in. diameter wheels, 8in x 12in. cylinders and driving gear were screened from view by a metal vallance round the sides and ends extending to within a few inches of the ground. The exhaust steam was turned into a condenser mounted in the roof, and so they were normally quiet in operation.

The Corporation renewed their licence for the steam engines for a further six months in March 1882, but meanwhile the

Company, wishing to continue the use of the steam engines, sought to ensure their freedom of action by promoting a Bill to give them specific powers to use mechanical traction without reference to the Board of Trade or the local authorities. The Bill was not well received, and while Portobello's opposition was withdrawn in consideration of some street paving concessions, both Edinburgh and Leith opposed it. In the event Parliament did not mind the Edinburgh Street Tramways Company being authorised to use mechanical power, but felt Edinburgh and Leith should have the usual safeguards of licensing regarding the number and type of engines, their speed and the routes to be worked. So the Edinburgh Street Tramways (Mechanical Power) Act of 1882, (passed 12 July 1882), really did no more than continue the existing system of operation by licence from the Corporation. This Act limited the number of cars to be drawn by an engine to two. Consent or revocation by the local authority required a majority of at least two-thirds of the votes. The attached Schedule required the engines to be numbered, fitted with effective braking, a bell or whistle, speed indicator, fender, and a seat for the driver affording a full view. They were to be free from noise and clatter, and the fire and machinery were to be concealed to within 4in. of the rails. Maximum speed was to be 8 m.p.h. When the Company applied in September 1882 to continue steam traction on the Portobello route, Edinburgh Corporation now had the last word and on 12 September declined to renew their licence so the engines were withdrawn. However as no reply to their application had yet been received from the Portobello authorities a steam car service on the route was reintroduced outside the City boundary on 23 September. Passengers changed to horse cars for the Edinburgh portion of the route, but two or three days later the cars were taken right through hauled by horses within the City boundary and by the steam engines beyond. The Company then realised their existing licence did not expire until 27 October and so, on 6 October, they recommenced steam working through to Waterloo Place. The Portobello authorities now also declined to renew the licence for the steam engines and so 27 October was the last of them. There had been the usual complaints of smoke and noise and so on, and Edinburgh would not contemplate for its street transport that which might be, and indeed for several years was, accepted in the industrial areas of England and elsewhere.

Before we leave this matter mention must be made of other possibilities which were tried too: Moncrieff's compressed-air car; and even a machine assisted by a form of spring-wound device. These were far from satisfactory. In October 1884 a small electric car which had been shown at a local exhibition was also demonstrated, but this was not much more than a toy. A further approach to the Corporation to allow steam engines to be used was made in

30

July 1886. This time the Company hoped to use a "Greens" improved noiseless engine on the Portobello route. The ratepayers objected and although the Edinburgh Council voting was 18 for and 15 against, the two-thirds majority approval required by the Act was thus not attained and approval could not be given.

Now let us return to 1882.

Work on the various extensions authorised by the 1881 Act was commenced early in 1882 and pushed ahead vigorously. At the same time another Act was obtained, the Edinburgh Street Tramways Act 1882, (3 July 1882), authorising construction of another single line branch, from Churchhill as far as Morningside Drive with a passing loop just short of the terminus. Three years were allowed for its completion.

The first of the new extensions to be opened to traffic was the foot of Leith Walk to Restalrig Road on 1 May 1882, the service running to the Waverley via York Place. Junction Bridge to the foot of North Junction Street was opened early the next month, and the services from these two new termini were then run to Haymarket. In the following spring however, a single sharply curved connecting line was laid from Junction Street to join the Constitution Street line before the junction leading into Duke Street, and on 30 April 1883 the aforementioned two services were replaced by a penny fare shuttle service from North Junction Street to Restalrig Road. This was decidedly unpopular and Leith Town Council protested. The old services were therefore restored within a few weeks but ran only to the Waverley.

The other extensions were completed soon afterwards and the doubling of the route to Portobello was also completed during 1882.

It will be recalled that the 1881 Act also authorised the Company to run buses, and they lost no time in starting up that business. Stables were acquired in the summer of 1881 at Corstorphine, on the south side of the main road a little way beyond Manse Road. There was also a grazing field for the horses, which thus became known as Tramway Park. So a bus was put on between the Coltbridge car terminus and Corstorphine where the terminus was at the Oak Inn. It ran every hour.

On 1 February 1882 the Dalkeith "coach" was taken over by the Edinburgh Street Tramways Company together with the stables at Dalkeith, and they ran their bus four times a day from the Waverley Steps. The Loanhead service, and stable, was taken over too, running four times daily; and in the summer of 1882 a bus was run to Roslin at a fare of 9d.

On 1 May 1882 another bus was put on between the Portobello tram terminus and Musselburgh, but this did not do so well. Musselburgh traffic had long passed to the railway, and Elliot's old Edinburgh — Musselburgh coach had made its last run in February 1878. Fares, times, and stances for the new service were revised in July 1882 in an attempt to popularise it, but it had to be withdrawn a few weeks afterwards.

Then in September 1882 it was proposed to divert the Mound — Newhaven bus from Goldenacre via Granton to Newhaven; but instead, a separate service was run from Granton to Newhaven and continued on to the Custom House at Leith. The other obligatory service from Waterloo Place to Stockbridge of course continued too. The vehicles used were of orthodox pattern, seating about 12 inside and with either a "knifeboard" seat or "garden seats" for 14 on the roof, reached from a small rear platform by a narrow curved stair. Three horses were used to haul them.

However, prior to this, in December 1878, a bus was put on between Tynecastle Toll and the Tron Church, running via Dalry Road, Morrison Street, Tollcross, Lauriston Place, George IV Bridge and High Street. It was probably run by Croall, but the Edinburgh Street Tramways Company, despite their lack of authority at that time, were the licensees. The fare was twopence inside and one penny outside, but these were increased in March 1880, again on the Edinburgh Street Tramways Company's application, on the ground that the service didn't pay. Not long afterwards this service ceased.

With all this development and the increase in their establishment the Edinburgh Street Tramways Company drew up their first Rule Book which was approved by the Directors on 25 September 1882 and printed and issued to the staff in 1883. The services quoted were :

> Post Office to Newhaven
>
> Haymarket to Bernard Street
>
> Powburn to Coltbridge
>
> Post Office — Grange — Churchhill circle
>
> Newington to Bernard Street;
>
> Waterloo Place to Portobello;
>
> Bernard Street to Tollcross
>
> Post Office to Morningside
>
> Granville Terrace to Princes Street and Post Office, and back by High Street and Lauriston Place, both ways round
>
> Post Office — West End — Tollcross — Lauriston — High Street, circle

32

Bernard Street to Tollcross via High Street and Lauriston
Post Office to Commercial Street
Post Office via High Street, Lauriston, Lothian Road,
    and West End to Ardmillan;
Tollcross via West End to Ardmillan
Restalrig Road to Haymarket

It is probable that some of these services were not worked regularly. Each route was divided up into quarter-mile distances for the purpose of calculating fares to which a special page was devoted. "The fare chargeable by Act of Parliament by car or omnibus is 2d. either inside or outside for the first two miles or any part thereof, even a fraction of one mile". There were however, as already noted, a considerable number of "special" penny fares. These were, outside only :— Junction Bridge and Stanley Road; Leith Walk Station to Junction Bridge, or to Bernard Street; Post Office and Haymarket, or Tollcross, or Salisbury Place; West End and Coltbridge; West End and Barclay Church; Tollcross and Churchhill; Churchhill and Salisbury Place; Salisbury Place to Powburn; West End and Ardmillan; Tollcross and Granville Terrace : Note the one-way downhill stages. Inside penny fares were limited to :— Foot of Leith Walk to Commercial Street, or Bernard Street, or Restalrig Road; Haymarket and West End, or Coltbridge, or Ardmillan; Waterloo Place and Norton Place. There were also a few 2d. and 3d. "bargains".

The conductors carried in a "distributor", rolls of tickets of the "cloakroom" style, numbered consecutively and showing also the car number. There were 1d., 2d., and 3d. values, the 1d. ones being blue. Fares above 3d. were met by issuing more than one ticket. The flat fare on the Leith — Granton bus was 3d. inside or 2d. outside, the other local buses charged a 2d. fare. The Loanhead bus was 6d. outside or inside, as was the outside fare to Dalkeith. Inside fares to Gilmerton were 7d. and to Dalkeith 8d. Gilmerton — Dalkeith was 4d. outside and 6d. inside, and Eskbank — Dalkeith 1d. outside and 2d. inside. To Greenend was 6d. outside or inside. "From Stockbridge to Newington or vice versa by omnibus and car 3d. inside and 2d. outside, available only on day of issue and by next car or omnibus only. Passengers pay whole fare to conductor of car or omnibus in which they first travel, and will have their tickets checked with the date of issue, by the checker at the Register House. This fare carries to Salisbury Place or Blackett Place only, — Powburn and Grange not included."

There were eight "sections" for the inspectors as follows :—
No. 1 got the cars out in the morning,—workmen's cars,—relieved the Register House "checker" at dinner time, and finished early "about 2.00 p.m." No. 2 took North of Pilrig and the Granton bus.

33

Courtesy Inglis

HORSE CARS AND BUSES AT THE POST OFFICE

The bus turning round in Waterloo Place is running from Post Office to Stockbridge. Note the horses trying to take car 36 the wrong way and the man pulling the car t o the right track: "Points" were open,—without blades.

34

No. 3 Waterloo Place to Coltbridge, and Corstorphine, Stockbridge and Trinity buses. No. 4 Post Office to Newington and George IV Bridge, also Loanhead and Dalkeith bus stance. No. 5 West End to Morningside and Grange. No. 6 Portobello route. No. 7 Merchiston, Dalry and Lauriston; and No. 8 was the checker at the Register House. In those days, while there were a considerable number of fixed stopping places, cars normally stopped anywhere when hailed, but exceptions were made for some of the up grades, viz : between Pilrig and Leith Walk station, then to Annandale Street; to London Road; to Picardy Place; to foot of Leith Street; and to Post Office. Similarly between Bright Crescent and Mayfield; to Blackett Place; and to Salisbury Place. Also between No. 77 South Bridge and Surgeon's Hall, Waterloo Place and the Calton Hill stairs, Abbeyhill to Abbeymount, and Barclay Church to Bruntsfield Terrace. Cars would not stop between these points. Further, cars were to be "walked"* at the following places : Register House down to Nottingham Place; Foot of Leith Walk into Junction Street; curves at either end of Newhaven Road; Register House to St. Andrew Street; Salisbury Place; Clinton Road; at Crosscauseway, Causewayside, and Whitehouse Loan; from Tron Church to Post Office; Abbotsford Park to Morningside School; and on the passing loops on the Portobello route.

This first Rule Book merits further notice. From it we learn that drivers and conductors were appointed by the General Manager and applicants had to be under 35 years of age, with extension to 40 years in the case of ex-police or ex-railway applicants as conductors. Conductors had to deposit £1 as security, and "must possess and constantly wear a good time-keeping watch". Fares were to be collected before starting from termini, and thereafter "as far as possible from the passengers on entering". They were not to be off the platform when the car was travelling. No standing passengers were allowed. There were, of course, stringent rules regarding sobriety, cleanliness, and improper language while it is intimated that "the Company is determined to render every possible assistance to conductors in resisting the fraudulent demands of drivers and others". "Any driver soliciting money from a conductor is liable to instant dismissal". Trace boys were to walk their horses back and if they rode them "at a walking pace" they did so at their own risk. Inspectors were to "look after the trace boys . . . and see that the horses are properly treated". A driver, too, "shall be careful and considerate in the treatment of his horses". There was a carmen's shelter at Morningside which could be used between 11.00 a.m. and 7.00 p.m. All sections of the establishment were covered. Those relating to "Workmen in the Car-Making, Smith, Farrier, Saddlery, and Lighting Departments" make strange reading today. Let us be content with the

* i.e. the horses were not to be allowed to trot or gallop.

working hours, viz :— Monday to Friday 6.00 a.m. to 9.00 a.m., 9.45 a.m. to 1.00 p.m., and 1.45 p.m. to 5.00 p.m. Saturdays 6.00 a.m. to 9.00 a.m. and 9.30 a.m. to 1.00 p.m. It is interesting to note however that in the summer of 1883 a hinged stool was provided for car drivers.

In January 1884 the timetables showed tramway services as follows :—Bernard Street to Haymarket; Bernard Street to Newington; Grange — Morningside Circle, each every 10/15 minutes : Newhaven to Register House; Portobello to Register House every 20 minutes: West End to Morningside Toll; Coltbridge to Powburn; Polwarth Gardens via Dalry to Powburn; Tron Church to Colinton Road, every 30 minutes, (every 15 minutes between Tron Church and Granville Terrace): North Junction Street to Register House; Restalrig Road to Register House, every hour. The Morningside Toll and Colinton Road services did not run in the late evening. The bus services were as already described. There were now 18½ miles of tramway route and 88 cars and buses.

Clifton Robinson who went off to London early in 1884 was succeeded by the first of the really "well kent" managers. John Erskine Pitcairn came from the North British Railway where he had been in the Traffic Manager's Department. The Edinburgh Street Tramways Company's undertaking was now thriving and under "Johnee" Pitcairn it continued to flourish.

About May 1884 there were some alterations. The services from Restalrig Road and from North Junction Street to the Register House were extended both to Haymarket and to Salisbury, then described as Newington; while the Morningside Drive to West End service was extended to the Register House. Other services were increased in frequency. About October the Restalrig Road and North Junction Street services were again extended from Haymarket to Coltbridge, and an additional hourly service given between Granville Terrace and Post Office via Lothian Road. The following month the Restalrig Road — Coltbridge service was diverted to North Merchiston, and the North Junction Street — Salisbury service ceased. The Restalrig Road — Salisbury service ceased too, early in 1885.

To revert to the bus services, a coach was run nine times a day in August 1881 between Waverley Steps and Corstorphine, but this venture seems to have been by some other operator. John Player of Dundas Street was taking up this business, and in May 1883 bought a small ten-seater bus, six inside and four outside, which had been in use at an exhibition at Craiglockhart. With this he ran a half-hourly service from the Mound to Howard Place at a twopenny fare. In February 1884, in spite of some opposition, his route was extended to Newhaven in competition with the

E.S.T.Co. HORSE CAR WITH "GARDEN" SEATS ON TOP

'STARBUCK' TYPE HORSE CAR WITH 'KNIFEBOARD'
SEAT ON TOP IN E. & D.T.Co. LIVERY AT MURRAYFIELD

Edinburgh Street Tramways Company who had to provide a statutory service on the route. Player was finding plenty of traffic too for his "brakes" to Roslin in the summers of 1883 and 1884, and in August and September 1885 he also ran excursions further afield such as Carlops, Hopetoun, and Dirleton. Meanwhile in 1884 George Hall was running to Queensferry, to be joined by the Edinburgh Street Tramways Company in 1885, and later Croalls. One of the latter's vehicles rejoiced in the name "Chevy Chase". Another route running in January 1884 was from the east end of Princes Street to Cramond, three times daily, with fares of 9d. and 6d.

On 1 June 1885 the Edinburgh Street Tramways Company started a new service from Waverley Steps to Bonnington Toll via York Place and Broughton Street, but it was taken off again early in the following year.

In 1886 the Edinburgh International Exhibition of Industry, Science and Art was held in the Meadows and drew big crowds. To cater for the traffic the North Junction Street — Coltbridge service was run to Tollcross instead during August, and diverted at the other end to Bernard Street in September. The service to Colinton Road was now run to Post Office via Lothian Road, and a ten-minute service provided between Tron Church and Tollcross via Lauriston Place. North Merchiston to Powburn was replaced by a North Merchiston to North Junction Street service. Thomas Blair of Glasgow secured a licence to run a bus between Waverley Market and the Meadows for the Exhibition. The electric light was a feature of the Exhibition and a short demonstration electric tramway was also laid down on the north side of the grounds, upon which two cars supplied by the North Metropolitan Tramway Company ran. The Edinburgh Street Tramways Company also exhibited their latest tram fresh from the Shrubhill works, seating 16 inside and 18 outside, weighing two tons, and fitted with a special life-guard, emergency brake, and railcleaner.

Mr. Pitcairn favoured long routes, and with the Exhibition over, some reorganisation was effected about December 1886. The services were then distinguished by a coloured board and a lamp at night, and were :

Portobello to Colinton Road	Yellow	every 20 minutes
Newhaven to Morningside Drive	White	every 20 minutes
Bernard Street to Tollcross	?	every 20 minutes
Bernard Street to Newington	Blue	every 10 minutes
Morningside Circular	White	every 10 minutes
Tron Church to Tollcross	?	every 10 minutes

Coltbridge to Powburn	Blue	every 15 minutes
North Merchiston to		
North Junction Street	Red	every 30 minutes
North Merchiston to Restalrig Road	Green	every 30 minutes

Also some journeys Bernard Street to Haymarket. No regular service was given on Harrison Road. There were no material changes in the bus services. The Bernard Street — Tollcross service was dropped soon afterwards, but apart from frequency changes the foregoing remained the pattern for a long time.

Player's Newhaven bus was taken off early in 1887, but in that summer a bus was run in from Penicuik in the morning and back out in the afternoon.

In January 1888 the Edinburgh Northern Tramways Company commenced tramway operation between Hanover Street and Goldenacre as mentioned in the next chapter and in accordance with Section 74 of their original Act took over the Edinburgh Street Tramways Company's statutory obligations on the route. Accordingly the Edinburgh Street Tramways Company's Mound — Newhaven bus was withdrawn and the Edinburgh Northern Tramways Company bus put on a bus connecting with the car service at Goldenacre. This was a small bus with no outside seats. The new service ran every twenty minutes from Goldenacre to Newhaven and for the first week was extended to the Custom House, Leith except in the evenings. Another bus was run every half-hour from Goldenacre to Granton. In that year too, an independent group of promotors proposed to lay a tramway from Coltbridge to Corstorphine. The Town Council agreed to support their projected bill, but nothing came of it.

At the beginning of 1889 the Edinburgh Northern Tramways Company put on another bus every half-hour from Goldenacre to Trinity Crescent, while a year later the Edinburgh Street Tramways Company's Stockbridge bus was withdrawn consequent upon the opening of the Edinburgh Northern Tramways Company's Comely Bank cable car route.

The working conditions of the Edinburgh Street Tramways Company's employees were improved in 1889, the weekly hours being reduced from 76 to 68. Drivers were then paid from 21/- to 26/- per week and conductors from 20/- to 25/- per week.

In the summer of 1890 the International Exhibition of Electrical Engineering, General Inventions and Industry was held at Meggatland on a site on both sides of the Suburban railway north of Craiglockhart station and the Union Canal. The main entrance was from Polwarth Terrace between Ashley Terrace and Colinton Road, and a large loop line was laid in past the gate,

39

just short of the Colinton Road terminus. For this traffic the Restalrig Road-North Merchiston service was extended up Harrison Road to the Colinton Road terminus, to which the Tron Church-Tollcross service was likewise extended.

Bernard Street to Salisbury Place was at this time extended to Powburn and new services run from North Junction Street to Powburn, and Bernard Street to Colinton Road. All routes ran at twelve minutes frequency, though this was soon altered to fifteen minutes, and the North Junction Street to Powburn service diverted along Grange Road to Marchmont Road. This carried a blue board and lamp. A bus was also tried from Churchhill to the Exhibition, but did not pay and was taken off. After the Exhibition the Bernard Street — Colinton Road service was cut back to North Merchiston, and the service from Tron Church reduced, and later abandoned. The Restalrig Road — North Merchiston service was altered to Gorgie Road about August 1891.

But now the Company's first twenty-one years were drawing to a close, and we must leave the development of the services meantime to deal with the coming important political phase. The Company would afford no more experiments or expansion. Instead they sought from Edinburgh, from Leith, and from Portobello town councils an indication of their intentions. Edinburgh town council, in August 1890, announced their intention of taking over the system within the City. Leith were in favour of discussions with the Company. In fact they didn't like Edinburgh's unilateral action, for a unified system was clearly desirable. There was a meeting between Leith Town council and the Edinburgh Street Tramways Company in November 1890, and another between Edinburgh and Leith town councils in May 1891. The Company offered substantial wayleave payments, revised fares, mechanical power, and profit sharing above 6% in return for a further twenty-one years lease. But Edinburgh wanted to own the tracks and on 1 December 1891 decided to buy them up, expressing the hope that Leith town council would do the same.

Leith, of course, wanted to know what arrangements would be made for joint control of the whole system if they bought their part, and suggested the whole undertaking be bought jointly, but Edinburgh refused to discuss these aspects of the matter, and insisted on going ahead alone. This was an awkward situation, which Portobello was meantime watching. Leith town council were not at that time keen to buy up the system and resented the suggestion of Edinburgh's dictation. So on 7 June 1892 Leith town council entered into an agreement with the Edinburgh Street Tramways Company for their continued operation in the burgh. At the end of the year Portobello town council likewise decided not to purchase the lines in their area.

The Edinburgh Street Tramways Company of course hoped they would be able to lease the Edinburgh part of the system from Edinburgh Corporation when the City acquired it, as local authorities still had no power to operate tramways. If this had materialised the running of the whole system would have remained with the one company with obvious advantages to all parties. But it was not to be. In any event a new Act was called for, enabling the Company to enter into leases, contracts, or agreements for working the tramways, to introduce mechanical or electric power, etc. These objects were secured in the Edinburgh Street Tramways Act 1892, — passed 27 June 1892, — which also provided for alterations in the Company's capital and other matters. The agreement with Leith town council was scheduled to the Act and provided for the following : The Company undertook to promote a bill in the next Parliamentary session to cover extensions from Restalrig Road to Seafield Place, and from North Junction Street along Commercial Street to the Custom House; also additional connections at Junction Bridge and at Foot of Leith Walk. They undertook to continue through services to Edinburgh and if Edinburgh introduced mechanical power on Leith Walk not later than 1 June 1899, (other than experimentally), promised to do likewise. Penny outside fares were to be available, and penny inside fares too, within $\frac{3}{4}$ mile of termini, (up to one mile if mechanical power was introduced). They also agreed to pay a wayleave of £500 per year for seven years and £600 per year thereafter. In return Leith town council promised not to exercise their option of purchase for fourteen years from the date of the Act, and for twenty-one years if mechanical power should be introduced on Leith Walk.

Accordingly the Edinburgh Street Tramways Act 1893, (passed 9 June 1893), authorised the construction of the aforementioned two extensions, and connections from Ferry Road into North Junction Street, and from Great Junction Street to Constitution Street. It will be recalled that the latter had been laid as a single line ten years previously. There was a trailing crossover in Junction Street and a facing one near the foot of Leith Walk. Two years were allowed for completion and the extensions were duly opened well within that period.

Meanwhile on 12 August 1892 Edinburgh Corporation had given statutory notice to the Edinburgh Street Tramways Company and to the Board of Trade, of their intention to exercise their powers of acquisition in terms of Section 43 of the general Tramways Act 1870, of that part of the system within the City boundaries, but excluding the line from Waterloo Place towards Portobello. The Board of Trade duly gave its approval in spite of protest from Leith. The Edinburgh Street Tramways Company as "sitting tenants" endeavoured to negotiate with Edinburgh

41

Corporation for a lease of the system and offered as much as £10,000 a year. But Edinburgh wouldn't accept the company which now had an agreement to continue operations in Leith, and so thirty years of inconvenience at Pilrig was precipitated.

Edinburgh Corporation were also deliberating on what form of mechanical traction to adopt. Clearly the days of horse haulage were numbered. Although experiments were taking place with electric traction in various parts of the world, cable haulage was acknowledged to be the cheapest method so far devised, and its future was considered bright. The Edinburgh Northern Tramways Company's system, — to be described in the following chapter, — was operating successfully and economically, although it comprised only fairly short reasonably straight routes not complicated by numerous junctions etc. There really was little option, for steam engines had been found ineffective and unpopular, and overhead wires for electric traction would have been quite unacceptable in Edinburgh at that time: No one would have dared to try to instal such a system.

So the Corporation promoted their Edinburgh Corporation Tramways Act 1893, which was passed on 29 June 1893. Section 4 authorised the use of cable power with the consent of the Board of Trade who were also empowered to make various byelaws. Other Sections referred to borrowing powers for money, and duties regarding road levels, water and gas mains and such like matters. Local authorities of course, still had no general power to work their tramway systems, and the Board of Trade had to approve the terms of such leases as were arranged. In this case provision was made for the Board of Trade to license the Corporation to work the system themselves, temporarily, should no satisfactory offer to lease it be forthcoming.

So offers to lease the system on certain terms were then sought. These provided for a rental of 7% per annum on the purchase price to be paid by Edinburgh Corporation to the Edinburgh Street Tramways Company, plus taxes and feus etc. The lessees were also to maintain and renew the system. It was provided that the Corporation should acquire or build other lines and convert the lines to mechanical traction, and the lessees were to pay the 7% rental on the capital cost of these works also. The staff's working week was to be reduced to 54 hours.

Three offers were received, namely from the Edinburgh Street Tramways Company, Messrs. Dick Kerr & Co. Ltd., and the Glasgow Tramways Company. Messrs. Dick Kerr & Co. Ltd. accepted all the Corporation's terms and also offered to introduce penny fares when cable traction was brought into operation.

The Edinburgh Street Tramways Company preferred to offer a sum of £13,000 per annum initially, which was rather more than the Corporation would have received on the 7% basis. They also agreed to pay 7% on the cost of cabling certain specified main routes, but, prudently would not bind themselves to this in respect of other routes or new routes without their prior consultation and agreement. They also urged that it would be better not to interfere with the men's working hours. The Glasgow company's offer was not disclosed.

The council met on 11 October 1893 when Messrs. Dick Kerr & Co's offer was accepted, and it was arranged they should enter on the property on Monday 20 November. Approval of the Board of Trade was then sought, but as the terms of the lease made no mention of through running to Leith, Leith town council petitioned the Board of Trade to insist on such a clause.

There was thus some delay, and at the last minute a judicial factor had to be appointed to run the system, in law, from 20 November until approval of the new lease was forthcoming. This was duly given by the Board of Trade on 24 November, but with the added clause requiring the Company to arrange for the interchange of traffic between the Edinburgh and Leith systems.

The Corporation thereupon took possession of the Edinburgh Street Tramways Company's system within the City, with the exception of the section from Waterloo Place to Jock's Lodge, on 9 December 1893. This amounted to about 11¾ miles. About 60 cars and some 600 horses were taken over at a valuation of about £40,000 and immediately resold to Messrs. Dick Kerr & Co. Ltd. who took over the working for twenty-one years from that date.

However, there was another problem still to be resolved. The price to be paid to the Edinburgh Street Tramways Company was still unsettled. Section 43 of the 1870 Act provided for the appointment by the Board of Trade, of an arbiter, who was to consider "the then value (exclusive of any allowance for past or future profits of the undertaking, or compensation for compulsory sale, or other consideration whatsoever), of the tramway, and all land, buildings, works, materials, and plant of the promotors suitable to and used by them for the purposes of their undertaking". The arbiter appointed by the Board of Trade was Mr. Henry Tennant the well-known General Manager of the North Eastern Railway, then recently retired. He held this to mean the cost to construct the lines less an allowance for depreciation, and on 13 November 1893 had announced a figure of £185,000. The Company disagreed with this reasoning, holding that they were entitled to a value which took account of the rental which the property would command, and they appealed, seeking interdict in the meantime.

43

The arbiter's decision was however upheld in both divisions of the Court of Session and the Company then appealed to the House of Lords. A similar action by the London Street Tramways Company was proceeding through the English Courts at the same time. The cases excited much interest in tramway circles, the Edinburgh one opening first on 8 June 1894. On 30 July the decision was given upholding the arbiter's decision. While this was doubtless legally correct it did not commend itself as fair to tramway companies.

In the meantime, in January 1894, the Edinburgh Street Tramways Company had bought some property in the Leith part of Leith Walk near Smiths Place to make a new depot and stables. Until these were ready they continued to occupy part of the depot and stables at Shrubhill now leased to Messrs. Dick Kerr & Co. Ltd. Of course at this stage the tramways were still functioning as one undertaking with the same staff. Mr. Pitcairn, the manager, and Mr. Adam, the treasurer, had the unenviable task of serving two masters, i.e. both companies. At the staff Annual Dinner in March 1894 the two owning companies were jointly toasted with enthusiasm! There was a kind of "common purse" arrangement and the old company received a quarter of the receipts taken on the Leith part of the system by the Dick Kerr cars. Then on 9 June 1894 the 29 cars and 298 horses remaining with the Edinburgh Street Tramways Company were moved down to their new premises on the site of the later day Leith Depot. The operating arrangements continued as before, but as the owning companies still could not reach any permanent agreement regarding through traffic, the Board of Trade appointed an arbiter in the matter in August. Again it was Mr. Henry Tennant, and it was some time before he gave his decision.

In the interval another problem arose. Shortly after Messrs. Dick Kerr & Co. Ltd. concluded their lease of the Edinburgh system, they approached the Corporation for permission to sublease the undertaking to a new company which they proposed to form. This was with a view to raising additional capital for their Edinburgh activities, and they deemed it sound to attract this capital locally and invite some prominent local gentlemen to join the Board. They had indeed already registered the Edinburgh Tramway Co. Ltd. on 8 November 1893, (dissolved in June 1895), but this never functioned at all, since for some reason or other the Corporation would not entertain this apparently quite reasonable scheme. After a few months discussions the Company withdrew their request and the council were left wondering what all the bother had been about. Then, as a more sensible attitude became evident, the matter was raised again and in July 1894 the Corporation agreed to the existing lease being determined, and entered into a new lease jointly with Messrs. Dick Kerr & Co. Ltd.

and their new Edinburgh & District Tramways Co. Ltd., which had been incorporated on 6 March 1894. The first directors were B. Hall Blyth (chairman), Alex. Fleming, G. H. Geddes, John Kerr, and F. Manuella. Part of this bargain was that inside fares on a penny per mile basis would be introduced on 1 September 1894 instead of within a month of the introduction of cable cars as provided for in the original lease. The rolling stock henceforth carried the name of the Edinburgh & District Tramways Co. Ltd. in place of Dick Kerr & Co. Ltd., the latter company remaining liable to the Corporation for the financial affairs. Mr. Adam now became manager of the Edinburgh Street Tramways Company while Mr. Pitcairn remained with the new Edinburgh and District Tramways Co. Ltd.

The new fares were introduced on 3 September 1894, and some service changes were also effected. The Commercial Street and Marchmont Road service was extended to Churchhill, while the Newhaven-Morningside Drive, and Seafield or Bernard Street to Gorgie and North Merchiston services were diverted from Leith Street to the York Place line.

Adjudication on the through services had still not been given, but on this same date the companies decided to discontinue the through service over the Portobello route, and the cars from Portobello and from Colinton Road were turned back at Waterloo Place and the Register House respectively.

At last, on 4 December 1894 the arbiter announced his interim award in the through services question. To avoid passengers having to change cars, the cars were to be taken through from the one system to the other, but in order to avoid any suggestion of running powers, horses, drivers and conductors were to be changed at the boundary at Pilrig. There was in fact no crossover at Pilrig by which the cars could have been turned back. To meet the terms of the original Act certain through fares were to be made available, and he went on to specify these and other fares adjustments. Some of these new fares were less favourable than the current ones, and Leith town council objected to the Board of Trade that such matters were outside the arbiter's terms of reference. The Board of Trade however claimed they could not interfere.

Nevertheless the companies announced that on Monday 24 December 1894 through working in terms of the arbiter's award would commence. Twopenny through tickets would be issued for journeys between Post Office and Bernard Street, Junction Bridge, or the Seafield terminus, for which the second conductor would give an exchange ticket. In Leith penny fares applied from Pilrig to the aforementioned points, while to Stanley Road was

45

twopence. Other penny fares were Stanley Road-Junction Bridge; Bonnington Terrace-Smiths Place; and Fort Street or North Junction Street to Lorne Street. A halfpenny fare was made available between Pilrig and Smiths Place or Annandale Street. There was no longer any distinction between inside and outside fares. Some workmen's cars with a halfpenny fare were run in Leith, but the Edinburgh Street Tramways Company pointed out that they would not be able to run through workmen's cars, and could not run connecting cars to Pilrig as there was no crossover there. They asked Leith town council's approval of laying in one, but were refused. On the same date the through working between Portobello and Colinton Road was resumed on the same basis. A general range of halfpenny fares was introduced in Leith on 1 July 1895.

The traditional animosity between Edinburgh and Leith now reached new heights. Contemporary tentative proposals by Edinburgh for annexation of the port did not help matters. Conditions at Pilrig were chaotic. The Edinburgh Street Tramways Company on their relatively level routes in Leith could manage with two horses per car; the Edinburgh & District Tramways Co. needed four from Pilrig to the Register House. The crews got muddled up: A car would set off with the wrong conductor, — or even two leaving the next car without any. The press complained bitterly and were at pains to point out the stupidity of it all and indicate the culprit. It was observed that Dick Kerr & Co. had undertaken to pay 7% on the cost of any new route for which Edinburgh would borrow the money at 3%.

Edinburgh Corporation were now seeking the Board of Trade's approval of the new Edinburgh & District Tramways Company lease, and so Leith sent a public petition to the Board of Trade demanding the insertion of a clause to end "The Muddle". The matter was however put so clearly and pointedly at a meeting of Leith town council on 4 January 1895, that from the following Monday, 7 January 1895, the companies at any rate reverted to the old fare scales. The Lord Provost now held out an olive branch and sought a meeting with Leith, though apparently with little support from his colleagues. Meetings were duly held and it was suggested Leith might now buy the system in the burgh and lease it to Dick Kerr & Co. Leith might have agreed to this arrangement if they could have bought on the statutory bargain terms which Edinburgh had secured. But this sale could now only be a voluntary one on the part of the Edinburgh Street Tramways Company who refused to sell under their own valuation of £155,000. Leith of course declined. Then Dick Kerr & Co. offered to buy up the Edinburgh Street Tramways Company's system in Leith, but the latter refused to sell unless their whole undertaking including the

Portobello line and their buses were included, and this Dick Kerr & Co. would not undertake to do. So in June 1895 Leith town council resolved to proceed no further with the question.

Meanwhile Edinburgh Corporation withdrew their application to the Board of Trade for approval of their new lease to the Edinburgh & District Tramways Company. This action of course prevented Board of Trade intervention in the through running dispute as sought by Leith, but gave rise to the charge that Edinburgh was not complying with the law. The Edinburgh Street Tramways Company then pressed Mr. Tennant for a revised award regarding through services. Much ridicule was poured on the legal quibble of what constituted running powers. Mr. Tennant met the parties in Edinburgh on 24 May 1895 after spending some time at Pilrig, and decided to seek legal advice in the matter; but in the end he felt unable to pronounce any more useful ruling and his interim award still stood.

Another anomaly had arisen. Dick Kerr & Co. had undertaken to reduce the crew's time to a nine hour day as stipulated by Edinburgh Corporation. But the men's wages were then correspondingly reduced, and so the Edinburgh Street Tramways

Horse Cart and Country Buses at the Waverley Steps. Note the hoarding in St. Andrew's Street where the new cable pit is under construction

47

Company's men had seven shillings or so more per week. Probably Edinburgh Corporation did not forsee this aspect of their effort to ease the men's lot.

On 26 December 1894 the first staff "Rules and Regulations" for the new organisation were approved by the Company's directors and issued under the joint names of the Edinburgh & District Tramways Company and Dick Kerr & Co. Ltd. Its contents were little different from the earlier Edinburgh Street Tramways Company's book.

Proposals for a tramway to Corstorphine had again been aired in the summer of 1893, — this time by an electricity company who announced their intention of seeking authority for an electric line, — but the Corporation opposed it.

Notwithstanding the terms of their 1893 Edinburgh Corporation Tramways Act, several Edinburgh councillors were still not happy about cable haulage and the question of whether or not to go ahead was still being hotly debated. It was not until March 1895 that a decision was reached, and in July they appointed Mr. W. N. Colam and Mr. John Cooper as Engineers. The latter was Burgh Engineer at the time. Tenders were invited and that of Dick Kerr & Co. accepted to carry out the work of conversion. Mr. Colam appears to have become Engineer for the Company also, though this was denied in the press. The original intention was to use the existing rails but it was later agreed that it would be preferable to reconstruct the track entirely, and to compensate for the additional cost on which they would have to pay the 7% rent, the Company were relieved of their future obligation to renew the tracks.

It was also decided that some extensions to the system should be made, and these were provided for by the Edinburgh Improvement and Tramways Act of 1896. Passed 7 August 1896, this contained an important section, 26, authorising the use of electric power, or mechanical power, (other than steam locomotives), on the Corporation's tramways. No doubt this pacified the anti-cable element, who were now no longer bound by the 1893 Act if a change of plan became possible later. The new lines authorised were :

1. A double line extension from the Powburn terminus to Lady Road.
2. A double line extension from the Morningside Drive terminus to the Braid Burn.
4. A double line branch from Dalry Road along Gorgie Road as far as Robertson Avenue.

5. A double line extension from the Coltbridge terminus to Murrayfield Avenue.

6. A new double line from Earl Grey Street, through Brougham Street, Melville Drive, and Marchmont Road to join the Grange route towards Salisbury Place.

7. A single line from Home Street round Thornybauk to the proposed new Tollcross cable power station and car shed.

8. A similar single line from Earl Grey Street by Wellington Street to the new car shed.

9. Doubling of the single line track in North Bridge, — together with street widening.

10. Doubling the existing Churchhill — Morningside branch.

11. Doubling the single line parts of Dalry Road.

There was difficulty over No. 3 and this was dropped out, but came up again as No. 6 in the following year's Act, which see. There had also been a proposal to seek a route via the Middle Meadow Walk to Warrender Park Road with automatic barriers to exclude other vehicles from the Meadows, but this was not pursued.

Meanwhile twenty-one years had now elapsed since the Portobello route had been completed, so the Corporation gave notice and duly took over the line from Waterloo Place to Jock's Lodge on 31 January 1896, whereupon it became part of the system leased to the Edinburgh & District Tramways Company. The changing of horses and men at Jock's Lodge, which of course followed, was not such an inconvenience as at Pilrig, there being only a relatively sparse service. As at Pilrig the cars were taken through. The arbiter awarded the Company £13,615.

Another Act of 1896, the Edinburgh Extension Act brought the burgh of Portobello within the city's boundaries. By this Act Edinburgh had sought also to annex Leith, but the Leithers still would have none of it, and secured the rejection of that part of the bill. While Leith's insistence on her continued independence was quite natural, her council's attitude to the tramway situation now became somewhat difficult to understand.

The Edinburgh Improvement & Tramways Act of 1896 has already been dealt with, but one of its proposals which did not materialise sought power for Edinburgh Corporation to purchase the Edinburgh Street Tramways Company's system in Leith, subject to the Company's willingness to sell, and to certain rights reserved to Leith Corporation. Both the Edinburgh Street Tramways Company and Leith Corporation petitioned against the Bill, and the Select Committee examining it would not agree to this power unless with Leith Corporation's agreement, which was not forthcoming. The Select Committee then went on to examine another Bill promoted by the Edinburgh Street Tramways Company which contained a counter proposal seeking running powers for them over the whole of the Edinburgh system, again with the object of providing through services and avoiding changing horses and men at Pilrig. Mr. John S. Adam, the Edinburgh Street Tramways Company's Secretary and Manager, and others, made much of the delays at Pilrig. Of course the Edinburgh & District Tramways Company objected to this proposal, and the Committee rejected it too, so that neither side gained any advantage.

The Edinburgh Street Tramways Act 1896, passed 7 August 1896, did however provide for the Company selling their undertaking by arrangement, and with Board of Trade approval, at any time notwithstanding the terms of the agreement attached to their 1892 Act. Section 27 provided for the winding up of the Company in this event. Some further extensions were also authorised however.

1. A double line extension from Portobello to Joppa. This was to be completed by 1 September 1897, and if the Portobello tracks were acquired by the local authority this extension was to be included.

2. A short single line linking up the Bernard Street and Commercial Street termini.

3. An extension, partly double and partly single, from the Stanley Road terminus, down through Newhaven and along Annfield and Lindsay Road to join the Commercial Street line.

4. A double line junction from the foregoing into North junction Street.

Although the Bernard Street and Commercial Street termini were quite close there was of course the Harbour between, spanned by an old narrow drawbridge. The need for a new bridge was in any case generally accepted. It belonged to the Dock Commission; the Tramways Company wanted to use it; who was to pay? The result was that the Dock Commission agreed to build a new swing bridge, Leith Corporation and the Edinburgh Street Tramways Company each to contribute £1500 towards the cost. The foregoing tramway extensions in Leith were to be completed within three years of the completion of the new bridge.

The Edinburgh authorities were still continuing their overtures for the extension of the cable system into Leith, but notwithstanding the undertaking in the 1892 Act, Leith town council seem now

50

to have made up their minds to keep the cables out of the burgh. Nevertheless when the plans for the new bridge were put before them in January 1897 they refused to approve them on the ground that they did not appear capable of accommodating a cable system, and argued against paying their contribution to the Dock Commission. On the other hand the Edinburgh Street Tramways Company approved the plans.

Sir William Armstrong's tender for the new bridge was accepted in February 1897 and on 24 May the old bridge was closed. Construction of the new bridge proceeded slowly and there was much complaint at the delay. A newspaper leader referred to the presence of "occasionally two men and a boy" and "the clang of a hammer may even be heard". However early in February 1898 the new bridge was at last ready. It had cost £8000, and when the Dock Commission sought their £1500 the Tramways Company declined to hand over the money till they were satisfied of its suitability by actual use. This quibble caused a further week's delay and the bridge was then opened for ordinary traffic on 17 February. It was worked by hydraulic power from the Bernard Street side.

Preparation of the plans for the haulage cables in Edinburgh was now under way, and eventually in March 1896 Dick Kerr & Company's tender for the work was accepted from among fourteen offers. Soon afterwards a start was made on the construction of the two new power houses at Shrubhill and Tollcross, and on the laying of the aforementioned extensions, as cable tracks, the policy being to work from the termini inwards towards Princes Street. Temporary tracks were laid through James Street and Dryden Street to enable the horse cars to reach the Shrubhill stables. These were lifted again in 1903.

But again the plans were amended as further extensions were thought desirable. Accordingly the Edinburgh Corporation Act 1897, (3 June 1897), provided for the following new tramways :

1. A further extension from Lady Road to Liberton Dams.
2. A further extension from the Braid Burn to the City boundary.
3. A further extension from Robertson Avenue to the City boundary.
4. A further extension from Murrayfield Avenue to the City boundary.
5. A double line from George IV Bridge down to the foot of the Mound.

6. A line, partly single and partly double, from the top of Marchmont Road through Strathearn Road and Strathearn Place which was to be continued through into Greenhill Gardens by the acquisition and demolition of some property. Thus this new line would join into the existing line again in Churchhill.
7. A double line from Lothian Road down Morrison Street into Dalry Road.
8. A double line from Leith Walk along London Road to Abbeyhill.
9. A single line extension from the Colinton Road terminus to the City boundary. It also provided that the old routes from George IV Bridge down the High Street to Tron Church, and from the top of Marchmont Road via Hope Terrace and Clinton Road to Churchhill would be abandoned and lifted.

An important part of the 1897 Act was Section 20 which authorised the Corporation to acquire the Edinburgh Northern Tramways Company's existing cable system which is described in the next chapter.

Meanwhile the Edinburgh Street Tramways Company's extension to Joppa had been opened early in 1897. A local group proposed an independent extension to Musselburgh but nothing came of the proposal at that time. The Portobello outpost of the Edinburgh Street Tramways Company was of course now within the City of Edinburgh and the Corporation would have the option to purchase in 1899.

Throughout 1897 and 1898 the tramway situation was debated at length by Leith town council. The Edinburgh Street Tramways Company sought permission to instal cable traction between Pilrig and the Foot of Leith Walk in accordance with the terms of their 1892 agreement. For the sake of through running with Edinburgh's future cable system one section of the council would have agreed to this being done if the cable could have been continued to Bernard Street, but the Company pointed out the narrowness of Constitution Street and to their lack of authority for such extension. Most of the council however had already come to the conclusion that electric traction was the coming thing, and thought it better to suffer the Pilrig muddle rather than commit Leith to cables. A passenger shelter could be erected at Pilrig. The Edinburgh Street Tramways Company were not now in a good financial position; their system was now too small to be profitable. They were however making the most of their opportunities with their buses which now outnumbered their tramcars. There was some scope for bus activities at this time as the tram services in Edinburgh were being subjected to delays on account of the extensive relaying for the cable system.

So in April 1897 the Edinburgh Street Tramways Company offered their system to Leith Corporation at a figure of about £80,000, but Leith considered this too much. Negotiations were continued slowly however, and the Edinburgh lessees were asked if, and on what terms, they would lease the Leith part of the system from Leith Corporation if the latter bought it.

Early in 1898, Edinburgh Corporation agreed to purchase, on 30 June 1898 by voluntary agreement, the remainder of the Portobello line, for £40,000, and this induced the Edinburgh Street Tramways Company to tentatively agree to a reduced price for the Leith system. Although this was still a good deal higher than the maximum which Leith town council had had in mind in 1895, they now agreed to proceed with the deal, — the Provost alone objecting. It was intended that the change of ownership and leasing to the "Edinburgh lessees" should take place at the end of June 1898, and with this in view the two Companies set out to negotiate a temporary arrangement whereby the horses and men would run through at Pilrig as from 15 March. In the event a dispute developed at the last minute regarding the apportioning of the receipts and the arrangement fell through. The Edinburgh & District Tramways Company now fully expected a twenty-one years lease of the Leith system from 30 June 1898, and as will be seen in the next chapter arranged a new lease with Edinburgh Corporation to run concurrently from that date.

It will be remembered however that the Edinburgh & District Tramways Company's present lease from Edinburgh Corporation had never been ratified by the Board of Trade, and when Leith town council held a special meeting in April 1898 to confirm their decision, the question was asked; Who are the legal lessees of the Edinburgh system? This was sufficient to defer the matter again while enquiries were made regarding the legal standing of the Edinburgh & District Tramways Company. So another special meeting was held on 24 May, at which no answer to the enquiries about the Edinburgh & District Tramways Company was available. It was moreover now suggested that there was "friction" between the Company and Edinburgh Corporation. In addition there was now a hitch regarding the taking over of the Edinburgh Street Tramways Company's contract with an advertising concern. So again there was no action. By the next special meeting on 14 June the matter was no further forward, and the same situation pertained on 5 July. The Leith councillors were by now losing interest and on this occasion there was not a quorum for the meeting. For the time being therefore the whole matter was dropped, and Edinburgh Corporation advised accordingly.

The latter thereupon asked Leith Corporation to allow them to buy the system from the Edinburgh Street Tramways Company, as they had wanted to do two years earlier. As before, Leith town council were not interested in this suggestion, and after allowing the holiday period to pass, replied that they intended to buy the Leith system themselves, and could not agree to its purchase by Edinburgh. After so much vacillation, this gave the local press much ammunition. Why not let Edinburgh buy it and get rid of "The Muddle" at Pilrig?

In view of the foregoing, the Edinburgh Street Tramways Company of course, had done nothing about their authorised extensions, but as it was now evident that Leith Corporation were not going to take over the system, nor allow cable traction below Pilrig, the Company made a start with the connection between Bernard Street and Commercial Street. This was completed early in 1899. The new line from Stanley Road through Newhaven, Annfield, and Lindsay Road to Commercial Street was also put in hand, and this was ready and inspected by Col. Yorke for the Board of Trade on 29 March 1900.

During all this period there had been few material alterations in the pattern of car services other than those mentioned. At the beginning of 1896 an hourly service was run from Post Office to Polwarth Terrace via Dalry, while during that summer an additional service was provided between Post Office and Meadowbank. Towards the end of that year a service was tried between Tollcross and Haymarket, no doubt to meet the bus competition, but by May 1897 it had been taken off again, and the Post Office to Polwarth Terrace via Dalry followed at the end of the year.

The extensions to the Edinburgh system were completed during 1897 and on 18 December the services were pushed out to the new termini at Murrayfield, Gorgie, Braid Hills, and Nether Liberton, The new lines along London Road to Abbeyhill and from Tollcross via Melville Drive to Marchmont were also completed. The Braids to Post Office service was extended over the former to Meadowbank and a service over the latter from Post Office to Marchmont started in the summer of 1897. At the beginning of 1898 a new afternoon service was put on between Newington Station and Braids ; — later extended to Nether Liberton and then cut to Morningside Drive. Some cars were also run through between Portobello and Murrayfield. About July 1898 the service on the new line along London Road to Abbeyhill was altered to a fifteen minutes service between Meadowbank and Post Office by this route.

As is related in the next chapter the Edinburgh & District Tramways Company succeeded in making a trial of the first part of their cable system between Pilrig and St. Andrew Street on 1 June 1899, and so claimed that the cable system should now be introduced below Pilrig also, in accordance with the terms of the 1892 agreement between the Edinburgh Street Tramways Company and Leith town council. To this it was retorted that a trial over part of the system could not be accepted as implementing the conditions which would call for such action, and a regular cable service not having been introduced by 1 June 1899 there was no longer any obligation to instal the cable in Leith.

On 1 June 1899 also, the Board of Trade inspected the new route along Strathearn Road and Strathearn Place, and the horse car service was transferred to it from the narrow twisting Hope Terrace and Clinton Road route. Strathearn Place was also narrow, but instead of having an orthodox single line, was laid with closely interlaced rails with one common conduit and slot for the future cable. The object of this was to avoid the noise associated with points. The old line through Clinton Road was lifted in February 1900. On 31 July 1899 the Post Office, — Melville Drive — Marchmont service was extended by Grange Road and the Bridges to form the circular route so well known in more modern days. It was however then called the Inner Circle to distinguish it from the old Morningside Circle proceeding via Churchhill. This Inner Circle with a ten minutes service and a fare of threepence was however run in the anti-clockwise direction only, the other direction being covered by the diversion of the Commercial Street to Churchhill cars down by Marchmont Road, Tollcross, and Princes Street back to Leith. At the other end of the route, the rails in Bernard Street having been linked to Commercial Street via the new bridge the cars to Bernard Street and to Commercial Street were making a circle of the two routes back to town.

Then on Monday 23 October 1899 the major change took place due to the introduction of cable haulage from Pilrig to Edinburgh as will be dealt with in the next chapter. Through services between Edinburgh and Leith then ceased, and the Edinburgh Street Tramways Company were left to provide services between Pilrig and Seafield, (every fifteen minutes), Pilrig and Bernard Street, (every seven minutes), Pilrig via Commercial Street and Bernard Street, (every fifteen minutes), and Pilrig and Stanley Road, (every ten minutes). On 2 April 1900 the latter was extended along the new route through Newhaven, Commercial Street and Bernard Street back to Pilrig forming the Outer Circle, though the Inner Circle which had been formed on the connection over Bernard Street bridge then ceased, a fifteen minutes service being provided from Pilrig to Commercial Street, and additional part-day cars from Pilrig to Bernard Street. On 5 April 1900 the Edinburgh Street Tramways Company announced their intention of turning back the Seafield cars at Pirniefield, but on representations, agreed to run every third car to the end of the line. The halfpenny fares were withdrawn at this date also.

At this time horse cars were still at work on various routes in Edinburgh pending their conversion to cable haulage, and it will be convenient now to leave their dwindling record till we deal with the installation of the cables in the next chapter.

Returning to the political scene, negotiations were re-opened between the Edinburgh & District Tramways Company, — who were now undoubtedly the Edinburgh lessees, — Leith town council, and the Edinburgh Street Tramways Company. In January 1900 the former company made an offer to lease the system from them if they would purchase it from the Edinburgh Street Tramways Company, as had been proposed in earlier years. Their offer did not satisfy the council however, and in March the Edinburgh & District Tramways Company made a further offer. In this they undertook to extend the cable system to the Foot of Leith Walk, and to electrify the remainder of the Leith system. They offered Leith 7% on the capital expenditure on the cable system and 5% on the remainder. Edinburgh Corporation of course would have received 7% on the additional capital expenditure at the Shrubhill power station where provision had been made for installing power to drive a cable in Leith. By April figures had been more or less settled in respect of the Edinburgh Street Tramways Company's assets, and the Edinburgh & District Tramways Company had amended their offer to 6% on the whole system, undertaking to carry out the cable part immediately and the remainder within four years. The Leith folk and their council were still divided on the question, one objection still being the change from cable to the future electric car being transferred from Pilrig to the hub of their system at the Foot of Leith Walk. A special ratepayers meeting was held. However when the town council discussed the matter on 18 May 1900 they were unable to come to terms with either party, the Edinburgh Street Tramways Company refusing to make a reduction in the price asked for their Morton Place premises, and the Edinburgh & District Tramways Company refusing to agree to the Corporation's proposed charge of 1½d. per unit for electric current from their new electricity station. It all had a familiar ring; and so the matter was dropped once more.

By 1902 public dissatisfaction with the position in Leith was nevertheless increasing. The cars were said to be dirty and obsolete. Once again, in March 1903 a special committee of Leith town council met to consider the matter: Something really had to be done now, — before the statutory opportunity of taking over the Company arose again in 1906. A further valuation of the Edinburgh Street Tramways Company's undertaking was made and on 1 June the Committee met the Edinburgh Street Tramways Company's chairman James Clark and the directors, and offered

£60,000 for their system. The Company's financial position was now such that the directors found this acceptable. Consequently a formal resolution was passed by the council on 23 July and confirmed on 1 September. There was still some opposition from a section of the ratepayers and a plebiscite was sought, but this was rejected. Accordingly a Provisional Order was promoted to enable the Corporation to work the system, and Board of Trade approval for its transfer from the Company sought. In order to protect itself from possible competition by the old Company continuing its bus operations, Section 12 of the Agreement scheduled to the Order required the Company forthwith to wind up its affairs and "cease to exist".

With the matter now so far arranged Leith town council this time made an approach to the Edinburgh & District Tramways Company. They suggested the Edinburgh & District Tramways Company might lease their system and electrify it, and also equip the route up Leith Walk and York Place to a proposed siding in the south side of St. Andrew Square for electric traction. If Edinburgh Corporation refused permission for this, they suggested the electric cars could be taken on over the cable system by putting on a cable gripper at Pilrig. Visits were paid to London to see such a scheme in operation there. The Company however rejected this as impracticable. While they were not anxious to extend the cable system, they considered the only way of providing through cars between Edinburgh and Leith was to extend the cable to the Foot of Leith Walk, on which they again offered 7%. But Leith was by now firmly against any cable traction in the burgh, and so negotiations terminated again, — this time finally. All that remained to be done now was the transfer of the Edinburgh Street Tramways Company's undertaking, including 29 cars and 200 horses, to Leith Corporation as provided under their Provisional Order of 1904, and this is recorded in the chapter on Leith Corporation Tramways, which also continues the final months of the horse cars in the burgh.

Finally, we have to revert to 1891 to complete the story of the horse bus services. This was a decade of considerable activity by the Edinburgh Street Tramways Company in this field, but it may be noted that one or two of the services to be mentioned were possibly run by other operators.

First, some provisions of the Edinburgh Municipal and Police (Amendment) Act 1891 should be mentioned. By Section 64 of this Act "It shall be lawful for the Magistrates to license all tramway cars, omnibuses, brakes, or other carriages . . ." Drivers and conductors had similarly to be licensed, and the licence fees were stipulated. Section 65 empowered the Magistrates to make Bylaws to prevent the running of unlicensed or unsound vehicles and the use of unlicensed drivers and conductors, the prevention of over-crowding, and the regulation of stances and times. Railway Companies' vehicles plying from railway stations were exempted from the Act.

The Bylaws under the Act were duly drawn up and approved by the Sheriff. They provided for the licensing, maintaining in good repair, brakes, steps, handrails, seating, lighting, ventilation, etc. of all tramcars; required the display of licence number, seating capacity, maximum fare, and route, all in letters and figures of stipulated size; the behaviour of drivers and conductors; stances and places where cars may, or may not, stop; and many other similar matters. A separate but similar set of Byelaws was issued for omnibuses. At that time of course only horse buses were thought of, and only horse and cable trams.

Thus was a most effective control over bus services secured by the Corporation, and the system remained in operation until the introduction of the Road Traffic Act of 1930, which put the matter on a nation-wide basis. Edinburgh had led the way forty years before. The Bylaws were of course amended from time to time. Provision had to be made for changing circumstances, the introduction of motor buses and other matters, as well as new routes and stances. Many of the requirements regarding tramcars were later dropped when the tramway system came under direct Corporation control, and were also subject to Board of Trade, and later, Ministry of Transport safeguards. Until 1930 buses continued to be inspected by the Corporation's Hackney Carriage Inspector.

About August 1891 a bus was put on running every fifteen minutes between the Mound and the foot of Easter Road via London Road. About November 1891 another service was started between the Mound and Warrender Park, via George IV Bridge and Bristo, while the Edinburgh Northern Tramways Company took off their Goldenacre — Trinity Crescent run for the winter. November 1891 saw two more Edinburgh Street Tramways Company services, viz. — Cameron Toll to Angle Park Terrace every half-hour, which was a revival of an earlier route; and West End to Ravelston Park every half-hour, which was quite new. In the summer of 1892 the Edinburgh Northern Tramways Company's Newhaven service was increased to fifteen minutes frequency, alternate journeys proceeding via Trinity and the Chain Pier, then popular with bathers. A service from Waverley Steps to Lasswade, four times a day was also put on during this summer, and the following.

Early in 1893 the Coltbridge — Corstorphine service was increased in the afternoons, and shortly had a competitor running approximately every two hours from West End (Hope Street) to Corstorphine, but this did not last out the year. The Goldenacre — Granton, West End — Ravelston Park, and Mound — Warrender Park services were also withdrawn. About the end of 1893 a fifteen minutes service was tried between Post Office and Haymarket, but lasted only some weeks. In the summer of 1894 the Angle Park Terrace — Cameron Toll route was cut to Hope Park Terrace except during "rush" hours. A new country connection was available between Dalkeith and Pathead. This was provided by one named Cowing using "brakes". On Sundays he started from Eskbank, In October 1894 the Cramond bus ceased to run consequent on the opening of the railway branch to Davidson's Mains and Barnton. The Mound — Easter Road route was also withdrawn.

On 20 May 1895 a bus was again started by the Edinburgh Street Tramways Company between Portobello and Musselburgh, and ran every hour. For the summer the Roslin route was reinstated on 17 June, and the other country routes increased in frequency, It is interesting to note that at this time the Glasgow Tramways and Omnibus Company took up the hiring business in the Edinburgh district, having bought some of Croall's premises. Whether they actually ran any bus services is not clear. From 30 September 1895 the Edinburgh Street Tramways Company put on a bus every hour between Trinity Crescent and Seafield car terminus via Commercial Street and Bernard Street, but on 4 November this was replaced by an hourly Bernard Street — Granton run. There was already an established service on this route of course, and three weeks later Mr. Henry Whitelaw took over the operation of the route from the Edinburgh Street Tramways Company. On 28 December 1895 the Edinburgh Street Tramways Company started an hourly service between Junction Street and Dean Park Street, Stockbridge via Bellevue. This proved popular and was soon increased to a half-hour frequency, and extended via Henderson Street to Bernard Street. In the following spring the Bernard Street — Dean Park Street, and Bernard Street — Granton routes were linked up to form a circular route.

At this time the construction of the cable tramway system was in full swing, and the work thereon inevitably caused delays and inconveniences to the horse car services. The bus operators, including the Edinburgh Street Tramways Company, made the most of the opportunity. In May 1896 the latter advertised their services as follows :—

1. Echo Bank to Gorgie every half hour.
2. Hope Park Terrace to Gorgie every quarter-hour.

3. Bernard Street — Dean Park Street and
4. Bernard Street — Granton, running through to form a circle, every half-hour.
5. Coltbridge to Corstorphine every half-hour.
6. Portobello to Musselburgh every half-hour, (hourly in the mornings).
7. Loanhead, four journeys daily.
8. Dalkeith, four journeys daily.
9. Roslin, three journeys daily.

On 4 May the Company put on a new service every fifteen minutes from Grange Loan to Haymarket via Marchmont Road and Tollcross. Also that summer a bus was run between Morningside station and Mortonhall. There was one morning journey and then hourly from 11.0 to 4.0 On Tuesdays and Thursdays the morning and one afternoon trip were extended to Lothianburn. The Portobello — Musselburgh Cross service became half-hourly and the Hope Park Terrace — Gorgie service every fifteen minutes. The Grange to the Mound route was restarted. Then on 10 August 1896 they introduced another fifteen minutes service from Grange Loan to West End running via Oswald Road, Grange Terrace, Causewayside, Bristo, George IV Bridge, Johnston Terrace and Castle Terrace. The Grange to the Mound route was also extended to West End. New fare stages including halfpenny and threehalfpenny fares were introduced, but although the Company's bus traffic generally was flourishing, the Grange district was being over served and retrenchment became necessary. The new Grange to West End via Johnston Terrace route was therefore withdrawn from 2 November, while the older route via the Mound was again shortened to the latter point, and the Grange Loan to Haymarket route became Marchmont Road to Haymarket. At the same time some of the Company's other services were increased in frequency, and the Cameron Toll to Angle Park Terrace route extended along Slateford Road.

From 14 December 1896 the Corstorphine bus was extended in to Haymarket and combined with the Haymarket — Marchmont route. The Edinburgh & District Tramways Company had itself entered the field earlier in that year with the circular horse bus service running via London Road, Easter Road, Albert Street, and Leith Walk, every half-hour. This however lasted only till the following summer. About the end of 1896 a fifteen minutes service was put on between the Mound and Blackford Avenue via Causewayside. There was also a short-lived fifteen minutes service in the afternoons from Foot of Leith Walk to Newhaven. In the spring of 1897 another South side route was started between the Mound and Mayfield Road, (Wilton Road) integrating with the Blackford Avenue one.

E.S.T.Co. THREE-HORSE BUS FOR COUNTRY ROUTE TO ROSLIN

E. & D.T.Co.'s. HORSE BUS. 1896

For the summer of 1897 the Edinburgh Street Tramways Company's Portobello to Musselburgh run became Joppa to Levenhall, as the car service was now extended to Joppa. Later in the year, the Corstorphine to Marchmont route was cut to Corstorphine and Tollcross, and soon afterwards Corstorphine and Haymarket.

During the summer of 1898 a bus was again run to Cramond, four times daily. The Hope Park — Dalry service was increased in frequency, some journeys being extended to Cameron Toll and to Slateford. Later in the year the Corstorphine bus was extended to West End, and early in 1899 again extended to the Mound. About May 1899 every other bus on the Slateford route was extended to Inglis Green, but this only lasted a few weeks. The Musselburgh — Portobello bus was extended through to Bernard Street Leith for the summer on 27 May; fare 5d. In June the Wilton Road terminus was altered to Lygon Road from where the vehicles returned by way of Wilton Road. November 1899 saw further services to the South side, viz. — Mound to Newington and Echo Bank, and Mound to Melville Terrace. These direct Mound to South side services had become popular and it became the custom for the Edinburgh Street Tramways Company's manager to receive a subscription from the regular travellers for the bus crews at New Year time.

From 2 April 1900 the Leith — Granton bus ran only between Newhaven and Granton by reason of the tramway extension through Newhaven. In the summer of 1900 some of the Loanhead buses were extended to Lasswade, and an additional service run from Waverley Steps to Liberton via Captains Road, but the former did not last many weeks. On 29 October 1900 the Edinburgh Street Tramways Company started a new fifteen minutes service from Bonnington Terrace via Bonnington Toll, East Claremont Street, and Broughton Street to the Mound. This lasted until about the following April, when the Captains Road and Liberton service also disappeared. The Lasswade route was revived in the summer of 1901, but soon after, the Dalkeith route was cut short at Gilmerton. A new fifteen minutes service was started between Angle Park Terrace and Tron Church via Tollcross and Chambers Street. For the summer of 1902 the Dalkeith and Lasswade runs were revived and the Corstorphine bus started from the Waverley Steps along with the other country services.

Improved alternative transport making itself felt however, included the cable car service which was now in full swing. Some of the Edinburgh Street Tramways Company's services became uneconomic and a retrenchment was necessary. By the end of 1902 the only remaining horse buses were plying between Leith and Stockbridge half-hourly; Tron Church-Tollcross-Robertson Avenue every ten minutes; Angle Park Terrace—Tollcross every ten minutes and extended to Hope Park Terrace in the afternoons. There was also a half-hourly service from Tron Church to Slateford on Saturday afternoons; and of course the half-hourly services from Goldenacre to Newhaven, and Newhaven to Granton. The Musselburgh — Portobello route still ran, extended to Bernard Street in the summer, while the Corstorphine bus was now only hourly and from Haymarket. Then there were still the other country routes to Gilmerton, Loanhead and Roslin, with Dalkeith in the summer also.

Later in 1903 some of the Hope Park Terrace buses were again extended to Echo Bank, while others went to Montague Street. When the Leith Corporation Tramways Order was before Parliament in 1904, the Edinburgh & District Tramways Company lodged a petition to secure their release from their obligation, as successors to the Edinburgh Northern Tramways Company, to run the Goldenacre — Newhaven service. Though this did not materialise, the Company interpreted the provisions of the Leith Act as transferring the obligation to Leith Corporation. The latter of course disagreed but the Company ceased to run the service after 27 August 1904 in spite of protest.

At the end of 1904 by the foregoing Act, the Edinburgh Street Tramways Company had to be wound up and its operations ceased. The Newhaven — Granton bus was taken over by Leith Corporation who maintained the route till the extension of their tramways to Granton in 1909, after which it was tried briefly from Seafield to Portobello. George Hall, the Edinburgh Street Tramways Company's contractor for the Corstorphine route continued this route, and the Leith — Stockbridge route, the Tron Church — Tollcross — Robertson Avenue route, and the Angle Park Terrace — Hope Park Terrace route were also continued by other contractors. The other routes ceased. A bus painted red and cream, which the North British Railway had run to Levenhall, connecting with the trains at Musselburgh station also ceased with the opening of the Musselburgh tramways. In January 1905 the Leith — Stockbridge route was extended to Craigleith station and Blackhall but this lasted only a couple of months. In April the Angle Park Terrace—Tollcross—Hope Park route was diverted via Lauriston Place to the Infirmary, but soon ceased altogether.

So at the beginning of 1906 there were only the Leith-Stockbridge, and Tron Church-Robertson Avenue routes left in addition to Leith Corporation's Newhaven — Granton route. The Corstorphine route had succumbed immediately to the newly formed Scottish Motor Traction Company's motor bus. The horses had served us well and were still trundling the old trams from Tollcross to Colinton Road. As this tram route was not run on Sundays a horse bus now covered the route on that day. But horses were displaced there too on 24 August 1907 by which time Leith Corporation's horse bus route was the only regular one left. The Leith — Stockbridge route apparently ceased regular operation in the summer of 1906 but continued to be run spasmodically until early in 1907.

Nevertheless, even though the buses had gone, "four-in-hand" "brakes" were still to be seen running to Roslin, Carlops, Cramond, Queensferry, etc. in the summer. Croall, Player, George Hall, Adam Cramond, and Dan T. Munro were the principal proprietors, the latter's five named "Lord Roberts," "Waverley," "Defender," "Queen Mary" and "Ivanhoe." George Hall's fare to Queensferry with his "Rob Roy" was 1/- single, 1/6 return. The first world war brought a drastic reduction in the number of these, though such machines were occasionally seen in use in the early twenties. A small horse-drawn wagonette still plied between Barnton station and Cramond on Saturday afternoons in 1919. George Hall still advertised his "brakes" to run to Carlops up till the Spring Holiday in 1922. The return fare was then 4/-. Afterwards these firms concentrated on the cab and taxi business.

A few years ago the remains of one of the old horse buses was discovered on a farm near Pencaitland. With a fitting appreciation of its historical value, the dilapidated machine was acquired for preservation by the City Transport Department, who thoroughly rehabilitated it, and painted it in dark blue and cream with the Edinburgh & District Tramways Company's name and crest etc.

Before concluding this chapter some notes on the tramway rolling stock may be given.

The Edinburgh Street Tramways Company's initial order was probably for sixteen cars and with the sixteen added in 1872 made a fleet of thirty-two in 1874, apparently numbered 1-32. These cars were of orthodox pattern with a "knifeboard" seat on the roof, the first lot having six windows with rounded tops and the second lot seven windows with square corners.

The colour scheme in Edinburgh & District Tramways Company days was apparently that which has persisted in the City, but for the Edinburgh Street Tramways Company period evidence is not conclusive. Some vehicles at least were blue and in those early days the dash panels seem to have been painted a light colour like the rocker panels, while the car number on the dash was enclosed in a circle. No lettering appeared on the rocker panels but as the cars were kept to their allocated routes the destination was painted on the outside stair stringer in most cases. Later the Company's name appeared in full on the rocker panels, and it has been suggested that the dash panels were then painted the colour of the route for which the car was licensed.

By 1875 the fleet had grown to forty or more, the additions being of the standard seven window pattern, though about this period there were some similar cars on which the windows had rounded tops and separate ventilators above. The cars built by the Starbuck Company which started to appear in 1876 were rather longer and had eight windows, but the standard seven window type continued to be built at the Shrubhill works. The earliest cars appear to have been replaced in due course, usually by cars of this type also, though there were some similar cars with only six windows.

Later, probably in the eighties, an improved version with a flatter roof and transverse reversible "garden" seats outside appeared. The first of these had seven windows but six windows then became the usual pattern for this type. The older standard cars were also converted to "garden" seats outside by building up the sides of the roof to give a level floor. An "Eades" reversible car was tried for a time. In this vehicle the whole body revolved on a centre pin on a "truck" so that the horse merely walked round with it at the terminus. The orthodox method of unhooking the spreader bar and shaft from the car and walking the horse round with the driver holding up the spreader bar was really simpler however.

The fleet had increased to seventy-three cars by 1889, of which ten were "toast-racks". Four of these were scrapped the following year but eight single-deck saloons were added, followed by two more and two further standard cars in 1891. At the end of 1892 there were eighty-four cars and another six were added during the next year.

By this time the numbers had become more random and a few known examples at this period can be quoted* :—

Standard cars seven windows : 2, 5, 36, 39, 47, 57.

Standard cars six windows : 14.

Starbuck cars eight windows : 25, 26, 107.

Later "garden seat" six windows : 72.

"Toast-rack" : 87.

Single-deck saloon : 63, 90, 92, 95.

* It is probable that a car permanently changed to another route was renumbered, taking one of the licence numbers for that route. This arrangement did not apply to cable and electric cars, though the practice of keeping a car on one route often persisted. For example, electric car No. 1 spent nearly all its life on service 15.

The twenty-nine cars which the Edinburgh Street Tramways Company retained in Leith in 1894 appear to have included Nos. 2, 7, 14, 17, 22, 26, 28, 38, 39, 54, 63, 75, 79, 82, 83, 84, 87, 90, 95, 100 and 110, and these passed in due course to Leith Corporation who later sold Nos. 26 and 110 back to the Edinburgh & District Tramways Company. It may also be mentioned that Leith Corporation sold Nos. 39 and 83 to the Stirling & Bridge of Allan Tramway Company. The remainder of the cars in 1894 of course passed to Dick Kerr & Comany and subsequently the Edinburgh & District Tramways Company, the companies' names appearing in full on the rocker panels. As the cars retained by the old Company in Leith no longer ran in Edinburgh after 1899 some of their numbers were then apparently re-used by the Edinburgh authorities, e.g. horse-car No. 14, and several cable cars.

II

CABLE TRAMWAYS — THE MECHANICAL MARVEL

We have seen how the Edinburgh Street Tramways Company abandoned the idea of laying tramways down the steep hills on the north side of the City, making do with the little horse buses. This was clearly not satisfactory; five horses were often required to one bus and they just could not be run in snow or icy weather. The steam engines which had been tried on the Portobello line had not been well received, and in any case they would have been impracticable on such steep grades as these. Some other mechanical system would have to be devised.

In San Francisco, also abounding in steep hills, a new idea had recently been developed by A. S. Hallidie, namely cable haulage. It was first introduced this side of the Atlantic by E. S. Eppelsheimer on the Highgate Hill line in North London opened in May 1884, but others had already seen in it the answer to the Edinburgh problem.

A Bill was therefore introduced in 1883 for tramways from Hanover Street via Canonmills, Inverleith Row, through Royston Terrace and Monmouth Terrace into Trinity Road, East Trinity Road, Main Street Newhaven, and Annfield to the Custom House, Leith. A double line was proposed as far as Canonmills, thereafter single with passing loops near Eildon Street, in Royston Terrace, in Trinity Road, in Annfield, in Portland Place, and near the terminus. At the foot of Craighall Road there was to be a double line triangular junction with another terminus in Maitland Place Newhaven. Another double line branch was to go off along George Street and down Frederick Street, through Stockbridge to Comely Bank. Any form of power could be used including ropes or electricity. From a contemporary article it seems that flat rails were at first envisaged for a cable system, the centre slot serving for guidance. A meeting was held in Newhaven to explain the system, tramways in the narrow streets being regarded unfavourably by the residents. To secure Leith Town Council's support the promotors agreed to divert their line from the narrow Main Street to Pier Place and to continue behind the back of the Peacock Hotel.

They also agreed to charge penny fares and to run a bus at a penny fare between Newhaven and Granton. However there was other opposition and the Bill failed.

Dick Kerr & Co. were behind the scheme and they came back next session with a similar Bill. This time it was proposed to take the line round Goldenacre to Trinity Road instead of by Royston Terrace and Monmouth Terrace, and to reach Newhaven via Primrose Bank, Trinity Bridge and Trinity Crescent. There was to be a double line throughout except through Main Street. The Comely Bank route was to be separate, starting in Frederick Street. The gauge proposed was 3ft. 6in. Again there were discussions with Leith Town Council who now raised many objections but principally about the use of Main Street. Edinburgh Town Council however supported the Bill and as they were responsible for two-thirds of the whole route Leith's case was not strong. Nevertheless the promotors agreed to amend their Bill, making Newhaven their terminus, and adopting the 4ft. 8½in. gauge. Cable operation was specified, and sufficient inside accommodation at a penny per mile fare, though a first class compartment at a higher rate was allowed. Single-deck cars were originally envisaged.

This time the Bill was passed and the Edinburgh Northern Tramways Company was thus formed on 7 August 1884. John Waddell was chairman and W. Hamilton Beattie, engineer. Three years were allowed for completion of the works.

Construction was of course an entirely different proposition to that of horse tramways, and though preparatory work by the contractors, the Patent Cable Tramways Corporation, was in hand in 1885, it was October 1886 before track laying started on the route between Hanover Street and Goldenacre, along with the erection of an engine house in Henderson Row. The contractor's engineer was a young man William Newby Colam who had been Eppelsheimer's chief assistant. He was to play an important part in the development of cable traction.

Both the Trinity and Stockbridge routes included a long hill at the town end, as steep as 1 in 11 near the top. The Company decided to finish the 1½ miles of route to Goldenacre first and as they had also decided to locate the engine house and car depot in Henderson Row, a hundred yards or so off this route near the bottom of the hill, and to make it serve the Stockbridge route as well in due course, a new Act was required to authorise the connecting lines to the depot. As the time for completion had nearly expired and the Stockbridge route was not yet started, the Edinburgh Northern Tramways Act 1887 (5 July 1887) allowed a further two years for the construction of this route as well as the two connecting lines to the depot, for which three years were allowed. The powers for the continuation from Goldenacre to Newhaven were allowed to lapse and it was never constructed, a bus being run instead as required by Section 74 of their original Act as already mentioned.

At last the Hanover Street to Goldenacre line was ready at the end of 1887 and its opening was planned for 2 January 1888. Some hitch, however, arose concerning an agreement with the Patent Cable Tramways Corporation, and the Board of Trade inspector also called for some modifications to the cars. The steps had to be arranged to fold up when not in use as the maximum width was otherwise exceeded. The opening of this route took place on 28 January 1888 without ceremony though there was considerable public interest. A five minutes service of cars was run with connecting buses to Granton, Trinity and Leith, as already recorded. The old Edinburgh Street Tramways Company's buses on the route of course ceased. Major John Boulton, one of the promotors was appointed Manager.

About a week later, on a Saturday, the first breakage of the cable occurred, but repairs were completed ready for the Monday morning service again. The system worked well however, and early in 1889 work was started on the 1¼ mile Stockbridge route. This was duly opened with a five minutes service of cars on 17 February 1890, again replacing the Edinburgh Street Tramways Company buses.

The gauge of these lines was, of course, 4ft. 8½in. 75lb. rails were used. The conduit was formed of concrete with cast iron frames embedded to carry old rails which formed a centre slot ⅞in. wide. The cable, of 3½in. circumference 6/13 steel wire rope, was carried over 14in. dia. cast-iron pulleys placed in recesses at 50ft. intervals. Horizontally mounted pulleys with one deep flange on the bottom were used on curves. At the town end terminus of each line the cars ran into the "stub end" by gravity while at the other end the cars ran out of the "stub end" by gravity on to the double line where the returning cable was picked up. At Comely Bank the grade was so slight that a little persuasion was sometimes needed to get the car to run out. The cable was returned round a large horizontal pulley in each case.

As already mentioned the power house and car shed were situated in Henderson Row, a hundred yards or so from the Goldenacre route near the bottom of the hill. The cable was diverted from the down line into the power house where it was driven by a 10ft. 6in. dia. driving pulley. After passing round a tension pulley loaded to 7 cwts. it returned to the down line. Cars on the down line passed Henderson Row by gravity. There was both a facing and a trailing connection on the down line connecting with the single line in Henderson Row which led into the car shed. The car shed had a number of stalls, access to and from which was gained by a traverser. There was originally no slot in this part of Henderson Row and the car grippers had to be lifted out through a small hatch before leaving the "main line" and running by gravity through the facing connection into Henderson Row from where a horse pulled them along to the shed. Similarly the horse took them out to the trailing connection where the cars gained the down line and the gripper was inserted through another hatch. At a later date the slot was provided in Henderson Row as in the case of the Comely Bank route and the grippers remained on the cars, the services of the horse being normally obviated.

To reach the Comely Bank route the cars came off the opposite end of the traverser, which lay parallel to Henderson Row. They had to travel on the single line to the other end of Henderson Row where there was a passing place and continue along Hamilton Place on single line and over a trailing connection onto the up line of the Comely Bank route, again near the bottom of the hill. Again the cable was diverted from the down line to reach its driving pulley in the Henderson Row power house. This was about 550 yards and too far for the cars to be effectively dealt with by horses however, so that the cable was used in both directions. The outgoing and incoming cable being under the same slot in the single line care was necessary to see that the car gripper got the correct cable. Cars going to the car shed were run back by gravity round the trailing connection from the up line into Hamilton Place, but to proceed onto the up line round the curve from Hamilton Place, a separate short auxiliary cable was provided. This was driven from the shaft of one of the main cable diverting pulleys there and was put into operation when required by means of a clutch operated by a key. Latterly this was removed and in the mornings the cars were pushed and pulled round the curve onto the "main line" in groups of three, the last one using the Hamilton Place cable and pushing the two in front till the first one was on the "main line". It then took the "main line" cable and pulled the other two round behind it. As at Henderson Row on the Trinity route, two crossovers were provided, the facing one on the town side and the trailing one on the Comely Bank side. It had been originally intended to provide two connections at Hamilton Place but experience at Henderson Row indicated that one would be sufficient.

An innovation was tried at the Hamilton Place junction. It will be appreciated that if the driver of a car coming down the hill towards Comely Bank did not, through forgetfulness or some other reason, release the gripper at the corner of Hamilton Place where the cable was diverted to the power house, the cable would be pulled from its pulley and considerable damage and dislocation of traffic would ensue. Approaching the critical point, therefore, the cable was led a few inches out of line with the slot, and if it were pulled into line under the slot by a car gripper, it bore against a cast steel lever in the form of an inverted "L" pivoted at the bottom. When this lever was moved by the cable bearing against it, the top leg moved across the underside of the slot and therefore arrested the progress of the gripper, and of course the car. This device, which was known as a "pawl", had to be of great strength, since it had to absorb the energy of a car running into an immovable object. Such an occurrence was naturally fraught with considerable danger to the passengers, and so at a point just before the pawl would come into action, another striker was arranged which made contact for a large electric bell. It was hoped that this would warn the driver in time for him to release the gripper before bringing the pawl into action, but it seems to have been found that the bell was ineffective and it was subsequently removed. The pawl device remained however and was provided also on the later lines in the city.

The power house was provided with two non-condensing horizontal steam engines of 300 h.p. by Messrs. Dick Kerr & Co., Kilmarnock. Each engine was capable of working either or both of the cables. Messrs. Babcock & Wilcox provided the boilers.

HANOVER STREET ROUTE CABLE CAR AT GOLDENACRE
IN E. & D.T. Co.'s. LIVERY

The Company possessed eighteen tramcars. The first eight were built by the Metropolitan Carriage Company and were numbered 1 to 8. The saloon seating 20, had six windows each side and was divided into two sections forming first and second class. The platforms were rather longer than normal and the dash panel was continued part of the way along the "step" side leaving a comparatively narrow access adjacent to the saloon on both sides, passengers entering and leaving the forward saloon by the front platform. This arrangement was subsequently abandoned and the partition in the saloon removed. The steps were mounted on the bogies and as previously mentioned had to be arranged to fold up. A full-length square-ended canopy was provided and the 32 "outside" seats reached by a "reversed" stair. These cars weighing 6 tons, were kept on the Goldenacre route and carried the legend "Trinity Route" on the canopies. The square-ended tops earned them the nick-name of "coffins". The second batch of eight cars, presumably Nos. 9 to 16, worked the Comely Bank route carrying the inscription "Stockbridge Route". These were built by the Falcon Company and were somewhat shorter having that firm's peculiar corner entrance platforms, "ordinary" stairs and very short canopies. There was no division in the saloon and the seating capacity was 18 inside and 22 outside. They were 23ft. 3in. overall and weighed about four tons.

Both types of car ran on bogies with outside plate frames. The gripper at each end of the car was a single jaw arrangement, the subject of a patent by Mr. Colam, mounted in a frame behind the leading axle and operated by a horizontal wheel on a pillar which protruded through a hole in the floor of the platform. The hole was slotted to allow for movement on curves. A small horizontal ratchet lever by which the gripper could be kept tight protruded underneath the handwheel. Brake blocks were provided to all wheels. On the "Metropolitan" cars these were applied by a foot pedal on the platform which operated the brakes of the bogie underneath. If the driver required the wheel brake at the back of the car he had to give three beats on the bell which was the signal for the conductor to press the pedal on the rear platform. The "Falcon" cars had orthodox inter-connected brake gear applied by one of two large levers to the left of the driver. The other lever similarly worked track brakes. The track brakes on the "Metropolitan" cars appear to have been worked by a separate horizontal handwheel. An oil lamp was provided at each end of the saloon, and the driver gave warning of approach by striking a brass bell suspended from the canopy.

There were two other cars of which little is known. They were long single-deck vehicles and said to have been of American construction. They were apparently found unsuitable and little used.

72

Nevertheless one at least was still to be seen in Henderson Row car shed during the time of the first war. Numbered 137 and 138 in 1897 they were subsequently renumbered 7 and 13. The Northern Company's cars were painted blue with cream panels and adorned with a hand-painted crest depicting a car encircled by a rope.

The Board of Trade Regulations, repeated in the Company's Rule Books, limited the speed to six miles per hour, and were very emphatic in prohibiting gravity running except at the special places, mentioned earlier, where this was necessary. Cars were not allowed to pass one another on the Canonmills curve. An increase in speed to 8 m.p.h. was soon sought, but was not sanctioned.

The fare from Hanover Street to Goldenacre was 3d. first class and 2d. second class or "outside", and the tickets were available for the bus journey to Trinity or Granton without extra charge. Intermediate fares were also available. The first class was discontinued after a time and the fares were reduced, halfpenny stages being introduced in 1895.

In September 1890 the Company suggested an extension by way of the Mound and George IV Bridge to the Grange district but Edinburgh Corporation refused to support the scheme and it was dropped. The following year the Company's chairman, now John Paterson, proposed an extension at the other end, from Goldenacre down Ferry Road and over the Edinburgh Street Tramways Company's tracks to Junction Bridge, with possibly a branch down Craighall Road. Nothing was done at the time but in 1896 the Company prepared a Bill on these lines for the 1897 Parliamentary Session. In this they proposed the following extensions:

1. From Goldenacre down Ferry Road as far as Craighall Road.
2. A continuation of this along Ferry Road to Newhaven Road;
3. A branch from these down Craighall Road as far as Stanley Road
4. A continuation of this down the hill to Newhaven.
5. From the Comely Bank terminus to Crewe Road.
   All were to be double line and worked by cable.

However proposals for unification with the new system being planned for the City were in the air, and the Company's activities ceased on 31 December 1896, the foregoing project being apparently withdrawn. It had been arranged for the Edinburgh & District Tramways Company to run the system meantime until formalities could be completed for the acquisition of the line by Edinburgh Corporation. This was accomplished by Section 20 of

73

the Edinburgh Corporation Act of 1897 (3 June 1897) and the whole undertaking passed to Edinburgh Corporation on 1 July 1897 for the sum of £110,000. The rolling stock etc. was immediately resold to the Edinburgh & District Tramways Company and the vesting was back dated to midnight of 31 December 1896. It then became part of the Corporation's system leased to the Edinburgh & District Tramways Company, and the Edinburgh Northern Tramways Company's affairs were wound up as provided for in the 1897 Act. Nos. 1 to 16 were renumbered 121 to 136.

In the half-year to 30 June 1894 the Northern Company ran 173,791 miles and carried 1,697,639 passengers, with receipts at 10.89d. p.c.m. and expenses of 5.33d. p.c.m. of which 0.73d. represented motive power. The figures include the horse bus service on which there was a small loss.

Now reverting to the Edinburgh & District Tramways Company's horse car system in 1896 we saw in the last chapter how plans for the cable installation were in hand. As mentioned, the construction of the two new power houses at Shrubhill and Tollcross had been started, and also the relaying of the tracks with the heavier rails and conduits. A formal start was made at Newington by Lord Provost McDonald on 9 September 1896. Reconstruction was generally commenced at the outer termini and progressed inwards to Princes Street where work was not commenced till 5 April 1897. 83lb. rails in 32ft. lengths were used, and 200 to 300 yards were usually done at a time, the horse car service being carried on over the other single line by means of temporary crossovers and transferring to the new lines on completion. The junction work was left to the last as this was quite complicated, involving the construction of extensive pits under the roadway. A good deal of delay arose through alterations and extensions which from time to time, right up to 1897 as we have seen, were proposed and incorporated, often entailing considerable changes in the equipment which had already been designed.

All the extensions authorised in the 1897 Act were not fully carried out, but most of the 1896 ones were. The Newington line was extended as far as Nether Liberton, at Gilmerton Road end. The Morningside line was extended as far as Braid Hills Road. The line along Gorgie Road was laid as far as Saughton Park, and the old piece of line up to Polwarth Terrace abandoned. The Murrayfield line was extended to the boundary at Saughtonhall Drive, the railway arch at the old terminus having to be replaced by a girder bridge to allow for this. The Gilmore Place to Craiglockhart route was not included in the conversion scheme at all, the traffic being considered insufficient at that time, and it remained a horse car line until a much later date. Nor were the triangular junctions at St. Andrew St. and West End perpetuated. For the time being also, plans for the Portobello route power house, were deferred as Dick Kerr & Company suggested that it might be suitable for an experiment with electric traction.

Provision was made in the Shrubhill power station for driving a cable to Leith, and in February 1898 Mr. Colam produced a scheme whereby the cable system could be continued right round the circular route by Bernard Street, Commercial Street, and Junction Street, including the new swing bridge over the harbour! In this scheme the cable would have been led via Junction Street to the Commercial Street side of the bridge and back via Foot of Leith Walk to the Bernard Street side of the bridge, and then back to Shrubhill. Constitution Street would have been single line. The swing bridge itself was to be provided with an auxiliary cable driven from the Bernard Street side. Unfortunately precise details of this ingenious scheme are lacking, but the difficulties will perhaps be better appreciated when we come shortly to describe the method of operating the cable system generally. Leith, however was still not interested in cables.

With all these delays, it is perhaps not surprising that contracts for the construction of the various junction pits were not signed until April 1898, and since so much time had already been spent on the still far from complete construction work, the two companies approached the Corporation for an extension of their lease, which as things stood, seemed likely to allow them only about eighteen years operation. Further, negotiations for leasing the Leith system from 30 June 1898, then seemed likely to materialise, so this would be a suitable date for a fresh start. The current lease had never received the Board of Trade's approval, and as Sections 22 and 23 of the Edinburgh Corporation Act of 1897 had empowered the Corporation to work the tramways themselves or to lease them without seeking Board of Trade approval, the opportunity should be taken to regularise the position. Thus the three parties entered into a new lease in July 1898, by which "the Corporation let to the Tramways Company the whole tramways belonging to or that might hereafter be constructed or acquired by the Corporation, and relative lands, premises, and works, for a period of twenty-one years from and after 30 June 1898". The Company undertook to pay the Corporation 7% on the capital expenditure, as from the date of commencing the public service. As each section was opened the 7% became payable on the corresponding proportion of the capital expenditure incurred, the sums involved being the subject of negotiation over which little difficulty seems to have arisen until the final stages were reached.

With the first part of the new system nearly ready the Company abandoned the idea of electric traction to Portobello, and the Corporation thereupon authorised a start on the power house for that route too. At first it had been intended that this be situated in the vicinity of Meadowbank, but later a site in Portobello High Street was decided upon. The Edinburgh Corporation Act 1899 (13 July 1899) authorised :

1. Doubling the Portobello line between Fishwives Causeway and Hope Lane.

2. Doubling the junction leading to the depot at Livingstone Place.

3. A slight shortening of the single line in Strathearn Place at Whitehouse Loan.

The present schemes were then completed by the Edinburgh Corporation Act 1900 (30 July 1900) which provided for access to a new Portobello depot and power house near Pipe Street; a trailing junction into Thornybauk leading to Tollcross depot; doubling the curves at Salisbury Place junction, and at Churchhill junction, and doubling the line between Tollcross and the Infirmary.

Returning to 1899, the Council, and the public, were getting impatient for the cable cars. The Tramways Committee met regularly and heard Mr. Colam's progress report. Fourteen cars had been delivered, and over a hundred more were ready at the maker's works awaiting completion of the depot accommodation. Then, on 23 May, the Shrubhill engines were put in motion for the first time, though the cables were not as yet laid.

Two pairs of horizontal compound non-condensing engines each of 500 h.p. were provided, one being kept as a reserve. The high pressure cylinders were 23in. dia. and the low pressure 40in. dia., the stroke being 5 feet. They were supplied with steam at 160lbs. per sq in. and ran at 45 r.p.m., governors keeping the speed within 10% with 100% overload. Three boilers were installed. The engines drove a countershaft by means of a series of driving ropes and the grooved cable-driving pulleys of 10 feet dia. were driven on this counter-shaft by means of Lindsay coil clutches. Provision was made for driving three cables, though the third one, for Leith, never materialised. The balance weights of the tensioning carriage were arranged on the wall of the engine room. The Shrubhill to St. Andrew Street cable was put in on 29 May and a car tried on the line late the following night. The new cables were of $3\frac{7}{8}$ in. circumference, and were drawn in as follows : Lengths of light cable were dropped through the slot, spliced together below and led round the cable driving pulley : The engine and light cable then pulled the main cable into place over the route.

1 June 1899 was a red-letter day. The Tramway Committee, the Lord Provost, Mr. Pitcairn the Manager, Mr. Colam, Mr. John Kerr and Mr. Moir of Messrs. Dick Kerr & Company, and several other notabilities assembled at Shrubhill at 12.30 where they boarded one of the new cars, No. 142. Promptly on the sound of Edinburgh's well-known one o'clock gun, the car moved off and made the inaugural trip to St. Andrew Street and back without any hitch. Thereafter from 3.00 p.m. till 6.00 p.m. that day the car plied the line giving free rides to all and sundry, and naturally it was always well filled.

The line was not yet available for public service however. Much pit work remained to be done also at the Post Office, the West End, Tollcross, and most of the other junctions. The horse cars were running past these obstructions on temporary single lines at the side of the street. The work was considerably held up by delays in deliveries of the steel troughing which was required for the roofing of the pits. However the West End pit was completed

Credited E.O.C.

SHRUBHILL CABLE POWER STATION

on 3 July, and as from 23 August the horse cars from Craiglock-hart were turned back at Gilmore Place to ease matters at Toll-cross. There were hopes of starting the Pilrig to Braid Hills Road service at the beginning of October. Leith asked the Board of Trade not to sanction the opening until arrangements had been made for through running to Leith, but this was of course still impossible.

The public grew more impatient. The Company was criticised for not employing a night shift, but replied that they had not enough suitable labour. However, the Tollcross engines were now ready and the Tollcross — Braid Hills Road cable was drawn in on 18 and 19 September. To expedite the Salisbury Place pit the horse cars on the Grange Road route were turned back either side of the junction as from 25 September, and now the Post Office, Morrison Street, and Haymarket pits were the only ones still to finish. The Princes Street cable from Tollcross, was ready on 27 September and on Sunday morning 1 October a trial car was run from Tollcross to Shrubhill, and from there right to Braid Hills Road, and back to Tollcross. This ran well and accordingly the Board of Trade were asked to inspect the line on 11 October. Meanwhile another successful trial run at full speed, i.e. 8 m.p.h., was made over the same route on the morning of 8 October. The trip was repeated in the afternoon, with the directors, officials and press on board, but this was not so auspicious, as on proceeding from Shrubhill to Braid Hills Road and approaching Tollcross, the car "hit the pawl"! Although the party were considerably shaken no one was really hurt. However the car was taken into the depot and the rest of the trip abandoned. This mishap was ascribed to the mistaken action of a workman in the Tollcross pit, the Company explaining that such a thing would not happen normally!

Sir Francis Marindin, the Board of Trade Inspector, came on 12 October. The inspection party included the Lord Provost and the Tramways Committee, and of course Mr. Pitcairn, Mr. Colam, and several others. The Tollcross power house was visited first and there Mr. Colam described and showed to the Inspector the intricacies of the system in the extensive pit running out to the main line, and full of whirring cables and pulleys etc. The Lord Provost and his colleagues seem to have been particularly impressed by the magnitude and complexity of the undertaking. The engines, boilers and driving gear here were similar to those at Shrubhill, but there were four boilers and three pairs of engines arranged for driving five cables.

The party then boarded one of the cars in the depot, and at 11.15 a.m. set off for Pilrig. A "slight hitch" at the St. Andrew Street junction is recorded, but Pilrig was reached safely and the return trip to Braid Hills Road also passed off without untoward incident. Returning from Braid Hills Road a brake test was satisfactorily carried out, the cable being released coming down the hill and a speed of 15 m.p.h. gained before applying the brakes. The Inspector had not forgotten the St. Andrew Street incident so the journey was continued thence and this time there was no hitch, and the party adjourned to a luncheon provided by the Tramways Company at the Royal Hotel.

A few days later, on 19 October, the Town Council held their "official" inspection of the system, and made a trip from Tollcross to Pilrig. Again there was a hitch at St. Andrew Street, the auxiliary cable for the curve being too oily for the car to grip, but Mr. Colam jumped into the pit and by the application of some sawdust soon had the trouble overcome. After this trip it was stated that if the Board of Trade Certificate was received in time, public service would commence on Monday 23 October, and it was intimated that the through service of horse cars to Leith would cease on that date. The Certificate did not arrive in time, but meantime the Company were running a few trial cars empty every day to accustom the drivers to their somewhat complicated duties.

One of these trial cars came to grief on 23 October, again at St. Andrew Street junction, where the points were lying for the public horse car service towards the Post Office. The cable was pulled out of the car gripper and "stranded". It continued to run all right until the stranded portion reached the Tollcross pit where it caught in another car's gripper. Warning of the impending danger arrived just in time and the cable was stopped, but the entangled gripper had to be removed from the car at Tollcross and of course with the cable stopped, all the other trial cars between Tollcross and St. Andrew Street were halted : Consequently the public service of horse cars was also held up. That was the end of cable running for that day and the cable cars had to be brought in by horses. Such mishaps had already occurred once or twice on the Northern lines.

The Tollcross depot was reached by a short line through the lane known as Thornybauk. There were facing and trailing connections on the incoming track at the foot of Home Street which came together with their inner rails against one another in Thornybauk. They then spread to provide a passing place from where a single line ran straight into the depot. The entrance was opposite Thornybauk, further west than in electric car days, and the floor was higher so that there was a slope up inside onto the traverser, from which cars could be run out by gravity. An auxiliary cable was provided to take cars through Thornybauk to and from the main line, and crossovers were laid in Home Street and Earl Grey Street. The former would be worked by gravity. The latter, being level, cars had to be pushed over by man power. The cars being relatively light this was fairly easily done once it was started by means of a pinch bar under the wheel. The main cables were taken out to Earl Grey Street direct under the street called West Tollcross and not round Thornybauk. Other crossovers were provided at the Waverley Steps, — worked by the returning cable, at the foot of Lothian Road and at Morningside Station, — which could be used by gravity, and at West End of Princes Street, — "push".

At last the Board of Trade Certificate arrived and the Company gave notice on 26 October that commencing that day a number of cable cars would be introduced into service between Pilrig and Braid Hills Road between 8.10 a.m. and 8.30 p.m. Eight cable cars carried passengers that day and there is no record of any mishaps. Two days later however a Pilrig bound car failed to release the cable in time at Tollcross and the cable was knocked off its pulley. A few hours delay ensued during which the horse cars did their best to provide a service, The number of cable cars on the line was increased gradually and the horse car service correspondingly reduced. Thus without great ceremony was the cable car introduced to public service in Princes Street.

Meantime work was proceeding as fast as possible on the remaining junction pits, and the other new routes.

It is now necessary to attempt to describe the method of operating the system at junctions etc. The Byelaws stipulated that gravity or impetus was not to be used, and to meet these conditions Colam designed for the new cars an improved gripper with jaws on either side. This was mounted ahead of the first axle and its operating rod provided with a knuckle-joint and sliding coupling so that its top part was carried in a fixed pedestal on the platform and operated by a vertically mounted spoked wheel. By this means the objectionable hole in the floor was avoided. It was arranged that the driver could disengage the front gripper operating rod and work the rear gripper instead. This was effected by means of a small lever on the pedestal which transferred the motion of the driver's hand-wheel to the gripper rod at the other end of the car by means of a shaft running underneath.

The method of working at junctions can be illustrated by considering a left-hand junction. It would be arranged for cars to approach with the cable in the right-hand jaw of the gripper, and on reaching a pre-determined mark in the roadway just before the junction the car was stopped. At this point the centre slot was diverted to the left for about two inches, and when the gripper which followed the diverted slot was opened the main cable jumped out of the right-hand jaw to take up its normal straight position. At the same time the auxiliary cable for the curve which was close to the left-hand side of the gripper slipped into the left-hand jaw as it opened. After rounding the curve with the auxiliary cable, the car was again stopped and the other main cable similarly picked up. A car going straight across the junction instead of round the curve, also stopped before the junction, and took the main cable in its rear gripper. It moved forward again thus until the front gripper had passed clear over the auxiliary cable of the curve into the main line. It then stopped again and dropped the cable from the rear gripper picking it up in the front one and proceeding once more, the rear gripper then passing clear over the said auxiliary cable. The main cable passed underneath the auxiliary cable on the curve, and so cars proceeding from the curve into the main line did not let go the auxiliary cable until they were on the main line and ready to pick up the main cable. In the case of the St. Andrew Street junction the auxiliary cable was pulled into position in the gripper of a car for St. Andrew Street by means of a pulley actuated by the pointsman pulling up a chain. In Earl Grey Street the Princes Street cable and the Braids cable similarly overlapped so that cars stopped to drop the one and pick up the other. At Shrubhill depot entrance the main cable was diverted from both lines into the power-house and the auxiliary cable used for taking cars out from the depot was used for the short distance down to the terminus at Pilrig where the cars ran into the "stub end" by gravity. There was an overlap with the main cable at the depot entrance on the up line. It should be mentioned that when the Shrubhill cable reached St. Andrew Street it was returned round a large vertical pulley and after doubling back a short distance served a crossover, and so enabled cars to be turned back towards Pilrig. An extension on the shaft of the vertical returning pulley drove the auxiliary cable which worked the junction curves at half speed, and this cable had its own tensioning device in the pit. The auxiliary cables were $3\frac{1}{2}$in. circumference. Pawls were provided at all points where it was essential for the main cable to be released.

There were no other complications on the Pilrig to Braid Hills Road route when first opened but with the coming into operation of other routes shortly afterwards, involving numerous such complicated manoeuvres at the many junctions, the whole system became very cumbersome to operate. For various reasons many simplifications became imperative, one of the earliest and most obvious being the securing of authority to run cars by gravity at certain places. But meantime the initial cabling arrangements and opening of the various routes had to be dealt with.

The winter of 1899-1900 was severe and it was not until 7 March that a trial car could be run on the next section to be cabled, viz. — Tollcross to Salisbury Place, from where the cable returned up to Churchhill, and back to Marchmont Road and Tollcross again. Crossovers were provided in Salisbury Place, Churchhill, and the top of Marchmont Road and equipped with the returning cable as at St. Andrew Street. This cable also drove auxiliary cables for the curves at the junctions at these three places. That at Churchhill was probably led underneath the main Braids outgoing cable as the Churchhill auxiliary did not see normal service. In the other two the auxiliary was uppermost round the curve as was normal. The Grange route horse-cars were replaced on 4 April by a cable car service between Post Office via Tollcross and Marchmont Road to Salisbury Place on a temporary permit prior to Board of Trade inspection. It would appear that the section between Marchmont Road and Churchhill was covered by a shuttle service from Salisbury Place.

The next step was the pulling in of the Nether Liberton cable from Shrubhill. This was 33,500 feet long, the longest on the system, and was installed on 18 April. It was arranged meantime to run "blind"* from Shrubhill to Picardy Place junction, and it also ran "blind" from Leith Street to North Bridge using a separate and straighter pipe for part of the distance. The outgoing cable came up to the incoming line in North Bridge and was used to work a crossover in gaining the outgoing line there. An auxiliary cable was provided between Leith Street and Princes Street and another one from in front of the Post Office round into North Bridge, which on its way back passed over the top of the former one going to Princes Street. Other crossovers which could be used by gravity were laid in Leith Street, South Bridge, and Newington Road, the latter "facing".

On 22 May Col. Yorke carried out his inspection, starting from Picardy Place junction and proceeding to Nether Liberton, thence back to the Post Office. Back again as far as Salisbury Place and along Grange Road to Churchhill and down to Tollcross. From here the party returned by Churchhill and Salisbury Place again to Post Office. Everything proved satisfactory and cable car service was provided between Post Office and Nether Liberton the following day. Two days later the cable cars commenced working the complete route from Pilrig to Nether Liberton. The Churchhill to Salisbury Place service was also extended to Pilrig.

Horse-cars were still operating on Princes Street to Murray-field, to Gorgie, and to Craiglockhart, but a siding was laid from Home Street to the south side of Tollcross and the Company gave notice that as from 4 June the Craiglockhart cars would operate in to Tollcross only. The service was arranged to run in connection

* i.e. the cable was not located under the slot and could not be picked up by a car gripper.

with the cars on the Marchmont route and a penny transfer ticket made available between West End and Merchiston Avenue. This was valid on any incoming car from Tollcross, but outwards from West End it was at first issued on Marchmont Road cars only.

The Princes Street cable was extended on 5 August. Reaching the West End from Tollcross it was turned left to Haymarket, to a crossover on the Murrayfield side of the Haymarket junction, and returned through this crossover back to West End before proceeding along Princes Street to Post Office and back to Tollcross. An auxiliary cable was provided for the curves to and from Lothian Road. It was arranged for cars proceeding towards Haymarket to use the rear gripper in Princes Street, and stopping on the Lothian Road curve crossing they picked up the cable for Haymarket in the front gripper.

The extension to Haymarket was inspected by Col. Yorke on 9 August and cable cars were running between Post Office and Haymarket the following day. It was announced that horse-cars would cease to operate on Princes Street from 13 August, Haymarket becoming an interchange point, but there is some doubt as to whether this was achieved so promptly. The auxiliary cable for the curve between Princes Street and North Bridge was also inspected by Col. Yorke on 9 August, so that the Marchmont Circular route was completed again. This was carried under the auxiliary cable from North Bridge towards Leith Street, so cars from Princes Street to North Bridge used the rear gripper and stopped on the crossing to change to the front gripper.

The Murrayfield route was completed next and the cable car service inaugurated on 10 September, prior to Board of Trade inspection. The Gorgie route, much of which was new, and the new Morrison Street line were completed soon afterwards, but in this case the change-over was withheld until, at last, after much prodding, Col. von Donop arrived on 14 December. He inspected all these lines, travelling from Haymarket to Gorgie, thence to the east end of Morrison Street and back to Haymarket. Boarding another car he then went to Murrayfield and back. The public service of cable cars between Pilrig and Gorgie via York Place, and also between the east end of Morrison Street and Gorgie was put on right away. The latter was very short lived. There being very little traffic it lasted two weeks.

Both the Gorgie and Murrayfield cables were driven at Tollcross power station, and the Morrison Street route was built mainly to take them to Haymarket. From Tollcross they ran in a "blind" tube to Morrison Street. The Murrayfield cable then continued "blind" to Haymarket where it took up its position under the Murrayfield track, and returning from Murrayfield as far as the

Haymarket crossover it entered the "blind" tube up Morrison Street for Tollcross. The Gorgie cable operated the Morrison Street tracks starting with a crossover at the Lothian Road end. An auxiliary cable was provided for the Lothian Road junction and appears to have been led under the main north-going cable in Lothian Road since it was not intended for normal service. Another auxiliary cable was provided between the Haymarket junction and the junction between the Morrison Street and Gorgie lines, and was led over the outgoing cable between West Maitland Street and the Murrayfield direction, and under the cable from Gorgie into Morrison Street. Both termini "stub-ends" were worked by the cable in both directions. Crossovers were provided at Shandwick Place, the east end of Dalry Road, west of Ardmillan Terrace, and at Westfield Road. Some were "facing" to suit gravity operation in the desired direction.

With the end of 1900 we have reached the stage where most of the system had been converted, only the Mound route and the Portobello route with its new London Road branch to Leith Walk being uncompleted, though these new tracks had been finished for some time. Since 1897 a horse-car service had been running between Meadowbank and Post Office on the new London Road line, but in order to advance the cabling this was withdrawn on 20 February 1901 and replaced by a shuttle service of horse cars between Abbeyhill and Leith Walk only. Henderson Row power station was being enlarged and an additional pair of engines of 500 h.p. provided to drive the Mound route cable.

About this period however there were a number of serious breakdowns which put sections of the system out of action for several hours. On these occasions the stranded cable cars were drawn away by horses to adjacent sections which were still functioning and temporary shuttle services of horse cars provided. It is interesting to note too, that at this period early morning workmen's services continued to be provided by horse cars. There was some complaint in the Town Council regarding these mishaps and the Company seems to have been apprehensive too for in April 1901 they quietly reverted to the service from Post Office via Tollcross and Marchmont Road to Salisbury Place instead of the Circular route. The Churchhill to Pilrig service also reverted to its former Churchhill — Salisbury Place run. The Salisbury Place auxiliary cable thus dropped out of normal use and was altered to lie under the main cable coming in from Nether Liberton instead of over it. The pawl on the incoming main cable was removed as cars gripping it did not require to let go.

At first the public were led to believe this was a temporary measure, but after a week or two it became known that the Company had no intention of restoring the Circular service. The matter was raised in the Town Council and the Town Clerk instructed to write to the Company demanding the restoration not only of the so-called inner circular service but also an outer circle via Churchhill as well. The Company declined and announced that as from the following Monday, 22 April, the Murrayfield — Nether Liberton service would also be cut, cars working between Murrayfield and Waverley Steps, and between Nether Liberton and Post Office only. Transfer tickets were made available but the inconvenience of changing cars at this important point raised a further storm of protest. The Company said delays were avoided by the new scheme which was therefore in the best interests of the public. The latter were not slow to allege the failure of the cable system. The Town Council for their part would accept no excuses and insisted on the restoration of the former services, but without effect. They had a meeting with the Company who then alleged insufficient traffic to warrant the circular services. In July the Town Clerk issued a comprehensive report on the situation. It was disclosed that of the £32,210 2s. 11d. rental due at Whitsun the Company had defaulted to the extent of £20,500. The Company had alleged that the auxiliary cables were unworkable and that under present conditions they were unable to earn sufficient revenue to enable them to pay the sum due. They had suggested that at certain places the main cables should be used instead of the auxiliaries, and that the rental should be reduced to 5% rising to $5\frac{1}{2}$% in 1902 and by $\frac{1}{2}$% each year till 7% was reached in 1905, the abatement to be made up in later years. If these proposals were accepted they would agree to work the system, but they were not prepared to relinquish their lease unless upon adequate terms. The Town Clerk had replied to the Company pointing out that the Company knew all about the estimated capital costs and about the auxiliary cables when they undertook their lease, and it was suggested that the difficulties with the auxiliary cables were exaggerated.

It must be admitted that the method of working the junctions was very cumbersome. For example, the average time taken to proceed from St. Andrew Street junction to North Bridge is said to have been nearly four minutes. The Company therefore had already started working cars by gravity at certain places, though of course without official sanction. Cars from St. Andrew Street were being run by gravity into Princes Street, and shortly afterwards the auxiliary cable was altered similarly to that at Salisbury Place. Also, at Haymarket, outgoing cars were running by gravity from West Maitland Street to the point at which the main Murrayfield or Gorgie cables were picked up. At Tollcross, cars proceeding towards Braid Hills were run by gravity across the junction, and at Marchmont Road cars from Churchhill direction crossed the junction by gravity. Yet another example was between Picardy Place and London Road where cars from Post Office were run gravity, picking up the York Place cable for Pilrig after passing London Road.

While this was going on, the Mound route was completed. On Sunday 25 August the Goldenacre cable was altered to run between Goldenacre and Henderson Row and a new cable put in between Henderson Row and Hanover Street and continued in a "blind" tube under Princes Street to the Mound and up to Tollcross and back. An auxiliary cable was provided for the junction into Brougham Street. Col. von Donop inspected the new line on 10 September and the public service between Mound and Marchmont Road commenced the following day. The horse car line in the High Street was apparently abandoned at this time or perhaps earlier. Crossovers were provided in George IV Bridge and in Lauriston Place at Tollcross.

The dispute between the Company and the Corporation lingered on. In November the Company again paid over only about half of the sum due in rent, and offered to sell their assets to the Corporation so that they could take over the working of the system themselves. The Corporation then initiated legal action for recovery of the sums due, and a novel turn followed. On Saturday 30 November the Company announced that as from the following day they would run their cars on Sundays between 10 a.m. and 10 p.m. This upset the Corporation further, who claimed the Company had to obtain their permission for Sunday services. All day on the Saturday they tried to stop the scheme, but on the Sunday the cars ran as announced, and indeed proved very popular with the public. Eighty-two cable cars were operated, but the horses had their day of rest as usual, and only the Salisbury Place — Churchhill section suffered poor patronage. Another innovation on that day was the introduction of "Bell-Punch" tickets with the stage names printed on them. It is believed that hitherto thin paper tickets torn off a roll had been used.

The Corporation again invoked the law and sought to interdict the Sunday service, but the Court refused to intervene. The drivers and conductors were not entirely satisfied however. They had been paid at time-and-half rate, but sought a limitation of their weekly hours and also a two shillings per week increase. The company for their part would not immediately agree, and wished to await the outcome of the legal question. So on the fourth Sunday, namely 29 December the car crews didn't turn out though the engineering staff did. By the afternoon however Mr. Pitcairn had gathered together some inspectors and others and a skeleton service with eighteen cars was provided between Pilrig and St. Andrew Street, and between Post Office and Haymarket, Morningside, and Newington; also Hanover Street to Goldenacre. The following week the Company conceded the two shillings increase for cable car crews, the Colinton Road horse car crews to receive a shilling a week as from the date of cable car operation to Portobello, and this was accepted by the men.

Meantime at their meeting on 4 December the Corporation reiterated their intention of recovering the sums due in rent, opposing the Sunday service, and declining the Company's offer to sell. This time however they decided to leave the question of the restoration of the through services until these more important issues were settled. The Company's answer to the Court was to the effect that the sums claimed were not justified since the tramways capital account had been wrongly debited with the cost of street widenings and acquisition of properties therefor. Also that the allegedly experimental auxiliary cables should not have been so charged. They pointed out that many of these were disused and they made the system unworkable. They claimed the right to run the cars on Sundays if necessary and pointed to the need to obtain all the revenue they could get. Shortly afterwards the Company offered to pay in £20,000 if the Corporation would drop the legal proceedings and take the matter to arbitration, but still the latter declined.

On 20 December the Mound to Marchmont Road service was altered to work only between the Mound and Tollcross due to insufficient through traffic, but on 8 March following it reverted to the former arrangement and was divided into three halfpenny stages with a penny fare for the full journey.

In February 1902 the financial dispute was considered by the Court and the Company ordered to pay over £20,000, the balance to await settlement of the matters raised by the Company. A more amenable spirit on both sides was arising however, and the Company actually paid over £30,000, while the Corporation conceded that there might be a case for amending the tramways capital account in respect of street widenings, etc.

While these affairs were being negotiated, pressure was applied for the completion of the Portobello route, — by the April holiday if possible. To enable the pit work outside the depot to be expedited the horse cars were temporarily withdrawn between the depot and Joppa from 10 February.

On 24 February the Company made a further gesture and reintroduced working round the Salisbury Place junction, cars proceeding round the curve into Salisbury Place by gravity. The Pilrig—Churchhill service was thereby restored, though the circular route was still cut at the Post Office, cars working from Waverley via Tollcross, Marchmont, and Salisbury Place to Post Office and back. From 9 March this route ceased to operate on Sundays.

Meantime a great effort was being made with the Portobello route. The power station with two 500 h.p. engines driving the cable drums through gears instead of ropes as in the earlier power stations, and supplied by three boilers with automatic stokers was complete, as was also the depot with accommodation for 22 cars. Then on 16 April the cable between the Portobello power station and Waterloo Place was installed, followed by the shorter one between the power station and Joppa on 19 April. The two cables overlapped outside the depot and an auxiliary cable was put into operation when required to take cars into the shed. Cars ran out of the shed by gravity. At the Joppa terminus the cars were worked both in and out of the "stub-end" by the cable and two stopping places provided, with means to ensure the right cable was picked up. At Waterloo Place the double tracks made connection with the Princes Street tracks though the Portobello cable was turned back just short of the junction. This connection was not then normally used and could only be worked by means of a "fly-shunt". A facing crossover was provided in Waterloo Place through which cars gravitated before returning to Portobello and Joppa. Other crossovers were provided at Montrose Terrace, Cadzow Place, Meadowbank, Piershill, King's Road, at either side of the depot, and at Pitt Street in Portobello. On the following day, Sunday, two trial trips were made successfully, but the Board of Trade Inspector had not yet visited the line and on the holiday on the Monday the public had to be content with the horse cars. Col. von Donop made his inspection on 1 May. It was over by 9.30 a.m. and the public service of cable cars commenced immediately with thirteen cars. Outgoing cars were arranged to run by gravity over the junction with the new London Road line at Abbeyhill, but it does not appear as though the London Road cable was then installed.

This London Road cable was an extension of the Pilrig to St. Andrew Street cable which, on its run back down Leith Walk was diverted under the up main line cable at London Road junction, and taken to Abbeyhill where, after passing the junction, it was returned and passing over the outgoing Portobello cable, ran back along London Road and round the curve onto the up line in Leith Walk, from where it was again returned and took up its place on the down line beyond the London Road junction. No auxiliary cables were therefore provided at the London Road and Abbeyhill junctions. All cars were run down Leith Walk between Picardy Place and a point beyond London Road junction, or round into London Road, by gravity. Crossovers were provided at each end of the London Road line. There was also one in Leith Walk above the London Road junction.

The cable was extended along London Road in July 1902 and a service provided between Meadowbank and the Leith Walk end

JOHN E. PITCAIRN
Manager E.S.T.Co. and E. & D.T.Co. 1884-1906

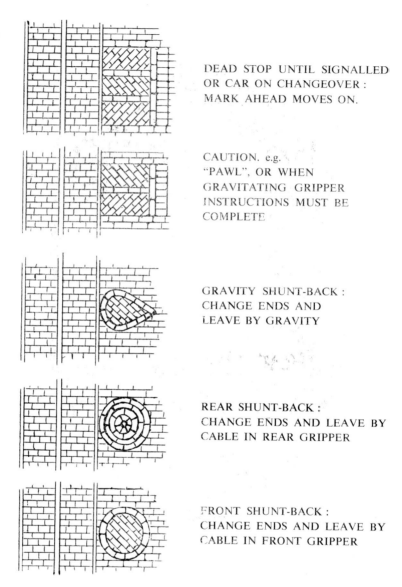

DEAD STOP UNTIL SIGNALLED
OR CAR ON CHANGEOVER :
MARK AHEAD MOVES ON.

CAUTION. e.g.
"PAWL", OR WHEN
GRAVITATING GRIPPER
INSTRUCTIONS MUST BE
COMPLETE

GRAVITY SHUNT-BACK :
CHANGE ENDS AND
LEAVE BY GRAVITY

REAR SHUNT-BACK :
CHANGE ENDS AND LEAVE BY
CABLE IN REAR GRIPPER

FRONT SHUNT-BACK :
CHANGE ENDS AND LEAVE BY
CABLE IN FRONT GRIPPER

ROAD MARKS, EDINBURGH CABLE TRAMWAYS

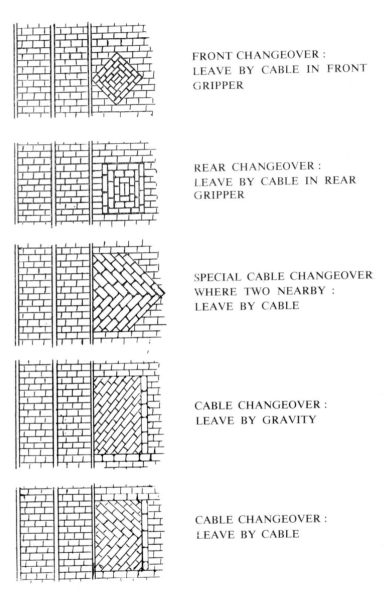

FRONT CHANGEOVER :
LEAVE BY CABLE IN FRONT
GRIPPER

REAR CHANGEOVER :
LEAVE BY CABLE IN REAR
GRIPPER

SPECIAL CABLE CHANGEOVER
WHERE TWO NEARBY :
LEAVE BY CABLE

CABLE CHANGEOVER :
LEAVE BY GRAVITY

CABLE CHANGEOVER :
LEAVE BY CABLE

ROAD MARKS, EDINBURGH CABLE TRAMWAYS

of London Road. The public desired a through service to Princes Street however, so on 20 October 1902 this was replaced by a service between Abbeyhill and Morningside Station via London Road and York Place.

The system now extended for 21¼ miles and was considered complete. Meanwhile the negotiations between the Company and the Corporation had been proceeding, and on 29 July 1902 a new agreement between them was signed. This resolved all the matters which had been in dispute including reduction of the capital account and the sums due by the Company, the future rates of rental, through working and Sunday services.

On 21 December 1902, the Marchmont Circular route and the Murrayfield — Nether Liberton service were restored, the auxiliary cable from Princes Street to North Bridge having been altered to lie above the other auxiliary from North Bridge towards Leith Street. Cars for the latter direction were then run by gravity.

The system was now operating quite successfully. In January 1901 the Company had placed the drivers under the control of the engineering department, and later in the year an Instruction Book was issued to them, containing an Appendix wherein was laid down the correct procedure in regard to left or right hand jaw and front or rear gripper for each section of every route. The precise spots at which cars had to stop to change cables or carry out other manoeuvres were afterwards marked by squares, circles, or other special shapes, each with its own meaning, laid in setts between the two pairs of rails, and pointsmen were provided to ensure by examination, that all was correct before cars were allowed to proceed at the various junctions. See diagrams on pages 90 and 91.

Nevertheless minor mishaps continued to occur from time to time, and there were also instances of cars hitting pawls. Some of these latter occurrences were accompanied by injuries to the passengers and gave rise to discussions with the Board of Trade regarding the use of pawls. The Company believed the prevention of serious damage, and hence dislocation of the service, justified their use where really necessary, but the introduction of gravity running at various places, as already mentioned, had enabled several of them to be eliminated. Further improvements of this nature were effected from time to time. On 17 January 1904 the main cable was extended from Shrubhill to Pilrig and its diversion to and from the power house arranged on the down line. Cars proceeding towards Pilrig passed Shrubhill by gravity, and had a clear run with the cable coming up from Pilrig. At Tollcross junction the declivity was too slight for effective gravity operation, and the cable heights were adjusted, also early in 1904, to allow of safely "fly-shunting" cars proceeding towards Braid Hills. The same scheme was put into operation at the West End for cars proceeding towards Haymarket, in October 1905.

These and other minor alterations considerably lessened the risk of accidents as well as simplifying the operation of the system, and enabled driving by the rear gripper to be dispensed with except in one or two special places. The pawls were still retained at certain necessary locations however, and were again under discussion later as we shall see.

In 1903 there was a strike by the car crews over the introduction of a new pay system, and there were unfortunately instances of assault and sabotage. Mr. Colam retired in December 1904 and was succeeded by Mr. E. F. Harris.

In 1904 the question of the Company's payments to the Corporation came up again. The capital expenditure on constructing the system was said to amount to approximately £1,000,000, but the Company had been paying the 7% on an estimated total of £1,250,000, which included the cost of purchasing the Northern Company's system. The Corporation now said their total was higher, — nearly £1,300,000, while the Company wanted a reduction. Some reduction appears to have been made and in 1905 the position appears to have been more amicable, as a further revision was agreed upon. The Company's "Deferred" shareholders did not receive their first dividend till 1908.

An increase in speed was considered desirable and feasible, and as the maximum speeds had been fixed in the local Acts, the Corporation secured an Order in 1905 to permit the Board of Trade to fix the speeds notwithstanding the Acts. The cable speeds then became as follows :—

Mound	7¾m.p.h.	Braids, and Princes St.	10¼m.p h.
Stockbridge	8 m.p.h.	Joppa	10½m.p.h.
Goldenacre	8¾m.p.h.	Portobello	11¾m.p.h.
Liberton, York Place, Grange, Gorgie, Murrayfield			9½m.p.h.

It is opportune now to review the services and fares in operation. The "Tickets and Fares" Book dated 1903 quotes the following services, the identifying letters being used for ticket purposes only :

A	Murrayfield & Nether Liberton
B	Pilrig & Gorgie
C	Pilrig & Braid Hills
D	Abbeyhill & Morningside
E	Marchmont Road Circle (Not on Sundays)
F	Mound & Marchmont Road
G	Pilrig & Churchhill
H	Pilrig & Nether Liberton
J	Post Office & Joppa
L	Tollcross & Colinton Road (Horse cars)
M	Princes Street Goldenacre
N	Princes Street & Comely Bank
BX	Post Office & Gorgie
CX	Post Office & Morningside or Braid Hills

The "Bell-Punch" type tickets were : 1d.-white; 2d.-pink; and 3d.-mauve, the fares conforming fairly closely to those in force prior to the second world war. Separate issues of tickets were provided for routes A, B, C/D, E/F, G/H, J, L, M/N. Children under 10 years paid 1d. for any one journey. There were certain $\frac{1}{2}$d. stages on E and F routes, also from Pilrig, Joppa, and Goldenacre, and certain special children's and workmen's $\frac{1}{2}$d. stages also, and a blue ticket was available for these. A pale brown 1$\frac{1}{2}$d. ticket was provided for four 1$\frac{1}{2}$d. stages on E, J, and M routes, while there was quite a selection of 1d. transfers for which a green ticket was used. These however were soon withdrawn with only four exceptions. Special 1d. tickets were sold at the Company's office for use of scholars, messengers, etc., and Season tickets could be obtained for the Joppa route. The Season ticket scheme was introduced in January 1903. A parcels delivery service was started in October 1904.

The frequency of the various services was altered from time to time but each service generally had cars every three, four, or five minutes, which compares well with service frequencies today. Some changes were made in the services later. Commencing about September 1904 a service was put on between Ardmillan Terrace and Salisbury Place, but on 1 October 1906 this was altered to Ardmillan Terrace and Abbeyhill via York Place and London

THE PILRIG "MUDDLE" c.1905-6   Courtesy Inglis
The cable car driver is waiting with his hand on the gripper-wheel ready
to tighten it and put the car in motion : The Pointsman has already checked
that the cable is in place in the gripper, and the brakes are off. Leith car
No. 32 emerging from Pilrig Street.

95

Road, the Morningside Station and Abbeyhill service being changed to Morningside Station and Pilrig. Also on 1 October 1906 the Mound to Marchmont Road route was again terminated at Tollcross, and the Pilrig to Churchhill service shortened to Pilrig and Salisbury Place. The Marchmont circular service was cut once more this time at the top of Marchmont Road, and the cars run on an increased frequency from there via Tollcross, Princes Street, and Salisbury Place to Churchhill, and back again. This alteration was not popular and after considerable discussion the Corporation referred the matter to an arbiter, — the Dean of the Faculty — who, in February 1908 decided that the Company must operate the circular service if required to do so by the Corporation. Pressure being brought to bear this was restored later in the year and the Pilrig — Salisbury Place service extended to Churchhill. The public were still dissatisfied with the service provided however, and in February 1909 the Council agreed to the Marchmont-Tollcross—Post Office-Salisbury Place-Churchhill scheme, the Pilrig-Churchhill service again being cut back at Salisbury Place. The junction at the top of Marchmont Road was then taken out, as had already been done some time previously at Churchhill and at the east end of Morrison Street. Meanwhile a new fare table was introduced on 1 April 1906 giving longer stages and more transfer facilities again.

Mr. Pitcairn retired on 30 August 1906. He had been appointed Manager of the Edinburgh Street Tramways Company in 1884 and had come to be very highly regarded by his staff and directors alike. He was succeeded by Mr. C. W. Shepherd, who had been Traffic Superintendent.

In January 1907 most of the routes were given numbers, and these were displayed on a coloured oval board mounted on the upper deck rail. The numbers and colours were as follows :—

1	Murrayfield & Nether Liberton	Red	board
2	Pilrig & Gorgie	Blue	board
3	Abbeyhill & Ardmillan Terrace	Blue	board
4	Pilrig & Braid Hills	Green	board
5	Pilrig & Morningside Station	Green	board
6	Marchmont & Churchhill	White	board
7	Pilrig & Nether Liberton	Red	board
8	Pilrig & Salisbury Place	Red	board

The Hanover Street route, Comely Bank route, Mound route, and Joppa route never carried numbers. The bulls-eye light in the saloon bulkhead was then arranged to show the corresponding colour at night. Later the long destination board carried above the saloon windows was discarded in favour of a more conventional small board carried at the bottom of the centre window. About 1911 the bulls-eye light in the saloon bulkheads was removed and a slide arranged with opaque glass behind took its place. Into this slide a metal stencil was inserted after dark, being illuminated by the saloon interior lighting. These stencils showed only the termini and the name was often abbreviated; hence a long-standing designation "Toll-X". The old Northern section cars were not provided with these amenities. At the end of 1907 the Company agreed to fit higher handrails to the outside of the car stairs. In October 1907 the Board of Trade sanctioned an increase of speed for the Henderson Row cables to 9 m.p.h.

Reverting to 1905, the question of extensions and future policy was under discussion in the Town Council. The Musselburgh Company were already inside the City boundary with their line to the cable terminus at Joppa, though the City had powers to acquire it upon six months notice if they wished. Other electric tramway promotors were seeking routes into the City. The Town Clerk was asked to report and he recommended the Corporation to ensure ownership of all lines constructed within the boundary, and to consult the present lessees in regard to any extensions. It was considered the conversion of the Gilmore Place-Craiglockhart horse-car line to either cable or electric traction was now necessary.

The Corporation's Provisional Order for 1905 therefore sought authority for the reconstruction of the Craiglockhart line, which it was proposed to extend to the City boundary, and beyond it to Craiglockhart Avenue. The line was then to go down Craiglockhart Avenue to Slateford and back to town by Slateford Road and Fountainbridge. In May 1906 however the Corporation decided to withdraw from their application all but the reconstruction of the existing line and its extension as far as the top of Craiglockhart Avenue. Even so, the portion outside the City boundary was not included in the resulting Edinburgh Corporation Act 1906, (passed 4 August 1906). Authority for another new route was included in this Act however, namely down Broughton Street from the foot of Leith Street to Canonmills, with a branch down East Claremont Street to Bonnington Toll: Also connections from York Place and from Picardy Place. Cable traction was to be used for the Craiglockhart line unless the Company agreed to some other system; while if cable traction was not provided for Broughton Street that line was not to be included in the Company's existing lease. The Corporation might then work it themselves.

The Corporation were now thinking hard about the high capital cost of the cable system, which many already regarded as obsolete, and a considerable controversy arose. Sir Alexander Kennedy was consulted and favoured a surface-contact electric line.

A full size demonstration of the "Kingsland" surface-contact system had been given in the North Bridge Arcade in June 1906. A council deputation therefore set off to inspect the various systems to be seen at work in the country. Their tour took them to London where the conduit system was seen. They saw the "Dolter" surface-contact system at Hastings, and also at Rotherham and Mexborough; the "Lorain" surface-contact at Wolverhampton, and the "G.B." surface-contact at Lincoln. The "Kingsland" surface-contact system was also further explained to them at the Traction Corporation Ltd.'s London office as they had as yet no line in operation in this country. This company were anxious to provide a six months trial on the Morrison Street route, or from the Mound to the High Street, and while the Corporation were willing, the Edinburgh & District Tramways Company were not. The Dolter concern offered to equip the Craiglockhart line on a sort of "not satisfied no payment" basis. The Edinburgh Suburban Electric Tramway Company, to be mentioned in a later chapter, and who were then in course of negotiating an agreement with the Corporation, offered to extend their proposed system along Melville Drive to Tollcross and connect up with the Craiglockhart line on the overhead system. This however was rather ruled out as the Corporation did not want to turn out their present lessees, who for their part, preferred to continue a uniform system, which meant cable. They were however prepared to agree to an electric system if the Craiglockhart route was continued from Tollcross down to the Mound, and with certain safeguards on costs. On the other hand they refused to agree to electric traction for Broughton Street.

The Council deputation duly reported. They felt the "G.B." surface-contact system most suited Edinburgh, but the difficulties of installing this on a cable line, as would be necessary between Tollcross and Gilmore Place, did not appear capable of solution. Only the overhead electric system could be used there, and to bring that system down the Mound in view of Princes Street just would not do. So on 5 February 1907 the Council decided to reconstruct the Craiglockhart line for cable traction. As before, Mr. Colam was offered the joint appointment as Engineer for the new works, but this time refused, so Sir Alexander Kennedy was appointed. On 26 February 1907 the Town Council decided to construct the Broughton Street line to Canonmills, likewise for cable traction.

The contracts were let, to Dick Kerr & Co. Ltd., in July, and the three horse-cars withdrawn from the Craiglockhart line on 24 August 1907, to allow work to proceed. So ended horse traction in Edinburgh.

The residents beyond the Craiglockhart Station terminus had been pressing for the extension of the line to be carried out at the same time, as they claimed it would be less costly than adding it later. The Corporation agreed on 11 June 1907, and the construction of the extension to the City boundary was put in hand also. The first half-mile or so of this route had interlaced tracks with a single slot, and there were two passing places. The extension was nearly all interlaced track, but on this section separate slots were provided. Where a single slot was used great care was necessary, and the Rule Book pointed out that the gripper could not be opened more than two turns with safety. If opened further the cable was liable to slip out altogether. Opening the gripper one turn to let the cable slide through while holding the car with the brake was normal traffic stop procedure. Seven turns ensured the cable was dropped for change-over purposes.

The new cable was driven from Tollcross power station, provision having been made in the original design for additional power output. During the alterations in the power station there was a serious mishap in the early hours of 3 November 1907 resulting in the Grange and Murrayfield cables being out of action that day, though by great effort full service was restored for the following day.

An auxiliary cable was provided at the Gilmore Place junction, and manual signal lamps were installed on the sections which were in effect single line, for use in fog.

On 14 April 1908 Major Pringle inspected the whole line for the Board of Trade, starting from Princes Street in one of the new top-covered cars. Everything proved satisfactory and a five minute service between Post Office and Craiglockhart was inaugurated immediately after the inspection was completed. This service was numbered 9, displayed on a yellow board.

Meanwhile construction of the Broughton Street line was proceeding. This was to be ready for service on 1 June 1908 under a penalty of £20 per week. The work was not so straightforward however and necessitated some rearrangement of the cables. The Henderson Row — Goldenacre cable was led "blind" as far as Canonmills where it then took up the line to the foot of Leith Street, returned to Goldenacre, back to Canonmills, and then "blind" to Henderson Row. An auxiliary cable driven from it served the short distance between Henderson Row and Canonmills where, in returning, it worked a crossover. The facing crossover below Henderson Row was relaid in the trailing direction and apparently worked by one of the cables. Another trailing crossover was provided above the junction also. The junction to the Broughton Street line and its pit were not constructed however, there being a gravity crossover at the end of the new line. No auxiliary cable was provided at the junction at the foot of Leith Street, the main Broughton Street cable being taken through the junction into Leith Street, and cars for Pilrig gravitating across it.

Some difficulties arose with the pulleys in the dip in the line near the Canonmills terminus, which further delayed the opening, and in the event, it was not until 20 October 1908 that Col. von Donop inspected the line for the Board of Trade. A top-covered car was again used for the inspection, and the Craiglockhart—Post Office service was extended to Canonmills the same afternoon. Some modifications to the cables at the Post Office had also been required for this service, probably involving a lowering of the two auxiliaries for the two North Bridge curves so that the cars from Leith Street to Princes Street could safely make the two "flying-shunts" over them. At the Town Council meeting on the same day that the line was opened, the Corporation called upon the Company to complete the junction at Canonmills so as to enable the Broughton Street route cars to run through to Goldenacre. The Company demurred, but in face of public clamour for the through service, started to build the junction, pointing out at the same time that through running would still not be possible owing to the differences in the old Northern system pulleys etc. A transfer ticket was made available from 9 November. The Corporation insisted that through running was necessary and authorised the expenditure on the necessary modifications between Henderson Row and Goldenacre. The work was completed in due course and the Broughton Street cars extended to Goldenacre early in 1910. The cars on this service showed "Leith Street & Goldenacre" on their destination board. When the junction was made the Canon-mills—Henderson Row auxiliary cable was led under the main Broughton Street — Goldenacre cable, and cars from Goldenacre to Hanover Street took the junction by gravity. This new link provided an orthodox route by which the Northern section cars could be hauled to the Shrubhill workshops when necessary. Hitherto such transfer had been effected by means of a single trailing connection from Hanover Street eastwards to Princes Street laid in 1906. This connection had no conduit and was removed on the opening of the Broughton Street route.

After clearing the junction at the foot of Leith Street, the Broughton Street tracks were interlaced with a single slot for a short distance, and just before the end of this section the York Place route was crossed at right angles. Both routes were on gradients but the new line being the steeper, the York Place cables were led underneath and cars proceeding up York Place had to take a good "flying-shunt". This raised the question of pawls again. It was intended to provide pawls here but on account of strong objections by certain parties they were not put in. The first

100

accident due to a York Place car not releasing its cable occurred only five days after the opening of the Broughton Street line. Several passengers were injured and the Broughton Street line put out of action for the rest of the day.

Early in 1909 Sir Alexander Kennedy, who had now been appointed permanent Consultant to the Corporation Tramways Committee, was asked to report on the subject of pawls in general. He considered that the risk of injury to passengers was not increased by the use of pawls and felt unjustified in recommending their removal. Nevertheless an alternative was suggested for the Broughton Street-York Place crossing, viz. — a permanent "pointsman" to warn York Place drivers to release their gripper. The Board of Trade concurred with Sir Alexander Kennedy's report and the provision and duty of the pointsman at the Broughton Street-York Place crossing incorporated in the Byelaws. The branch to Bonnington Toll and the connections to York Place and to Picardy Place were not constructed.

Towards the end of 1907 a Mr. N. Thomson proposed a sixty years lease of the whole system with a view to electrification but this found no favour with the Council.

An improvement was effected at the London Road junction in 1908 when a new pit was built and an auxiliary cable provided, apparently for the benefit of upgoing cars. Another alteration was made at the Lauriston Place-Brougham Street junction where the original auxiliary cable had earlier been removed and the main cable extended in its place for taking the Mound route cars to and from the depot. A new pit was built in Lauriston Place in 1909 and an auxiliary cable provided for the junction curve again.

One other extension to the cable system remains to be considered. This was to the Gorgie route which it was intended to extend for about half a mile from Saughton Park to the then new road called Chesser Avenue, and then to continue along Chesser Avenue to the new Cattle Markets. The Corporation sought powers for this line in their 1908 Provisional Order, and also for a new link from the Murrayfield terminus to the Gorgie line along what is now Saughtonhall Drive, then being constructed. This latter was however withdrawn. In March 1908 when the Cope Collis Syndicate Ltd. sought permission for a conduit electric line along Saughtonhall Drive it was refused. Preparations were in hand for the Scottish National Exhibition to be held at Saughton Park in that year however, and it was urged that if part of this extension could be laid in time for the Exhibition opening on 1 May it would be very useful for storing cars to meet the expected heavy traffic. In October 1907 the Board of Trade agreed to work being put in hand for this purpose forthwith, notwithstanding that Parliamentary sanction could not be obtained for some time. The Company agreed to compensate any affected parties. The work was pushed ahead as far as Chesser Avenue and finished in time for Major Pringle to inspect it on the same day as the Craiglockhart line, namely 14 April 1908. The extension was then available for storing cars for the Exhibition traffic; the normal service not being extended to the new terminus until after the Board of Trade's Certificate arrived in September, the Provisional Order by that time having passed through Parliament. A service from Lothian Road via Morrison Street to the Exhibition was proposed but did not materialise. Traffic was very heavy leaving the Exhibition and queue barriers had to be installed. The Tramways Company issued an illustrated Guide.

On the excuse that a threehalfpenny fare was inconvenient with the Exhibition crowds, the Company raised the Gorgie and Murrayfield fares to twopence. After the Exhibition closed a deputation to the Company sought a restoration of the old fare, but the Company then revised their scale to give three stages for a penny and six for twopence throughout the system, dropping the threehalfpenny fares.

The remainder of the proposed Chesser Avenue extension was never built. Messrs. Dick Kerr & Company were ready to start work on it in February 1910 when it was pointed out that there would be difficulties with the cable on account of the rise over the bridge at the Cattle Market. So the matter was reconsidered, and instead, the Corporation decided on a new line from Ardmillan Terrace along Slateford Road to the Cattle Market. It has to be mentioned however that another concern, the Colinton Tramways Company proposed to build a tramway on private ground from Slateford to Colinton, and also a line from East Fountainbridge to Ardmillan Terrace, as related in chapter V. With all this in view it was decided that the Slateford Road line should be electrically operated, and that it should be excluded from the subjects of the 1898 lease to the Edinburgh & District Tramways Company. Accordingly a Minute of Agreement was drawn up on 14 June 1910, by which the Slateford electric line was to be worked by the Edinburgh & District Tramways Company "as a line distinct and separate from the Tramways let under the Lease of 1898" to the thirtieth day of June 1919. Provision was made for through running over the Colinton Tramways. The line made a single line trailing connection with the outgoing Gorgie line at Ardmillan Terrace, and was single with passing places. The overhead system was adopted, current being supplied from the Corporation's Dewar Place electricity station to a feeder pillar at the foot of Ardmillan Terrace. The work was put in hand very quickly and the line was opened on 8 June 1910, prior to date of the Agreement. The Company converted four cars for this service, the two normally in use being hauled to and from Shrubhill depot night and morning by cable cars.

On Saturday and Sunday afternoons in the summer of 1908 a service had been run between Ardmillan Terrace and Joppa, proceeding via Waterloo Place on the outward journey, but using the London Road and York Place route on the return. This return route avoided the additional complications at the Post Office junctions entailed for west-going cars. There were several requests for such a through service to be provided regularly in both directions between Regent Road and Princes Street but these were turned down on account of the aforementioned complications for west-going cars.

Further changes were made in the services. In the summer of 1909 the number 3 service was altered to run from Ardmillan Terrace to Pilrig and number 5 became Abbeyhill to Morningside Station again but near the end of the year the previous arrangement was reverted to, though the aforementioned alteration was tried once more in the following summer. A penny transfer ticket between Abbeyhill and Surgeon's Hall was made available from 24 September 1909, while in July 1909 a penny fare for dogs or luggage, using a brown ticket, was introduced. The opening of the new amusement park at the Marine Gardens brought additional traffic to the Portobello route for the summer, and through services were sometimes run.

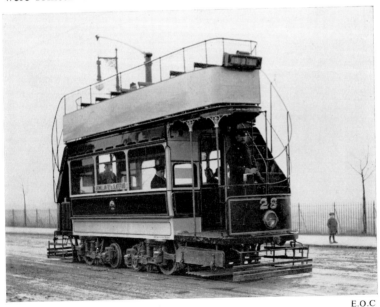

E.O.C

SLATEFORD ROUTE ELECTRIC CAR
Note the "country" road and fields

Long service stripes and merit medal awards for the staff were introduced about the end of 1908, and in 1909 a comprehensive Rule Book was issued. A glance at some of its contents is interesting. There was a page of instructions on "How to deal with offenders against the Bye-Laws". Another on "How to report street accidents": Several on "General Instructions", and several more on "Special Instructions to Drivers and Conductors". The first of these is perhaps of particular interest in showing the exacting nature of the driver's duties: "No one shall be appointed a driver unless he is under thirty-six years of age and can produce a written character for carefulness and sobriety, and is in possession of the necessary technical certificate. He must then qualify to drive on all routes". For the necessary technical certificate the man had to know :

1. The construction of grippers, bogies, and brakes, with the names of their parts.

2. How to use the grippers and gearing, brakes and sand.

3. How to drive a car.

4. How to deal with a faulty gripper, slot-roller, sleeve, die, guide-pin, cradle and slide-bar.

5. How to deal with a faulty friction-plate, gripper-centre, gripper leg, and screw-fork.

6. How to attach and detach a gripper.

7. Names and positions of changeover marks.

8. Examinations of grippers and cables at changeover marks.

9. Names and positions of cables on all routes.

10. Position and displacement of cables on curves, crossings, and supporting pulleys.

11. Names of all junctions.

12. Use of slot and track points, and how to rerail bogies.

13. Use and position of slot-stops. (i.e. pawls).

14. Management of gas generators and car lighting.

There were seventeen pages explaining the various road marks and special detailed instructions for working cars at certain junctions etc. The book was completed with the inclusion of the Board of Trade and Corporation Bye-Laws.

Attempts were being made to devise a better form of lifeguard for the cars. Electric cars normally had the gate and automatic tray device under the platforms, but there was no room for this on the cable cars which were provided only with a fender. It was a problem which proved intractable. However another safety measure applied in 1909 was fitting of wire mesh between the top deck rails of the cars. The Princes Street tracks were relaid in the sumer of 1910. Passenger "islands" were introduced at Antigua Street and at Easter Road in 1911, also a passenger shelter, — Edinburgh's first, — at Ardmillan Terrace in February 1911. At this time the only transfer fare in operation seems to have been that to Slateford. A decorated car ran during the Royal visit to the City in the summer of 1911.

There was labour trouble again on 18 July 1913 when the men ran their cars into the depot and came out on strike for an additional halfpenny per hour, having refused the Company's offer of a farthing. New men were gathered from around the country and lodged at Shrubhill while undergoing intensive training in the strange technique of driving a cable car. A row developed over these men not having licences, and when application was made for these on 29 July the Magistrates refused them. Thirty-five cars were by then in service, and one or two hostile acts occurred However a settlement was effected on 30 July through the mediation of the Lord Provost, and normal service resumed the following day.

The question of the further development of the City's transport was again to the fore at this period, though it was realised that extension of the cable system could not now be profitable. There had recently been proposals for a line from Fountainbridge through the Grassmarket, Bristo, Preston Street, and Duddingston to Portobello, and also via Palmerston Place to the Queensferry Road. In July 1911 the Burgh Engineer inspected the petrol-electric tramcar running at Morecambe, and suggested a trial with such a machine in Edinburgh. Three months later a report on Motor Bus Traction and the "Rail-less Trolley Car" was submitted. Three routes were suggested. However in September 1912 a review of the various systems of street traction was called for, and the Burgh Engineer's resulting document was a comprehensive survey of the possibilities of all kinds of tramways, trolley-buses, and motor-buses.

Mentioning that 25¾ route miles of cable tramway were operating in the City, the cost of construction, track work only, was given as £29,000 per mile of double track. Working expenditure was shown as 5¼d. per car-mile and rent and rates worked out at 4d. per car-mile. Since the revenue averaged 10½d. per car-mile, the Company apparently made a small profit of 1¼d. per car-mile. It may be remarked that the horse-power per car employed worked out at the very low figure of about 15. The capital costs were of course very heavy, and although up to that time the operating costs at 5¼d. per car-mile were the lowest in the country, Leith Corporation's electric tramways had succeeded in reducing their operating costs to a new low record figure of 4½d. per car-mile. So, to quote the review, "It is not likely, in face of these facts, that any extension of the cable system will be contemplated". This of course proved to be the case.

For the future, the Burgh Engineer ruled out the conduit electric system on account of cost, and the surface-contact electric system mainly on the grounds of potential danger. The overhead electric system he considered suitable except for Princes Street, and it was shown to be economical. For lighter traffic routes, petrol-electric cars, trolley-buses, or motor buses were considered again. The three proposed new routes were considered further. These were : The Northern route, from Blackhall via Stockbridge and Broughton Road to Pilrig. The Central route, from Ardmillan Terrace via Fountainbridge, Bread Street, and Johnston Terrace to the Tron Church. The Southern route; A circular run via Preston Street, Dalkeith Road, Lady Road, West Mains Road, Blackford Avenue, Marchmont Road, and Melville Drive. It will be noticed that these mostly covered roads which had earlier been served by horse buses.

For the first two, trolley-buses were suggested, though were it not for the narrowness of Fountainbridge and the old canal bridge, a tramway would have been preferred here. For the Southern route, only the motor bus was considered likely to pay, though a trolley-bus route from the foot of Marchmont Road via Preston Street and Dalkeith Road to Cameron Toll was put forward as an alternative. The Town Council deliberated on these proposals: In any event Parliamentary powers would be required, and the lessees of the existing tramway system would have to be considered too.

However in the Edinburgh Corporation Act 1913 (passed 15 August 1913), it was secured that the Corporation "may provide maintain repair work and use (but shall not manufacture) motor omnibuses or may lease or otherwise arrange for maintenance repair working and running of such motor omnibuses". The Corporation could impose such reasonable charges as may be approved by the Board of Trade. Arrangements made had to have the consent of the Edinburgh & District Tramways Company, and if the buses were driven by electricity there was the usual clause for the protection of the Post Office telephones.

The Corporation then entered into an agreement with the Edinburgh & District Tramways Company to work motor buses for them at bare cost, the Corporation to purchase the vehicles. At the end of 1913 it was decided that the Southern circular route should be tried and tenders were invited for three single-deck and three double-deck petrol-electric buses. In the event six single-deckers were bought, three Leylands and three Tilling-Stevens, only the latter being petrol-electric. All had 29 seat rear entrance saloon bodies with clerestory roofs. The Leylands were Nos. 1, 2 and 3, registration numbers S4440-2, and the Tilling-Stevens Nos. 4, 5 and 6, S4443-5. All were lettered Edinburgh Corporation.

The Tramways Company housed the buses at Tollcross depot and the service commenced on 3 August 1914. However on 19 October 1914 the War Department commandeered the three Leyland chassis. A reduced service was then maintained by two of the Tilling-Stevens, — the third being under repair, — but this was not effective and the service operated for the last time on 31 October 1914. Thus ended for the time being, supplementary forms of transport under Corporation auspices. The three Tilling-Stevens were sold to the Scottish Motor Traction Company for £2400, and later the bodies off the three Leylands were sold to Munro of Auchendinny. The proposed Northern and Central routes were of course dropped until after the war.

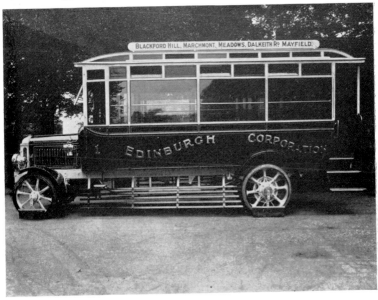

ORIGINAL CORPORATION LEYLAND BUS OF 1914

The Corporation had already decided on 31 October 1912, to take over the tramway system and operate it themselves on the expiry of the Company's lease, and towards the end of 1914 a Minute of Agreement was drawn up with the Company regarding this. In the agreement the Corporation were to be allowed to experiment with petrol-electric tramcars as long as they did not hinder the Company's traffic and the Company agreed to work them on certain proposed extensions, which were included in the Corporation's Provisional Order in 1915. In this Order authority for the following tramways was sought. An extension from Craiglockhart to Colinton. A tramroad from the Braid Hills terminus through the Braid Burn valley to join up with the proposed Colinton extension at Firhill, and most of which would have been on its own private right-of-way. An extension from Murrayfield terminus to Corstorphine, the proposed new terminus being just beyond Templeland Road. A siding into the old stable premises near the Corstorphine terminus. A short line from Shandwick Place into Hope Street. Connecting lines between Morrison Street and Haymarket Terrace, and between Lauriston Place and Home Street. The extensions were of course outwith the then City boundary. It was envisaged that the overhead electric system or petrol-electric tramcars would be adopted. The Colinton proposal was however complicated by the existence of the already mentioned Colinton Tramways Company, and the Commissioners enquiring into the Corporation's Order would agree to the Corporation's proposal only if the latter bought up the Colinton Company for £9000. Although the Company were willing to sell and the War Office offered to relieve the Corporation of the Company's agreements with them, provided a through car service to the barracks was given, the Corporation would not accede. There was thus a year's delay and the Edinburgh Corporation Order Confirmation Act 1916, (passed 17 May 1916) did not include the Craiglockhart to Colinton line, though the other routes sought were authorised.

The war however was putting a stop to any such schemes and nothing could be done till afterwards. Indeed its impact was making itself felt on the cable system, so dependent as it was on coal, steel, and skilled labour. While electric cars could quite well be handled by women, the arduous duty made it hardly feasible with the cable cars. Women conductors were not employed until June 1915 as the men had been very averse to their use.

There were proposals that the Corporation should buy up the operating Company at a negotiated figure without waiting for the expiry of the lease, but no agreement could be reached. There was however an increase in fares about the end of 1915, and through fares to Leith were withdrawn.

By the end of 1915 the condition of the system was engaging public attention. The position certainly was bad, though the difficulties of the period have to be appreciated. 5,000 of the 13,000 pulleys were defective, — or missing! Stoppages occurred daily. Even the Company's chairman at its annual meeting on 4 February 1916 admitted it was "not in the condition it ought to be". He indeed ascribed the unfortunate situation to "inefficient inspection", and the many inexperienced drivers. Mr. Wilson had replaced Mr. Harris as the Company's Engineer on 1 January 1916. Mr. Shepherd resigned a week afterwards, but continued to act as Secretary to the Company. He was succeeded by Mr. J. D. R. Cox. The Council were considering what redress they had for "the collapse of the tram services". Some of the cars too, were in bad condition, and as the Magistrates were the licensing authority for the cars, the Company were allowed to continue operations on a month to month basis while they got the system into order, as they promised to do. Indeed a good effort was made. In April 1916 stoppages of the cable had averaged three per day. By October it was reported there had been only 33 stoppages over the preceding 41 days. The longest one however, had been for nearly seven hours. Still, the Lothian Road and Shandwick Place tracks were relaid, and a new cable installed on the Portobello route.

At this dark period the public were, naturally, exasperated. Passengers having no sooner paid their fare when the system broke down, demanded their money back. On refusal one enterprising gentleman walked off with the spare driving wheel from the car! He was handed over to the police, but was not charged. Another threatened the Company with a charge of obstruction of the streets under the 1879 Act. Yet another, having twice taken a penny transfer ticket from the West End to the Infirmary and found the Mound route at a standstill, took a cab on both occasions and sued the Company for his 2/- cab fares. The Court ruled he had a case, but as the Company had now offered to repay his two penny fares, he was advised it wouldn't be worth pursuing. A mishap which could have been serious but which, in retrospect has its humorous aspect, was reported on 28 April 1916. The Liberton cable got stranded and entwined in the gripper of an outgoing car near Hope Park. As the poor driver could not release it, his car was carried forward, willy-nilly, at cable speed, he tolling his bell and doubtless shouting his predicament. First one car and then another were overtaken and pushed relentlessly onwards. At Preston Street a refuse cart failed to get out of the way of the cavalcade and was pushed into a motor lorry which thereby had a wheel knocked off. By the time the cars had got well down the hill towards Newington Station someone had telephoned to Shrubhill and the cable was stopped. It was fortunate no more damage was done.

Economy measures became necessary, and the number 3 Abbeyhill—Ardmillan Terrace service disappeared entirely in the summer of 1916, the number 5 service being again and finally diverted to Abbeyhill.

In October 1916 the Corporation obtained a further report on the future transport possibilities, prepared jointly by the City

Engineer, Mr. J. B. Hamilton the Leeds Tramways Manager, and Mr. Brodie the Liverpool City Engineer. Soon afterwards negotiations commenced between the Corporation and the Company regarding the terms of taking over by the former. In this the Corporation had the advice of Mr. Hamilton who suggested £25,000 for the rolling-stock. The Company wanted £75,000. Eventually £50,000 was agreed upon for not less than 200 cable cars, 4 electric cars, and 14 spare bogies, all in good condition. The track was to be handed over fit for six years work, except in respect of curves and junctions. On 30 July 1918 the Corporation appointed Mr. R. Stuart Pilcher, of Aberdeen, as their Tramways Manager, so that he had a year to lay his plans for taking over the system on expiry of the Company's lease and for its future.

In August 1917 the Company had increased the fares, the alternative of a reduced rental having been refused by the Corporation. Another increase took place in April 1919, when 1½d. became the minimum. The 1½d. ticket was "white" with a pink stripe. The Corporation however announced their intention of reintroducing the penny fare immediately they took over the system. The Company's lease duly expired on 30 June 1919 and the system passed into the City's hands. The story of its last few years will be dealt with in another chapter. Meanwhile the rolling-stock has still to be described.

ROLLING-STOCK

The type of car running on the Northern lines was not considered appropriate for the main part of the system, a larger and more orthodox design being desired. Accordingly the Edinburgh & District Tramways Company designed and built at the Shrubhill works a prototype car, the main features of which were orthodox platforms, entrances and stairs, though the full-length canopy did not enclose the latter. The saloon had three large windows to each side. The car ran on inside-framed bogies with the gripper mounted ahead of the first axle and its operating rod provided with knuckle joints and a sliding coupling operated by a spoked wheel vertically mounted on a fixed pedestal as described earlier. This car was turned out in 1897, numbered 112 and originally painted red, instead of the Company's usual chocolate and cream style. It normally ran on the Comely Bank route, and the braking arrangements were similar to the other cars on that route.

Six similar cars were obtained from Messrs. G. F. Milnes & Co. Ltd. Birkenhead later in the same year. They were primarily intended for the increasing traffic of the Northern lines and were therefore 17in. shorter. Otherwise there were only minor differences from No. 112. These six cars were numbered 139 to 144, one of them, as already noted, making the inaugural trip on 1 June 1899.

From No. 112 the standard design was evolved. The standard cars were a little longer and roomier, the saloon accommodating 20 passengers as against 18 in the earlier cars. Both types seated 28 on top. The overall length was 26ft. 6in. and the weight about 4¾ tons. They cost £445 each complete. The destination was indicated on a small board hooked on to the edge of the canopy and generally it named an intermediate point and the terminus. The other side was lettered for the return journey the board being reversed at the terminus. A long board carried on the panel above the saloon windows gave the termini and principal points passed. Orders were placed with Messrs. Brown, Marshall & Co., Birmingham totalling 120 cars and Messrs. G. F. Milnes & Co. also supplied 25. The saloon ceilings of the Brown-Marshall cars were finished in decorative white panels, and those of the Milnes cars were polished brown panels. When the service started 24 cars had been received and delivery continued through 1900 and 1901. The cars were numbered in scattered fashion, the highest number being 208. (See list in Chapter 7.)

Twenty additional cars were obtained from the Preston works of Messrs, Dick Kerr & Co. Ltd. in 1903. These were of the standard pattern but of a more solid appearance, the windows having square corners and small lights above as was usual practice at the period. They seem to have had the seats covered with cloth when built. Their numbers were 209 to 228. A neater style of painting was adopted, the Company's name previously emblazoned on the sides in large letters was omitted, and much smaller numerals were used for the car number on the dash. This style then became standard for all cars.

The saloons were lighted by oil lamps, but in 1905 acetylene lighting was introduced, though this improvement was not extended to the old Northern section cars.

At this time it was evident that additional rolling-stock would soon be required and the Company turned to building cars at the Shrubhill works themselves. In 1906 Nos. 25 and 27 appeared, being almost identical with the Dick Kerr cars of 1903. A new development was afoot however, and people were asking why top-covered cars should not be provided. After all Leith Corporation who had by now bought up the old Edinburgh Street Tramways Company lines and electrified them were running top-covered cars. The matter was considered at intervals. It was calculated that the Murrayfield and Dalry Road railway bridges could be negotiated by top-covered cars at a squeeze, but the Gorgie Road bridge beyond Ardmillan Terrace would be too low. The chief difficulty was that all the depot roofs would have to be raised. However the Town Council pursued the matter, and so Tollcross depot roof was modified; and two further cars built early in 1907.

These were Nos. 37 and 48. The former had an all-enclosed top saloon and appears to have originally had somewhat square ends over the canopies though latterly they were of the normal rounded shape; while the latter had ordinary open balconies. In each case the stair was outside just as on the standard open-top cars. There was a ceremonial trial trip to Braid Hills, and No. 48 was decided upon as the more acceptable pattern. Similar top-covers were thereupon fitted to Nos. 25 and 27 and to all the Dick Kerr cars of 1903, the weight of which with top-covers became 9 tons 8 cwts. The Shrubhill and Portobello depot roofs were then raised also.

In view of the forthcoming extensions to the system a further twelve top-covered cars were built by the Company at Shrubhill between 1908 and 1911, while all the standard "Milnes" cars, (except Nos. 28, 38, 64, and 74, which were converted in 1910 to electric cars for the Ardmillan Terrace to Slateford line,) were provided with top-covers also. The programme was completed with seven more top-covers which were fitted to "Brown-Marshall" cars in 1912. These were Nos. 12, 24, 111, 137, 151, 152, and 206. About 1915 estimates were considered for fitting top-covers to further "Brown-Marshall" cars but nothing came of this.

It remains to mention that five of the newer horse cars were reconstructed as standard pattern open-top cars. They were however rather shorter, similar to No. 112, though differing in minor details. These cars were Nos. 15, 17, 19, 53, and 113. It may also be mentioned that there were no cable cars with the following numbers : 75, 76, 84, 86, 87, 90, 92, 93, 95 to 99, 102, 108, 110, 170, and 171.

To conclude this chapter a few general notes on this marvel of mechanical ingenuity may not be out of place. It is rather sobering to think today of the miles of conduit under the streets and the vast pits under the main junctions, — the locations of the pulleys and cables etc. being precise to fractions of an inch. These pits were provided with electric lighting, and there were telephones too. Throughout the streets there was the continuous faint rumble of the cable over its pulleys, — a sound to which residents were so accustomed they would wake up when it stopped for the night after the last car was in. There were the complexities of operation, with pointsmen to inspect that all was well with each car at the main junctions so that no accident to the cable occurred. Snow caused little difficulty : the cars kept running and acted as snow-ploughs. On the other hand there was the necessity of regularly cleaning out mud and sludge from the conduit, — a job undertaken by the City Cleansing Department. Severe frost could however give rise to trouble by swelling and closing in of the slot, and the slot was subject also to malicious mischief by the insertion of pieces of wood, horseshoes etc. A good deal of trouble of this sort seems to have been experienced around 1900. Then there was a favourite prank of the youngsters: to tie a tin can on a piece of string which was then let into the slot and dangled on the cable till it got caught on it. Authority however was not amused at the sight of the can rattling along the street at cable speed. Many an apocryphal story has been told involving the system, such as the "drunk" wont to guide himself home by hooking his walking stick through the slot on the cable finding himself one night at Murrayfield instead of Gorgie.

Although Edinburgh's cable cars were a music-hall joke, it must be acknowledged that the system worked remarkably well on the whole, and economically too in its earlier days, besides sparing the city the overhead wires to which there was such strong objection at that period.

III

LEITH CORPORATION TRAMWAYS

The Schedule to the Provisional Order under the Leith Corporation Tramways Order Confirmation Act of 22 July 1904 empowered the Corporation to purchase the whole of the Company's lines in the burgh, to use mechanical power with Board of Trade consent and to construct additional tramways. The clauses covered the usual variety of matters, including the question of junctions with other systems including Edinburgh, and Edinburgh's interest in their side of Pilrig Street; parcels, workmen's cars, fares, which were not to exceed one penny per mile, and safeguards concerning the use of electric or steam power. The work was to be completed in five years and there was permission to run buses over the routes while construction was proceeding and over contemplated extensions. Such buses were not to be electrically driven unless by batteries. Apart from the reconstruction and doubling of the existing lines, the new routes authorised were: From Pilrig by a junction facing upgoing cars in Leith Walk, down Pilrig Street to join the existing route in Newhaven Road; From Pilrig by another junction facing into the foregoing, by Iona Street and Easter Road to a triangular junction with the Seafield route; A link across the Foot of Leith Walk from Junction Street to Duke Street and to Constitution Street; A line along a proposed new road from Pier Place to Annfield to bypass Newhaven, and which road has still not been built. The Iona Street and Easter Road route was never constructed.

At the beginning of August 1904 the Corporation appointed a sub-committee to consider the form of traction to be adopted, and this committee thereupon inspected the tramways operating in several other cities and towns. Stirling's Motor Construction Company hoped their petrol-driven tramcar would be adopted. On 11 October it was resolved to adopt the overhead electric system, and that the work be carried out by direct labour. Mr. James More was appointed Consulting Engineer. Leith Walk, Junction Street, and Commercial Street were to be provided with centre poles to facilitate the movement of ships' boilers through these streets.

The Edinburgh Street Tramways Company handed over their system to the Corporation at 2.00 p.m. on 23 October, though their activities officially ceased after the previous day. Mr. Adam retired and their Traffic Superintendent, Mr. J. Wilson was appointed interim Manager for the Corporation. The staff were issued with new uniforms and the Bell Punch ticket system introduced. The Corporation continued the horse car services as before except in Craighall Road where the "Outer Circle" cars were turned back at the top and bottom of the hill. The half-hourly horse bus service from Newhaven to Granton also continued.

The committee and officials were now busy with estimates, designs and tenders for rolling-stock etc., and proposals for routes, frequencies and fares. On 10 January 1905 the Council decided to order thirty open-top and six closed-top cars, half from the B.T.H. Co. and half from the Brush Co. The cost of the whole conversion and equipment including rolling-stock was estimated at just under £122,000.

At the beginning of February 1905 Mr. Relph was appointed Construction Superintendent, and work on the new Pilrig Street route was commenced on 6 February. During subsequent reconstruction of the other routes single line working with temporary crossovers was adopted on the double-line sections, but service had to be temporarily suspended over the single-line sections. An "instruction car" for training drivers was ordered at the end of March, and a sprinkler car in April, both from the B.T.H. Co. A ratepayer's plebiscite declared in favour of Sunday services being run, though there was some high feeling about it. Mr. Wilson was confirmed as Manager on 11 May.

Work proceeded quite rapidly. The Town Council and Col. von Donop for the Board of Trade inspected the Pilrig Street route on 7 June 1905 and it was passed for use by horse cars which commenced to run on 15 June, giving a seven minute headway from Pilrig Street to Stanley Road. The new electric cars were now arriving from the B.T.H. Co., but acceptance of some was deferred for not having the specified type of controller. It was proposed to start the first electric section on 21 July but this had to be postponed. There were difficulties with the new depot being built near Smith's Place and its access tracks, and it seems that some of the new cars had to be left out in the street. However an electric car was tried over the line to Stanley Road at 3.00 a.m. on 28 July. A certain baillie, having heard of the intended expedition, turned up and was said to have driven the car part of the way, his unofficial precedence causing some ill-feeling among his colleagues!

LEITH CORPORATION OPEN TOP CAR, 'BRUSH' BUILT, ON TRIAL
RUN AT BONNINGTON TOLL
Showing also the Caledonian Railway's massive girder bridge

At last the Leith Walk, Pilrig Street, Newhaven Road, and Stanley Road sections were duly passed for electric cars by the Board of Trade on 12 August, and a service of eight electric cars was run over the route from 18 August 1905. The fare was 1½d., with a 1d. fare from Foot of Leith Walk to Bonnington Terrace, or from Pilrig to Stanley Road. There was also a ½d. stage from Foot of Leith Walk to Pilrig. Four B.T.H. and four or five Brush open-top cars were used, and the latter did not escape some criticism of details of their equipment either.

The remainder of the circle round to the Foot of Leith Walk by Newhaven and Junction Street, and also the Ferry Road link, were completed and inspected by the Board of Trade on 14 September and the service was operated round the circle from two days later. The circular fare was 2d. Ferry Road was catered for by a service between Pilrig and Stanley Road via Foot of Leith Walk.

By October, all but the Brush Co's closed-top cars had been delivered, and the remainder of the system was ready except for the Seafield line and the equipment on the Bernard Street swing bridge.

The Bernard Street and Commercial Street sections were inspected by Col. von Donop on 19 October and services commenced the following day.

An official opening ceremony was arranged for 3 November 1905, and at 4.30 p.m. that day five cars, the leading one (believed to be No. 6) decorated with yellow, white, and pink chrysanthemums, laurel, and holly, and with palms on top, left the depot for a trip over the main parts of the system. The other four cars were top-covered ones. The official party of some 150 persons led by Provost Mackie, who drove the first car along with Mr. Relph, included the Leith Town Council and officials, representatives from Edinburgh Town Council, the Edinburgh and District Tramways Company, the Chambers of Commerce, Merchant Company, and other public bodies and all the various contractors concerned. After proceeding via Pilrig, Pilrig Street, Newhaven, North Junction Street, and Foot of Leith Walk to Bernard Street, the party returned to the Foot of Leith Walk, where the Provost addressed a large crowd from the top of the leading car and declared the tramways open. The party then repaired to a celebration dinner in Smith's rooms, followed by speeches in the usual congratulatory vein, and also the plea for through electric cars to Edinburgh. The employees were also entertained to supper at the same establishment after finishing duty early at 10.30 p.m.

THE OFFICIAL OPENING OF LEITH CORPORATION TRAMWAYS
Decorated car at the depot.

117

A trial over Bernard Street bridge took place on 10 November and this and the Seafield line were inspected and passed by the Board of Trade on 21 November 1905, services commencing at once. The circular route was altered to proceed to and from Newhaven via Bernard Street, and new services run between Pilrig and Caledonian Station via North Junction Street, and between Seafield and Stanley Road via Pilrig and Pilrig Street. Extra cars ran from Pilrig to Bernard Street, and to Bonnington Terrace via Ferry Road. A range of halfpenny fares was then introduced, followed on 26 November by penny transfer through tickets from Foot of Leith Walk to Post Office or St. Andrew Street over the Edinburgh system, with a similar 1½d. transfer between Bernard Street, Seafield, Junction Bridge, or Bonnington Terrace, (later Stanley Road), and Hanover Street or Tron Church. The maximum speed authorised was 12 m.p.h. subsequently increased to 15 m.p.h.

The Corporation were fortunate in obtaining their materials at very favourable prices, and the system was well constructed. The gauge was of course the standard 4ft. 8½in. and 45ft. rails of a special section weighing 106.7 lbs. per yard were used. They were obtained from the North Eastern Steel Co., Middlesborough, and rested on a 6in. bed of concrete. Points and crossings were of Hadfields "Era" manganese steel. The layout at the Foot of Leith walk was quite a complicated piece of work but having been preassembled by the makers was duly installed in twelve days. The system was double line throughout except for a short length in Duke Street, the curves at either end of Stanley Road, and the junction at Bonnington Terrace.

The overhead trolley wire was of 4/0 gauge grooved section, which was then still a novelty. Apart from the centre poles already mentioned they were used also in Bernard Street and Craighall Road. Side bracket-arm poles were used in Ferry Road, part of Newhaven Road, Stanley Road, Duke Street, and at certain other locations. Elsewhere span wires were provided. Quite elaborate wrought-iron scroll-work was provided together with a short ball-and-spike shape finial, and a tall fluted cast iron base bearing the burgh coat of arms. Overhead fittings were by S. Dixon & Sons, Ltd, Leeds, who also provided six sets of automatic point controllers and automatic signals for the three single-line curves. Guard wires to prevent telephone wires falling on the trolley wire were provided where required. Current for the system was supplied from the Corporation's electricity generating station near Junction Street by p.i.l.c. cables pitched in troughing to feeder pillars in Leith Walk near the depot entrance, Newhaven Road near Bonnington Toll, Lindsay Road, Junction Bridge, Constitution Street, and Leith Links. The first two were 0.5 sq. in. section, the remainder 0.25 sq. in. There was also an extension feeder of 0.25

sq. in. section from the Newhaven Road pillar to another at Stanley Road. The side-feed cables to the line were taken through a short conduit into the base of the pole and out through holes near the top making a neat arrangement. Negative feeders were laid to Foot of Leith Walk, Lindsay Road, and Bonnington Terrace. Pilot cables for testing and telephone circuits were also provided, and were run overhead where suitable. The price of current was initially 1¼d. per unit. A horse-drawn tower-wagon was provided, there being also a second temporary one during the construction period.

The swing bridge across the Harbour at Bernard Street involved some interesting problems. The bridge in those days was owned by the Leith Dock Commission, and was operated by hydraulic power. Before swinging it was arranged to lift on its centre pivot with a tilting action whereby the attachments above the ends of the 2/0 gauge bridge trolley wires supported from girders spanning the bridge dropped out of complementary spring-loaded forks on the fixed land girder at one end. The other end was similar, the spring-loaded forks being on the bridge girder and lifting upwards off the attachment on the fixed girder. The trolley wire attachments were thereby kept in alignment when the bridge was in position, and were clear for swinging when it was tilted. The approach tracks on either side were provided with trap points electrically controlled from the tilting movement of the bridge and the position of these was indicated by a semaphore signal arm mounted on the adjacent pole. The trolley wire over the approach track in each case was fed from the line on the other side through the bridge trolley wire so that it also became dead by the disengagement of the attachments when the bridge was tilted prior to opening. This equipment was also provided by S. Dixon & Sons Ltd.

The car depot had eight lyes (i.e. tracks) fanning from trailing connections to each track in Leith Walk. A two lye repair shop was provided on the south side.

The electric system was now in full operation. The remaining 22 old cars and most of the 37 horses had been disposed of. The old Morton Street premises had been given up. There were suggestions for extending the Seafield line to connect with the Musselburgh system, for replacing the Newhaven — Granton horse bus by a motor bus, though a tramway extension was also being mooted, and for running a bus to Easter Road, but none of these materialised. The "Brush" closed-top cars were at last delivered. The instruction" car was no longer of use as such and it was proposed to convert it to a "toast-rack" car for summer service. Instead a further open-top body by the Brush Co. was obtained for it.

Mr. Relph resigned in May 1906 and was replaced by Mr. F. A. Fitzpayne as Engineering Superintendent. For the summer of 1906 services were given as follows : The Newhaven circular via Bernard Street and via Pilrig Street every ten minutes; Pilrig to Stanley Road via Ferry Road every five minutes; Seafield to Stanley Road via Pilrig Street every ten minutes; Pilrig to Pier Place via Bernard Street every ten minutes part day except on Saturday afternoons when these cars ran via North Junction Street. A workmen's ½d. fare and certain 1d. transfer fares were introduced, and on 12 November 1906 the Seafield — Stanley Road 2d. fare was reduced to 1½d. and nearly all the 1½d. fares reduced to 1d. The ½d. fares had proved unremunerative however, and though some additional ones had been tried, they were at this time all withdrawn except Foot of Leith Walk to Pilrig or Junction Bridge. which survived till August 1907. A parcels service was started on 10 June 1907.

The undertaking was proving successful. By 1911 the operating expenses had been reduced to 4.5d. per car-mile, the lowest figure attained by any tramway undertaking in the kingdom. In the last half-year of horse operation the cost had been 8.32d. per car-mile, and the average speed only 6 m.p.h.

It was not long before extensions were being proposed, and Portobello, Granton, and Davidson's Mains were considered. It was agreed that Newhaven to Granton, and also a line along Ferry Road to Goldenacre and Granton would be justified and powers were obtained for these in the Leith Burgh Act of 1908. As in the case of the Pilrig Street line, one track in Ferry Road and Granton Road lay in Edinburgh, the boundary being in the centre of the road. Negotiations resulted in Leith owning the pair of tracks, Edinburgh retaining a right of purchase, as had been arranged in the earlier case. A suggestion to lay sidings into the C.R. and N.B. railway stations and the Newhaven fish market and thus carry fish to the trains was not proceeded with.

In April 1908 the platform staff were provided with new cap badges showing the burgh coat of arms instead of the initials L.C.T. as previously. Another through booking was arranged the following month in connection with the Exhibition at Saughton Park that year. At a fare of 2½d. this was available from any part of Leith, and Leith Corporation's share was ¾d.

Two new crossovers were provided in Commercial Street early in 1909 and work on the Granton extension also started then. Commencing with a junction in Pier Place there was a double line by Lower Granton Road to Granton Square thence by (High) Granton Road and Ferry Road back to Bonnington Terrace where single line junctions were formed onto the existing lines leading to Junction Bridge and to Pilrig. The "S" bend under the railway bridge at Trinity Crescent had to be a short single line section and was provided with automatic signals. These were also fitted up at the Bonnington Terrace junction in the summer of 1911. The overhead was span wire construction throughout, and there were feeders to pillars in Ferry Road near Clark Road, in Granton Road near Wardie Crescent, and in Lower Granton Road. A junction was laid in Ferry Road at the top of Granton Road ready for the proposed extension to Davidson's Mains. Thermit welding and chilled blocks were used, the latter preventing wear of the setts adjacent to the rail by cart traffic. There were crossovers at Granton and Granton Road station, and a facing one at the top of Granton Road too.

The low road is mostly narrow and while construction was proceeding the bus from Pier Place was started from Stanley Road and proceeded to Granton by East Trinity Road, a transfer ticket being made available from Pier Place. This diversion lasted from 18 February till early in May.

Mr. Wilson the Manager died suddenly on 6 April and Mr. Fitzpayne was put in charge meantime, being confirmed as Manager on 27 July 1909.

The low road to Granton was ready first. The Council had a trial run on 14 April and then on 11 May 1909 the bus was withdrawn and the Pilrig to Pier Place via Bernard Street car service was extended to Granton. This now ran via North Junction Street in the evenings as well as on Saturday afternoons. A twenty minutes service was run between Pilrig and Caledonian Station via North Junction Street during the day. The fare from Pilrig to Granton was 2½d.

Col. von Donop inspected this part of the route for the Board of Trade on 2 June, and came back and passed the next section from Granton up to Goldenacre on 2 July, the car service being immediately extended accordingly. A formal opening of the new circle was proposed for 22 July, but the portion between Bonnington Terrace and Goldenacre was not ready, and it was 3 August when this was passed by the Inspector and the new circular service commenced. The speeds authorised were Trinity Bridge — Granton, Trinity Road — top of Granton Road, and Bonnington Terrace—Craighall Road 12 m.p.h. elsewhere 15 m.p.h. except the usual 4 m.p.h. for curves. The cost of the extension was put at £50,390.

The Granton Circle via Bernard Street and via Pilrig Street operated on a ten minute headway each way, the fare for the circle being 4d. The old "Outer Circle", now a misnomer, was now run during the morning "rush" and afternoon only, on a ten minute headway. Seafield to Stanley Road via Pilrig Street, and

121

also Pilrig to Stanley Road via Ferry Road continued to provide ten minute services. At certain times of the day the latter was increased to a five minute service while the former was extended via Newhaven, Bernard Street and back to Pilrig, a curious working known as the "figure nine car". Additional cars worked Pilrig to Bernard Street. Another "part-day" service was started shortly after, from Pilrig to Goldenacre via Junction Street, but this only lasted a few weeks, till 2 September. The Pilrig and Caledonian Station via North junction Street service was also dropped on account of poor receipts.

Courtesy E. R. L. Fitzpayne

F. A. FITZPAYNE
Manager Leith Corporation Tramways 1909-20
Manager Edinburgh Corporation Transport 1929-35.

Meantime the old Granton bus was experimentally put on between Seafield and Kings Road from 15 June 1909 at a fare of 2d. with transfers available also. But a horse bus was by now an anachronism and the service was withdrawn at the end of October. The bus was put up for sale and all but one of the twelve horses disposed of. The Fire Department took five for £100, viz. "Yankee", "Willie Watson", "Duncan", "Soldier", and "No. 1". The Cleansing Department paid £15 for "Kirky". Who bought the other five is not recorded, and one wonders what other intriguing names we might have learnt. Again was the unfortunate "No. 1" just that or was he rather "Number One"? The one horse retained was for the tower-wagon, but the poor animal went lame within a year and was replaced by an "outsider", hired while the Council made up their minds about a motor tower-wagon.

From time to time pressure was brought to bear for the re-introduction of ½d. fares, and after several refusals these were conceded again from 15 August 1910.

For the winter of 1910 the Granton Circle was reduced to a twenty minute headway during the slack periods, although the ten minute service was maintained to Granton via Bernard Street. Certain early morning cars ran to Granton via North Junction Street as did a Saturday afternoon service, and some early morning cars ran via Junction Street and Ferry Road. The Council kept a very close watch on the services and their earnings, and it is interesting to note that the Granton extension was provided with services without any additions to the rolling-stock. The Bernard Street — Pilrig part day cars were experimentally extended to Stanley Road for a month or so, and the old "Outer Circle" completely dropped. Then the full ten minute Granton Circle service was restored from 1 April 1911. The pattern of the regular services was now set for some years, viz. Granton Circle; Pilrig — Stanley Road via Ferry Road; Seafield — Pilrig — Stanley Road — Bernard Street — Pilrig, "figure nine"; and Pilrig — Bernard Street. There was thus no regular service on North Junction Street.

Further extensions were considered in 1911. Seafield to at least the burgh boundary, or to the top, or the foot, of Kings Road, and the Easter Road route were reported upon, but the question was complicated by Edinburgh's current thoughts on railess traction (trolleybus) routes in the district including Easter Road and Bonnington Road. Nothing came of these proposals however. They were again under active consideration in 1913-4 when meetings were held with the Edinburgh authorities and the use of motor buses, possibly as a joint undertaking was discussed. Then of course the war ended all such schemes.

In 1912 it was felt that there should be more top-covered cars and tenders were called for twelve top covers to be fitted to existing open-top cars. These were duly received from the Brush Co. at the end of the year and cost £111 each. Vestibule screens for the driver were also proposed and a car was fitted with these the following year. Two forms were tried, an orthodox wood framed screen above the ordinary rounded metal dash panel at one end, while the other end was provided with a new angular dash as well, having a flat front and two flat corner sections, all built up with vertical wood matchboarding. This latter type was adopted when it was eventually agreed to equip further cars.

The motor tower-wagon was finally decided upon and a Halley machine ordered. It was received and registered WS194 in March 1914 whereupon the horse was sold, — for £8. The disadvantages of the centre poles in the narrower streets were being felt and it was proposed that those in Junction Street and Commercial Street be replaced by span wires using rosettes where possible, and this was eventually done.

In the spring of 1914 restoration of the North Junction Street service was requested and also a five minute service to Seafield. Although the Manager reported adversely, a ten minute service in "rush" hours from Pilrig to Pier Place via North Junction Street, and an increased service between Pilrig and Seafield was instituted on 13 April. In the summer an early morning service to Seafield was run for golfers! A 3d. fare for the Granton Circle was also proposed. Traffic continued to be heavy at times and trailers were proposed but turned down. Eight more top covers were however ordered from the Brush Co. at a cost of £968. It was now realised that the equipment, though well maintained, would not last for ever and a renewals fund was started. A "windscreen" device was tried on car No. 20 but was found unsatisfactory and the drivers asked that complete vestibule screens be fitted to the platforms of all the cars. They also asked that the front destination boards be dispensed with, believing the roller blind screens to be sufficient. After some consideration it was agreed to fit a further six cars with vestibule screens. A full drop window was provided in these in place of a circular shutter in the first one.

In December 1914 an experimental "island" was installed at the Foot of Leith Walk. This was of wood and in the following February it was agreed to extend it and make it permanent. Complaints of noise, due to rail corrugation, called for investigation, and the watering car was fitted with grinding blocks to deal with the problem.

The war was now on, and the curtains on the car windows served a real purpose in the partial blackout. As they suffered from passengers' attentions however, other methods of shading had to be tried. Workmen's fares were granted to the Forces except on Sundays as from 16 May 1915. In July a decorated car toured the system for a fortnight to stimulate recruiting. Its furnishing was carried out by Sir Robert Maule. One of the minor sidelights of the prevailing conditions was the inability of the uniform contractors to provide the brass buttons, and the old ones had to be re-used! Of more import was the decision in October to recruit women as conductresses. The first eight started on the Ferry Road service in December, which was increased to a five minute headway. The through tickets to the Edinburgh system were withdrawn in December, at the instigation of the Edinburgh & District Tramways Company.

Traffic was still increasing, and so were costs, though Leith still boasted the lowest figure in Scotland, viz. 5.65d. per car mile. The ½d. fares were abolished in March 1916. To deal with lunch time crowds two conductors were carried on the 1.02 p.m. journey from Bernard Street to Pilrig. The Caledonian Railway found it necessary to renew the girders of the bridge at Lindsay Road, necessitating single line working, so the old temporary crossovers used during the horse car conversion were laid down in April.

The crews again pressed the nuisance of changing the front destination boards, and this time a compromise solution was found. The coloured boards lettered according to the route were replaced by coloured boards without any lettering as follows: Granton Circle, red; Granton via Junction Street, red and white; Pilrig and Stanley Road via Ferry Road, white; Seafield and Stanley Road or "figure nine car", green; Pilrig and Bernard Street, yellow. These of course did not require changing at the termini. At the same time new screen blinds showed both destination and via . . . . This scheme was introduced towards the end of 1916. At this time too, it became necessary to train women as drivers, or "motoresses", as they were termed. Small folding seats were provided on some cars for conductresses.

On 27 October 1916 a subsidence occurred in Duke Street, and for the next week Seafield was served by one car left beyond the obstruction. Early the next year single line working had to be introduced between Pier Place and Trinity Bridge during repairs to the sea wall. Signals were provided. About this time the Corporation contracted with the Post Office to convey the Granton mails to and from the Foot of Leith Walk for 3d. per bag. As many Post Office telephone wires were replaced by underground cables a start was made in removing the guard wires which were redundant.

Traffic continued to increase, particularly in the industrial parts of the burgh and to Granton, and early in 1917 the Bernard Street—Pilrig cars were extended to Bonnington Terrace, and later, at the other end to Caledonian Station. There were complaints of over-crowding and poor timekeeping aggravated by the partial blackout. To improve matters the Stanley Road — Pier Place — Benard Street — Pilrig leg of the "figure nine car" was abandoned and a five minute service run from Pilrig to Granton via Bernard Street instead. This carried a yellow board. The service via North Junction Street now ran on Saturday afternoons only. These changes took place on 15 March 1917 and resulted in there being then no service in Craighall Road.

At the beginning of 1918 the war effort was pressing still harder. The authorities asked if Leith could spare any rails, poles, or cars, but there were only a few rails and twelve poles in stock and certainly no cars could be spared. On the other hand Leith managed to buy ten "Brush" controllers and four motors second-hand from Belfast. Staffing was difficult and women were appointed as inspectors The last car times were brought forward from 11 April, and several stopping places were eliminated in July, while by September an effort had been made to reduce the services where possible in order to save coal at the power station.

With the war over many difficulties remained, especially costs, and a new fare table was introduced on 16 May 1919. The child's minimum fare rose to 1d. and other concessions were withdrawn. Early next year another increase was called for and a 2d. transfer introduced. Some of the stopping places were being restored and in July an evening service by North Junction Street was again tried. The King's Road extension was discussed once more but other events were pending and powers for this line were included in Edinburgh Corporation's Act of 1920 which also provided for the amalgamation of the Burgh of Leith and the City of Edinburgh.

So on 20 November 1920, after much negotiation and considerable opposition, amalgamation was effected and the Leith tramways merged with the Edinburgh undertaking. The Leith Manager Mr. F. A. Fitzpayne was appointed Deputy Manager in the combined undertaking.

As far as is known the following are the colours of the various tickets used on the Leith system :

½d.	bright brown	
1d.	pink	
1½d.	pale brown	
2d.	white	(at another time, yellow)
2½d.	blue	
3d.	mauve	
4d.	green	
6d.	brown	
1½d.	transfer, pale brown with blue stripe.	

The rolling stock remains to be mentioned in more detail. The open-top cars by the B.T.H. Co. and the Brush Co. were fairly similar, though the latter had only three windows whereas the former had four. The B.T.H. cars were 27ft. 6in. long and ran on four-wheeled trucks of the Brill 21E type with a six foot wheelbase and 32in. dia. wheels. The two motors were GE54 type, and B18 controllers with provision for rheostatic braking were supplied. There were 22 seats inside and 36 outside. The Brush Co's cars were 6in. longer and seated two less outside. Their trucks were the Brush AA type with 1002B motors and 3A type controllers. The top-covered cars were similar, the top deck seating being two less in each case. The Brush cars had a more domed roof, but the B.T.H. cars on the other hand were provided with an opening portion down one side of the roof, the panels sliding under the other half. All the cars had longitudinal wooden seats in the lower saloon and the usual transverse reversible seats upstairs. The stairs were of the ordinary pattern. There was a headlamp in the centre of the dash panel and a roller blind destination screen was mounted above the upper deck rail. Later these were removed to beneath the canopy, No. 29 being the first car so altered in December 1909. A coloured board lettered according to the route was carried on the upper deck rail, and side destination boards were also carried on the windows. The conductor's bell was of the cord type. Platform gates were originally proposed but these were cancelled. The folding steps, originally of metal, were replaced by wooden ones when they wore out. Curtains were provided for the lower saloon windows. The colour scheme was "Munich lake" and white, similar to that in Edinburgh, but the gold lettering "Leith Corporation Tramways" on the rocker panels and the car number on the dash were shaded in blue.

The B.T.H. open-top cars were numbered 1 - 15 and the Brush ones 16 - 30. The three B.T.H. top-covered cars were Nos. 31, 32, and 33, while the three Brush top-covered cars were No. 34, 35, and 36. The "instruction car" previously mentioned was originally numbered 61, but when converted to a normal Brush open-top car became No. 37. The sprinkler car was numbered 60 and painted green. It had a tank for 1000 gallons of water together with sprinkler pipes, two revolving brooms, and snow plough. GE58 motors and B18 controllers were fitted. The Brush top covers obtained in December 1912 were fitted to twelve B.T.H. cars, as also were three of the further eight obtained in December 1914, so that all the B.T.H. cars became top-covered though most of them hybrids. The other five of the eight obtained in December 1914 were fitted to Nos. 16, 17, 18, 19, and 37. The top-covered cars were also fitted with "Peacock" brake gear. The windscreen obtained from the Equipment & Engineering Co. in

May 1914 was tried on No. 20 while the experimental vestibule screens of 1913 were fitted to No. 35. In 1917 this car was provided with new truck side frames with a seven foot wheelbase. New wooden dash panels and vestibule screens were subsequently fitted to No. 29 in March 1915, followed by Nos. 10, 8, and 11 during the next two months, when it was decided to cancel the other two sets authorised on account of the war difficulties. No. 29 was the only open-top car so fitted.

IV

THE EARLY MOTOR BUSES

Edinburgh was the scene of some of the earliest motor services. Pioneers in this field were John Love, Norman Doran Macdonald, and Rowland Outhwaite who formed the Edinburgh Autocar Co. Ltd. in May 1899 with a capital of £50,000, the latter acting as manager.

The Company ran a fleet of thirty-one "public motor cars" which are believed to have been Milnes-Daimlers, fitted with wagonette type bodies, i.e. a seat for four along either side facing inwards, with another one or two beside the driver. Entry was at the back and the whole was surmounted by an awning. One is said to have been registered number S73. These were run between Post Office and Haymarket, and Post Office and Newington, both at a fare of one penny. The service started on 19 May 1899.

Other owners using one or two generally similar vehicles set up competition, but information on these activities is scanty. Some were run possibly to other districts wherever or whenever there was traffic offering. If there was a breakdown on a section of the cable tramway system, the "motor car" service was intensified and they did a roaring trade. At the end of 1899 the Edinburgh Autocar Company put on a service to Corstorphine (?) operating to a time-table and a fare ½d. more than that charged by the horse buses. The journey time was 20 minutes against 40 minutes by horse bus. The Autocar Company sometimes carried as many as 5,000 passengers per day, but generally the "penny stinkers" as these cars were dubbed, had more enemies than friends. The time was not yet ripe, and the Autocar Company failed after about eighteen months. The service to Corstorphine (?) had lasted only three months. The fleet was sold in July 1901 and then also included an 18 seater "Lifu" steam-driven bus.

John Love, himself, seems to have acquired some of the vehicles and continued to run these services to Salisbury Place and Haymarket, however, operating from a small garage in Abbeyhill. About 1902 he also retired from the scene and Messrs. Rossleigh & Co. of Annandale Street, one of the pioneer motor firms in the city, took over the route for a month or two. There does not seem to have been any regular operation thereafter. Nevertheless there seems little doubt that the machines were effective, for the Autocar Company had successfully used them on private trips as far afield as Inverness and London. Indeed several of them served other owners for many years, including one said to have been registered S56. Four were licensed in the city in 1913, and even after the first war one or two were being run between the Murrayfield tram terminus and the Zoo on busy days, and could bustle along at a smart pace with a full load.

An early manufacturer of motor vehicles was William Peck whose Madelvic Motor Carriage Company started producing electrically-driven cars in a fine new building at Granton in 1898. One is said to have run for a time in public service between Granton and Leith. The firm changed hands in 1900 and became the Kingsburgh Motor Construction Company, turning out a 12 seater petrol-driven machine with the driver seated over the bonnet. New owners took over the concern in 1902 and developed a small business in motor buses and petrol-driven tramcars under the name of Stirling's Motor Carriage Company, later, Stirling Motor Construction Company (1903) Ltd. The firm produced double-deck buses of the then orthodox pattern which were known variously as the "Granton" and "Stirling" models. An effort was made to interest Leith Corporation in the firm's products as alternatives to the proposed electric tramways, but none were put to work there. Some of their "Kingsburgh" buses were ordered by a London firm, and the manufacturers are said to have run a demonstration service for a while between Post Office and Haymarket. John Stirling and his associates formed the subsidiary Edinburgh Motor Omnibus Syndicate Ltd. on 21 May 1903, but no further operations materialised, and the Company was dissolved in September 1905. John Stirling, who came from Hamilton, had built the Edinburgh Autocar Company's vehicles, and was one of the earliest men in the business in Scotland. He died in Vancouver in 1945.

Another operating concern was formed in 1904, known as the Scottish & Irish Motor Service, J. G. W. Butler being Managing Director at a later period if not initially. This Company operated what they called the "Green Busses" and survived until about the time of the first war. Little has been traced regarding their earlier operations however.

Someone inaugurated a service from West Linton in to Edinburgh via Penicuik on 1 July 1904.

At the end of 1904 the old Edinburgh Street Tramways Company had statutorily to be wound up, though consideration had been given to reconstituting the Company to provide country

130

motor services. A new company was required however. Clearly there was scope for development of this traffic. This led to the formation in June 1905 of the Scottish Motor Traction Company Limited, which weathered all the difficulties of those days and of the war years to develop into the national network of today. Its story is therefore the subject of a separate chapter. The policy of the S.M.T.Co. was not competitive with the tramway company, but they had competition to meet from several firms besides those already mentioned.

The activities of these other operators are difficult to trace. Many services were short lived and the press took little notice of the "public motor cars". Even the inauguration of the S.M.T.Co's service is unrecorded in the daily press.

One, Henry C. Baillie, of Stenhouse, Liberton, ran a service, — eight trips a day, — from Nether Liberton to Gilmerton, commencing about April 1906.

Motor services were run between Levenhall and Port Seton and Tranent by the Musselburgh tramway company in connection with their trams, from 1906, and are referred to in the chapter dealing with that company.

Norman D. Macdonald came back to the scene also in 1906 with his new Edinburgh & District Motor Omnibus Company of which J. Morris was appointed managing director. He started off with a fleet of five open-top double-deckers of Dorkupp and Vulcan make with London-built 34 seater bodies. They were brightly painted in blue and white, picked out in gold, and with scarlet frames and wheels. Acetylene lighting was provided.

These were put on a service between Post Office and Murrayfield which commenced on 27 October 1906. Halfpenny fares were offered. What was described as an "experimental" service was also run between Craiglockhart station and Tollcross and sometimes to the Post Office. A circular route to the south side was started shortly after. This ran via Princes Street, Tollcross, Melville Drive, Marchmont Crescent, Sciennes Road, St. Catherine's Place, Salisbury Place, and the Bridges. It was followed early in 1907 by a service from Post Office to the Foot of Leith Walk, though difficulty was experienced in obtaining a licence for this.

It appears that the Dorkupp machines were ineffective and the E. & D.M.O.Co. acquired a "Granton" double-decker of 40/50 h.p., registration number S702. Another interesting early vehicle whose ownership has not been traced, and may have been one of the E. & D.M.O.Co's fleet, was a Leyland with a curious "Milnes" double-deck body having its platform with a reversed staircase, — tramcar style, — beside the driver. It was registered S678.

DENNIS "TOAST-RACK" CHARABANC OF 1906 USED BY
W. CESSFORD ON DALKEITH—BLACKSHIELS SERVICE

As with so many of the early motorbus operators, and in spite of Norman Macdonald's early optimism, the Company got into difficulties. On 20 March 1907 the firm went into voluntary liquidation. They then had eight buses in running order, and seven chassis. There had been an action against the suppliers of the Dorkupp, and two Vulcan charabancs were to be delivered the following month. It was said the charabancs were profitable but there was no room in Edinburgh for the Company's buses. Norman Macdonald alleged the trouble was mismanagement. An extraordinary general meeting was held in London on 3 April and broke up in disorder, though an investigating committee was formed. The bus services had now ceased and the Company retained only four employees. There does not seem to have been any further effective operation.

Norman Macdonald was well-known as a lawyer and he also took much interest in railway matters. Both he and Rowland Outhwaite lived to a good old age, surviving until a few years ago, and so seeing the eventual triumph of their protégé.

Another operator was styled the "Edinburgh & Loanhead Motor Service", and used Edmundson card type tickets, like the railways.

Motor services also replaced the Eskbank to Pathead coaches. This route was extended to Blackshiels and run by W. Cessford who used four Dennis "toast-rack" charabancs. He had competitors, and the rivals found themselves in Court, having come to blows in July 1906. A competitive service between Dalkeith and Pathead appears also in the timetables for March 1909. This would doubt-less be Adam Young whose route from June 1909 became Eskbank — Blackshiels and was run in connection with the S.M.T.Co's services, appearing, — though as a separate section, — in their timetables.

About 1912 Dan T. Munro bought a Maudslay charabanc, painted red, and with a wooden roof, which he put on the Queens-ferry route in the summer. However the War Department com-mandeered this vehicle on the outbreak of war, and he was left with only his horses and the "four-in-hand brakes".

In December 1912, Jordan, of Broxburn, started a service into Edinburgh, — four trips a day with an extra late one on Wednesdays and Saturdays, (three trips on Sundays), with Waver-ley Bridge as the Edinburgh terminus. The following April this service was extended to Uphall, and was subsequently increased in frequency though some journeys ran as far as Broxburn only. This service assumed the title "Seat of Comfort" though those who remember it had other ideas. The buses were single-deck Halleys with a platform entrance at the rear, one being SX275.

March 1913 saw a new service by the Scottish & Irish Motor Service to Gilmerton, Dalkeith, and Newtongrange, by "cars . . . comfortably upholstered and fully protected from the weather and lighted by electricity".*

* Handbill in possession of Scottish Omnibuses Ltd.

Courtesy R. L. Grieve

JORDAN'S "SEAT OF COMFORT" 1912

In April 1913 the Levenhall — Tranent service was recast and provided seven trips, (eight on Wednesdays and Saturdays), between Musselburgh station and Tranent, with "extra cars Levenhall — Tranent on Saturdays and Sundays".

November 1914 brought another operator into the field with Munro's Motor Bus Service from Waverley Bridge to Penicuik, some journeys proceeding via Liberton village, and others via Liberton Brae and Roslin. This lasted until the following June. Straker-Squire saloon buses with clerestory roof appear to have been used, one being registration number S4615. Munro's garage is thought to have been at Auchendinny.

There is said to have been another operator to Penicuik about this time, known as the Edinburgh Northern Automobile Company using two Commer double-deckers.

A small concern known as the Edinburgh & District Motor Co. Ltd. was formed on 30 March 1914 and ran a few charabancs on the Queensferry route, until shortage of petrol curtailed their activities. Their garage was at Dunedin Street.

The difficulties of the war brought most of these independent services to a close. Jordan's service to Broxburn and Uphall succumbed to the S.M.T.Co. in February 1917, followed by the Edinburgh & District Motor Co. in September 1918. Only the Musselburgh — Tranent service carried on for a time in addition to the S.M.T.Co's services. The post-war period will be dealt with in a separate chapter.

V

SOME OTHER TRAMWAY SCHEMES

In preceding chapters several proposals for tramways outside the city have been mentioned, most of which never materialised. Let us now deal with one which did, and some which at least got to the length of securing statutory powers.

About the turn of the century the Drake and Gorham Electric Power and Traction Co. Ltd. were active in promoting electric tramways in various parts of the country, and at this time reconstituted themselves as the National Electric Construction Company. One of the schemes they pursued was the oft mooted proposal for an extension of the tramway from Joppa to Musselburgh.

The Portobello and Musselburgh Tramways Order 1900, confirmed 6 August 1900, authorised this company to construct a tramway to be worked by electrical or mechanical power, — but not by steam or by animals, — from the Joppa terminus of the Edinburgh system, through Musselburgh to a point in what we now know as the "Coast" road, four chains east of the "pub." at Levenhall. The route was to be a single line with seventeen passing loops. A spur from each direction was to give access to a depot and generating station on the south side of the High Street in Musselburgh east of the Town Hall, while a branch thirteen chains long with a triangular junction at the Mall was to run to Inveresk Road. The gauge was not stipulated but there were all the usual provisions and safeguards. Cars were to be run at least every half-hour on weekdays between 8.0 a.m. and 10 p.m., and in connection with the last car from Edinburgh. Sunday services had to have the consent of the local authority, as also had the carriage of goods and animals. Maximum fares were 1d. per mile and workmen $\frac{1}{2}$d. per mile. The portion within the Edinburgh boundary was not to be constructed for twelve months unless the Corporation agreed and they had the right to buy it from the company if they wished.

Matters moved slowly however, and later the Board of Trade gave a special direction of extended time for completion of the system except for the portion within the Edinburgh boundary, which the Corporation thought of building itself.

By 1903 there was still no progress, and the position was retrieved by the Portobello & Musselburgh Tramways Order 1903, — confirmed 11 August 1903, — which authorised a subsidiary company, — the Pioneer Electric Company Ltd. to construct the portion of the route between the Edinburgh terminus at Joppa and the city boundary at the Brunstane Burn. Edinburgh now had no veto except in respect of an actual connection to their system. An extension of time until 6 August 1904 was given for the remainder of the Musselburgh system and the name of the new company brought in.

There was still no move to build however. The company were interested in trying the "G.B." surface contact electric system, and in January 1904 got Edinburgh and Musselburgh to agree. In March this plan was abandoned. Time was running out, and so at last, construction was started about a month or so later, the orthodox overhead electric system being adopted. The line was not completed by 6 August 1904 however, and it was 2 December before the first trial was run. Access to the depot was by a trailing connection towards Joppa only, and the branch down the Mall to Inveresk Road was never built. The depot itself was a corrugated iron shed with four tracks in a yard behind the buildings on the south side of the High Street, the single line connection leading through a high arched gateway. The rails in the depot and yard remain still. The steam generating station was at the back of the car shed and consisted of three water-tube boilers and three Davey-Paxman engines driving 100KW dynamos, boosters and batteries being incorporated in the installation.

In later years the steam power was shut down and the rotaries driven by a high-tension supply from Portobello through the associated Lothians Electric Power Company's network.

The gauge was of course 4ft. 8½in. and 45ft. rails weighing 90 lbs per yard were used. From Joppa to Bridge Street a double line was laid, the bracket-arm poles being on the north side. 2/0 gauge trolley wire was used with the usual section insulators, and feeder cables as shown on the diagram. The permitted speed was 10 m.p.h., but 12 m.p.h. was allowed on the "country" portions.

The Board of Trade inspection took place on 9 December 1904, and the public service commenced after a ceremonial trip on 12 December. The weather was most inauspicious. There was already two inches of snow on the ground and it was still snowing

Courtesy "Buses Illustrated"

MUSSELBURGH ORIGINAL OPEN TOP CAR OF 1904

heavily. Nevertheless a large company gathered in the "dynamo room", where the wife of Musselburgh's Provost Simpson switched on the machines. Lord Provost Cranston expressed the hope that electric cars would be extended to the G.P.O., but no further! Thereafter some of the party braved the elements for the inaugural run, in four cars, to Joppa. An entertainment was provided in the evening, but the snowstorm prevented several guests from attending.

A ten minutes service was run, increased to five minutes on Sunday afternoons, Musselburgh Town Council having agreed to the running of Sunday cars. The horse bus which the North British Railway ran from Musselburgh station to Levenhall was consequently withdrawn. The full journey cost 2d. and ½d. and 1d. fares were offered.

William Bain, who had been the construction engineer was interim manager, becoming manager a few months later. The promotors now formed a local company which took over the system by agreement and also its local electricity supply interests. This was the Musselburgh & District Electric Light & Traction Company, incorporated in August 1905, apparently by the Portobello & Musselburgh Tramways (Amendment) Order 1905. The car service proved popular and the company started to think about extensions.

The Portobello & Musselburgh Tramways (Port Seton Extension) Order 1906 was the result. This sought a single line route, with twelve passing loops, from the Levenhall terminus to Port Seton at Barracks House. Musselburgh town council however raised objections to the short length between the Levenhall terminus and the burgh boundary. Road widening at three points was asked for and when the company agreed to this the council threatened to restrict Sunday services and asked for a substantial proportion of the receipts. The Company urged that this issue be discussed separately to which the council first agreed, then reversed their decision in favour of submitting the dispute to the Board of Trade. When the representatives of the council and the Company arrived there they found a telegram from the council cancelling the mandate. So the 1906 Order had to go forward without the opposed portion within the Musselburgh boundary, and was confirmed in this form on 4 August 1906. The same provisions were included, and the local authorities were to use the poles for lighting.

Courtesy "Buses Illustrated"

MUSSELBURGH SINGLE-DECKERS EN-ROUTE FOR STORAGE ON
LAST DAY OF SERVICE
Musselburgh closed-top car still in traffic

The Company naturally waited developments before proceeding with their new separate tramway, but meantime, on 11 August 1906, put on a Thornycroft charabanc between Levenhall and Port Seton. This was followed a month or two later by a Napier bus between Levenhall and Tranent, every hour. At this time the Company were seriously considering a tramway for this route.

The Burgh of Cockenzie and Port Seton had also objected to the line through their area as proposed in the 1906 Order, but had been persuaded to give their assent on the Company promising to endeavour to obtain power for the alternative route the council wanted. Accordingly this gave rise to the Portobello & Musselburgh Tramways (Port Seton Deviation) Order 1907, — confirmed 29 April 1907, — which provided for the route being taken northwards at the Tranent Road corner, and along Main Street, Red

Row, and past Rose Cottage to join the original route. There was also a formidable list of road widenings to be carried out, though in a few cases this was not to be done until the extension was connected to the existing line at Levenhall. In the event this deviation was never carried out.

The Company also went ahead with another Order to get their two lines connected before proceeding with construction, and at the Inquiry at the Justiciary Court in Edinburgh on 29 April 1907 the difficulties with the 1906 Order were related. The Musselburgh council were now agreeable if the three road widenings were carried out, and the Company as before, were willing. The Portobello & Musselburgh Tramways (Levenhall Extension) Order 1907 was therefore confirmed on 26 July 1907, and authorised the 34.47 chains of line between the existing terminus and the previously authorised tramway starting at the burgh boundary. Four years from the date of the Inquiry were allowed for completion and all the provisions of the earlier Orders applied.

Construction of the new line was now started and the Levenhall — Port Seton bus withdrawn after the summer of 1907, the Tranent one becoming Saturdays and Sundays only at the same time.

There was much trouble in Musselburgh in the summer of 1907 however. Drivers were being paid $4\frac{3}{4}$d. per hour with an extra $\frac{1}{2}$d. after six months service and a further $\frac{1}{2}$d. after eighteen months while free from accidents. Conductors earned $\frac{1}{4}$d. less. The men demanded an increase of $\frac{1}{4}$d. throughout this scale, conductors to get the same as drivers, a fifty-six hour week, and some minor alterations. This not being forthcoming they came out on strike on 1 August. Three cars were taken out by inspectors but were attacked and damaged in Bridge Street, and they had to be replaced. This time they carried two policemen each and the trolley ropes were wound round the booms to prevent interference. But the crowds were hostile, windows were smashed, and the crews roughly handled. Passengers wouldn't risk travelling and the cars went in early. Thomas Hunter was now the manager, and new drivers were obtained from allied companies in the south, so a few cars were run next day too. The rioters appeared in Court and were duly fined, but they seem to have had much public support. On the following day, Saturday, only one car was left with any glass in its windows. They were taken in to the depot in the early evening, after some derailments. The manager was stoned and injured. On the Sunday the progress of the cars was blocked by large crowds lingering on the track. During the following week an increasing number of cars continued to run, still accompanied by police, and still subjected to rowdyism. Twenty police were sent from Edinburgh. Musselburgh town council tried to mediate, and met the Company, but new men were signing on and the Company refused arbitration or reinstatement. The strikers held meetings at which public enthusiasm gradually waned, though rowdyism and obstruction continued including detonators and the use of a flock of sheep! A "strikers'" opposition motor service was well patronised, but ran only for a few days. After the next weekend conditions became normal again: It was all over. The Company had won, but some Musselburgh councillors wanted to ban Sunday services as a reprisal. Later the Company claimed £220 from the town council for damage done, and eventually recovered about half.

A passenger shelter at Joppa was proposed towards the end of 1907. Edinburgh at first considered a joint building, but in the end left the Company to provide it on their own.

On 5 August 1909 the new extension was opened as far as Tranent Road Cockenzie, and to the Port Seton terminus a few months later that year. A twenty minutes service was given to Port Seton, increased to ten minutes in the summer. The last few hundred yards of the route was laid on a reservation raised slightly from the south side of the roadway. Most of the route lay along narrow roads. Through Prestonpans in particular was a very narrow, and there were some sharp curves and scanty clearances from buildings. Bracket-arm poles were used for the overhead, and due to the considerable offset between wire and track in places trolley ropes had to be abandoned.

About this time the halfpenny fares were withdrawn, though a 1½d. fare was subsequently introduced. Tickets at first had the stage names printed, but latterly numbers were shown. The colours then were : 1d. - white; 1½d. - pale brown; 2d. - blue; 3d. - pink; 4d. - green; 4½d. - purple; 6d. - brown; 7d. - white with red stripe; 9d. - yellow with blue stripe. The Company's operations were no gold-mine, though they had managed a 2% dividend.

In 1911 the service was still every ten minutes to Levenhall and every twenty minutes to Port Seton, reduced to thirty minutes in the evening, but increased to ten minutes for the summer months, when the Company also intimated "A more frequent service is run on Sundays and holidays". On such occasions it was necessary to run the cars in groups of two or three, they having to shunt round one another on the shorter passing loops. A bus service to Tranent was revived in the spring of 1913 starting from Musselburgh railway station.

In 1913 C. W. Bentley was appointed manager but he resigned early in the following year and was succeeded by R. Watson who had been secretary since the Company's inception. D. L. Winter was appointed engineer.

There was another strike of car crews on Saturday 20 February 1915, but the men went back after an hour. It was an uneasy truce however, — wages and overtime being the issue, — and following the "sacking" of three crews a fortnight later, only a skeleton service could be run by inspectors. The Industrial Commissioners held an Inquiry on behalf of the Government on 19 March at which Mr. W. B. Cownie, the Company's managing director declined to reinstate the six men. However reinstatement of the others was offered, together with payment of a war bonus, and on 22 March the services were running normally again.

In June 1915 the time-table for Port Seton intimated till "11.20 p.m. which stops at Levenhall if no passengers beyond that stage, and 11.45 p.m. provided passengers board car at Joppa". By the end of the year the Joppa-Levenhall cars were extended to Prestongrange Colliery.

The Company had seen several managerial changes and more were to come. The engineer having joined the forces in February 1916, E. J. Walsh came to succeed him, but four months later the manager resigned whereupon Walsh became manager and engineer. He in turn resigned in December 1919 and was succeeded by H. C. Babb who was still in command when the Company's transport operations ceased.

The rigours of the war made maintenance difficult, and it is said that the service became even less reliable than the Edinburgh cable system. As so much of the route lay along the sea shore the car windows on that side were painted over to screen them from the sea at night. There was of course no means of turning cars end for end. Miners' traffic called for additional cars, and here the rolling-stock may well be dealt with.

The initial fleet consisted of ten orthodox open-top cars seating 22 inside and 32 on top with three windows and reversed stairs. They were built by the British Electric Car Company and ran on 6ft. wheelbase trucks. The electrical equipment was by B.T.H. with G.E.C. motors. Numbered 1 to 10 the cars were painted red with ivory pillars and rocker panels, lettered Musselburgh Electric Tramways, but later this was gradually altered to M. & D. E. L. & T. Co. Ltd. Roller-blind destination screens were mounted above the top rail, and it may be noted that the Joppa terminus was called Portobello. About the autumn of 1905 four further cars Nos. 11 to 14 were obtained, the order being sublet by the B.T.H. Co. to the Brush Company. These were similar but had ordinary stairs. Later these four cars were fitted with closed tops with the usual open balconies. The trolley bases were fixed to one side of the roof, nearest the shore, to assist in reaching the overhead wire, and the destination screen-boxes were refitted below the platform canopies. Two more similar closed-top cars were also obtained from the Brush Electric Co. in 1909, and numbered 15 and 16.

Nos. 5 and 13 were involved in a somewhat violent collision, and the former was so badly damaged that it was scrapped. The latter however was duly repaired and was then renumbered 5. During the war not much could be done with the rolling-stock and for such painting as was possible an overall chocolate colour was used. Some of the old cars lost their destination screens. After the war an overall green livery was adopted.

As has been mentioned, additional cars were required, and three old single-deckers with 28 seats were acquired from Sheffield Corporation about 1918. These were numbered 17, 18, and 19, and were followed in 1923 by three closed-top double-deckers from the same city which became Nos. 20, 21, and 22. These latter had short top saloons, open stairs and very short platform canopies. About this time, — probably while awaiting these cars, — one of the Slateford electric cars was borrowed from Edinburgh for a short period. As might be expected fares had to be increased in 1920-1.

The arrangements for through running with Edinburgh Corporation are dealt with in that chapter. The Musselburgh closed-top cars were smartened up with two shades of green, the upper deck sides of some enjoining passengers to "enjoy the sea breezes" of "11 miles ride beside the sea". One car, No. 11, was repillared giving it five windows each side to the lower saloon and about 1926 this car and also No. 5 were fitted with transverse seats in the lower saloon.

By now the system was getting into an unsatisfactory condition, and as recorded in the Edinburgh Corporation chapter, the Company ceased tramway operation after 1 March 1928. A fleet of buses took over the route, starting from the top of Waterloo Place, but were diverted around Portobello by Baileyfield Road and Milton Road. To make room for them in the depot the open-top and single-deck cars were cleared out a few days beforehand and taken to Edinburgh's Gorgie depot where the remainder duly joined them for storage until a contractor bought them for scrap soon afterwards. The fate of the tramway route thereafter is related in the chapter on Edinburgh Corporation, while the Company's bus operations will be found in the chapter entitled "Some Independent Bus Operators".

Another route which attracted tramway promotors over many years was that to Queensferry. It was a popular drive in summer and thirty "brakes" were in use on the route. The National Electric Construction Company brought forward a scheme in 1905, proposing a Dolter surface-contact system from the West End and with a connecting line from Goldenacre to Davidson's Mains. Capital was to be £150,000. Linlithgow County Council and others objected at the Inquiry in April 1905, and so the necessary authority did not materialise.

At the same time Mr. Colam of cable car fame was interested in a competing concern, the Edinburgh Suburban Electric Tramway Syndicate who proposed to lay their lines by Belford Bridge, and to have two other connecting lines, one from Comely Bank, and another from Bonnington Terrace via Ferry Road. This scheme did not go forward either, but the idea of a tramway to Queensferry came up from time to time, until, towards the end of the first world war, Edinburgh Corporation themselves sought powers to build such a line. At this time there was heavy traffic in naval personnel to and from the bases at Port Edgar and Rosyth and this was expected to continue. Although warned that a tramway of this nature was unlikely to pay the Corporation went ahead with a Provisional Order in 1918.

The scheme envisaged a double line from the West End, at Hope Street, and also another from the Comely Bank terminus, to Cramond Brig, which would be widened. Over the widened bridge and onwards to beyond Burnshot the tracks were to be laid on the south side of the road. Thereafter a reserved track to the south of the roadway was to be built, diverging around the small wooded plantations, as far as Chapel Gate, from where the south side of the roadway was to be used again for a short distance before resuming the reserved track around the next plantation, and on to the top of Hawes Brae. The roadway was to be used down the brae, and after passing the pier the line would become single through the town to Hopetoun crossroads, with six passing loops. A double line reserved track would then continue south of the Hopetoun road, which was joined a short distance before the proposed terminus at the west gate of Port Edgar naval base.

The proposals also included an alternative line from a point near the top of Hawes Brae, cutting across the fields to a point east of Dalmeny station, from where a single line would be laid along the road, including a passing loop under the station bridge. From there a double line reserved track south of the road was to be laid as far as the Kirkliston Road, which it would cross and then cut through the fields to join the first route beyond Hopetoun crossroads.

Although the plans covered the laying of tracks, it was proposed that the portion of the route between New Halls pier and the terminus be constructed as a trolley-vehicle system.

Many objections were lodged and to placate some, the alternative line by Dalmeny station was dropped. There was much public opposition to the project which was regarded as a waste of money, and a ratepayers' petition was drawn up. The Admiralty then insisted on the Dalmeny line and also reduced fares for naval personnel as the price of their support, whereupon the town council held a special meeting on 20 September 1918 and decided to withdraw their Order and abandon the scheme. An alternative route from the authorised Corstorphine extension, to Queensferry via Kirkliston was then suggested in the town council, but got no further than a suggestion, and that was the last of tramways to Queensferry.

Reverting to 1905, the Edinburgh Suburban Electric Tramways Company proposed to build an electric line from the Nether Liberton terminus via Gilmerton and Eskbank to Bonnyrigg terminating along the Lasswade Road, with a branch from Eskbank to Dalkeith terminating near the Palace Gates. The Company secured their powers by the Edinburgh Suburban Electric Tramways Order Confirmation Act 1906 (passed 21 December 1906). The route was to be single with passing places and with a triangular junction at Eskbank. The usual provisions were included; the gauge to be 4ft. 8½in. or as approved, the overhead or other system as approved; poles to be lighted, and painted not oftener than three-yearly as required by the local authority. Five years were allowed for completion. A fifteen minutes service to Dalkeith and a thirty minutes service to Bonnyrigg were stipulated, and the Company were to carry all the passengers off the last tram from Edinburgh, though if they averaged less than twelve over six months the Company need not run after 11 p.m. The fare to Dalkeith was to be 4d. and to Bonnyrigg 5d.

The Company had already thought it better to get their line right in to the city if they could and to this end proposed to extend from Nether Liberton by way of Lady Road, Dalkeith Road, Pleasance, and Jeffrey Street to a terminus at the Waverley Bridge. They also proposed a branch along Melville Drive to Tollcross and suggested to the Corporation that they be allowed to provide the Craiglockhart route, about which the Corporation were then deliberating. The surface-contact system was proposed for these new lines within the city, and the conversion of the Mound route to work in conjunction with the Craiglockhart route was also suggested. Edinburgh town council were interested but as we have seen they preferred to hold with their existing lessees, and did not support the new Company.

So nothing further transpired. Dalkeith town council asked the Company about starting, but there appear to have been financial difficulties. The Company obtained another Act in 1911 (passed 18 August 1911) extending their time for construction until two years after 21 December 1911. Nevertheless nothing was ever done and the powers lapsed. A similar trolley-bus route had been proposed by the Dalkeith Railless Electric Car Company in 1908.

One other concern has to be mentioned. About 1909 the War Office had decided to build the new barracks at Redford.

This led to a company known as the Colinton Tramways Company seeking powers for a line from Craiglockhart terminus to the Loan, Colinton, with a branch to Slateford station and along Slateford Road, Angle Park Terrace, and Fountainbridge to East Fountainbridge. At the Inquiry in July 1909 there were objections from Midlothian County Council and from Edinburgh Corporation who had an eye on the route themselves. Nevertheless the Order was passed on 25 November 1909 as the Colinton Tramways Order Confirmation Act 1909. This authorised a line through the fields between Craiglockhart and the barracks site, with the branch to connect with the line the Corporation were now projecting to Slateford station, and another branch to the Caledonian Railway sidings behind Slateford station. The contractor for the barracks buildings was to have the right of using the line for materials. Steam power could be used for this purpose for four and a quarter years: Thereafter the line was to be electrically operated and a generating station allowed for. Later, power from Edinburgh Corporation was agreed. The gauge had, of course, to be 4ft. 8½in. and five years were allowed for completion. As with the Edinburgh Suburban Company buses were authorised within five miles of the line over contemplated extensions.

In April 1910 a contract was let to William Jackson, Edinburgh, to make the formation through the fields and construct the bridge over the canal near Slateford. Temporary railway track was laid the following month for use by the contractor building the barracks, and two steam locomotives were used on it.

By 1913 the Company had made no effective progress, only the reserved track formation being made, from which the barracks contractor's rails were now removed. They then sought powers for a line from Angle Park Terrace via Dundee Street and Fountainbridge to a terminus just west of Earl Grey Street, with running powers over the Corporation line along Slateford Road. Edinburgh Corporation objected to this and considered electrifying their own line inwards from Ardmillan to Haymarket and the east end of Morrison Street. The Company's Provisional Order failed, and so they then suggested the Corporation might build the line from Craiglockhart to Colinton themselves, offering, in March, to sell their rights to the Corporation for £10,200. The Town Clerk drew up a report on the matter, suggesting the Corporation should accept in the public interest, as a service would be required by the War Office, yet such could not now be provided by the Company.

The town council deliberated and thought of building the line through the fields from Craiglockhart for operation by a self-propelled car. No action materialised however, and in November the Company sought an extension of time for the compulsory purchase of a certain field at Slateford, between the canal and the station, belonging to the Corporation, without which they would not be able to complete their route to Slateford. This was refused though continued temporary access across the field to the railway sidings was agreed.

The Company then obtained the Colinton Tramways Extension Order Confirmation Act 1914 (passed 8 July 1914) which granted them a three years extension of time from 25 November 1914, and also power to sell their concern to the Corporation at any time if the latter secured Board of Trade approval to purchase. In 1915 the Corporation again refused to buy up the Company, as already mentioned in chapter II and consequently failed to secure powers to build a line to Colinton themselves. Nevertheless the Company secured extensions of time annually until 25 November 1920. It was now evident the Colinton Company would have to be liquidated to clear the way for the Corporation to serve the expanding city, and so at last, early in 1920, the Corporation agreed to purchase the concern for about £5,000. The Corporation found the bridge over the canal useful for carrying some new water mains.

The old formation through the fields remained for several years until building developed. Part of the route then became Craiglockhart Road including the spur to the old Craiglockhart terminus. The other portion northwards towards Slateford station and the bridge over the canal can still be seen, and is now in use as a footpath leading to Allan Park Road.

VI

THE RISE AND FALL OF SUBURBAN RAILWAYS

The surrounding places which could be reached by rail at the beginning of the "seventies" have been recorded in the introductory chapter. The main lines should need no description, but the branches may be less well-known today.

The Peebles branch left the south main line at Hardengreen junction just beyond Eskbank, and climbed steadily upwards to its summit just beyond Leadburn whence it followed the Eddleston Water to Peebles. Single beyond Hawthornden, passing loops were provided at Leadburn and Eddleston, but not at Peebles station where the one platform was on the up side, as were the other platforms on the single line. The loop at Eddleston was later taken out leaving only the down platform in use. The Dolphinton branch from Leadburn meandered down into the Lyne valley where it became flatter. The first small platform was on the down side, the others on the up, and at the terminus an end-on connection was made with a Caledonian branch from the west, that Company's station being beyond an intervening road bridge.

The Polton branch left the Peebles line a short distance beyond Hardengreen junction, and climbed steeply through Broomieknowe, over its summit and down through a curved tunnel to immediately enter Lasswade station, over a viaduct, and then on down into the North Esk valley to its cramped little terminus. All platforms were on the up side of the single line. The Dalkeith branch was a short spur off the main line just after it crossed the North Esk, the terminus having a single platform and a short roof.

The Haddington branch was far from flat but calls for no comment, the terminus with platform on the up side being on high ground to the west end of the town. The North Berwick branch was similar, but had a more commodious two-platform terminus. There was a deep cutting before reaching the short platform on the up side at Dirleton.

The Macmerry branch left the East-Coast main line at Monktonhall junction, where it crosses the Esk, and climbed steeply on embankment to Smeaton, from where it doubled back round

147

into a reverse curve, still climbing, and now through a very deep cutting, to eventually emerge on more level ground at Ormiston, and on to the terminus, with another intermediate station at Winton. Platforms were on the down side except Smeaton which had an island platform. A goods branch from here linked the south main line at Hardengreen Junction until closed about the first war period.

Finally the Queensferry branch descended from the main line just before Ratho, at which it had its own adjoining platform at the lower level, on the down side. Curving away across the Almond valley Kirkliston station, on the down side, was reached, after which there was much heavy cutting until the line turned westwards to descend steeply down the hillside forming the shore of the Forth.

Much railway development was still taking place however. On 20 June 1870 a branch from Hawthornden to Penicuik was authorised and duly constructed. Passenger service from Waverley commenced on 2 September 1872. It was an interesting line, single all the way, with intermediate stations at Roslin Castle, Auchendinny, and Eskbridge. A short distance beyond Roslin Castle, the line ran through an artificial wooden tunnel erected at the behest of the Board of Trade on account of the proximity of the old gunpowder works in the valley below. Following some open country there was a substantial viaduct over the North Esk and the line immediately plunged into a lengthy tunnel emerging to pass through a paper mill with a siding. This was again immediately followed by another short but curved tunnel, at the other end of which lay Auchendinny station with another bridge over the river squeezed in between. Onwards to Eskbridge was more straightforward, but thereafter the course followed the winding river, with several paper mill sidings, to its terminus at the south end of the town. All the station platforms were on the up side, except at Auchendinny.

A further Act on the same date had authorised another branch on the other side of the North Esk valley, to Roslin. This left the main line at Millerhill, and had stations also at Gilmerton, some distance south of the village, and at Loanhead. The line, single with a passing loop at the latter station, was heavily graded and served several collieries. Beyond Loanhead, Bilston Glen was crossed on a massive girder viaduct. This branch was opened on 23 July 1874, and in accordance with a further Act of 5 August 1873, was extended to Glencorse, the extension thereto being opened on 2 July 1877. The approach to Glencorse was over a graceful viaduct across the golf course, while beyond the station the rails continued for about another half mile to the gasworks on the northern outskirts of Penicuik. Station platforms were on the down side except at Gilmerton.

The Caledonian was also building its goods branch, authorised on 7 July 1862, from Crew on the Granton branch, down to Leith. A connection was also made from the Granton direction, and in order to be able to run trains between the Lothian Road station and the Leith and Granton branches, a line was built in 1864 from Dalry junction to Coltbridge junction. The Leith branch was a double line, the terminus being immediately west of the Docks. An Act of 30 June 1874 authorised the West Dalry branch from this route to form a link for main line trains down to the North British main line, and this was opened in July 1876.

Another Caledonian branch of this period was the sharply curved but very picturesque single line up the valley of the Water of Leith to Balerno. Authorised on 20 June 1870 this left the main line beyond Slateford, and was provided with intermediate stations at Colinton, Juniper Green, and Currie, the latter having a passing loop. The branch was opened to passenger traffic on 1 August 1874. Its course took it first through Colinton Dell, followed by a curved tunnel immediately beyond which lay Colinton station, on the up side. Scott's oatmeal mill and siding was then passed on the left, and the twisting line continued up the narrow valley to Juniper Green station, also on the up side. There was then a dip past Kinleith paper mill and siding before the line climbed again up to Currie station with its two platforms. The rest of the route though still tortuous was more open. Balerno passenger station though having a passing loop had a platform on the down side only. It was situated immediately beyond the bridge under the main road, some distance from the village. The goods station was nearer the village and reached by a spur leaving the passenger line before it passed under the main road. Beyond the passenger station the branch was continued down to the main line again at Ravelrig.

Perhaps the weakest feature of the local railway services at this time was the premises which formed the main termini of the two companies, viz. Waverley station and Lothian Road station. Several writers tried, but felt they could not do justice to the inadequacies of the former. The latter was dismissed as a "wooden shanty", Clearly neither was worthy of the city. The local trains too were spartan. Narrow four-wheeled carriages were practically universal, and three classes were usually provided, the third class being quite devoid of upholstery. The North British carriages might be described as a plum colour; those of the Caledonian a dark chocolate, the newer ones being relieved by cream upper panels. The engines however brought a touch of colour, the North British with their green-brown so difficult to describe, and the "Caley" with their beautiful blue: And in those days trains were really clean, at least outside.

The North British trains were mostly hauled by old main-line engines or in some cases by old saddle-tank engines, till the late "seventies", when Dugald Drummond, the Company's locomotive engineer introduced a class of very neat little 0-6-0 tank engine. Their wheels were 4ft. 6in. diameter and the cylinders 15in. x 22in. These engines were adorned with names chosen from the places on the branches which they normally served, and hence we had "Haddington", "Granton", "Bonnington", "North Berwick", "Polton", "Queensferry", "Dalkeith", "Leith", and Musselburgh". In 1880 a rather similar 4-4-0 tank type appeared having driving wheels 5ft. dia. and solid bogie wheels 2ft. 6in. dia. The cylinders were 16in. x 22in. The local names on this class were "Dirleton", "Roslin", and "Penicuik". Names such as "Haymarket", "Corstorphine", "Gogar", "Ratho", "Peebles", and so on were in use on main line engines. The use of names of this kind however had several disadvantages and after Drummond had been succeeded by Matthew Holmes in 1882 they were all discarded.

The Caledonian trains were in the hands of old tank engines or the somewhat ungainly 0-4-2 tender engines with 5ft. 2in. dia. driving wheels and 17in. x 24in. outside cylinders. Names were not used. Some neater 0-4-4 tank engines were however appearing, with 5ft. 9in. dia. driving wheels and 18in. x 26in. cylinders, and for the Balerno branch J. F. McIntosh, the Caledonian locomotive engineer, produced a smaller version with 4ft. 6in. dia. driving wheels and 17in. x 24in. cylinders.

Much has been written elsewhere regarding locomotives and railway rolling-stock, and it is not proposed to deal with them in detail here. Readers interested may refer to the usual works on the subject. However let us have a look at the train services themselves, taking the 1876 summer time-table for our example.

There were stopping trains in the Dunbar direction, all with connections to Haddington and to North Berwick, at 7.5, 10.5, 3.55, and 6.30, also semi-fasts at 2.5, and 5.10, there being connections into these from South Leith at 10.0, 3.50, 4.25, and 5.55. Joppa and New Hailes were, however, generally served by the Musselburgh branch trains at 8.20, 9.35, 11.20, 1.10, 3.0, 3.45, 4.40, 6.0, 8.30 and 10.0 Macmerry had two trains only, viz. 7.15 a.m. and 4.40 p.m. Trains in the Galashiels direction ran at 6.20, 9.45, 1.45, 3.30, and 6.40, with connections from South Leith at 6.12, 9.25, 1.0 and 5.55.

Stopping trains from Waverley to the west ran at 6.50, 11.0, 3.0, 5.0, and 8.0 The Queensferry branch trains left Waverley at 9.10, 12.10, 4.45, and 7.15, all but the last connecting with ferries to Fife.

The Penicuik branch was served at 10.27, 1.30, 4.0, and 8.15, all but the last also having a portion for Polton, which place also had trains at 7.40 a.m. and 9.45 p.m. The Roslin branch trains were at 11.0, 4.50, and 9.0 with connections also from the 7.40 and 1.30 trains. The Peebles line trains with connections on the Dolphinton branch were at 7.0, 10.40, 4.15, and 7.0 The middle two ran non-stop from Portobello to Hawthornden, the afore-mentioned branch trains providing connection from intermediate stations. The Dalkeith branch trains ran at 10.45, 12.20, 2.10, 5.20, 7.35, 9.25, and 10.45.

To North Leith there were twenty-eight trains between 5.30 a.m. and 9.55 p.m., and to Granton, eighteen trains between 6.5 a.m. and 10.20 p.m. Four of the five of the latter which connected with the ferry to Burntisland ran non-stop or called only at Leith Walk. The Granton and North Leith branch services were arranged to make connection between one another at Leith Walk.

The Caledonian had a few stopping trains on their main-line and others running to Midcalder via the Balerno branch at 6.20, 10.5, 2.0, 4.10, and 6.35, with another at 8.20 p.m. on Saturdays, while there was an 8.0 p.m. as far as Balerno only, Saturdays excepted, when it terminated at Currie.

The pattern on the return services was similar. On Sundays, only some of the main-line stations, and the Haddington and Peebles branches were offered a service, though there were also two trains on the Granton branch to connect with the ferries.

During the "seventies" the horse-tram services began to have their effect on the local railway traffic, but this was not taken lying down. The North British Company's frequent service to Leith in 1876 will be observed, and they also now offered very cheap fares between Waverley and/or any stations on the branch, as follows : First class 2d., second class 1½d., third class 1d. single. In addition third class return tickets available by specified trains at times suitable for workmen could be bought in advance at 1/3d. per dozen, and each half ticket could be used in either direction.

It will be remembered, nevertheless, that the public were not entirely pleased with the horse-trams at that time, and the railway could still hold its own. It was cheaper and quicker, though the poor access to Waverley station gave cause for comment. The Caledonian indeed, thought there was plenty of traffic to and from Leith for them too, and in 1878 set about laying separate passenger lines from Newhaven on their Leith goods branch to a new passenger station at the foot of North Junction Street. The passenger service of twelve trains a day between Lothian Road station and the new Leith station was opened on 1 August 1879, and proved very popular. Extra trains had to be put on for the first Saturday's traffic. The fares charged were: First class 3d. single, 5d. return, third class 2d. single, 3d. return. The North British had already made a general reduction of their third class fares at the beginning of the year. The Caledonian Leith branch was a double line, and there was much deep cutting and embankment particularly between Murrayfield and Craigleith where passenger stations were provided. Other passenger stations were at Granton Road and at Newhaven, and at these and also at Craigleith the station offices were built on a bridge spanning the lines and adjoining a road bridge. The Leith station had an island platform with one track either side, and a short overall roof. There being no provision for the engine to run round its train after unloading, the coaches were pushed back up the grade out of the station : the engine then retired to a siding, and the coaches returned into the platform by gravity.

On the "Caley" main-line, a station which became very useful as the district became built up, was opened on 1 July 1882, named Merchiston, and served of course, also by the Balerno branch trains. Improvement in the approach tracks to the Lothian Road station were also prepared.

A bigger scheme was now afoot however, the Edinburgh Suburban and South Side Junction Railway, authorised by Acts of 26 August 1880 and 24 July 1882. This was really a North British scheme and was amalgamated with its parent company on 1 May 1885. The route was double-line and branched off the main-line beyond Haymarket after crossing Russell Road. Diving under the Caledonian's West Dalry branch it joined a connection coming in from westwards on the North British main-line, and then climbed steeply around the south suburbs of the city with a summit just west of Morningside Road. On reaching Duddingston it joined the more level course of the old "Innocent Railway", which it used before curving northwards again to join the "Waverley route" main-line just before it passed under Milton Road. The old "Innocent Railway" connections southwards and a new connection eastwards to the "East-Coast" main-line continued to be used for goods traffic and occasional passenger specials, and the line has thus always been a useful bypass for such. Passenger stations were provided at Gorgie, reached from either Gorgie Road or Slateford Road between which two roads it lay; Morningside Road, Blackford Hill, Newington, and Duddingston, and a circular passenger service from Waverley, where a special new through platform on the south side of the station was built, started on 1 December 1884.

The rather circuitous route put Newington and Blackford Hill stations at some disadvantage for passengers to and from town. Nevertheless the line was popular and an additional station at Colinton Road, known as Craiglockhart, was opened on 1 June 1887. Much of the western end of the line lay in deep cutting, and except at Gorgie and Duddingston the station offices were on the adjoining road bridges.

A useful loop was laid by the North British eastwards from Abbeyhill to join the line from North Leith and Granton and so reaching the main-line just beyond the St. Margaret's loco. depot. This was constructed under the Company's Act of 22 July 1885, and came into use on 1 October 1886. A passenger station at the eastern end of this line, Piershill, was opened on 1 May 1891.

It should be mentioned that a station to serve the little village of Philpstoun, on the main-line between Winchburgh and Linlithgow had been opened on 12 October 1885, and a new goods station for the North British near the Docks, at South Leith, on 2 February 1885. The passenger station at Portobello had long been criticised, but a fine new station with an island platform was completed in June 1887. The branch trains to South Leith continued to use their separate old platform however. For the International Exhibition in 1890 the Caledonian built a temporary station east of Slateford, just to the west of the bridge across the North British line. A small electric railway operated in the Exhibition grounds from this point to near the North British Craiglockhart station. The Exhibition was also served by electric launches on the Union canal,* as well as by the tramways.

The Forth Bridge was now under construction. This was, of course, a most important development. Much has been written elsewhere about the bridge, and here it will be sufficient to record the incorporation of the Forth Bridge Railway Company, and its Act of 12 July 1882 to build the bridge and its immediate approaches, the interest being guaranteed by the North British, North Eastern, Great Northern, and Midland Railway companies. The North British built new main lines leading to it from the then Corstorphine station, and from the west beyond Winchburgh, the old Queensferry line from Kirkliston also joining them. A new station, subsequently called Dalmeny, was provided near the south end of the bridge. After some trial runs and tests the ceremony of the "last rivet" was performed in a gale by the Prince of Wales on 4 March 1890, and traffic commenced the following day, a passenger service being given from Edinburgh via Kirkliston and across the bridge to Dunfermline in place of the service on the old Queensferry branch which was then withdrawn. The new connecting lines on the south side and others in Fife were not opened until 2 June when through traffic commenced. A major change was thus effected in the whole pattern of the North British Company's operations. There was still some local traffic to Granton and one of the passenger ferry boats, the long remembered

* The Union Canal, opened in May 1822, had its Edinburgh terminus at Port Hopetoun which was where Lothian House now stands. The canal connected with the Forth and Clyde canal by a flight of locks near Falkirk and had carried much passenger traffic in its first twenty years. Soon afterwards it came under the control of the Edinburgh and Glasgow (later North British) Railway. It was shortened to its present terminus near Leamington Terrace about 1921 and is no longer connected to the Forth and Clyde canal at the Falkirk end.

"William Muir" continued to ply between Granton and Burntisland. The other three, "Auld Reekie", "Thane of Fife", and "John Stirling" were sold. The goods train ferries of course ceased and the special vessels "Leviathan", "Balbirnie", "Kinloch", and "Midlothian" also disposed of. The goods and passenger traffic handled by the ferry boats had been very substantial: For example the figures for the year to 31 January 1873 were :—

Passengers (exc. season etc. tickets)	464,147
Parcels	58,732
Horses	675
Goods (tons)	232,782
Coal (tons)	90,033
Minerals (tons)	35,772
Livestock (wagon loads)	3,729
Fish (tons)	2,986

It should here be mentioned that in 1890 a Captain Arthur took over the Queensferry passage from the North British Railway, where the "John Beaumont" continued to ply until Arthur was succeeded in 1893 by D. Wilson & Son, who put the "Forfarshire" on the run. Further, in 1891, the North British Railway through the North British Steam Packet Company acquired a controlling interest in the Galloway Saloon Steam Packet Company, operating between Leith and various Forth resorts.

On 1 September 1897, a station was opened at Turnhouse on the new main-line from Corstorphine. It is interesting to note that fares to stations on the Fife coast continued to be calculated on the shortest route, as was then the normal railway practice, — in this case via the Granton-Burntisland ferry. Places such as Dunfermline were not so well off in this respect: the Forth Bridge counted as ten miles in calculating fares.

A disruptive railway strike broke out just before Christmas 1890 and lasted over the New Year.

We are now at a most interesting period of local railway development. Both companies had their eyes on Leith and the provision of increased facilities, both passenger and goods, there. At the end of 1889 the two companies put forward their schemes.

The North British proposed a branch from Abbeyhill to a new station right at the foot of Leith Walk, together with a connecting link on to the new Piershill loop towards Portobello. The Caledonian, being further away, had to be more ambitious in order to reach central and south Leith, and they put up two schemes. One was for a line from a point west of Newhaven on their existing Leith branch, which would curve away south and east, passing

Bonnington Toll, then down beside the North British's proposed new station at the foot of Leith Walk, thence to sweep up round Lochend and circle in to a station near Salamander Street, with a spur leaving further out, to cross over Seafield Road and the North British lines, to reach the new Edinburgh Dock. There would be a triangular connection at Newhaven, and passenger stations on the new line at Newhaven, Leith Walk, and Lochend.

The other scheme was more grandiose. No less than a line diving underground from outside the Lothian Road station and proceeding under Charlotte Square, George Street, and the Calton Hill, then out onto a viaduct and embankment over Greenside and Hillside, and sweeping on over Easter Road to join the afore-mentioned scheme at Lochend. A branch to a proposed station at the Waverley Market was included. Leith Town Council were agreeable to all the foregoing schemes. Edinburgh Town Council, not surprisingly, objected to this second "Caley" proposition, and the Act which the Caledonian succeeded in obtaining on 4 August 1890 did not include this part. The "Caley" expressed themselves as disappointed and brought forward a similar scheme next session.

This time the North British were brought into the plan, and spurs were proposed from the North British at Haymarket, and from the "Caley's" Morrison Street goods station as well as the original Rutland Street spur, all uniting under Charlotte Square. This time the line was proposed to join the North British west of Easter Road, and a new connecting line built between a point east of there and the proposed new "Caley" South Leith line at Lochend. Instead of the branch station at Waverley Market, a larger one was proposed under St. James' Square. This Edinburgh and Leith Junction Railway was also rejected. Perhaps it was as well: it would have been a very expensive line to construct. Only the link from the N.B. at Easter Road to the C.R. at Lochend was authorised by the Caledonian Act of 3 July 1891, and it was never constructed.

The impact of the new route across the Forth was however calling for extensive improvement of the North British's facilities, and an Act was obtained on 5 August 1891, and the work promptly put in hand, for doubling the line to give four tracks in from Corstorphine, through Waverley, and on to Abbeyhill junction. New tunnels at Haymarket, the Mound and Calton were necessary, and the Waverley station itself was also drastically rebuilt and improved. The separate long through platform on the south side remained for the Suburban circle trains. The powers previously sought for the new Leith branch were now also granted by this Act.

155

**NORTH BRITISH RAILWAY TRAIN OF OLD FOUR-WHEELED
CARRIAGES WITH SMALL 4-4-0 TANK ENGINE AT
NORTH LEITH STATION**

The Caledonian also felt it essential now to do something
about their principal station, and the new structure was put in
hand and opened piecemeal in 1894. Both stations when finished
were a great advance on the previous premises, and while public
access to Waverley was not as convenient as might be desired, the
Caledonian's Princes Street station was perhaps ideal in its easy
level approach to the concourse and platforms from such a focal
point as the West End.

The Caledonian, under an Act of 25 July 1890, then built its
double-line branch from Craigleith to Barnton with an intermediate
station at Davidson's Mains. The summit of the line was just
beyond this station. The terminus was provided with an unroofed
island platform, the neat station buildings being behind the buffer-
stops. This branch was opened on 1 March 1894, the terminus
being called Cramond Brig until April 1903, while the Davidson's
Mains station was known until then as Barnton Gate.

The North British added Powderhall station on their Granton
branch at Broughton Road on 1 May 1895. Further east the
Aberlady, Gullane and North Berwick Railway Act of 24 August
1893 resulted in the single-line branch leaving the East Coast
main-line near Redhouse Castle and curving to within a half-mile

of Aberlady where a station was provided, before curving round again in a big sweep to reach Gullane. This branch was more or less at ground level, and the platforms were on the down side. The branch was opened by North British trains on 1 April 1898, and never got any further than its station at the east end of the village of Gullane. The nominally separate company was amalgamated with the parent North British in 1900.

The North British Corstorphine station was too far from the village to be of much use, and on 12 August 1898 an Act was obtained for a short branch leaving the main-line where it crossed the Water of Leith, and after running alongside for a short distance, curving northwards and westwards to a terminus in the village of Corstorphine. An intermediate station was provided at Pinkhill, which later proved convenient for the Zoo. The new terminus had long platforms either of which could be used for arrivals or departures, a scissors crossover providing for engine release. The old station on the main-line was renamed Saughton when the new double-line branch was opened on 1 February 1902.

C.R. SMALL-WHEELED 0-4-4 TANK ENGINE AND TRAIN OF OLD FOUR-WHEEL COACHES AT DAVIDSON'S MAINS STATION
Note Semaphore head code on engine

In 1899 the Caledonian at last made a start with their South Leith line. There had been difficulty in acquiring some of the ground between Bonnington Toll and Leith Walk, and a further Act had been required in 1894 to cover a deviation at this part. In consequence the line crossed Leith Walk some little distance from the foot of the Walk, viz. immediately south of Manderston Street. The line crossed over Bonnington Toll diagonally, and here and at Leith Walk and at Easter Road massive lattice girder bridges were required. A goods station was built on the west side of Leith Walk, and there was a temporary passenger station for a military occasion nearer Bonnington Toll. A double line was laid but it was singled in 1917. Although the passenger station platforms at Newhaven were built as proposed, they were not completed, and the ordinary passenger service never materialised. Nor were the rails laid on the east side of the triangle there. A similar connection at Crew from the Granton direction was abandoned soon after. In recent years this has been partly covered by a housing scheme.

A useful new station on the Leith and Barnton branch was opened on 2 July 1900, at Dalry Road. This had an island platform and could be reached at either end from different parts of Dalry Road and also from Fountainbridge.

The North British were now building their new double-line branch down to the foot of Leith Walk, where much property had to be acquired and some demolished, and also streets closed and altered to make room for the large terminus which they called Leith Central. This was undoubtedly a convenient and worthy terminus with four platforms and a high overall roof, but it is doubtful if such a large station was really justified. It was opened on 1 July 1903, and the South Side suburban trains were run into and out of it on their journeys round the circle. Passengers on trains on the inner circle rails could change into a main-line train at Portobello for a direct run to Waverley, and similarly in the opposite direction. Some main-line trains to Glasgow or Dundee also started or terminated at Leith Central, and the then 8.5 a.m. from Polton ran direct there. With the opening of the new station, the service to South Leith was much curtailed, ceasing altogether in September 1904 by which time only three morning trips to South Leith were being run from Portobello.

Two North British country branches have now to be mentioned. In the east, an Act of 3 July 1891 provided for a twelve mile branch from Ormiston to Gifford and Garvald, but a further Act of 24 August 1893 authorised instead, an alternative line, seven miles long, to Gifford. Still nothing was done however, till a Light Railway Order under the new procedure for such undertakings, was obtained on 14 July 1898, and this resulted in a single-line railway with some steep grades and sharp curves, from Ormiston as far as Gifford, with small intermediate stations at Pencaitland, Salton, and Humbie. The platforms of the first two were on the down side, the latter and the terminus on the other. As built it was nine miles long, and opened on 1 November 1901, by the North British, though the Light Railway company remained nominally independent until the grouping of the railways in 1923.

To the south, the Lauder Light Railway was incorporated in 1898 and constructed under a Light Railway Order of 30 June 1898 as a single-line branch, ten miles long through the hills from Fountainhall to Lauder with an intermediate station at Oxton. It was very heavily graded and for much of the way sharply curved. The North British opened this line on 2 July 1901, though it also remained nominally independent till 1923. Both these lines were of course subject to the speed, weight, and other restrictions of the Light Railway Acts, and crossed the public roads by unguarded crossings without gates except where the Lauder branch crossed the main road just after leaving Fountainhall on its way up the hillside. Here the trains stopped while the guard opened and closed the gates. Both branches were worked by the small 4-4-0 tank engines and four-wheeled carriages.

A short branch line to Bangour Hospital was built under the Edinburgh District Lunacy Board's Act of 30 July 1900. This left the Bathgate line west of Uphall, and was opened on 1 July 1905, being worked by the North British. A new station was built on the Galashiels main-line nearer the village of Newtongrange, replacing the old Dalhousie station on the other side of the South Esk on 1 August 1908.

Returning to the Caledonian, a connection from the Granton branch was laid in to the new Edinburgh and Leith gasworks which had been built alongside the branch about a mile from its terminus. This was then open country and as most of the gasworks employees would require transport to and from Edinburgh, a small station was built on the gasworks estate, and a passenger train service, third class only, run at suitable times to and from Princes Street. This was started on 1 November 1902, but the trains were not shown in the public time-tables beyond Craigleith. Nevertheless people from the few cottages in the vicinity of the gasworks occasionally made use of them.

There were other proposals about this time for extending the Barnton branch to join the North British near Queensferry, or alternatively near Gogar, or by a loop back to Corstorphine, but nothing came of these.

For the Scottish National Exhibition at Saughton Park in 1908 the North British built a temporary wooden station on the Corstorphine branch where it crossed Balgreen Road. A fifteen minutes service was run on the branch at busy times during the period of the Exhibition. A useful halt, Crossgatehall, in the deep cutting between Smeaton and Ormiston was opened on 1 September 1913. Another, on the East-Coast main-line between Prestonpans and Longniddry, called Seton Mains, was opened on 1 May 1914, but this was too far from Port Seton to attract much traffic.

About this time there was much development of coal traffic from the Lothians coalfields, particularly to Leith for export, and though we are really concerned only with passenger traffic, the resulting construction of new railways should be mentioned. The Lothians Lines of the North British, authorised by Act of 15 August 1913 comprised an additional single-line from Monktonhall junction beside the river Esk on the East-Coast main-line, rising and curving westwards to join similar lines from the Millerhill and from the Duddingston directions near Niddrie junction, where the main-lines passed underneath the new line. The new line then crossed over both the main-lines again, just west of Joppa station, and curving westwards again dropped down on a high embankment to join the Portobello-South Leith line where it left the main-line at Portobello station. There were also improved facilities on the approaches to South Leith and the Docks. A special signalling system was adopted for the new mineral line, instead of the usual methods in use on single-lines, and the lines were opened for the mineral traffic on 26 September 1915.

The unique route indicator used by the Caledonian should here be mentioned. This consisted of small white semaphore arms mounted on the front of the locomotive and set as shown on page 164. The system continued in use until about 1930.

After nearly a decade of competition with cable and electric tramways, and also the developing S.M.T. bus services, it is opportune to take a look at the railway time-tables again. Let us take the summer of 1914 as exemplifying the services provided prior to the first war. These were as follows :

In the Dunbar direction, stopping trains at 6.43, 9.15, 2.2, 4.1, 5.18, and 6.30. There were Haddington, Gullane, and North Berwick connections from most of the above and trains for these branches also at 9.7, 11.15, 1.34, 4.30, and 8.10, though not all three branches were served in every case. There were also certain Saturday only or Thursday only trains. Joppa and New Hailes were still served only by the Musselburgh branch trains and the Macmerry branch trains, the former having twenty-nine services between 4.58 a.m. and 10.7 p.m. with three more on Saturdays, and the latter trains at 7.3, 12.44(SO), 5.10, and 10.45(SO), all with portions for Gifford, to which place there was a further train at 9.32 a.m. In the Galashiels direction there were stopping trains at 6.15, 9.35, 1.5(SO), 3.25, and 6.50, with some Saturday extras as far as Gorebridge. Lauder was served by the foregoing except the 1.5, and also by a semi-fast at 4.25 p.m. which caught up the 3.25 connection. Peebles trains were at 6.58, 10.32, 1.0(SO), 1.34 (SO and non-stop to Leadburn), 2.17, 4.32, 5.31, and 8.35, most of them fast to Hawthornden. The 1.34(SO), and except on Saturdays the 5.31 took through carriages to Dolphinton which came from West Linton only at 8.50 a.m. Most of the other services provided connections to Dolphinton. Penicuik trains were at 7.40, 9.54, 1.28(SX), 1.40(SO), 5.6, 8.3, and 10.40(SO), and those to Polton at 7.13, 9.38, 11.30, 1.17(SO), 1.52(SO), 4.8, 5.53(SX), 6.51, 9.40(SO), 10.18(WSX), and 11.0(SO). Most of the Polton trains had portions or connections for Glencorse, though in the afternoon and evening and also around mid-day on Saturdays separate trains were run to the latter branch. Dalkeith had trains at 10.48, 12.13, 2.36 (with Glencorse connection), 5.40, 7.21, 9.40, and 11.10, also one at 9.0 a.m. from Leith Central to which station the 8.10 a.m. from Polton ran direct.

Stopping trains to Linlithgow ran at 6.15, 9.35, 10.42, 2.55, 5.25, 8.0, and 10.10(SO), to Bathgate at 7.45, 8.49, 10.35, 1.40, 4.29, 6.56, 8.38, and 10.30(SO), and on the Dalmeny line at 5.47, 10.15, 12.12(SO), 12.58, 2.25, 5.1, 6.4, 7.15, 7.55, and 11.0(SO). There were four trains on the Bangour branch, the first one inwards in the morning running forward to make connection at Drumshoreland instead of at Uphall. Six trains traversed the Ratho-Dalmeny line and the Corstorphine branch was served by twenty-four trains between 7.15 a.m. and 11.10 p.m. There were twenty-nine trains, (one more on Saturdays) between 5.30 a.m. and 11.3 p.m. to North Leith, and eleven, (one more on Saturdays) between 5.25 a.m. and 8.20 p.m. to Granton. The South Side Suburban circle line had fifteen trains each way with another four to and from Duddingston covering the western side of the line. The "penny jerks" between Waverley and Leith Central were provided by these and other trains totalling fifty-four daily, several of which did not call at Abbeyhill. The workmen's tickets to North Leith remained in operation and were available to Leith Central as well. A useful feature of the North British time-table was that the number of the Waverley departure platform was given for the various trains.

The Caledonian ran stopping trains on their main-line at 6.30, 7.10 (as far as Curriehill), 7.55, 8.40, 9.40, 11.20, 1.20, 3.57, 5.0(SO), 5.10(SX and calling at Ravelrig on Wednesday), and 5.35, with two other evening trains missing Slateford and Curriehill. There were seventeen trains on the Balerno branch with three more on Saturdays, some of which continued on to Midcalder. The Leith branch had thirty-four trains between 5.28 a.m. and 11.10 p.m. while Barnton was served by twenty-four with five more on Saturdays.

On Sundays the services were restricted to the main-lines, one train each way on the Peebles line, the Haddington branch, and the Balerno and Barnton branches in addition in the summer.

It will be seen that the railways were providing good services, and indeed they were carrying a fair proportion of the traffic. There had been some improvement in the rolling-stock too, though four or six wheeled coaches were still almost universal on the branch line services. The motive power in use on the Caledonian had not changed to any extent, but on the North British new 0-4-4 tank engines similar to those on the Caledonian, and having 5ft. 9in. diameter driving wheels and 17in. x 24in. cylinders had appeared on a few duties from the "eighties". A new and neat 4-4-2 tank engine class was also appearing on the more important local trains. Driving wheels were again 5ft. 9in. diameter but the cylinders were 18in. x 26in. One of these was number one in the North British list, and as at this time that company commenced to paint the engine numbers in large figures between the initials N B for ease of identification with their new traffic control arrangements, this machine, familiar on the Corstorphine branch became affectionately known as "nib".

Then came the war. Though there was not much difference at first, coal and labour shortages began to have their effect and curtailment of service became necessary. On 1 January 1917 fares were increased and also a considerable number of stations throughout the country had to be closed to comply with a Government order for release of men and materials for use in other directions. Those in the Edinburgh area were: Piershill, Crossgatehall, Gilmerton, Roslynlee, Eskbridge, Broomieknowe, Blackford Hill, Craiglockhart, Saughton, Pinkhill, and Kingsknowe, in addition to which services were also suspended on the North Leith, Granton, and Dalkeith branches. After the war most of these were re-opened in 1919 as follows: The Granton branch on 1 February, followed by the North Leith branch on 1 April, except for Powderhall station which was never re-opened at all. Crossgatehall, Blackford Hill, Craiglockhart, Saughton, Pinkhill, and Kingsknowe stations were also re-opened on 1 February, and Piershill, and Broomieknowe on 1 April, but Gilmerton, Roslynlee, and Eskbridge remained closed till 2 June, and Dalkeith did not get its service back till 1 October.

There was a railway strike from 27 September till 8 October in 1919, but thereafter services returned to the normal pattern again. Road competition was however becoming keener, and the railways countered by offering reduced fares. Examples of cheap day return fares to and from Princes Street introduced at this time were: Craigleith 2d., Barnton 5d., Colinton 5d., Currie 8d.,

Balerno 9d., third class. The weekly season ticket was popularised, becoming known as a "Zone" ticket, of which the following sample third class rates may be quoted: Merchiston 1/4d., Murrayfield 1/4d., Leith 1/9d., Barnton 2/4d., Balerno 4/-, Musselburgh 3/1d.

In 1919 the North British resumed the working of the Queensferry passage, bringing in the "Dundee" which continued until Denny's took up the ferry in 1934. A halt was opened on 1 December 1919 at the east end of Queensferry on the old branch to Queensferry and Port Edgar and a service of five trains daily was provided to it. On the other hand trains ceased to call at Ravelrig after May 1920, though until the early "thirties" a Saturday afternoon train from Balerno returned to Edinburgh via the main line, reversing at Ravelrig Junction. Saughton station was closed on 28 February 1921, and later entirely demolished. It was several years before building development reached its old location. Some "pleasure" steamer sailings were restarted from Leith in 1919.

In 1921 the Caledonian built some new four-wheeled coaches specially for the Balerno branch, and built them to "main-line" standards of comfort with high curved roofs. These coaches were sometimes used for Barnton and Leith trains too, though by the middle "twenties" the six-wheeled coaches on those branches were being replaced by older main-line bogie coaches. Coaching improvement on the North British was slower, and it was not till about 1925, under L.N.E.R. auspices, that new bogie coaches, including the articulated train sets favoured by that company, appeared on some of the local services, particularly the South Side suburban, and Musselburgh. The "Caley" did much press and poster advertising in 1921.

In the early summer of 1921 the miners' strike brought about a serious coal shortage and the railway services had perforce to be much curtailed. The Granton, North Leith, and Dalkeith branches were suspended, while one of the services to be cut off and never re-opened was the Bangour branch. The so-called "Triple Alliance" of miners, railwaymen and other transport workers, threatened an extension of the strike to the railways and road services as well, but at the last minute the "Alliance" could not agree and transport continued to run. By the end of the year full services were running again. The time-tables of this early post-war period show the following services: Barnton branch 20 trains, Leith (C.R.) branch 23 trains, Balerno branch 17 trains, Corstorphine branch 17 trains, Musselburgh branch 24 trains, Granton branch 9 trains, Penicuik branch 7 trains, Polton branch 6 trains, Glencorse branch 6 trains, Gullane branch 9 trains, Haddington branch 11 trains, Gifford branch 5 trains, four with carriages for Macmerry. None of these ran on Sundays.

BALERNO   BARNTON   LEITH   DALRY RD.   EMPTY
(via Branch or   CARRIAGES
via Curriehill)

CARSTAIRS   GLASGOW   STATIONS   STIRLING
&c.   BEYOND   &c.
                                    GLASGOW

CALEDONIAN RAILWAY SEMAPHORE ROUTE INDICATORS

"MODERN" FOUR-WHEEL THIRD-CLASS-BRAKE CARRIAGE OF
THE TYPE BUILT 1921 SPECIALLY FOR THE BALERNO BRANCH
BY THE CALEDONIAN RAILWAY

Services continued more or less on this scale for the next few years, but road services were becoming steadily more competitive, and the new large L.M.S. and L.N.E. organisations, brought about by the grouping of the old companies on 1 January 1923 by the Railways Act 1921, were looking about for economies. On the old North British now L.N.E.R. system, the practice of keeping separate engines for some of the branches was replaced by a policy of using main-line engines, and later in some cases the main-line train sets too, in between their main-line duties. The practice was soon copied on the L.M.S., former Caledonian, also. Some engine power was thus saved, but it had the effect of reducing, to a certain extent, the local train services to such times as they could be fitted in with main-line requirements. The practice did of course lead to some of the local trains being hauled by a variety of locomotives of more ample power, of which there is no need to go into detail. The rolling-stock was also now appearing in the new colours. The L.N.E.R. express engines were green, the others black and coaches were varnished teak. The L.M.S. adopted crimson lake for both coaches and engines, except goods engines. Many however regretted the disappearance of the old "Caley" colours. Local trains were quite often hauled by black goods engines.

There have not been many serious railway accidents in the Edinburgh area, but on 28 July 1924 five passengers lost their lives, and fifty-four were injured when the 6.54 p.m. train from Waverley to South Queensferry ran into the back of the 6.50 p.m. Suburban train standing in Haymarket station. At that time manual signalling with a system of release treadles at the entrance to Haymarket tunnel was in use. The Ministry of Transport Inspector's report on the accident found that the driver of the Queensferry train, drawn by engine No.9338 running tender first, must have misread the north line signal at the tunnel as his. This signal was at "clear" but his signal on the south line was not. A warning bell inside the tunnel, to ring in such circumstances, was not heard. It was unfortunate that due to the holiday period the Suburban train was composed of older coaches which were not equal to the occasion though the speed of the colliding train was reckoned to be 10 m.p.h.

It was not long before there was another accident involving the loss of three lives and eight injuries, but this time the circumstances were quite different. The General Strike started on 4 May 1926. As with the road services, volunteers from various sources took over train crew and signalmen's duties as best they could, if even only to a limited extent. In these circumstances many signal-boxes were unmanned and the signals therefore could not be relied upon, so that trains had to a certain extent to be run "on sight". It happened that on 10 May the volunteer driver of the 1.6 p.m. train from Berwick to Waverley, who on the previous few days had had a clear run and a clear signal through St. Margarets locomotive depot, did not appreciate that on this afternoon the danger signal here displayed meant what it indicated. Some wagons were being shunted across the main-line, and into them the train crashed in the tunnel under London Road. The difficulties of rescue etc. were of course aggravated to some extent by trained staff and equipment not being so readily available. There were of course many other minor mishaps, such as the volunteer crew sent to pick up a train at Gorgie. Failing to locate their train they had reached Craiglockhart when they decided they had better go back and look again. This they did, down the hill, only to run their engine off the line into the side of the bank, at the catch-points. Although the General Strike was over on 12 May most of the railwaymen remained "out" for a further two days while their particular difficulties were resolved. Nevertheless a skeleton train service was maintained throughout, and one or two trains were even run on most of the branches.

Although two more L.N.E.R. branches had been closed, viz. Macmerry on 30 June 1925, *and Granton on 31 October 1925, and the service to South Queensferry reduced to one train out at 7.0 a.m. and three in during the afternoon, the L.M.S. showed some enterprise in continuing to run the Sunday service on the Balerno and Barnton branches in the summer time-tables. In fine weather large numbers of passengers were carried. A small unstaffed halt was also opened on the Balerno branch near Kingsknowe golf-course on 26 September 1927. Called Hailes platform, trains stopped only if required. The L.N.E.R. did not now run branch trains on Sundays. At the end of 1927 an interesting special train was run on Wednesday mornings from Dunbar to Gorgie Cattle Market for farmers.

In the late "twenties" the L.N.E.R. began to use "Sentinel" steam railcars for branch line work. These handy and economical light vehicles were painted green with cream upperwork and carried names. The first to appear in Edinburgh was No. 21 "Valliant" which was tried on the North Berwick service in 1927. This was a 64 seat car with chain drive and as it did not acquit itself very well, it was not retained. However in June 1928 the first of an improved type, with six-cylinder engines and 59 seats, arrived and proved popular. This was No. 35 "Nettle" which was exhibited at Waverley station on 1 July. These cars were used for many years on the North Berwick, Penicuik, and North Leith services, and those seen on these duties were: 31 "Flower of Yarrow", 32 "Fair Maid", 33 Highland Chieftain", 34 "Tweed-side", 35 "Nettle", 36 "Royal Eagle", 37 "Clydesdale", 38 "Pearl". Nos. 35, 36, and 38 survived in the district until after the war.

* Except where otherwise stated the date of closure given is the day on which the last trains ran, after which the station was locked up for the night never to reopen for passengers.

On the other hand a more powerful 2-6-2 tank engine with 5ft. 8in. diameter driving wheels and three 16in. x 26in. cylinders, the V1 class appeared in 1930 for the more important local trains, such as Musselburgh, North Berwick, and the Suburban. The tank engines of the L.M.S., and indeed all but the more important main-line passenger engines of both companies, were now appearing in black livery : railways were becoming less colourful. The vacuum brake had also become standard for passenger trains, though as this was unsuitable for the method of working at the Leith L.M.S. terminus, previously explained, "Westinghouse" air brake fitted coaches and engines had to be retained for these trains.

However, the period of retrenchment was setting in, as the following list of closure of service shows :

South Queensferry ;	11 January	1929
Gogar, Turnhouse, Kirkliston, Winchburgh, Seton Mains, Eskbridge ;	20 September	1930
Gullane branch, and Lauder branch ;	10 September	1932
Dolphinton branch ;	31 March	1933
Gifford branch ;	1 April	1933
Glencorse branch ;	29 April	1933

With the closing of the Gifford and Lauder branches the small 4-4-OT. engines finally disappeared from Edinburgh.

Nevertheless where traffic could be developed, the opportunity was taken, and the L.M.S. opened a halt at East Pilton on the Leith branch between Craigleith and Granton Road on 1 December 1934, and another, House o' Hill, on the Barnton branch between Craigleith and Davidson's Mains, on 1 February 1937. The L.N.E.R. looked out its old plans of the temporary Exhibition station of 1908 and again built a halt on the Corstorphine branch on the same site, calling it Balgreen halt and tapping a large season-ticket traffic in the now built-up district. This was opened on 29 January 1934. All these halts were of wooden construction.

The west end of Waverley station together with the tracks out as far as the Suburban line junction, - the old Haymarket Central signal-box, - were resignalled in 1937. Colour-light signals were installed, all controlled from a new box built into the wall of the gardens on the south side, east of the Mound tunnel, and brought into use in October of that year. The east end and tracks to beyond Abbeyhill were then similarly dealt with, and a new box built on the south of the tracks between the station and the Calton tunnel, this scheme being brought into use in November 1938. In the meantime the L.M.S. had renewed and simplified the signalling at Princes Street station in September 1937, but in this case the old box and semaphore type signals remained.

The train services had now dwindled in many cases, and the time-tables for the summer of 1938 show the following : Main-line stations to Dunbar at 6.53, 1.0, 3.45, 5.31, 6.23, 8.35, 9.50, 11.29. The Haddington branch carried thirteen trains most of which made connection to and from Edinburgh, and there was a through "market" train on Fridays only. The North Berwick branch had seventeen trains most of which carried through coaches to or from Edinburgh. Only four of them stopped at Dirleton. There were thirty-four trains to Musselburgh, - some non-stop. (These had been put on in 1934.) Main-line stations to Galashiels at 6.25, 8.18, 4.15, and 6.52, with others at 1.3, 2.30, 4.33 SO, 9.17 SO, 10.15 SO, and 11.20 WSO as far as Gorebridge. There were five trains to Peebles with two more on Saturdays. Penicuik also had five trains and two more on Saturdays; Polton seven, and Dalkeith four, with a fifth on Saturdays. Linlithgow and intermediate stations had trains at 6.3, 10.35, 1.26 SO, 3.23, 4.29, 5.25, and 7.55, while the Bathgate route was served at 8.3, 2.5, 2.30 SX, 4.40, 6.40 SO, 9.5 WSO, and 11.6 SO. The Dalmeny line had twenty-eight trains some of which did not run daily. There were still twenty trains to Corstorphine, but again not all daily. On the other hand North Leith had dwindled to eleven with no evening or Saturday afternoon trains. Twelve trains traversed the South Side Surburban line with another five to or from Duddingston round the west side. Waverley to Leith Central was augmented to about thirty trips.

The L.M.S. line to Midcalder showed ten stopping trains, the Balerno branch twenty-one, the last proceeding on as far as Addiewell on Wednesdays. The Leith branch carried thirty-three trains, and there were still four trips to Granton gas works. There were twenty-three trains on the Barnton branch, which also had sixteen trains on Sundays in August, one of which started at Dalry Road. There were now no other local trains on Sundays.

The special small-wheeled tank engines for the Balerno branch had now gone to the scrap heap and the similar standard machines with 5ft. 9in. dia. driving wheels were in use. It had also been found possible to use the shorter types of bogie carriage, and some of the trains were now composed of these. Flange oilers were fixed in the track at certain locations.

The war brought its problems to the railways no less than the road operators. At first coaches were fitted with dim blue lamps, though later most were fitted with the standard type of lamp shade which was devised and specified by the Ministry of Home Security. The main termini became gloomy places by night, and little better by day by reason of partial blacking-out of the roofs. The outlying stations offered little light at night and platform edges were painted white. In 1940 all name boards and other means of identification were removed, but this did not give rise to any real difficulty with the regular local travellers. The Granton-Burntisland ferry was suspended in March 1940, though another boat, "Thane of Fife", had replaced the veteran popularly known as "the Willie Muir", in 1936. The pleasure sailings of course also ceased. For many years the piers at Aberdour, North Berwick, etc. had become practically unusable, so that the sailings had become purely pleasure trips. With the development of road travel even that function was failing to attract much support.

The reduced road services gave a fillip to rail travel in several cases. The last train, at 10.40 p.m., to Barnton was later than the last bus which could not accommodate all the potential passengers anyway, so the train reaped the considerable surplus. On the other hand the train service to Granton gas works was withdrawn after 31 August 1942. As time went on some other services had to be withdrawn too. The Dalkeith branch was closed on 3 January 1942, and the last passenger train to Balerno ran on 30 October 1943. The era of public interest in "last trains" was beginning, and this train returned from Balerno at 8.19 p.m. to the accompaniment of detonator explosions etc., and carrying a dozen or two who had made the journey specially. To compensate Merchiston and Slateford stations, additional trains were then run as far as Kingsknowe on the main-line. The station at Fushiebridge was closed on 2 October 1943. The Sentinel steam railcars had gradually worn out and disappeared, being replaced by ordinary trains again. The last one in use locally was 38 "Pearl" which worked the North Leith branch until early 1947. In this case two old six-wheel coaches had to be brought up from the south to replace it as larger coaches could not be used. An engine of the J83 class as used for passenger shunting duties at Waverley took over this service. It was however short-lived for with the fuel crisis of 1947 this was one of the services suspended as from 16 June, and, as it happened, was never restored.

In many cases the post-war suburban railway service became a purely business-hours one, as the time-table for the summer of 1948 shows: Seven stopping trains to Dunbar, the last at 6.35 though the 9.5 p.m. to Dunbar stopped at Prestonpans, Longniddry, and Drem. There were fourteen trips on the North Berwick branch, one or two without main-line connection, but five had through carriages. Haddington still had eleven trains (twelve on Saturdays) most with main-line connections. The Galashiels line had four stopping trains with a further semi-fast, and two to Gorebridge only, — the last at 10.35 p.m. being Saturdays only. There were three trains on the Peebles line with another at 8.25 p.m. on Saturdays only. The Penicuik branch had four trains with another on Saturdays only. Polton had five daily, the 8.3 a.m. inwards still running direct to Leith Central. There were still twenty-one trains to Musselburgh, but Corstorphine now had only nine, there being none outwards in the morning nor inwards after 6.17 p.m. The Suburban had dwindled to six with two more round as far as Duddingston. There was no evening nor Saturday afternoon service. The same applied to Leith Central which now had only eight trips outwards, though eleven inwards to Waverley.

There were now five stopping trains to Linlithgow with a sixth on Saturdays, and only two, with a third on Saturdays, to Bathgate. Dalmeny was served by twenty-two trains with a few more on Saturdays, though some of these were long-distance express trains.

On the former L.M.S. line there were eight trains with three others to Kingsknowe only, while sixteen ran to Leith and eight to Barnton, none having an evening service. No local stations except Haymarket, Dalmeny, Portobello, and Eskbank, now had any Sunday service. The changing pattern was now very evident.

The railway company did not resume the Granton-Burntisland ferry, securing statutory power in 1947 to abandon it. Nevertheless a Mr. John Hall, of Kirkcaldy, invested in four converted tank-landing craft, and after negotiations with the railway authority and some alterations to the piers sold out to Forth Ferries Ltd. who started a Granton-Burntisland vehicular ferry service on 15 March 1951. This proved quite popular in spite of the longer crossing than at Queensferry, but the boats and their machinery were not really suitable for this job. A good deal of trouble was experienced and financial difficulties arose culminating in the final suspension of the service after 12 December 1952. The vessels were named "Bonnie Prince Charlie," "Flora Macdonald", "Eriskay", and "Glenfinnan".

In August 1948 there was severe flooding in south-east Scotland, and the East-Coast main-line was cut beyond Dunbar for several months while bridges etc. were rebuilt. The terminus at Haddington also suffered and the train service had to be withdrawn for a time. The passenger service was finally withdrawn from this branch on 3 December 1949.

On 5 May 1951 the Barnton branch was closed, and promptly lifted beyond Davidson's Mains goods yard, the bridge at Davidson's Mains station being demolished to the delight of Edinburgh Corporation who were thus enabled to run double-deck buses to Cramond and Barnton. The whole branch would have been lifted but the Davidson's Mains coal merchants succeeded in having a single-line left as a siding up to their yard.

Further stations were closed as follows :— Livingstone 30 October 1948; New Hailes 4 February 1950; Curriehill 31 March 1951; Ratho, Drumshoreland, and Philpstoun 16 June 1951; the Penicuik and Polton branches 8 September 1951; Leith Central 5 April 1952; Bowland (between Stow and Galashiels) 5 December 1953; Dirleton 30 January 1954; Leadburn 5 March 1955; Millerhill 5 November 1955; Uphall, and Bathgate 7 January 1956. It may be noted that the first station west of Haymarket was now Linlithgow, 16¼ miles away. On the other hand a platform for detraining football specials at Easter Road Park was opened on the Leith Central branch on 8 April 1950. No return services were given.

In the summer of 1956 a new diesel railcar set was tried for a few weeks on the service to Galashiels via Peebles, and then on a through service between Corstorphine and North Berwick. On both it attracted much extra traffic : No doubt the novelty of sitting behind the driver with a clear view ahead helped. This trial was followed by the regular use of these two-or three-car sets on nearly all the local services, which were later augmented. Their use has set a new standard for comfortable suburban and local travel in the district and with attractive cheap fare facilities should continue to draw an increasing proportion of the traffic to the railways which remain open.

In conclusion two recent local railway developments ought to be mentioned. The new connecting line between Craiglockhart and Slateford to provide a convenient means of transferring goods and mineral traffic between the two former companies' routes; and the large new marshalling-yard which is changing the face of the countryside at Millerhill, together with its new link to the East-Coast main-line near Monktonhall. *

* Craiglockhart-Slateford brought into use 18 December 1960. Millerhill yard brought into use 18 June 1962. Passenger services have since been withdrawn from the South Side suburban route, from the former L.M.S. line to Leith and from the Peebles line.

VII

THE CORPORATION TRANSPORT DEPARTMENT

1 July 1919 may be regarded as the real start of the Corporation's direct operations, as on that day the Tramways Department of the City, as it was then called, commenced to function under the managership of Mr. R. Stuart Pilcher. The occasion was marked by a civic luncheon in the City Chambers. The council had already decided on conversion to electric traction, and the Edinburgh Corporation Order Confirmation Act 1919 (passed 20 November 1919) provided for this being carried out from time to time in sections. Borrowing powers and the purchase agreements were also dealt with. All the existing staff were transferred to the City's employment except for the old Company's manager Mr. Cox. Arrangements were however made to dispense with the women conductresses who had served during the war, while the male staff were fitted out with new uniforms and caps of "cheese-cutter" style.

The council were now giving much thought to the methods to be adopted for the electrification, particularly in respect of Princes Street, and also a programme of conversion. It had been suggested that the Northern routes should be electrified first, but these tracks required reconstruction, so it was proposed that motor buses should be run until this could be accomplished. Meanwhile the Pilrig to Nether Liberton route could conveniently be dealt with. An important aspect of the electrification programme was the availability of power.

At that time there were two electricity generating stations in the city, namely at Dewar Place and at McDonald Road. Leith had their own station but were also taking power from Edinburgh. The output of these stations and the distribution network was fully loaded and a scheme for a high tension generating station and distribution network had been started just before the war. Suspended in 1916, it was now agreed that this new generating station at Portobello should be pressed forward and also enlarged. It was also designated the generating station for the Lothians district under the Electricity (Supply) Act of 1919. High tension cables were to be laid to converting stations located at Cowgate, Causewayside, Morningside, Robertson Avenue, and Granton, in addition to the two existing generating stations which would cease to function as such. The Leith station was similarly dealt with. Power for the electric tramways in Edinburgh was thus dependent on the progress of the Corporation's electricity undertaking.

Mr. Pilcher planned to use as much as possible of the existing tramway equipment, by converting the depots and rebuilding the rolling-stock. Clearly it would be some years before the conversion could be completed, and so steps were taken to improve the cable system meantime. Even before the Company's lease expired the Corporation accepted tenders for forty new top covers for open-top cable cars, and also ordered three motor charabancs and twelve buses. Of course the Company's crest disappeared from the cars to be replaced by the City's coat of arms, and there was much repainting of rolling-stock. Some of the oldest Northern cars had already been withdrawn. Enamelled plates of the same colour as the service number boards, and showing only the terminus, were screwed on to the destination boards used on the numbered services. In the aftermath of the war the financial position was difficult but penny fares were introduced immediately as had been promised.

The charabancs arrived in the late summer of 1919 and were put on to run three circular tours covering respectively the north, and south sides of the city, and round Arthur's Seat. These started from the Mound. The buses which followed inaugurated a route from Ardmillan Terrace to Abbeyhill on 29 December 1919 running by way of Fountainbridge, Bread Street, Johnston Terrace, High Street, and Canongate. While fuller details of the tram and bus rolling-stock will be given later, it may be mentioned here that both the charabancs and buses were Leylands with, of course, solid tyres, and were powered with engines rated at 35-40 h.p. The services filled a need and the Corporation were soon ordering more vehicles. Even the charabancs were pressed into traffic on winter Saturdays for football crowds. One difficult problem with these vehicles was the splashing set up by the solid tyres as they trundled over the setts on a wet day. Several types of brush hanging outside the wheels were tried in an effort to combat complaints but none proved really effective.

The Edinburgh Boundaries Extension and Tramways Act, 1920 (passed 4 August 1920) provided for extensions to the city boundaries, and at last accomplished the amalgamation of the Burgh of Leith with the City. This took effect on 2 November 1920, and so the Leith electric system thus passed into the control of the Tramways Department, the Leith manager, Mr. F. A. Fitzpayne becoming deputy manager in the combined undertaking. Until through services were accomplished the Leith system's accounts were to be kept separate. The lettering on the Leith cars was nevertheless changed from Leith Corporation to Corporation Tramways, and their fleet numbers increased by 230. The cable cars did not carry any such lettering, while the buses and charabancs, the earliest of which were lettered variously Corporation Tramways or Edinburgh Corporation Tramways, were altered to Corporation Motors. Buses were lettered on sides and back, charabancs on the back only.

The Corporation's Act of 1920 also included powers to construct further tramways, viz. — From the Nether Liberton terminus to Liberton crossroads; from Seafield Place to Kings Road; from Pilrig Street up Dryden Street to the back of Shrubhill depot; and connections between the Edinburgh and Leith systems at Pilrig. It will be remembered also, that powers already existed under the 1916 Act to construct tramways to Corstorphine, with a siding into ground on the south side of the road near the terminus; a terminal spur into Hope Street at the West End; and the Braids to Firhill tramroad. In the 1920 Bill the Corporation had further sought powers to run buses outside the city boundary. The S.M.T.Co., not un-naturally, objected to this and an agreement was come to, dated 12 May 1920, whereby the City dropped these clauses and the S.M.T.Co. agreed to provide efficient services on specified routes, including Gilmerton as a monopoly, and to charge a protective fare on tramway routes in the city. The agreement was initially for seven years, but continued in operation until 1954. They also agreed to pay the Corporation one halfpenny per bus mile run within the city unless future legislation required the Company to otherwise contribute towards road costs, which of course very soon came about. The necessity of securing Board of Trade approval for bus fares as required by the 1913 Act was eliminated in the 1920 Act.

With post-war costs rising it was soon found that the penny stages could not be maintained, and they lasted only till 31 December 1919 when the 1½d. minimum was reintroduced. Several fluctuations in fares followed in the next year or two. On 1 June 1920 the 2d. and 3d. fares were increased by a half-penny, and then on 7 September 1920 there was a further upward revision, but a short penny stage was included, and a 4d. maximum applied on the cable system. Workmen's return fares at one penny more than the single fare were available for the 2d., 3d., and 4d. stages on the tramways, the return journey being allowed on the top deck of the car only. There was a further revision of stages on 27 October 1921, by which a longer average journey was given. It should however be mentioned that the Leith system had continued on its old fares basis. The maximum bus fare was 5d. Tickets in the same format as those of the old Company and as of Leith Corporation continued to be used on the two parts of the system. Bus tickets were at first overprinted with a large B.

Early in 1920 it was decided that the Northern section of the cable system being worn out and uneconomic, it should be closed down and replaced by buses meantime. In view of the long gradients more powerful vehicles were ordered. These were A.E.C.s with 40-45 h.p. engines and improved brakes. The first tram route to be temporarily withdrawn however was the little electric service from Ardmillan Terrace to Slateford which suffered from its isolated location. The Ardmillan Terrace to Abbeyhill buses had been extended down Easter Road to Easter Road Station in March 1920, and on 18 October 1920 a proportion of them were extended from Ardmillan Terrace to Slateford and the electric trams withdrawn. On 31 October the Mound-Tollcross cars were replaced by a bus service, and on 2 December the Comely Bank route followed. About a fortnight afterwards the Comely Bank buses were extended from Frederick Street to St. David Street proceeding inwards via George Street and outwards via Princes Street. At the Comely Bank end the buses continued on to Fettes Avenue to turn, but in April 1921 the bus terminus was brought back to the old tram terminus. On 29 December 1920 the Mound and Tollcross buses were extended across Princes Street down Hanover Street to Goldenacre replacing the Hanover Street trams, leaving only the Broughton Street cable in operation from Henderson Row power station.

Some entirely new bus services were also started in 1920. The outlying districts now within the city's extended boundaries had to be catered for, and so the first was a morning "rush hour" and afternoon service between Craiglockhart car terminus and Colinton on 4 September, and soon afterwards extended to Juniper Green. At that time this was quite a country route. The next was on 27 September, from West End to Bonnington Toll via Dean Bridge, Henderson Row, and Broughton Road, and it was extended to Henderson Street, Leith about the end of November. The Easter Road Station terminus of the first bus route was at this time extended to the foot of Easter Road at Leith Links. A morning "rush" and afternoon bus service was also run between Murrayfield car terminus and Corstorphine (Victor Park), but on 17 January 1921 it was replaced by a service, approximately hourly, between Waverley Bridge and Corstorphine.

Some staff trouble was brewing in November 1920. Arising, apparently from grievances about shifts, cable car crews threatened to strike, and showed their displeasure by refusing to take standing passengers. On 12 November the Corporation cleared the deck so to speak, by announcing the revocation of the Byelaws covering this and other matters, and also the licences of drivers and conductors, which dispensation they had provided for by their 1916 Act. The following weekend there was much delay as drivers refused to start until standing passengers got off. The climax came on Monday evening 15 November when a man was "sacked" on the spot, and the rest of the crews then ran their cars into the depots at 9 o'clock. For the next two days only a skeleton service was possible, though the Portobello route, the Leith system, and the buses continued to run normally. Private buses were hired to help out mainly in the western suburbs. On 17 November agreement was reached and services were back to normal the next day.

On 24 January 1921 Henderson Row power station was finally closed down and the number 9 cars diverted from Broughton Street to Pilrig. To replace them a bus service was run from St. Andrew Street via Leith Street and Broughton Street to Goldenacre, proceeding to St. Andrew Street via York Place on the inward journey. At the same time the Henderson Street-Bonnington-West End route was extended along George Street, York Place, and Broughton Street to Goldenacre and on via Trinity Road to a terminus at Stanley Road. On 17 March the route was extended at the other end, from Henderson Street to the Shore at Leith, and about this time also the Goldenacre-Tollcross route was extended to Bruntsfield Place. Henderson Row depot having closed down it was converted into a bus garage, relieving pressure on the overcrowded yard at Shrubhill which had hitherto been their home.

On 28 February 1921 a new "country" service was started between Surgeon's Hall and Newcraighall serving the then villages of Craigmillar and Niddrie. At first this was also a morning "rush" and afternoon service only. It was now felt necessary to number the bus services, and so in addition to the roller-blind destination screens with which the vehicles were provided back and front, and the board carried on the middle side window, a kind of "ear" was fixed to the near side front edge of the roof of the buses and a stencil number displayed. The routes were numbered as follows, the various colours of the side window boards also being given :—

1	Easter Road and Ardmillan Terrace	Brown
2	Easter Road and Slateford	Brown
3	Goldenacre and Bruntsfield	White
4	St. David Street and Comely Bank	Green
5	Leith — Bonnington — West End — Broughton —	
	Goldenacre — Stanley Road	Yellow
6	St. Andrew Street and Goldenacre	?
7	Surgeon's Hall and Newcraighall	Blue
8	Craiglockhart and Juniper Green	Red
9	Waverley and Corstorphine	Brown

In the early part of 1921 there was a prolonged strike in the mining industry and to save coal at the power stations Tollcross power station was adapted to burn oil fuel, while some early morning cars were replaced temporarily by buses. Some of the charabancs were temporarily converted to lorries to assist in moving coal stocks. Nevertheless further expansion of bus services continued with a Wednesday, Saturday and Sunday afternoon service from the Mound to Cramond via Barnton as from 18 April 1921. The fare was 8d. and the buses, if full, often returned direct via Davidson's Mains, Quality Street. In those days a good deal of liberty was sometimes taken en route. When tarring and grouting was in progress on Queensferry Road it was usual for the buses to divert by way of Orchard Brae and Craigleith Road, or occasionally the shorter diversion by Ravelston Terrace and Queensferry Terrace. In the spring of 1922, during repairs at the Dean Bridge, Belford Road was followed. The S.M.T.Co's. drivers generally followed these diversions too. It was not long before the Cramond route became a daily morning "rush-hour" and afternoon service proceeding via Corbiehill Road, Davidson's Mains in both directions. It then became number 11 with a red side window board, and the fare was reduced to 5d. Another afternoon route from Seafield to Portobello started on 18 June, becoming daily on 29 June as number 10 which was displayed as X. Later this was extended to Bernard Street and on 19 February 1923 to Niddrie crossroads. As traffic was normally light a few buses were altered so that the entrance was at the front beside the driver, who thus collected fares from passengers as they entered and enabled a conductor to be dispensed with. A longer circular suburban route was added to the choice of tours for the 1921 summer season.

While all this was going on the cable car services were being improved by the rebuilding of many open-top cars with the new top covers. Other changes were made in an endeavour to simplify the system and reduce costs. The auxiliary cables had always been a major source of trouble as they were relatively easily dislodged from their pulleys. Some experiments were therefore made and it was found that satisfactory operation could be obtained by leading the main cables round the curves, the cars proceeding with the gripper slightly open and thus reducing speed. Accordingly the auxiliary cables from Leith Street to Princes Street and to North Bridge were removed and the main cable taken from its separate tunnel and put in place under the slot from Leith Street to North Bridge. The third auxiliary cable from Princes Street to North Bridge had to remain in use, and it is not clear what provision was made for cars proceeding between Princes Street and Leith Street, i.e. the number 9 service. It would seem that a long fly-shunt had to be made. This new arrangement left the trailing crossover at the foot of North Bridge without cable power, and in order to maintain facilities for turning cars back towards Nether Liberton a facing crossover was put in as well, making a scissors crossing worked by gravity. The main cable slipping through the partly open grippers in these new arrangements did not give rise to undue wear, and the practice was extended where possible. It seems probable that the auxiliary cable was removed and the main cable correspondingly extended round the curve at Salisbury Place junction. Also perhaps at London Road junction and Haymarket, but not, apparently, at Kings Theatre junction. The Craiglockhart, Grange, and Murrayfield cables were speeded up to $10\frac{1}{2}$ m.p.h. The crossover at the east end of Morrison Street was removed and the practice of running the Gorgie cars to that point when there was a stoppage of the Princes Street cable ceased.

Much welding of track joints was undertaken by the "Thermit" process in 1920 and 1921, and the "Sandberg" process of hardening the surface of the rails was also tried. Some rails in Morrison Street were lifted at this time and used for repairs elsewhere. On the Leith part of the system a considerable enlargement of the depot was being undertaken. The electric and cable tracks were connected up at Pilrig, a triangular double junction being formed, and a single line laid up Dryden Street from two trailing junctions in Pilrig Street. This gave access to the back of Shrubhill depot and was provided with a passing loop near the Shrubhill end.

An innovation was the appearance early in 1922 of two A.E.C. open-top double-deck buses of the latest London "S" type. The licences issued for them precluded their use on the Mound, Hanover Street, Frederick Street, east of the Tron Church, and also the Cramond route, because of the steep hills or low bridges, and they were put on the Waverley and Corstorphine service. The starting point for the tours was transferred from the Mound to the south side of St. Andrew Square in 1922.

In the early part of 1922 activity was concentrated on the erection of poles and overhead equipment between Pilrig and Nether Liberton, and along Grange Road to Churchhill. Picardy Place to St. Andrew Street, and London Road to Abbeyhill were also equipped. The old cast-iron centre poles for lighting in Leith Walk were replaced by tramway centre poles taken from Junction Street and Commercial Street in Leith, complete with their tall bases bearing the Leith coat-of-arms, span wires being then used for Junction Street and Commercial Street. The Electricity Department now had 550 volts D.C. power available at McDonald Road, Cowgate, and Causewayside substations, and feeder cables were laid and the rails bonded for the return current. A diagram of the ultimate feed arrangements is given at the back. New crossovers for the electric cars were laid at Surgeons Hall and Newington Station.

The inauguration of the new electric cars in Edinburgh from and to the Leith system and thus ending the Pilrig "muddle" of the previous twenty-two years, was arranged for 20 June 1922. That day at noon, the official first electric car, number 123, with Lord Provost Hutchinson and a select party aboard, came up from Leith, and amidst a large crowd of spectators, broke a blue ribbon at Pilrig to proceed on to the cable system. All went decorously until the car reached the University where it became surrounded by students determined to get aboard. In the general melee which developed bags of flour were flung around and some of the councillors and their friends suffered in consequence. Police appeals were in vain and the car proceeded to Nether Liberton with difficulty, carrying a much augmented and unauthorised load including a large number on the roof! One or two injuries were suffered before the car reached the University on its return journey, and there was a Court sequel at which it appeared the students had felt aggrieved at their exclusion from the original select party.

The public service cars followed up from Leith and as each one went into service to operate between Nether Liberton and Stanley Road via Pilrig, — No. 7, and between Churchhill and Stanley Road via Junction Street, — No. 11, a cable car was correspondingly run into Shrubhill depot. The Murrayfield, Craiglockhart, and Marchmont cars were turned at Waverley Steps or St. Andrew Street, but the Braids and Gorgie ones continued via York Place to Pilrig. The service on London Road to Abbeyhill was replaced by electric cars, No. 15 running to Salisbury Place, and No. 16 to St. Andrew Street. The Granton Circle cars were extended up to St. Andrew Street and numbered 13 and 14 on the outer and inner rail respectively. The Seafield to Stanley Road service was altered to run from Seafield to Nether Liberton, and numbered 12, and "part-day" cars run between Newington Station and Bernard Street or Newhaven, numbered 17. To compensate for the withdrawn Seafield-Stanley Road facilities a penny transfer ticket was made available between Bonnington Toll and foot of Leith Walk. This continued to be available until February 1951, many years after transfers generally were withdrawn. Other fares on the Leith part of the system were now revised in line with the Edinburgh section, the stages being extended and the $1\frac{1}{2}$d., $2\frac{1}{2}$d., $3\frac{1}{2}$d., and $4\frac{1}{2}$d. values discarded. Further transfer tickets of all values were issued to cover old cable through services temporarily withdrawn, and these were available where necessary until the conversion scheme was complete.

Apart from one or two minor mishaps the electric cars replaced the cables smoothly during the early afternoon, and the Liberton cable was finally stopped at 3.55 p.m.

FIRST ELECTRIC CAR CROSSING ON TO THE EDINBURGH SYSTEM
AT PILRIG 20 JUNE 1922

MIXED TRACTION ON LEITH WALK 1922

Cable car on service 4 followed by electric car on original service 12 to Liberton. The electric car is a converted cable car of the same build as the cable car, — Brown-Marshall. Note the cable car type of service-number board on the electric car.

The event was celebrated by a banquet in the City Chambers, at which Councillor Goalen was able to remark that he "was proud the first up-to-date tramcar in Edinburgh started from Leith!" The old rivalry was far from dead yet.

During the next few nights some interesting alterations were made to the cables. The Princes Street cable had been altered to run direct between Tollcross and Waverley without going to Haymarket, and also eliminating the auxiliary cable at the West End, while the Murrayfield cable was extended from Haymarket to the West End. The Princes Street cable was now extended down Leith Street to Pilrig in place of the now discarded Liberton route cable. The No. 2 Gorgie to Pilrig cable cars were then transferred from York Place to Leith Street, and the Braids cars terminated at Waverley Steps along with the Nos. 1, 6, and 9 services. This enabled the York Place cable to be taken out too and the Shrubhill power station to close down entirely, while still providing means of getting cable cars to Shrubhill depot each night, and also continuing a through service between Leith Walk and the West End. An unusual arrangement had to be adopted at

Waverley where most of the cable cars had of course to be reversed back over the crossover. A facing crossover was put in between the junctions opposite the North Bridge and cable cars coming up from Pilrig to Princes Street crossed with the cable to the "wrong" line here and regained the normal line with the cable at the Waverley Steps crossover in common with the other cars turning back there. The Grange cable may have been shortened at the top of Marchmont Road also.

Residents on the former Northern routes had long been vociferous with complaints about the noise and vibration caused by the buses; and with some justification. One claimed damages for ornaments in his house being broken by the shaking. Mr. Pilcher had however successfully fitted pneumatic tyres to one Leyland bus running on the Comely Bank route, and arrangements were made to effect this decided improvement on further buses. Meanwhile an 8 m.p.h. speed limit was applied in Inverleith Row where, due to the nature of the ground, the effects seem to have been particularly marked. But more satisfaction was found in the pressing on of the electrification of the Broughton Street—Goldenacre route. This was completed and connected to the former Leith tracks westward in Ferry Road, opening on 28 August 1922 with an electric service from Salisbury Place to Granton, — No. 8. Four days earlier the Nether Liberton route had been extended the short distance to Liberton Dams. With the introduction of the Broughton Street electric service, the No. 3 bus was curtailed at Canonmills, the portion of No. 5 between West End and Stanley Road abandoned, and No. 6 withdrawn. About this time the No. 7 tram service was altered to run to Stanley Road via Junction Street, the No. 11 taking the Pilrig Street route.

The scheme of conversion was now proceeding rapidly. Part of the Shrubhill depot was converted to an orthodox set of tracks though the old traverser was fitted with an electric motor and retained to give access to the body-building and paint shops on the one side. The redundant cable cars were being quickly rebuilt and turned out on electric trucks. Some did not get top covers but nearly all were provided with vestibuled platforms and balconies enclosing the stairs. Work also proceeded on poles and overhead equipment from Shandwick Place to Murrayfield and Gorgie. Princes Street was the great problem. Since the beginning of the year a terrific controversy had raged. Mr. Pilcher was disposed to recommend new tracks on the gardens side of the street as the clearance between the cable tracks was insufficient to allow of centre poles. This did not find favour however and after several meetings the town council decided that centre poles would be the best solution. To many citizens this was sacrilege, and the Cockburn Association and other bodies opposed the application to the Ministry of Transport, whose sanction had to be obtained for the use of centre poles anywhere. The "Citizens Protection Committee" showed films of the conduit system in operation in London and urged its adoption in Princes Street. Basset-Lowke's model shop in Frederick Street displayed a model tramcar running round their window with an overhead wire on centre poles to show what it would look like. A "question" was asked in Parliament. The Ministry of Transport held a public enquiry in the city on 29, 30, and 31 March 1922, at which many well-known personages gave evidence, those representing motoring interests or amenity being against centre poles, the others in favour. On 10 April the Government announced in the House of Commons their acceptance of the enquiry Commission's recommendation, viz. that centre poles be sanctioned. A special slender one-piece tapered pole with short bracket arms and scroll-work was designed and arranged also to carry new street-lighting lanterns parallel with the tracks. In the event few would doubt that this was indeed the right solution. To effect the conversion was, however, no simple matter and Mr. Pilcher prepared a well thought out scheme. The adjacent overhead equipment was ready and temporarily anchored at Shandwick Place and at Waverley and on Saturday night-Sunday morning 21-22 October 1922 the great change-over was made.

As much preparatory work as possible was done beforehand. The track on the south side was bonded. The holes for the centre poles were excavated and the poles themselves, painted complete with bracket arms and fittings, except the street-lighting gear, were laid out at the side of the street. Quantities of light contractor's type track consisting of low grooved rails resting on flat steel tie plates were also assembled. Then on the chosen night, which fortunately proved dry, some 300 men, watched by a large crowd of interested spectators, set to work even before the last cable car passed for Tollcross at midnight. The task was indeed formidable and Pilcher supervised personally. The cable had to be shortened at the foot of Lothian Road and the machinery cleared out of the pits. The temporary rails were laid on the surface of the street clear of the old cable track on the north side, but these temporary rails had to lead back on to and off the old track past the islands. This was arranged by short ramp rails leading into the grooves of the ordinary rails. Meanwhile the thirty centre poles were planted into their holes and concreted at twenty minute intervals. The first two at the Mound and West End, shortly after midnight, were cheered by the crowd. Then the trolley wires had to be run out, connected at each end and tensioned. Also on the same night the roadway and tracks under the Dalry Road railway bridge were lowered slightly to give increased clearance. It need hardly be added that food and refreshment were of course laid on for the well organised gangs. About 9.30 a.m. on the Sunday morning the first electric cars were able to run out over the old cable track and on to

Robertson Avenue on the Gorgie route. Returning they had to negotiate the temporary surface track in Princes Street, the object of which was of course to provide a path clear of the new centre poles which were foul of the old track on the north side; and there were some hitches with this during the day until it settled down. The achievement received widespread and well-deserved comment throughout the country and indeed abroad, vieing with a contemporary political crisis.

The Tramways Department were now a little ahead of the Electricity Department. The Murrayfield feeder cable from Dewar Place sub-station and also those from the new Robertson Avenue substation were uncompleted, so that the services initially provided along Princes Street were :—

1 Liberton Dams and Haymarket
2 North Junction Street and Robertson Avenue
3 Waverley and Robertson Avenue
5 Abbeyhill and Shandwick Place
6 Churchhill via Grange Road and Haymarket
9 Goldenacre via Broughton Street and Shandwick Place
16 Stanley Road via Junction Street and Shandwick Place

The 13 and 14 Granton Circles were also extended to Shandwick Place, and service 12 Seafield and Liberton Dams was altered to run between Seafield and Haymarket. A part-day service. No. 19, was run from Newington Station to Shandwick Place. Bus services were put on between Robertson Avenue and Gorgie, and between Haymarket and Murrayfield. When "juice" became available these were replaced and the cars extended, Nos. 1 and 12 running to Murrayfield and No. 2 to Gorgie, the former on 3 December and the latter on 21 December. The Braids, Craiglockhart, and Marchmont Road cable cars turned at the foot of Lothian Road.

Meantime the old north side track in Princes Street was torn up as quickly as possible and a new permanent track constructed at the requisite distance from the centre poles, the islands being also narrowed to accommodate it. As this was completed the temporary track was removed, the job being accomplished within a fortnight. The width between the tracks was increased by two feet. These pieces of temporary track were much used to provide temporary crossovers for single-line working during relaying work elsewhere on the system in the succeeding few years.

Before we leave 1922 it has to be mentioned that on 9 November the No. 5 bus service was extended by King's Stables Road and Grassmarket to Surgeon's Hall, but results were disappointing on this seemingly useful "short-cut" and it lasted only one month.

FIRST ELECTRIC CARS ON PRINCES ST. SUNDAY MORNING
22 OCTOBER 1922

Open top converted cable car No. 106 entering the temporary track on the
north side at the West End watched by interested spectators.
Note the driver looking out to see all's well and the conductor hanging
on to his trolley rope. Also buses on stand by service.

Then on 15 December 1922 the Edinburgh Corporation Order
Confirmation Act 1922 was passed. This provided for the construction of a tramway down Easter Road with triangular junctions at both the London Road and Duke Street, Leith ends. Also
for a long siding in Wheatfield Road which would be used for
football match cars to lift the crowds from Tynecastle. Neither of
these tramways was constructed, though the latter scheme
materialised in a different form in 1924. A proposal for a line
along George Street did not find favour at this time.

The next section of the conversion to be dealt with was from
West End to Marchmont Road and on 21 January 1923 the No.
6 service was extended there thus completing its old cable route.
A new service No. 18 from Bernard Street to Marchmont Road via
West End was also instituted. At the same time the other services
temporarily turning at Shandwick Place, Nos. 5, 9, 13, 14, 16, and
19, were extended to Tollcross. This left only the Braids and
Craiglockhart cables working from Tollcross.

INTERIOR OF LOWER SALOON OF CONVERTED
CABLE CAR OF 'BROWN--MARSHALL' BUILD. CAR No. 9

It will be recalled that the last half-mile of the Craiglockhart route was mostly interlaced track, and it was decided to get rid of this concurrently with the electrification. Accordingly the cable cars were withdrawn from this route and replaced by a temporary bus service on 18 March 1923, on which date the Nos. 13 and 14 electric cars were extended to the Braids and Nos. 15, 16, and 19 as far as Morningside Station, replacing the cable cars from Tollcross. At this time the Nos. 5 and 15 services exchanged numbers. Tollcross power station of course closed down and the redundant cable cars, minus grippers, towed to Shrubhill for rebuilding. Tollcross depot was also drastically altered. The old entrance opposite Thornybauk was abandoned and the floor lowered to street level. The single track round Thornybauk was continued round West Tollcross to form a trailing junction with the outgoing Braids line, and the facing connection at the Thornybauk end removed, — also the loop. A new oblique entrance to the depot was made nearer Tollcross and facing from there, and two fans of tracks provided inside, one lot at right angles to the street, the other parallel to it to the left.

The electric service No. 9 from Goldenacre, and also a new service from Waverley only, No. 10, were run to Craiglockhart Station on 15 April 1923 and extended to the old Craiglockhart

EDINBURGH AND MUSSELBURGH TRACKS AND OVERHEAD IN
COURSE OF BEING CONNECTED UP AT JOPPA 1923.
Edinburgh closed top cable car (Dick Kerr build) with
Musselburgh single-decker No. 17 (ex-Sheffield) behind.

FIRST THROUGH CARS EDINBURGH TO PORT SETON
24 JUNE 1923
M. & D. E. L. & T. Co. No. 15 for Port Seton. Edinburgh car on
service 20 behind.

187

terminus at "Happy Valley" soon afterwards. Work had also been proceeding on the Slateford route track, and providing a facing junction at Ardmillan Terrace, so electric cars were reintroduced on 29 April 1923 as service 4 from Waverley to Slateford. The No. 2 bus service was then withdrawn but it was to be revived again later as No. 4. A new direct bus service was also provided between Waverley Bridge and Juniper Green via Slateford at irregular intervals and numbered 8, the old No. 8 from Craiglockhart being renumbered 6 and terminated at Colinton. The fare from Waverley Bridge to Juniper Green was 6d.

The worst effects of post-war prices were now passed. Costs were being reduced, and a revision of fares giving longer stages was introduced on 21 January 1923. By now new tickets, longer and in a new clearer format, were in use.

Widening of Corstorphine Road was also in hand, and the tramway extension authorised in 1916 put down concurrently. For some distance west of Pinkhill the widening, on the north side, was considerable, and included a new entrance to the Zoo. A loop siding was laid on the incoming line here, with a crossover beyond. The next crossover was just east of Station Road, and the terminus was at the present shelter, east of Templeland Road. This extension was inspected by Col. Pringle for the Ministry of Transport on 20 June 1923. The No. 1 service was extended as far as Station Road the same day, and to the new terminus shortly afterwards. The No. 9 bus service was then withdrawn, the two doubledeckers transferring to the No. 5 route.

Electrification of the Portobello route was also under way and on 20 May 1923 the Nos. 5 and 15 services were extended from Abbeyhill to Piershill. An agreement was made with the Musselburgh and District Electric Light and Traction Co. Ltd. for the through running of both Corporation and Company cars between Waterloo Place and Port Seton and the tracks and overhead were accordingly connected up at Joppa.

Finally on Saturday night 23 June 1923 the last cable car trundled into Portobello depot — the engines were stopped and cable traction in the city was no more. Strangely there were no crowds — the occasion was almost un-noticed. The next day electric cars ran from Waterloo Place to Joppa, to Musselburgh Town Hall, or right through to Port Seton, numbered 20, 21, and 22 respectively. The Company cars shared in the latter service but did not display a service number. During the last two or three days of cable operation, a few No. 20 electric cars had been run amongst them. The Musselburgh Company's old open-top and single-deck cars were not allowed on the Edinburgh system and continued to provide additional local service on their own tracks. Conductors of through cars carried both Corporation and Company tickets for use on the respective lines, and also a special set of tickets covering through journeys. These were generally similar to the Musselburgh ones. The through fares were : Musselburgh 5d., Levenhall 6d., Prestonpans 8d., Port Seton 9d. The Corporation's fare to Joppa was 4d. but on 1 August 1923 this was reduced to 3d.

An Edinburgh electric car had been towed to Joppa for a trial over the line to Port Seton on 26 February, as a result of which some additional span wires had to be erected on the Musselburgh system. Even so, the layout of the Musselburgh overhead precluded the use of trolley ropes, so Edinburgh cars running beyond Joppa had their ropes removed and were provided with a hooked bamboo pole carried in clips above the truck. A hook was provided at each end of the roof under which the trolley-boom could be pulled down and held if necessary. All the cars allocated to Portobello depot were so fitted, and when extra cars were put on to the route on summer weekends, the trolley-ropes were wound and tied round the boom and the crew "hoped for the best." There would always be another car whose bamboo pole could be borrowed if it should be required. After a short time only the ex-cable cars were used over the Musselburgh line, but a few years later a number of the ex-Leith cars were drafted to Portobello depot for the Port Seton service, as the lack of headlights on the former was a difficulty on the sparsely lit route. It may be mentioned that the Post Office mail bags between Portobello and Edinburgh were carried by tram until after the war.

One of the old horse-bus routes was revived by a new half-hourly bus service started on 18 January 1923, namely Mound to Blackford Hill proceeding via George IV Bridge, Causewayside, Argyle Place, Marchmont Crescent, and Kilgraston Road. This was numbered 12, with a white window board. On 4 June 1923 the route was extended to Morningside Station. After the Corstorphine service No. 9 ceased, the No. 12 service took this number, and on 4 February 1924 the route was further extended to the west end of Morningside Drive. Another old horse-bus route was revived by a bus service started on 1 November 1923 between Cameron Toll and Haymarket, proceeding via Preston Street, Clerk Street, Lauriston Place, Bread Street, and Morrison Street. It was numbered 2 and the window board was white.

A further reduction of fares was effected on 28 October 1923 when the length of the stages was considerably increased.

The Northern and Mound tramway routes were the last to be electrified, much to the disgust of the residents. The Comely Bank line was finished and connected from Frederick Street eastwards into Princes Street. Being duly passed by the Ministry of Transport, service 24 from St. Andrew Street to Comely Bank commenced on 18 November 1923, replacing bus service No. 4. The Hanover Street and Mound routes were both connected to the Princes Street tracks adjacent and facing one another, the latter having to make a bulge westwards in doing so. At Tollcross the Mound tracks were extended across the Marchmont route tracks instead of joining them as before, and they were then connected to the Braids tracks in Home Street. Service No. 23 from Goldenacre to Tollcross via Hanover Street and the Mound commenced on 8 June 1924 replacing the No. 3 bus. The service was extended to Bruntsfield Place shortly after. For operating this and the Comely Bank route the Ministry of Transport stipulated that the cars be fitted with track brakes operated mechanically. The first few cars so fitted were tried on the No. 9 service before the Comely Bank route was opened. The drivers on these two old Northern routes were considered to have a greater degree of responsibility and for many years were paid a halfpenny per hour extra in wages. Eventually this differential was abandoned. A number of specially strong cast steel bollards were placed on the pavement at the sharp curve on the Mound, designed to stop a car going over the embankment in the event of derailment. Fortunately they were never called upon to perform this function for a tram, but skidding buses and other vehicles have been saved by them.

Meanwhile the extension up Liberton Brae to Liberton crossroads, authorised in the 1920 Order had been laid, and the No. 1 service extended to the new terminus on 28 April 1924. Some other small changes took place about this time as follows: Service 4 extended via Leith Street and London Road to Piershill; Service 5 extended from Salisbury Place to Churchhill; Service 12 extended to Corstorphine. Part day cars without a service number were introduced between Liberton and Stanley Road via Pilrig Street, and also between Restalrig Road and Salisbury Place.

A piece of ground was bought east of Westfield Road and the siding for the football match cars laid there instead of in Wheatfield Street. This would eventually become a depot for the west side of the City. In order to keep cars clear of the "main-line" at other termini, terminal sidings were constructed in Belhaven Place at Morningside, and in Northfield Broadway at Piershill. These seem to have been constructed with Ministry of Transport approval under the general authority to provide passing places, sidings, etc. in the original Acts, as was the Hanover Street-Mound connection. Several additional passenger islands were constructed in Princes Street and elsewhere on the system, while a very neat small cast-iron pole had been adopted to carry stopping-place "flags" where these were sited away from overhead or lighting standards.

R. STUART PILCHER, F.R.S.E., M.Inst.T.

General Manager, Edinburgh Corporation Tramways

1918 — 1928

These first five years of Corporation operation had been a period of great expansion. All the cable service routes had been electrified and some extensions added. Practically all the cable cars had been converted. Shrubhill being fully occupied on this work, new cars had so far been supplied by outside builders, but a start was being made on new construction now at Shrubhill. The bus services were firmly established too, covering 35 miles of route, while the tramways extended to 36 miles of route. Post-war housing schemes were well under way at Slateford Road, and Northfield, and the city's traffic was growing. Some comparative figures of passengers carried etc. are given at the end of the chapter. The tramway services displayed coloured lights at night in addition to the number, and a list of these should now be given together with the colour of the side window boards :—

No.	Route	Lights	Window-board
1	Liberton and Corstorphine	Red/Blue	Red
2	North Junction St. and Gorgie	Blue	Blue
3	Waverley and Robertson Ave.	Blue/White	Blue
4	Piershill and Slateford	White/Blue	Brown
5	Churchhill and Piershill	Red/Green	Green
6	Marchmont and Churchhill	White/Red	White
7	Liberton and Stanley Road	Red	Red
8	Granton and Salisbury Place	Red/Yellow	Yellow
9	Goldenacre and Craiglockhart	Yellow	Yellow
10	Waverley and Craiglockhart	White/Yellow	Yellow
11	Churchhill and Stanley Road	Red/White	White
12	Seafield and Corstorphine	Yellow/Blue	Red
13	Braids and Granton Circle	White/Green	Green
14	Braids and Granton Circle	Yellow/Green	Blue
15	Morningside and Piershill	Green/White	Green
16	Morningside and Stanley Rd.	Green	Green
17	Newington and Trinity Bridge	White	White
18	Marchmont and Bernard St.	Yellow/White	White
19	Newington and Morningside	White	White
20	Post Office and Joppa	Red	Brown
21	Post Office and Musselburgh	Green	Green
22	Post Office and Port Seton	Blue	Blue
23	Goldenacre and Tollcross	Green/Yellow	White
24	Waverley and Comely Bank	Red	Green
—	Liberton and Stanley Road	Yellow/Red	White with red letters
—	Restalrig and Salisbury Place	White	White

Until the introduction of the No. 4 service, No. 14's colours had been White/Blue. Most of the services ran at ten minute intervals.

Time-tables, fare-tables, maps, and other aids to passengers were issued. A Rule Book was issued to the staff in 1923. The rigorous disciplinary regulations of earlier times were no longer applied, and the contents were now mostly in the nature of instructions, including such pertaining to the electrical equipment of the tramways and the handling of motor buses. For the latter a speed limit of 6 m.p.h. was prescribed in Dryden Street, and Leslie Place, and 8 m.p.h. in Raeburn Place, Circus Place, Henderson Terrace, and Canongate. A staff magazine was produced quarterly. Later, from 1926, this adopted the title "Speed".

Now let us digress to record some of the constructional details of the electric system. As the cable tracks wore out they were relaid with heavier rails of B.S.7 section, and the conduit and slot was then of course removed. This was naturally a very gradual process, and a short length remained at the end of Waterloo Place even after the electric service ceased there in 1955. When the roadway was eventually re-constructed there this was lifted and reset safely behind a centre refuge as a reminder of the system, — a happy thought.

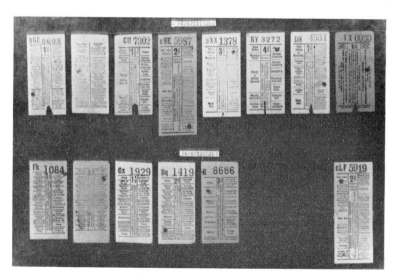

EARLY EDINBURGH CORPORATION TRAMWAY TICKETS IN THE
FORMAT OF THE E. & D. T. Co. AND OF LEITH CORPORATION
RESPECTIVELY
Note the Dog & Luggage ticket, top right.

193

As has been mentioned, centre poles were used in Princes Street and Leith Walk for the overhead equipment. Elsewhere span wire construction was used, wall rosettes being used where-ever possible, including some unlikely positions. There was how-ever one bracket arm pole at the short single-line outside the Theatre Royal. The poles used on the North Bridge had to be held in special base-sockets flanged on to the bridge decking. An effort seems to have been made to economise in spans and pull-offs and the general layout suffered somewhat in consequence. Small and medium standard poles were used equipped with a tasteful finial, cross-arm and scrollwork. Copper trolley wire of 4/0 round section was first used but having a very short life the cadmium copper alloy was soon introduced, followed by a very hard bronze wire for the busiest parts of the system.

Section insulators at the statutory half-mile intervals, or less according to the layout of the location, were of the air-gap type and provided with pavement boxes from which four cables were led up the inside of the pole and out along the span wire. The boxes were equipped with a panel carrying four switches for these side-feed cables and two larger switches for incoming supply cables, though in many cases of course these were idle as the box was not a supply point. There was also the usual choke coil and lightning arrestor. There were a few exceptions where no boxes and side-feed cables were provided such as North Frederick Street and North Hanover Street, and also, later on, at section insulators only a short distance from some of the extended termini. The underground feeder cables belonged to the Electricity Department, the Tramways Department taking the current at the pavement box though metered in the Electricity Department's sub-stations. Some of these feeder cables were composed of various discarded D C. cables and their route from substation to pavement box was some-times devious. Old tramway rails were sometimes buried and used to form negative feeders.

On the overhead line, facing "frogs" were of the so-called "poker" type, a short tongue being directed to the turnout by the hanging "poker" being lifted by the car's trolley-boom if it passed it at an angle. This somewhat "Heath Robinson" arrangement had to be judiciously positioned slightly ahead of the track point blades so that the trolley-boom lifted the "poker" neatly if the car had entered the turnout, yet missed it altogether if it passed straight on. Nevertheless they worked fairly well, though a trolley could not pass backwards through them from the turnout. For reversing back into depots or over crossovers "shunt frogs" were used, with a spring-controlled tongue which could be trailed through.

On account of the low bridges the trolley-bases used on the cars were of a specially low pattern, and the tension exerted on the wire varied from zero at roof level to about 25 or 28 lbs. at normal wire height, and then to zero again when free in the air.

Automatic trolley reversers were fitted up at the termini at Liberton, Stanley Road, Gorgie, and Churchhill. On the car reversing, the trolley was diverted back on to a "Y" from the leg of which it then trailed in behind again. They were however, inclined to be troublesome and all except the Stanley Road one were soon removed. This exception remained in use until after the second world war. More useful were the automatic point controllers provided at all the busier junctions except West End and St. Andrew Street which were always manned by a points-boy with "poker", and at the Post Office, Mound-Hanover Street, and Frederick Street where the electrically operated points were controlled by a boy at a switch-box on the pavement. All the automatic sets worked in the same way. If the driver wished to proceed straight ahead at the junction, he "coasted" while the trolley passed the "skate" on the overhead line. If he wished to diverge to right or left as the case might be, he passed the "skate" with power on and applied the handbrake to keep the speed in check. The "skates" used at that time consisted of a complicated treadle arrangement which actuated a pair of fingers one or other of which was allowed to make a contact feeding the requisite end of the solenoid in the ground connected to the point-rod, by the movement of another small solenoid mounted above the treadle and momentarily energised by the car's passage when drawing current. So many exposed small parts were inclined to give trouble especially in winter. A simpler skate arrangement at Pilrig operated for the curve only, and a resetting skate immediately beyond the frog on the curve ensured the points always lay for the straight as the car approached. The old Leith Corporation set at the Foot of Leith Walk was similar.

Proposals for further extensions to the tramway system were being advanced, and the Corporation had promoted a Parliamentary Order resulting in the Edinburgh Corporation (Tramways etc.) Confirmation Act 1924, (passed 1 August 1924). This authorised the construction of the following tramways : From Slateford terminus to Slateford village; From Gorgie terminus via Chesser Avenue to join the foregoing; Bernard Street via Salamander Street to Seafield, with a triangular junction at Bernard Street; Craiglockhart terminus to Colinton; Melville Drive from Marchmont Road to Clerk Street; and the George Street route, which was envisaged as a useful relief to the growing volume of traffic on Princes Street. Although all were authorised, the first three lines were never built, nor was an authorised connection from North Hanover Street eastwards into George Street. Consideration was also being given to laying tramways in Fountainbridge, Dalkeith Road, and to Lochend; also for extensions from Comely Bank to Cramond, and Braids to Hillend, but it was thought that such were unjustified for the time being. Most of Fountainbridge was too narrow to be really suitable. Only the Braids-Hillend proposal was revived some years later on.

In the meantime construction of the line from Seafield to Kings Road authorised by the 1920 Act was well under way, and it was opened on 26 October 1924, the No. 12 service being extended to Kings Road, described as Beach, Portobello. The "all-the-way" fare became 5d. No. 10 bus service was then operated only from Bath Street, Portobello to Niddrie, but was also extended on to Newcraighall. The old terminal stub on the outgoing line at Seafield remained, the new outgoing line to Kings Road branching off it while the new incoming track continued till it met the old track forming it into a crossover. Other crossovers were laid on the new line at Craigentinny Avenue and at Kings Road.

Another trackwork improvement was the shortening of the single line from the Theatre Royal to the north side of York Place by bringing the double line up to the south side of the York Place crossing. At the same time a double line connection was laid from York Place into Broughton Street towards Canonmills, though this was never used for normal traffic.

Some changes had been made in the services early in 1924. The junctions at Churchhill and Marchmont Road had been remade and service 6 then became the one-time familiar Marchmont Circle, while the Nos. 13 and 14 Granton Circles instead of proceeding to the Braids, circled back to the Post Office via Grange Road and the Bridges. Service 13 on the outer rails of the Granton circle took the inner rails of the Grange part, thus forming a "figure-eight" route. Service 11 then became Stanley Road and Braids via Pilrig Street and Princes Street. Service 16 was also extended from Morningside Station to Braids. A Wednesday, Saturday and Sunday afternoon bus service was put on between the Braids terminus and the recently opened Hillend Park.

Something now had to be done to serve the growing Lochend housing district, so a new bus service, No. 3, was started from St. David Street via York Place, London Road and Marionville Road, and shortly afterwards extended via Restalrig Road to Bernard Street. The side window board was originally white, and later yellow. It was, of course, usual to test the traffic with a bus service and consider from the results whether a tramway was justified. Another new bus service, No. 12 with a white side window board, was started on 5 April 1925. This was operated on a curious 60/30 minute time-table by the one-man type buses and ran from Surgeon's Hall via Clerk Street, Newington, Lady Road, Craigmillar and Duddingston, to Portobello Town Hall. From 19 July 1925 early morning buses were run on Sundays in the summer from Waterloo Place to Melville Street, Portobello for the benefit of bathers.

Several passenger shelters were now erected at various termini, including Port Seton. Portobello depot was enlarged by the conversion of the old engine-room, which was at a slightly lower level to the west of the main shed. All the tracks from both sheds trailed on to the incoming main line, except for one from the main shed which curved the other way on to the outgoing line. Next, a long narrow depot with three lyes and a further one outside was built on the site of the Westfield siding, and became known as Gorgie depot.

Early in 1925 work was also proceeding on the George Street route, from Shandwick Place via Hope Street, south side of Charlotte Square, George Street, and then round both the north and south sides of St. Andrew Square with double track, to junctions with the St. Andrew Street—York Place route. A new double-line connection was also laid in from North Frederick Street, eastwards into George Street. Crossovers were provided in Hope Street, the east end of George Street, and the south side of St. Andrew Square. In George Street itself centre poles were used although span wires had originally been intended.

Construction of the new Melville Drive line was also in hand. This formed a triangular junction with the Liberton route in Clerk Street, a crossover being provided in Hope Park Terrace. These two new routes were duly completed, and opened on 19 July 1925, service 2 being diverted to cover the George Street route, and service 3 extended to Gorgie. A part-day service, No. 25, had recently been introduced between Newington Station and the Zoo, and then altered to Restalrig Road and Zoo. This was likewise diverted to George Street. The service colour, originally white, was later changed to blue/yellow, with a white side window board. Another service to make use of George Street was the Comely Bank service, which on its inward journey, was diverted by George Street and the south side of St. Andrew Square to St. Andrew Street thus avoiding reversal there. The other services traversed the north side of St. Andrew Square. Soon afterwards both the junctions with the St. Andrew Street line were made into triangular junctions, and the George Street route was then much used for football match cars which were run right round St. Andrew Square on the "outer" rail, loading on the south side for Gorgie or Murrayfield.

For the new Melville Drive line a new service, No. 26, colours green/red, and with a white window board, was put on, starting from Newington Station and running to the West End, thence via Princes Street and the Bridges back to Newington Station, and of course operated both ways round.

The crossings and junctions at Bonnington Terrace on the Leith part of the system were reconstructed about this time. Instead of each line becoming single over the crossing with single-line curves south to west, and east to north, double lines were laid, including the two curves. Crossovers were provided at each side of both routes.

Many more buses were now running on pneumatic tyres, and the results were such that it was agreed that these should become standard.

An innovation on 19 October 1925 was the operation of an all-night bus service on two routes, for the duration of the winter. One bus ran hourly on each route between the Foot of Leith Walk and Bruntsfield, and between Salisbury Place and Ardmillan Terrace, connecting with one another at the Post Office. The fare to or from the Post Office was 4d., or all the way 6d. It took a little time for the public to get used to this facility, but it became especially popular with late dancers on Friday nights.

At this time the maximum speed authorised by the Ministry of Transport on the Edinburgh system was 16 m.p.h. and it was of course desirable to revise this figure which was doubtless frequently exceeded. It may be recalled that the maximum legal speed of motor buses was then still 12 m.p.h., to which the same remark may also be applied. For the Edinburgh tramway system, a revision was accordingly sanctioned on 9 November 1925, and provided for a maximum of 20 m.p.h. on the most favourable stretches, with, as usual, lower figures for various other specified parts.

Strangely, only a few weeks earlier, on 17 October, a serious accident had occurred. Fortunately such have been very few in the history of the tramway undertaking. It was a Saturday afternoon and the streets were busy when a car coming down the then single line in Ardmillan Terrace, apparently out of control, became derailed at the turnout on to the double line before the junction at the bottom. Careering right across Gorgie Road it crashed into the wall of St. Martin's Church on the opposite corner, trapping a boy in its course. The boy was killed and six other persons injured, two of them through jumping off the car.

Air-brake equipment operating on the wheels of the car instead of the track-brake shoes was now being tried and found very satisfactory, especially in view of the higher speeds to be run.

An experiment with the "Fischer" bow collector instead of the trolley-boom and wheel was tried on the Portobello route towards the end of 1925. The location of the overhead wire had to be adjusted to suit the path of the collector on all the curves. The Portobello route itself was fairly straight and so the amount of work required was limited, but if the whole system were to be suitably modified, including the Princes Street centre pole brackets, the cost would have been very heavy. Cars Nos. 67 and 110 ran in service with the bow for a few months before the trials were dropped.

Work had now been proceeding on the Colinton extension, and this was opened on 21 March 1926, service 9 going to the new terminus, and service 10 being extended to Craiglockhart Avenue where a crossover was provided. There were other crossovers at Firhill, Redford Barracks, and Redford Road, and at the terminus the track was laid over beside the south pavement at the beginning of Woodhall Road. There was a short piece of single line past Inchdrewer House just beyond Redford Barracks, where the ground could not be obtained for road widening. About the same time the single line section between Lower Gilmore Place and Merchiston Park was doubled, the new outgoing track being necessarily laid close to the pavement most of the way. The other single track section along Gilmore Place was however, never doubled. With the extension of the trams to Colinton the No. 6 bus service from Craiglockhart ceased.

Doubling of the single-line Slateford route was next undertaken, and again clearance between the incoming track and pavement was scanty east of Shandon bridge. An interesting feature was a few yards of interlaced track, incoming cars swinging over towards the other line in order to provide room for a vehicle to park outside Messrs. Lorimer & Clark's Caledonian brewery premises when required. On both these routes the work was started at the outer end and progressed inwards. Another section of single line was also doubled, namely Strathfillan Road to Whitehouse Loan, but again, the adjoining length to Greenhill Gardens remained single to the end. There was also a proposal to form a kerbside loading loop at the foot of Lothian Road but the idea was turned down.

In April 1926 the Town Council resolved to purchase the Industrial Hall, built only a few years previously, in Annandale Street at a cost of £30,000, and use it as a central garage for the buses and other motor vehicles. The building was taken over in May 1926, and although the lorries and such like vehicles remained at Shrubhill, the name of Central Garage stuck. The Henderson Row depot was then vacated and disposed of by the Tramways Department, eventually becoming the City Police

Traffic Department garage. The new bus garage was of ample size but had some disadvantages, particularly the main entrance and exit, which were not designed for vehicles and through which only single-deck buses could pass, and even then with only a few inches clearance each side. These inconveniences persisted for several years. The "pool" of motor cars which the Tramways Department maintained for the use of other City Departments was located at Central Garage, and the Parcels Department was also transferred there from St. James' Square. Vehicles for the expansion of the bus services had hitherto been available from other services replaced by electric trams, and no additions had been made to the fleet for some years. Continued expansion now called for new buses however and more modern types appeared. Included were four more open-top double-deckers, which ran on solid tyres for some time, and were used on service 5 together with the earlier two. One was once sent in error to Davidson's Mains to help lift a summer evening crowd. These double-deckers carried a route board back and front, similar to the arrangement used in London. A similar scheme was then applied to the old single-deck buses which carried a small board naming the main points on the route, alongside the front destination indicator. It was however difficult in general application and the practice soon ceased.

1926 was the year of the General Strike which started on 4 May, Students and others manned cars and buses, and indeed enjoyed it. Part of the Shrubhill workshops was transformed into a temporary dormitory for these crews, for whom pies and lemonade were also laid on. Those who essayed tram driving found it very easy to learn, and so quite an effective skeleton service could be maintained. Many a tale of their experiences, mainly humorous, was later recounted. On the other hand many vehicles suffered the attentions of strikers, and lost their windows. By the second day of the strike all the buses were manned and all districts were being served except the vicinity of Leith Docks. However, attacks on vehicles and crews developed in the afternoon, and the services were suspended after tea-time. The next day, Thursday, was similar, but on Friday and Saturday there was little trouble. The trams were not run on Sunday, but all the buses and 100 trams were out again on the Monday. On that day the maintenance staff returned to work, and the end was in sight. Many regular crews reported next day, whereupon all services were worked. The following day, 12 May, the strike was called off and the full normal services were running on the 13th.

A new terminal siding was constructed in Merchiston Place for service 23 trams, and a triangular junction formed at Churchhill. New housing areas were still expanding, and of course bus services developed concurrently. No. 2 bus service was extended from

Haymarket to Gorgie, and then early in 1927 again extended via Balgreen Road, Saughtonhall Drive, and Murrayfield, back to Haymarket to continue its return journey. Those going the other way round the Saughtonhall loop carried service number 6. These services had also been extended at the other end to Craigmillar cross roads, and from 15 September 1927 were diverted from Lauriston Place and Lady Lawson Street to run via Forrest Road, Grassmarket, and West Port. Service 5 was also extended from Leith Docks via Charlotte Street (Leith), and Lochend Road to Sleigh Drive, and on 9 October at the other end from West End to Bread Street. On 10 October 1927 a new service, No. 14 with a brown window board, was started from Leith Links to Juniper Green following the route of the number 4 service which had meantime been extended from Slateford to Longstone. Another new service, No. 13 with a green window board, started on 17 October 1927, from St. David Street via Princes Street, Coates Crescent, Melville Street, Manor Place, Chester Street, Palmerston Place, Belford Road, and Ravelston Dykes to a terminus at Murrayfield Road. The traffic was light and the one-man buses were used on it, — a part-day service only. On the tramways, service 9 was extended to Granton, and service 18 from Bernard Street to a somewhat ambiguous "Dock Gates", being in fact those at the old North Leith L.N.E.R. Station. Service 16 was diverted from Stanley Road to Granton Road Station. Service 25 was extended to Kings Road on Saturdays and on Saturday evenings extended also to Corstorphine terminus and run via Princes Street. The "extra" cars from Liberton to Stanley Road via Pilrig Street were dropped.

Meantime further tramway extensions were proposed, and the Corporation's Provisional Order and Act of 1927 authorised extensions from the Corstorphine terminus to a point 390 yards west of North Gyle farm; from the Gorgie terminus to Saughton Road including widening of the bridge over the Water of Leith; and from the Comely Bank terminus to a point just beyond Crewe Road. Part of the Corstorphine extension, as far as Drum Brae cross roads, was put in hand and opened early in 1928.

In the summer of 1927 the Musselburgh company experienced severe competition from the new "White Line" bus service and on 1 August cut their fares to meet it. The new fares were: G.P.O. to Hayweights 3d., to Levenhall 4d., to Prestonpans 5d., and to Port Seton 6d. Edinburgh accepted 2d. as their share as far as Joppa. On 28 August there was a general reduction of fares on the Edinburgh system whereby 4d. became the maximum fare except for the complete Granton-Churchhill circle, which became 6d., and certain of the longer bus routes, viz :— Nos. 2, 4, 6, and 14 which retained the 5d. fare.

The reduced fares did not greatly help the Port Seton traffic however, and the Musselburgh company decided they would withdraw their cars entirely and run buses instead. Consequently, on 1 March 1928, a supplementary agreement was concluded between the Company and Edinburgh Corporation, whereby the former resolved to lift their track beyond Levenhall, and while ceasing to run any cars, undertook to maintain the system and supply current as far as Levenhall, to which point Edinburgh Corporation were to run their cars as required. Receipts from the Company territory were paid to the Company less 8d. per car mile. Protective fares were to be charged on the Company's new bus service. The new arrangements were put into effect immediately.

At the beginning of 1928 the Department adopted the more embracing title of Transport Department, and "Tramways" and "Motors" disappeared from the vehicles. Services were still expanding. On the tramways service 5 was extended to Morningside Station part-day; service 10 to Colinton part-day; and service 15 to Kings Road. A new part-day service was started on 16 January 1928 from Pilrig to Tollcross via the Bridges and Melville Drive but later lapsed. These cars reversed at Tollcross in Brougham Street. An important amendment in fares was adopted in May 1928 whereby the twopenny fare from the Post Office took the passenger to any tram terminus.

To help serve the new housing area at Stenhouse, bus service 1 was extended there from Ardmillan Terrace via Gorgie Road on 30 April 1928. A connecting bus was put on between the Braids tram route and the City Hospital during visiting hours. On 7 June 1928 bus service 13 was diverted from Princes Street and St. David Street into Frederick Street from where it continued via Howe Street, Great King Street, north side of Drummond Place, London Street, Hope Crescent, Leith Walk, Albert Street, Easter Road, St. Clair Street, and Hawkhill Avenue to Lochend. The one-man buses were still used. On 11 November 1928 bus service 12 was altered to run via Causewayside, Mayfield Road and Esslemont Road; and on 28 November bus service 5 was extended from Bread Street via Fountainbridge to Ardmillan Terrace, while on 16 December it was extended at the other end from Lochend up to St. David Street. At the same time service 13 was extended from Lochend via Restalrig Road to Bernard Street. These latter two extensions, between them covered the route of bus service 3 which was later abandoned.

It may be of interest to mention in passing, that the city's first set of traffic lights was installed at the York Place-Broughton Street crossing on 21 March 1928. Other sets followed shortly afterwards and in several cases tram stopping places which had been beyond the crossings were brought back to the approach side.

so that following traffic halted for tram passengers boarding and alighting would not be waiting in the path of cross traffic. Another improvement at this time was the provision of new pawl posts* with lamps, on the "islands" at Castle Street, and subsequently elsewhere.

In November 1928 Mr. Pilcher was appointed general manager of the Manchester Corporation undertaking, and thus Edinburgh Transport lost its manager, — a gentleman respected by both staff and public. Mr. F. A. Fitzpayne, the deputy manager, who it will be remembered, had been manager of the Leith undertaking before amalgamation, was confirmed as his successor on 10 January 1929.

The extension at Comely Bank was now put in hand and this was completed and brought into use in June 1929. Mr. Fitzpayne also altered and extended a number of other tram services in 1929 as follows :— No. 17 extended to Granton on 8 May; No. 8 extended to Newington Station, and No. 10 extended to Foot of Leith walk on 2 June; No. 7 extended to Liberton terminus on 17 June; No. 3 extended to Newington Station, and service 19 abandoned on 14 July; No. 25 extended daily except Sundays to Corstorphine terminus and diverted via Princes Street on 15 July; No. 23 extended to Morningside Station on 28 July; No. 12 extended to Joppa, part-day, on 1 September. Service 18 was diverted from Marchmont Road via Melville Drive and Hope Park Terrace to Newington Station on 17 November replacing service 26 which then ceased. These lengthened routes still retained the 4d. maximum fare. The stages were also lengthened on the Cramond bus route, the only one on which 1½d. stages still obtained. Additional and longer circular tours were operated in the summer of 1929, and Nos. 21 and 22 were allocated to the Hillend bus and City Hospital bus services respectively. Bus service 2 was diverted through the Prestonfield housing scheme.

There was a spectacular accident on Saturday afternoon 1 June 1929. A driver and conductor having left their tram, No. 349, for a few minutes at Liberton terminus, found on returning, that it was moving off down the hill. The hand brake had not been used and the air-brake had leaked off. Gathering speed, they were unable to catch it. When the car reached the bend on the steep hill it left the rails and finished up in a front garden leaning against a tramway pole which cut well into its side. Of the four elderly passengers, the two on the top deck probably didn't realise what was happening: One, an old lady of 84 suffered only bruising and shock; the others were unscathed, and indeed the couple on the lower deck, — both over 70, — just proceeded home on a later tram !

* The term pawl-post for what would now be called a traffic bollard doubtless derives from the pawl of cable car days.

ACCIDENT AT LIBERTON BRAE, 1 JUNE 1929

In June 1929 an awkward piece of realignment of the track at the Waverley Steps was effected.

A summer bus service, No. 23 from the Mound to the Castle was started on 14 June 1930. The Sunday morning bus for Portobello Baths at Melville Street then took the number 24. On the night services restarting in October as usual, the Bruntsfield one was extended to Morningside Station and numbered 25, while the other night service, extended to Robertson Avenue, became No. 26. Most of the tram routes had been served by a few special early morning cars, but Comely Bank did not have this benefit and in this case an early morning bus was run over the route and numbered 27.

The tramway extension from Gorgie to the new Stenhouse terminus at Saughton Road was opened on 20 July 1930, prior to the Ministry of Transport's inspection five days later. A short extension at the Liberton terminus to keep waiting cars clear of the cross roads was also made. Passenger "islands" continued to be built at various additional places, and that at the West End of Princes Street on the west-going line was removed and replaced by new ones in Lothian Road and Shandwick Place. Some further increases in maximum speeds were also sanctioned.

At this time the possiblity of a universal penny fare was being mooted. While this could not be done, Mr. Fitzpayne's report showed that 70% of tram passengers paid penny fares and only

$1\frac{1}{2}\%$ paid more than 2d. However a further step in this direction was effected on 16 November 1931 when 3d. became the maximum tramway fare except to Levenhall. The child's fare, which now became a universal penny was made available up to 14 years of age instead of 12.

After the Musselburgh Company ceased tramway operations, the position there became increasingly unsatisfactory. No cars were running beyond Levenhall: the system was in poor condition and not being adequately maintained. Musselburgh town council asked the Ministry of Transport to make a closing order, but this was declined as the agreement for through running by Edinburgh was still in force. However a supplementary agreement was made on 7 March 1929 whereby the Corporation would then exercise running powers only as far as Levenhall, as they were in fact doing. Following this the Musselburgh & District Electric Tramways (Cessor of Powers) Order 1929 was issued, and the line beyond Levenhall officially abandoned, and subsequently lifted.

The Company still wanted rid of the remainder of their tramway between Joppa and Levenhall, and in February 1930 asked Edinburgh Corporation to buy it together with the bus service the Company were running to Port Seton in substitution of their tramcars. To do this, Edinburgh, of course, would have had to obtain further Parliamentary powers, and the S.M.T.Co. would have objected to Corporation buses running outside the city boundaries in competition with them. Musselburgh town council however urged Edinburgh to take over the remainder of the tramway. At the end of 1930 the Company arranged with the Corporation to attend to any necessary maintenance on their behalf pending negotiations which were now opened.

As a result, Edinburgh town council on 5 March 1931 resolved to acquire the tramway between Joppa and Levenhall and to seek the necessary Parliamentary authority in their next Provisional Order. A new agreement was therefore made between the Corporation and the Company whereby the Corporation would, on the granting of the necessary Parliamentary authority, buy the Company's tramway undertaking for £3000, while the Company undertook to continue to provide the traction current outside the city, and to charge protective fares on their bus service. Until the Parliamentary Order was confirmed, the Corporation undertook to maintain the system as agents for the Company as from 1 January 1931. This agreement was dated 7 May 1931, and the Corporation assumed responsibility the following day.

A new bus route, No. 15 with white side window boards, was started on 22 February 1931, at half-hourly intervals, from Eastfield to Juniper Green via Milton Road, Royal Park Terrace, High

Street, George IV Bridge, Tollcross, Bruntsfield, and Colinton Road. The fare all the way was 6d. The Cramond route was now extended to Barnton with a 5d. fare, reduced to 4d. in July 1931.

Some changes in tram window boards took place at this period. Service 4 was provided with blue boards and service 25 with yellow boards with blue letters, in November 1930. Service 2 carried a blue front board at the bottom of the driver's window lettered "via George Street", and services 13 and 14 similarly carried a white board lettered "Granton & Churchhill Circular Drive". A similar white board with red letters "via Melville Drive" was provided for service 18 in September 1931, at which time new side window boards, yellow with green letters were provided for service 23. The large destination boards on the remaining open-top double-deck buses were replaced by orthodox roller-blind destination and service number indicators in February 1931. In the summer of 1931 the City adopted the style City and Royal Burgh of Edinburgh and all vehicles etc. henceforth bore this lettering.

The Road Traffic Act 1930 brought about important changes for all bus operators. No longer could Edinburgh town council decide to run a bus service where or when they saw fit, or to decide the fares. The licensing of the vehicles was no longer in their hands. Road service licences were of course forthcoming from the newly appointed Traffic Commissioners for all the existing services. Subsequent alterations or additions required their approval, but there was seldom any difficulty. In April 1931, the public service vehicles, to give the buses their new official appellation, were being examined for fitness under the new auspices, and appearing with their new white enamelled oval licence plates on the back. The few remaining old buses and charabancs had only a limited life left and soon disappeared, among them the one-man buses. In any case a conductor now had to be carried on any bus with more than 20 seats. Coaches were then used for a few years on service 13 and elsewhere, and were provided on the front only with orthodox roller-blind destination and service number indicators. They were not entirely suitable for "stage carriage" work except where the traffic was light.

The Edinburgh Corporation Order Confirmation Act 1932 was duly passed 25 April 1932, and the Musselburgh tramway system then became vested in Edinburgh Corporation. The much needed reconstruction, estimated to cost £50,000, was started right away and continued over the next two years. A double line was provided as far as the slight bend in the road between Beulah and Windsor Gardens and crossovers provided at Eastfield, Bridge Street at Hayweights, and High Street just beyond the old depot entrance. The connection to the latter was of course removed. An extremely short piece of interlacing was introduced at the "bottle-neck" in the High Street at the Town Hall. For the last half-mile or so beyond Windsor Gardens a single line sufficed to the new terminus in Ravenshaugh Road opposite Hope Place. As before, there were three passing loops, the first between Windsor Gardens and Ashgrove, and the last at the junction of the main Tranent road just short of the terminus. The middle one rejoiced in the name of "tattie" loop from the product of the then field alongside. The short length of track between the new terminus and the Musselburgh boundary was abandoned as had been provided for in the agreement. The old overhead bracket arms were replaced by span wire construction throughout and a substantial number of new poles erected, most of which were obtained second-hand from England. The Musselburgh Company continued to provide traction current from their electricity undertaking as far as the Eastfield section insulators which then became the dividing point instead of Joppa. The feeder cables in Musselburgh became the Transport Department's property whereas in Edinburgh they remained Electricity Department property. With the system now in their ownership, the Corporation extended their 3d. maximum fare to Levenhall, and the 2d. fare to the city boundary at Eastfield on 19 July 1932. An additional Saturday service No. 22, colour blue, with blue side window boards, was put on between Post Office and Musselburgh Town Hall on 28 May 1932. By 21 January 1933, the overhead reconstruction permitted the use of the normal trolley-rope on the cars and the bamboo poles were discarded.

The Corporation also took the opportunity in their aforementioned 1932 Order to carry out a thorough tidying up of their transport legislation. All the Corporation's tramways Acts or parts of Acts relating to tramways, including those of Leith Corporation, and all the various old Companies' Acts, right back to 1871 and including the Musselburgh ones, were repealed. The existing tramways were all described in a schedule and declared vested in Edinburgh Corporation together with extensions unbuilt but authorised by the 1927 Order. Adequate powers were included in respect of bylaws, fares, luggage, parcels, freedom from licensing cars and crews, and to operate public service vehicles.

Reverting again to the development of the services, tram service 10 was extended to Bernard Street on 9 July 1932, and service 18 was cut back to Waverley except during rush hours, and later permanently. Bus service 9 was extended from the Mound to Blackhall via West End, Orchard Brae, and Craigleith Road to a terminus at Telford Road on 2 October 1932. Bus service 6 was extended to Harewood Drive about the end of the year, and this service together with Nos. 2 and 7 diverted from Nicolson Street to Davie Street, Pleasance, and St. Leonard's Street from 9 July 1933, the service 7 terminus being also altered to Davie Street. Then on

3 September 1933 bus service 1 was diverted from Gorgie Road via Westfield Road, Balgreen Road, and Stevenson Drive to Saughton Road to serve the growing housing area there. To cater for the many pupils of Daniel Stewart's College residing in the Corstorphine district a useful one way bus was run from Corstorphine to the College in the mornings. This was numbered 28, and there was no return service in the afternoon. Another hospital bus service started on 5 August 1933 from Granton Road to Pilton Hospital, No. 29. Tram service 22 became daily from 4 November 1933. Time recorders were introduced at several places on both tram and bus routes in an endeavour to better regulate the running of the services.

An interesting case of single-line working had to be practised in 1933 when each side of the North Bridge had to be closed for several weeks in turn to permit of repairs to the bridge fabric by the City Engineer. Crossovers were laid in to suit and work started on the bottom half of the east side in March. To ease congestion by waiting cars at the Post Office, services 4 and 10 were diverted via York Place from 24 April. Operations were transferred to the west side in August, the crossovers being relaid to suit, and the work completed in November. Only service 10 reverted to its former route, service 4 continuing to run via York Place.

White front window boards lettered in red "via Pilrig Street" were provided for service 11, while services 13 and 14 got similar new boards, green lettered "Churchhill via Princes St." and "Granton via Pilrig & Goldenacre", and red lettered "Churchhill via Bridges & Grange" and "Granton via Princes St. & Bernard St." respectively. Red letters appeared on service 8's side window boards. An interesting series of advertisements to "Travel by Tram" were applied on the inside of the cars. The Zoo was a favourite theme and these first enjoined one to see "A for Antelope". Eventually the whole alphabet was covered.

A trial with a pantograph collector was made in 1933. Again the Portobello route was necessarily used and side runners fitted to the poker frogs to keep the pantograph from fouling them. Such makeshift arrangements were again troublesome and car 73 carried the pantograph only from April till November.

An office building was constructed at Gorgie depot in 1933-4, and a start was made in extending the Central Garage. The parcels delivery service hitherto maintained by boys supplied with large canvas bags and who used the ordinary tram and bus services to reach their districts, was greatly improved by the inauguration of delivery by motor vans.

Of more direct interest to the passenger was the introduction of the ticket-printing machines. After one or two experiments, one hundred such machines, — "T.I.M.s" — were purchased and put into use with the conductors at Tollcross depot in January 1933. They found favour, — though not with the passengers, who complained of wet ink and the flimsiness of the tickets. So their number and use extended quite rapidly throughout the whole system, including some of the buses in 1935. To facilitate their use on all the bus services, the night services excepted, a 3d. maximum fare was eventually introduced on them too, on 5 December 1937. The 1½d. 2½d. and 3½d. fares on the Barnton route had disappeared in 1934. So did the old pre-printed coloured tickets disappear, — nearly. It was still necessary to carry a block of such tickets for 1d. 2d. and 3d. with universal stage numbers in case of failure of the machines. The colours of the 1d. and 2d. ones were as before but the 3d. ones were a sickly green shade. When these tickets had to be used they were cancelled by the conductor tearing out a small piece opposite the stage number. All the tram and bus stages had of course to be numbered, and to ensure common stage numbers on the tramway system, a clever scheme was devised whereby the Post Office or Waverley was called 12 in each direction on all services, except Nos. 20-23. A car leaving a terminus did not necessarily start at stage 1 but at such number as fitted 12 at the Post Office. Thus, for example, Haymarket, and Tollcross were always 10 inwards and 14 outwards. This scheme came into use on 8 April 1934.

An innovation for the Corporation was the first covered top double-deck bus which went into service between Surgeon's Hall and Craigmillar on 3 July 1933. Although a second one followed the next year, it was some time yet before the double-deckers became part of the accepted policy, although the S.M.T.Co. already had five years experience with them.

Work on a further extension of the Corstorphine route under the 1927 Act, from Drum Brae to a new terminus at North Gyle farm was started in November 1933. A trial run over the new line was made on 9 May 1934, but it was not opened for traffic till 1 July, all three services being then extended. This extension was useful on International Rugby Match days. Hitherto cars had been stored on the incoming line east of Drum Brae, in addition to four on the Zoo loop, ready to run in and lift the crowds from Murrayfield. This involved turning back the ordinary service at Corstorphine Station Road crossover and running a bus between there and Drum Brae. Now the ordinary service could continue to Drum Brae and only the much quieter length beyond had to be covered by the bus.

The main road east of Saughtonhall Drive having been widened on the south side, a new outgoing track was laid and the old outgoing track became the incoming line. The old track was slewed over at the east end to connect with the new, which were now centrally situated and in line with those west of Saughtonhall Drive, obviating the "double" bend there. The work took from September to December 1934.

The number of passenger "islands" was still gradually being increased and two were provided in Musselburgh, viz. at Hayweights and near the Town Hall. The last of the old cable tracks in Morrison Street and in Hamilton Place were removed in 1934, and several of the old cable junction and other pits were filled in.

Bus services 2 and 6 were altered on 16 September 1934, and instead of making the loop at the Saughtonhall end, both services proceeded via Whitson Road to the Stenhouse bus terminus. At the other end the terminus was extended from Harewood Drive to Hay Drive. Extra buses running from Surgeon's Hall to the latter were provided with green window boards with white letters in February 1935.

Mr. Fitzpayne died in harness on 3 March 1935. Of gentlemanly demeanour he had followed a progressive policy particularly in the engineering field. Robert McLeod, the traffic superintendent, who had come from Aberdeen with Mr. Pilcher, was appointed to succeed him on 2 May 1935.

Parliamentary authority was sought for further tramway extensions in the Corporation's 1934 Provisional Order, and were approved in February 1935. These were :—Braids to Hillend Park; Granton Road to Crewe Toll; and Liberton to Kaimes. On 4 April 1935 the Town Council decided to proceed with the extension from the Braids as far as Fairmilehead, and work soon commenced on this, together with a re-alignment of the existing track towards the centre of the widened roadway approaching the Braids terminus.

Meantime some new bus services were started on 7 April 1935, viz. — No. 3 St. David Street to Craigentinny Avenue via Lochend; No. 16 Willowbrae and Ardmillan, from the south end of Northfield Broadway via Willowbrae Road, Royal Park Terrace, High Street, and thence the No. 1 route; No. 19 West End and Pilton. The latter started from Randolph Place proceeding via Orchard Brae and Crewe Road. The window boards were respectively black with yellow letters, yellow with red letters, and white with red letters. In each case the service number was included at the left hand end, which innovation had appeared when new boards had been provided for bus service 9 two months previously.

A considerable extension at the back of the Central Garage was completed in the summer of 1935, together with a new fuel installation. Buses now entered the garage by the new entrance at the back in Green Street and were immediately re-fuelled, the operation being controlled from a gallery over the doorway, and hence the bus number was painted on the back of the roof where it could readily be seen by the attendant. Premises adjoining the Shrubhill depot were bought to which the parcels department was also transferred.

A touch of gaiety was added on the occasion of a Royal visit on 11 May 1935, when all cars flew a small coloured pennant from the trolley rope, a practice to be followed on future festive occasions. Traffic was specially heavy that day and practically every car was pressed into service.

On 4 August 1935 tram service 18 was extended to Liberton Dams, while a useful service, No. 19, started on 7 October, from Seafield Place to Tollcross via Bridges and Melville Drive. This was part-day only at first, but now proving popular became an all day service on 3 November. The crossover in Brougham Street was used for this service which on 6 April 1936 was extended to Craigentinny Avenue, and also to Kings Road at weekends. The service colour was green over red and the side window boards were green with red letters. At first a large paper label was stuck on the driver's window, but this was later replaced by a green board with red letters.

Modern covered-top double-deck buses began to appear towards the end of 1935, mainly on service 2 at first. Low bridges of course precluded their use on several of the other busy routes.

On 10 November 1935 tram service 2 was extended to Granton and service 17 cut back to Trinity Bridge again. Bus services 3 and 5 were slightly altered from 15 December, when they proceeded from the south side of St. Andrew Square via North St. David Street and Queen Street to York Place instead of from South St. David Street, Princes Street and South St. Andrew Street. Bus service 13 became an all day service on 13 January 1936.

The Carricknowe housing district was now being built up, and although the widening of Saughton Road had then only begun, bus service 1 was extended from Stenhouse through this area to Corstorphine High Street at the Library on 2 February 1936. A proposal to extend the Ravelston Dykes route down to Craigcrook Road was not approved. On 2 February also, the maximum bus fare was reduced to 4d. and workmen's fares were made available on the buses as well as the trams, thus satisfying a long-felt grievance in the new areas served only by buses.

In order to bring the Corstorphine route tracks nearer the centre of the traffic roundabout which had become operative at Haymarket, the junction was relaid. This was a rather complicated job as the overhead had to be altered to suit concurrently, and the

211

whole work was carried out on the night of 9-10 May 1936. Subsequently pairs of new "islands" were provided clear of the roundabout on each route. On 4 April 1936 the track re-alignment at the Braids was brought into use, followed on 19 April by the new extension to Fairmilehead, service 11 being extended there, with services 15 and 16 in addition on Saturdays and Sundays. Front window boards, white with red letters, were provided. The bus to Hillend Park then made Fairmilehead its starting point. Service 16 was also extended at the other end, to Granton, on 26 July, while a new service, No. 27 from Granton Road station, following the Hanover Street and Mound route, to Craiglockhart Avenue commenced on 6 September 1936. The colours displayed at night were yellow over red, and the side window boards were red with yellow letters. New white front window boards lettered in black "via Tollcross & Melville Drive" were provided for service 18 in the summer.

On 1 June 1936 there was a change in the bus stances in the city. The S.M.T.Co. vacated Waverley Bridge and the Mound in favour of St. Andrew Square, and the Corporation services 11 and 23 were changed from the Mound to Waverley Bridge, proceeding via Mound and Market Street on their inward journey. Service 7 was also extended there from Surgeon's Hall. Traffic arrangements were altered at the West End on the same date, no access being allowed between Princes Street-Shandwick Place directions and Queensferry Street—Hope Street. Buses proceeding between Princes Street and Queensferry Street now did so via South Charlotte Street, south side of Charlotte Square, and Hope Street. Trams however continued to use their tracks between Hope Street and Shandwick Place as an exception to the rule.

An interesting new summer tram service was provided on Wednesday, Saturday and Sunday afternoons, commencing on 12 July —it continued till 19 December that year, — and ran from Granton Road station via Ferry Road, Junction Street, and over the hitherto unused line across the Foot of the Walk to Duke Street, Seafield, and Kings Road. It was numbered 26, colours white, and carried pink side window boards lettered in black. Cars on various routes going to Kings Road or beyond were provided with new front window boards, white with black letters, "To and from Bathing Pool Portobello". The early morning bus service to Portobello on Sundays now terminated at the new pool.

When the all-night bus service re-started for the winter, a boon for early workers was a reduction to the ordinary day-time fares after 3.20 a.m. From 9 November 1936 service 25 was altered to work between Craigentinny Avenue and Drum Brae, new side window boards coloured yellow with blue letters being provided. Hitherto the first few early morning journeys on the Comely Bank route had been run by buses showing No. 27, but service 24 trams took over this duty at this time. Bus service 9 was extended to Greenbank Row, and bus service 3 to Portobello Town Hall on 3 January 1937.

The construction of the final piece of the Corstorphine tramway extension to the Maybury was undertaken, and this was opened on 14 February 1937, services 1 and 12 being accordingly extended. The crossover which had formed the previous North Gyle terminus was taken out shortly afterwards.

A considerable extension to Leith depot was being undertaken early in 1937. This included bringing forward the shed entrance, and widening to include the old workshop on the right hand side. Entrances were provided each side of the separate office block fronting Leith Walk, each giving trailing connections to each track in Leith Walk and forming a loop round the back of the office block, and the depot lyes fanning off it towards the middle. The crossover in Leith Walk was removed. If it were necessary cars could be reversed by going in one depot gate, round the loop, and out the other. A further office block, recreation room, and stores, etc. was also built to the right of the shed. 150 cars could now be accommodated. While the building work was proceeding, the old sand house and stores were out of commission, and bagged sand was therefore supplied from Shrubhill, being sent down in car 40 which was stripped of its seating and so used till March 1937. The body of car 82 served as a temporary store at the back of the depot.

About this period improvements to the power supply were effected by the Electricity Department who opened a new mercury-arc rectifier substation at Turnhouse Road to supply the Corstorphine route west of Belmont Crescent, as shown on the diagram. This was used during the night to feed back through the old Pinkhill feeder to their Robertson Avenue substation, and thence Gorgie depot, to avoid running the old rotary machines all night at the latter substation. Another rectifier installed at their Wardie substation was similarly used to supply Leith depot during the night. Both these substations were remotely controlled from their parent substation. The Leith Walk feeder was also extended into Leith depot where a new high speed circuit-breaker was provided. To meet the additional traffic load in the Lothian Road area, a new additional feeder was laid to a new pillar at Lothian House. A less successful scheme arose from the desire to load up new rectifier equipment in the Causewayside substation, by laying a new feeder to Greenhill Gardens, and taking the Bruntsfield and Churchhill area from the old rotary machines in Morningside substation. Such a long feed however gave rise to excessive difference in voltage from the adjoining substations and hence trouble at the section-insulators.

There was also difficulty with the return currents in the rails, which were wont to take strange courses even in orthodox circumstances. Improvement in the reliability of the side-feed cables from the pavement boxes to the overhead was obtained by leading these through a separate swan-necked pipe bracketed to the pole, straight out of the top of the box. This was of course done only as and when renewal was called for. A much improved design of automatic point controller was being installed at all junctions in regular use, apart from Princes Street. In this the trolley bridged a skate insulated from the trolley-wire, there being a path between the latter and one side of the skate through a relay contactor which operated in series with the car drawing power. Otherwise the skate being bridged completed a circuit from the other side of it through a second relay contactor operating on voltage, the first contactor not operating in these conditions. These relay contactors completed circuits to the points solenoids accordingly, and were housed in a box mounted on a pole so that there were no exposed moving parts.

In the Corporation's 1936 Provisional Order powers were obtained to extend the tramway from Stenhouse to the city boundary. Extensive housing was in progress in the area lying to the south of the main Calder Road which, of course, required widening. It was suggested that this extension might instead be laid on its own right of way to the north side of the road, but this did not find favour. There seemed a reluctance to proceed with the road widening too, but meanwhile, in order to provide street lighting on the usual arrangement of utilising the tramway standards, the positions for these were plotted out on the south side of the road and those which the City Lighting Department desired to use were erected on their behalf in 1937 in anticipation of the tramway extension proceeding. In the event this tramway was never constructed and these standards remained to serve only the Lighting Department.

To serve the district in the meantime, bus service 4 was extended from Longstone and out Calder Road as far as Sighthill Avenue on 26 September 1937. This was followed on 3 October by the extension of service 5 from Ardmillan Terrace to Stenhouse. At the same time service 16 was extended from Willowbrae to Portobello Town Hall via Duddingston Road. This service was again extended at the other end from Ardmillan Terrace via Stevenson Drive, Stenhouse, and out Calder Road to Sighthill Avenue on 30 January 1938. Tram service 17 was again extended to Granton on 15 November 1937 though it had been so extended on Saturdays a few months earlier, while tram service 27 was extended to Firhill on 6 February 1938 to cater for the new housing scheme nearby at Colinton Mains. This district benefited further

214

when on 14 August 1938 the Hillend to Fairmilehead bus service was extended via Oxgangs Road and Colinton Mains to Firhill as a daily service. At that time the traffic was mainly between Colinton Mains and the trams at Firhill, and transfer fares were made available between Colinton Mains and Tollcross. When issuing these tickets stage 99 was used on the ticket machines. On 31 October 1938 tram service 25 was extended to Kings Road daily. The all-night bus service was extended to Balgreen Road from 17 October.

Revised Regulations and Byelaws appertaining to the tramway system were made by the Minister of Transport on 17 August 1938, (S.R. & O. 1938 No. 822/S.53) and included an increase in speed up to 25 m.p.h. on the favourable stretches. The number of "compulsory stops" was also considerably reduced to the following, on the descending journeys :—Broughton Street at Forth Street, North St. Andrew Street at York Place, South St. Andrew Street at Princes Street, North Hanover Street at George Street, South Hanover Street at Princes Street, North Frederick Street at George Street, South Frederick Street at Princes Street, Howe Street at South-East Circus Place, Royal Circus at North-West Circus Place, Bank Street at North Bank Street, Pitt Street at Fettes Row, and Liberton Brae at Alnwickhill Road.

To cater for the increasing traffic to Portobello Bathing Pool on Saturdays and Sundays a service was run in the summer of 1939, — un-numbered, from Stenhouse to Bath Street via London Road. Service 5 was also likewise extended to Kings Road. At this time yellow front window boards, lettered in black "For Colinton Mains" were provided for services 9, 10, and 27, while similar boards "via Mound" were provided for service 23.

It will be clear that the bus services were now steadily increasing in importance, and indeed some of the extensions were having their effect on the revenue of adjacent or common tramway routes; but while additional plant was installed at Central Garage and more accomodation for bus body repairs and painting made available at Shrubhill the tramway policy still held good.

The council had decided on 6 January 1938 to proceed with the construction of the tramway along Ferry Road to Crewe Toll authorised by the 1934 Order, in conjunction with a road widening scheme. So far no rails had been laid but the road widening was nearly finished except for the short distance between Granton Road and Arboretum Road. Now, on 2 March 1939 the council had a recommendation from the Public Utilities committee that the previous decision be reversed. The council rejected this, but on 6 April 1939 the committee returned with the suggestion that as the trams would not serve the new housing schemes beyond the low railway bridges west of Crewe Toll, the extension should not be built and a bus service run instead. It was proposed that this should operate from Drylaw Mains via Ferry Road, Crewe Road North, Boswall Green, Afton Terrace, East Trinity Road, Craighall Road, Ferry Road, and Coburg Street to Dock Place.

Still the council adhered to the earlier decision that the line be built and so construction was at last started. In view of the road widening position work proceeded inwards from Crewe Toll, it being hoped that the short narrow stretch of road would be dealt with by the time the rails reached it. To facilitate welding of the rails the overhead standards were quickly erected and a wire strung along on small temporary brackets and insulators, a second wire being hung below for the return current. A feeder box was installed beside the first pole and a temporary connection made to the existing overhead line on the curve into Granton Road. The Electricity Department however, also laid a new feeder to this box from their new Pennywell substation, which was equipped with mercury-arc rectifiers, and this substation was then used to supply that section of the existing system alternately with the Wardie substation. Most of the poles had been erected; one track was laid as far as East Fettes Avenue, and the other for a short distance, when the fateful 3 September 1939 fell and work was suspended, never to restart, although this did nearly happen, as will be mentioned later.

The "blackout" was imposed on Friday 1 September and of course there was a great hustle to get office windows and depot roofs darkened in the quickest possible way for a start. The signal lamps for the single line sections had to be screened, and later modified. Tramcar bumpers and steps were painted white, and the crews continued to wear their summer white-topped caps all the year round. Buses had to run with their sidelights only, till improvised screens allowing a small patch of light from headlights were approved, followed later, by the slotted metal masks devised as standard by the Ministry of Home Security. Cardboard shields were fitted round some of the interior lights on buses, and the remainder removed. The trams faired rather better at first. The lamps were removed from some circuits and blue lamps used in the remainder. Blue lamps were a popular measure in the early days of the war, and for a week or two a large number were required every night until it was realised that traction voltage lamps had no domestic application. The glass of destination screen boxes was painted with a blue lacquer. The headlights on the newer cars were dimmed, but brake-stop lights and platform lights were removed. Aided by running on their defined tracks the trams managed very well though inevitably there were casualties. The dim blue light from the destination screen helped those cars without headlights, but when a "yellow warning" was in force on a dark night, and all these lights put off, it was a grim business creeping along in complete darkness. The blue lamp phase did not last long and in November 1939 200 volt carbon filament lamps with cardboard shades were used in the older cars, and on cars with long-series lighting circuits, these were connected into one circuit so that ordinary lamps gave only a suitably reduced illumination.

Contrary to many a rumour, the Transport Department were quite well off in their stocks of material of various kinds, and vehicle maintenance and painting continued more or less normally, though of course there was some reduction in staff, and the black-out halted night outside work apart from what could be accomplished by the aid of pocket torches. However the overhead linesmen were fitted out with caps carrying a small shaded electric lamp on the peak supplied from dry batteries strapped to a belt, and this enabled them to carry out localised work quite easily.

In addition to general A.R.P. measures, a number of staff were trained in decontamination duties. In order that they could function if the need arose a vehicle cleansing station was prepared outside the back of Gorgie depot early in the war and a tram track laid into it so that both trams and buses could be accommodated.

Of course no one knew what to expect and feared the worst would come at any moment. One thing was lacking which might well be a necessity,—a salvage wagon of some sort. So a de-licensed AEC Reliance bus SC3430 was partially stripped and equipped with a crane and other suitable gear, being ready early in 1940. One unfortunate decision was made when the council cancelled the enquiries they were putting out for a batch of new buses. In a year or two many of the older buses would run no longer and then replacements were unobtainable.

Services were maintained more or less normally except that from November 1939 the bus services had to be cut to save fuel, and an "Emergency" timetable was issued in which the times of the last buses were a little earlier. The last car times were also a little earlier, but still about 11 o'clock. The Corstorphine-Stewarts College bus ceased.

There was still dissatisfaction over the older trams running with no headlights, and so after some experiments with various marker lights, all these cars were fitted with a cylindrical form of lamp with red and white spectacles, and a similar shield fitted to the headlights of the newer cars too. This was done between February and June 1940. A white band was also painted right round the bottom of the body of all cars.

217

In 1939, before the war, renewals of some lengths of trolley wire had been carried out using a grooved section wire known as "Portsmouth" section, which was attached to the section insulators by means of detachable end pieces bolted thereto and formed with a groove into which the top lobe of the wire fitted and was held by pinching screws in the top. This gave a smooth under-run on to the section insulators and it was decided to standardise on this wire and provide frogs and other fittings with similar detachable end pieces. The suspension ears of course gripped only the upper lobe of the wire too. Another improvement was effected at crossovers normally used only in one direction, e.g. the Zoo, Newington station, etc., where the shunt frog was removed from the outgoing wire and the crossover wire led alongside it for a short distance and terminated separately. These measures helped to reduce arcing from the trolleyheads, which was a source of complaint in the blackout. So-called arc-springs were fitted to the section-insulators but these were not effective. Of course if the drivers shut off current when passing section-insulators and other fittings all was well, and to assist them to locate such places in the dark white glazed tiles were let into the setts between the tracks as markers. These were also used at automatic point skates, and, outside the rails, as stopping marks at passenger islands. Still arcing continued and many were the suggestions put forward to eliminate it. Some said bow collectors should be used, but experience elsewhere showed these to be even worse. It was even suggested that only buses should be used after dark.

The use of grooved wire had, however, been coupled with the idea of using carbon-shoe collectors instead of the old trolley-wheels. It would, of course be several years before even one route could, economically, be converted to grooved wire, and therefore experiments were made with a specially made, longer, and more robust shoe than those on the market, to see if such would have a reasonable life. This was tried on 23 November 1939 on car No. 22 to Levenhall, and proved promising. An improved simple production design was then got out and from 9 October 1940 all cars on services 21 and 22 were equipped with it. Some further modifications were made in the light of experience which gave a longer life to the carbon inserts and their use was extended all over the system. Conversion of all cars was completed by April 1942 and the design of the new trolley-head duly registered as the "Edinburgh" design No.839503. Edinburgh's requirements were produced in the Shrubhill workshops but it was successfully marketed by a well-known firm for use on trolleybuses elsewhere. These shoes were in fact more economical than the old wheels, and besides largely reducing arcing had the advantage of being quite silent. The noisiness of trolley-wheels was not realised until they had been superseded. It was considered that the use of the

218

shoes had a number of advantages over bow collectors, including their silence, and when the conversion was complete, complaints ceased. One of the difficulties which remained of course, was finding the wire after turning the trolley at the terminus in the dark, but in the winter of 1940-1 a device was produced to assist in this operation. The germ of the idea was the kind of overhead mat installed where streetcar or trolleybus lines crossed railway tracks in America so that if the trolley should become dewired the car would not become stalled in front of an oncoming train. So a metal plate about 18 in. wide and five feet long was clamped immediately under the wire, and having an angle 2in. deep along its edges which were tapered in to lead a trolley-head into the middle at the end, and so on to the wire as it left it. The first one was put up at Liberton. It proved a boon and the other termini were quickly equipped too except Stanley Road where the old trolley reverser remained. Later an improved version was devised with symetrical ends having a more gradual taper, and two grooves pressed into the plate which guided the top edges of the shoe straight through it if it entered the plate from the wire at the running-on end. This could therefore be used at crossovers such as Earl Grey Street etc., and worked satisfactorily provided the through-going car did not travel too fast.

At the beginning of the war the blackout had precluded renewal of trolley wire, but this could not continue to be deferred and so a method of doing so in daylight without interrupting the service was devised. The length of wire to be renewed was isolated by the section-box switches as normally, and trams were stopped and their trolleys transferred to the wire above the other line. Thus they proceeded, stopping to remove the trolley temporarily if they met a car coming the opposite way. If two or three cars made up on the wagon with the drum from which the new wire was being run out, before it reached the end of the half-mile length, it would just be drawn aside clear of the track to let the trams pass. With comparatively little general traffic about in a forenoon the scheme worked well and caused little or no delay, though it could not be applied in some of the busier narrow streets, nor where there were centre poles, except where the cars could coast downhill with trolley tied down as on Leith Walk. Renewals at these other places had to be planned for good moonlight nights.

Fortunately there was never any real shortage of wire, and overhead fittings were produced at Shrubhill in adequate quantity, so that it was possible by careful planning to incorporate the re-alignment of all curves for tangent running and also to reconstruct all the junctions. Combined with the shoe collectors the results were effective. Drivers soon found they could negotiate curves and junctions at normal speed, confident that the trolley was unlikely to come off. The number of dewirements was reduced, and of those which continued to occur most were attributed to the use of trolley-ropes which were so liable to get caught. These however, could not be dispensed with in the blackout. The breakdown squad found a difference too. Before the war there were usually eight or nine calls to the overhead equipment per day. By the end of the war there were often none.

The permanent way presented its problems too. It was soon found easy to put in new rails on ordinary track during the day without delaying the car service. The ground was of course prepared in advance and the gangs got so adept at cutting out the old and slipping in the new with temporary bolts and packing that two minutes was all that was required. So more complicated work was undertaken. Junction work was carefully prepared beforehand, and the pieces similarly fitted in piecemeal between cars. Even the busiest junctions such as the Mound and Post Office were renewed in this way during daytime without seriously delaying the service. On the other hand the supply of rails was not so good, and renewals could not therefore be afforded until essential, even though the inside or check rail had completely gone. The use of the track brake by drivers was discouraged and in some places the position of stopping places was moved ahead or back so that the increased wear on the rails was transferred to a less worn part. Nevertheless a satisfactory standard was maintained throughout the war.

There was an interesting suspension of all service from Levenhall to Kings Road and Seafield, also Bernard Street and the length of Ferry Road on the afternoon of 23 February 1940 to permit the passage of a shotdown German aircraft, on its wheels, from East Lothian to Turnhouse.

Now let us return to that hot June of 1940 when everyone was awaiting invasion. The roofs of trams and buses were quickly painted a mixture of brown and grey to be less conspicuous. Road blocks were being set up at many places, and even a tram route could be included. On 8 June concrete blocks were built across the road at the Esk bridge Musselburgh, leaving only a single line gap on the incoming side. Service 22 was terminated at Hayweights and single-line working had to be adopted for service 21 between Hayweights and Musselburgh Town Hall, a pilotman accompanying the cars to and fro. When thoughts calmed down after the initial excitement, this block was removed about the end of July and normal services restored. Rails were renewed at the top of Leith Street in July 1940 and service 10 temporarily diverted via York Place, other cars for Princes Street occasionally going that way too at times of pressure.

Twenty-five of the latest single-deck buses were requisitioned by the Forces in July, and so as many as possible of the old vehicles which had been laid aside had to be made to run again, some with second-hand engines. This was no easy task. Then in October the coaches were taken over for ambulance and fire service duties.

One of Edinburgh's "incidents" occurred in daylight about 7.30 p.m. on 18 July 1940, when a "hit-and-run" raider attacked the Leith Docks area, no alert being sounded. One of the bombs fell right on the junction at Portland Place forming a large crater. Only the point blades were left intact at one edge, the rest had gone and the overhead was all down except for a few span wires. The stone of the surrounding buildings was well marked by flying fragments, but car 365 standing just before the points picking up passengers for town, didn't even suffer a broken window! For the next few days cars were run to each side of the obstruction, while the crater was partially filled and rails supported across it connecting the Commercial Street tracks to Granton. This overhead line was also re-connected and these services restored on the afternoon of 22 July. At mid-day five days later, the junction had been rebuilt from stock materials and service 2 was restored also.

With rising costs an increase in fares very soon became inevitable. The first proposal was that the 1d. fare be increased to 1½d., but with a short 1d. stage in each direction from Post Office, West End or Mound. In March 1940 the council approved this scheme but restricted the 1d. stage to one only, viz. Post Office to West End. The Regional Transport Commissioner refused to allow this scheme however, and bade the Corporation think out a better all round revision of fares. The result was the dividing of the whole system, tram and bus, into stages of approximately half a mile. Two stages were given for 1d., three for 1½d., five for 2d. on trams (four on buses), seven for 2½d., and a 3d. maximum as before. This proved a good basis. Where buses followed tram routes no 1d. or 1½d. fares were given. The S.M.T.Co. considered their fare scale at this time and objected to the Corporation's 3d. fare to Juniper Green which they considered too low. So the Commissioner fixed the fare to Juniper Green at 3½d. and the Corporation had to use a preprinted ticket for this fare as no more values could be arranged on the ticket machines. This ticket, coloured pale green, was cancelled by tearing out a piece. These new fares came into operation on 4 August 1940.

Lighting was still to come in for more attention however. In October 1940 the lighting circuits were re-arranged so that normal traction lamps could be used, shielded in the case of the older cars, by cardboard box type shades. On the newer cars with inset lighting fittings a standard metal shield was fitted giving a directed ray of light through the slot along the middle. It was found that the slot could be widened without great difficulty and early the following year they all had to be reinforced to prevent this being done. In September 1940 small battery lamps were fixed above the car bumpers so that a light could be shown if cars became stranded without power in the blackout. Of course the batteries didn't last and for the following winter, were, in September 1941, replaced by small candle lanterns. New destination screen and route number screens had much thinner characters so that less light was shown through. In November 1940 a detachable hood was provided for the cylindrical type headlamps on the older cars, and in April 1943 this type of hood was fitted to the headlights of the newer cars also. In some cases these headlights were also replaced by the protruding cylindrical type. Signs, of A.R.P. type, were put up to warn traffic of trams swinging on to the passing loops at Levenhall.

The lighting was now, in the circumstances satisfactory, and this was the final form until the relaxations towards the end of the war. Nevertheless drivers sometimes lost their sense of location, and there was more than one case of a car shooting off the end of the rails at a terminus. Yes, the driver knew he went over the crossover but "thought that was only the Drum Brae"! Conductors too, had their difficulties, making up their waybills in the dim light; and the unscrupulous passenger who passed off the spurious coin in the dark. Another protective measure was taken in November 1940 when three cars had a white fabric stuck on the inside of most of their windows for protection against blast. The next month a further three cars had a black fabric similarly stuck on the outside of the lower saloon windows only, and transparent strips stuck on the platform windows. From January 1941 however all cars were provided with non-splintering glass for the platform and lower saloon bulkhead windows, and with the black fabric on the outside of the lower saloon windows only. Buses were of course treated similarly.

The welding plant car was of course now disused, and in December 1940 there was a proposal to build it into a tower from one of the old wagons so that the possibility of openwork track such as prevailed after the Portland Place "incident" could be negotiated for overhead purposes. The alteration, however, was never made, and fortunately the need for such a vehicle did not arise.

The air-raid warning system was altered in December 1940, when the Ministry of Home Security decided that work should continue through "alerts" until an "imminent danger" signal was given by telephone to large industrial establishments. This signal was given when raiders were approaching only a few miles away, but as it was not given publicly trams and buses were expected to continue to run until "things started happening". Aberdeen, right on the misty coast, had suffered much from "hit-and-run" raiders, and a useful scheme was thought out. It was arranged that cars' lights would be switched on during an "alert" and when the "I.D." message was received at the electricity undertaking's substations, the attendant opened the traction circuit-breakers twice for three seconds, with one second between. The crew kept an eye on their lights, and stopped and took shelter with their passengers if they saw the signal. Another longer interruption of supply was the "I.D." clear signal and might be seen from a shelter entrance. The crews of any buses that might be passing knew to follow the tram crews' actions. Edinburgh copied this idea from 18 January 1941, and found it useful, but at the end of the year the Ministry of Home Security vetoed it, as they ruled that the "I.D." signal was not to be allowed to be made public, and that the arrangement put tramway men in a privileged position compared to other transport workers!

From January 1941 firewatchers had to be provided for Shrubhill and Head Office. Nightshift workers were of course present elsewhere, although the winter evening hours had to be covered. The nights of 13 and 14 March 1941 had "alerts" all night while the raiders were on their way to the heavy attacks on Clydebank. In Edinburgh the trams stopped more or less where they were, and remained there until taking up service again in the morning with the early shift crews. Most of the bus drivers got tired of waiting and eventually took their vehicles back to the garage. In spite of the tension, only a few incendiary bombs fell on Edinburgh. A few landed just in front of a tram standing in Montrose Terrace, but the driver was on his platform and smartly reversed his car back out of danger. Throughout the war, as it happened, Edinburgh escaped remarkably lightly. By the spring of 1941 the A.R.P. organisations were becoming very centralised, and in conformity a control room was set up by the Transport Department at Central Garage, manned overnight by a rota of eight officials with authority to initiate any action deemed necessary if the appropriate officials could not be contacted.

There had been much snow in the winter of 1940-1, and the limitations of the very old salt cars for snow plough duties were becoming apparent. Early in 1941 therefore, arrangements were made to fix ploughs to some of the oldest passenger cars, though not much use was made of these.

Conductresses were taken on from the end of May 1941, first on single-deck buses, and soon spreading to all tram and bus services. Many served extremely well, and some are on the job still. Others, and some men too, under direction of labour, were unwilling. There was a high turnover of platform staff and discipline became very difficult. In the early part of 1941 some double-deck buses were lent to London, which was at that time in dire straits. They returned in September and subsequently carried small plates recording their war service. About this time most of the earlier Daimler single-deckers had their seats removed and ranged longitudinally down both sides to enable more standing passengers to be carried. In this Ministry of War Transport scheme up to 30 standees were allowed, but the idea was not popular, and no further buses were altered. Further cuts in the bus services were effected in April 1941, the last buses from the central points now being about 10.30 p.m. This nevertheless compared well with cities in the south.

In December 1941 the Ministry of War Transport provided the first of a few new buses for the City's fleet. Most of these were of makes strange to Edinburgh, some double-deck and some single-deck, but everything was welcome, even some of the Ministry's standard utility Bedford buses. Details will be found in the rolling-stock section. In May 1942 the army released the buses they had requisitioned earlier and these were duly overhauled, repainted, and restored to service. The utility Bedfords ran in the dark brown paint as supplied at first, but later these and some of the new double-deckers were painted grey though lined out as normally. The only standard vehicle to receive this grey livery was the single-deck bus A51. Otherwise the Department was able to continue, on only a slightly reduced scale, its regular repainting programme of trams and buses in the normal colours throughout the war. Dundee Corporation rejected two of their Daimler single-deckers released by the army. Both had been badly damaged, but Edinburgh seized the opportunity to acquire them and produced practically standard single-deckers with them, albeit in the grey livery.

Nevertheless travel was now becoming very difficult at rush hours. Edinburgh had never been queue conscious, and the scenes at some of the busier stopping places could only be described as disgraceful. No doubt the same happened elsewhere, and the Ministry of War Transport issued Regulations, soon afterwards amended, requiring the formation of queues. Even the Regulation of Traffic (Formation of Queues) (No. 2) Order, 1942, proved ineffective, until it was enforced by the use of inspectors, when the citizens gradually came to appreciate the advantage of orderliness. The older buses with double entrances had to have the front one barred up. Circular boards bearing a large "Q" and inscribed "this side" or "other side" were fixed to many stopping place poles. Later some of the principal passenger islands were lengthened and divided by a small barrier to segregate different groups of services. At the foot of Lothian Road a second island was laid down as well on 3 October 1942 to cater for three groups there. New islands were provided at Bernard Street, Portland Place and Tollcross. In an attempt to assist the longer distance passenger, it was proposed in June 1942, to charge a 2d. minimum fare on a proportion of the cars, suitably indicated, at rush hours. A trial was to be made on service 11 but was vetoed by the council.

To help in the collection of fares, little red boxes appeared on the vehicles into which the passenger was invited to drop his coins on alighting if they hadn't been collected. While these were fairly successful, the cost of emptying them proved uneconomic. Another scheme was the enlistment of the male office staff as auxiliary conductors on their journeys from and to work. A white linen armlet was issued to them. Soon afterwards the scheme was extended, volunteers being accepted from the public generally. A card of authority and a navy-blue armlet were issued for use within defined morning and evening rush hours, and the volunteers were not asked to pay their fare when acting thus. Many people did a useful job in this way, but the scheme was subject to much abuse, as some made a practice of doing all their travelling in this capacity whether their services were required or not. The scheme was of course terminated after the war.

In June 1942 the Ministry of War Transport asked that the number of stopping places be reduced in order to save fuel and wear and tear. This resulted in about 120 stops being removed on the tramway system. Others near the crest of a hill were moved over the top to lessen the re-starting effort. For the buses this meant many stopping-place poles and flags for hitherto the marking of bus stops had not been general away from the centre of the city. The buses might stop where hailed though regular travellers used customary places. Where stops were marked it sometimes applied to both directions though no pole or flag appeared on the other side of the street. The cast-iron stopping-place poles were no longer available, and a plain steel tube had to be used instead. For a time the use of these was restricted to suburban bus stops, but eventually tram stops too had to succumb to austerity.

One bus was spared to start a new service on 14 September 1942. This bus ran alternate trips from Pennywell Road to the Comely Bank tram terminus and to the Granton tram route at the top of Granton Road. Both routes were described as No. 18. There was considerable rush hour traffic on the latter route to Ferranti's factory, and as no more fuel could be spared for it the Ministry of War Transport wanted the Corporation to go ahead and complete the tramway extension to Crewe Toll, even if only one track were laid for a shuttle service of one or a group of cars. The Corporation were unwilling however and eventually succeeded in persuading the Ministry to drop the idea. However as the curve at the top of Granton Road was calling for renewal the new junction, already on hand in store, was laid in instead.

A canteen was provided at Central Garage and run by a staff committee. Opened on 12 October 1942, it was followed on 10 July 1944 by another at Leith Depot. Shrubhill works was, of course, situated quite conveniently for either.

Last car times were made a little earlier from 1 November 1942 and the buses followed suit too, three weeks later. There was a further cut in bus service frequencies, mainly in the forenoon and on Sundays from 1 March 1943.

The next "headache" was the instruction from the Ministry of War Transport that a proportion of the buses must be adapted to run on producer-gas in order to save fuel. A good deal of experimental work had been done in the south on petrol engines, but apart from some very old vehicles, Edinburgh now had only diesels and these were more difficult to deal with. The standard two-wheeled trailer units were supplied by the Ministry, some of the latest standard single-deckers fitted with towing gear, and experiments went ahead. Buses A71, A86 and A88 were among the nine adapted, and a fair measure of success achieved. About April 1943 the buses were run on the Barnton route, but the inherent difficulties of the system, lack of pulling-power, the use of trailers and the troubles with the gas plants themselves, made Edinburgh just as glad as every other operator in the country was to drop the scheme entirely as soon as the Ministry of War Transport allowed it. The last "gas" run was on 7 October 1944.

A new tram service was started on 19 April 1943, between Piershill and Drum Brae via London Road and Leith Street. This was number 26 and when route colours were restored after the war used blue over red. Side window boards were white, but at first paper bills were used, and the term Drum Brae South came into use. Some of the part-day extra cars and crews from services 1 and 5 were used for the new service. On 16 September 1943 service 16 was extended daily to Fairmilehead, while the part-day extra cars on service 11 then ran only as far as Braids, displaying no service number until June 1946 when No. 28 was brought into use for them. Colours, eventually, were blue over green. Bus service 9 was extended to Davidson's Mains on 14 November 1943.

In April 1944 the use of double-deck buses was extended to service 13 which was now serving Scottish Command H.Q., while the following month they were also used for part-day extra journeys on service 4 between Holyrood and Sighthill. Service 9 acquired them too. "Holidays at Home" brought increased traffic and in August 1944 tram service 4 was extended to Kings Road and tram service 15 to Fairmilehead. By the end of the year the position was becoming a little easier and some strengthening of tram and bus services became possible. The Ministry of Home Security was also persuaded to permit some relaxation of the blackout. From the middle of November 1944 the trams were wired with two circuits of lamps on each deck, one as then screened, and the other with unscreened lights as pre-war though of lower wattage. Normally both were used but the latter had to be switched off during "alerts". The platform light was also allowed again too, except during alerts". These concessions were indeed welcome.

New side window boards, yellow with blue letters, were provided in December 1944 for tram services 14 and 25.

Came May 1945 and "V.E." day. In the evening Princes Street was packed with humanity, many up to all sorts of pranks including pole climbing. But despite the crowds the services were kept moving and people did not have to walk home. Full normal lighting was quickly restored in the vehicles and as they went through the workshops the white paint was removed from the bumpers etc. The masks were removed from the headlights, the older type trams being left with an orthodox plain glass headlamp for the first time. Brake stop lights were also restored. The route colours were not restored on trams until 31 October 1946 however, and even then it was some time before crews got used to adjusting them. Most people had forgotten them anyway. Soon those few buses which had worn the grey livery were appearing in standard colours, and the wooden seats and other makeshift features of the utility and semi-utility buses gave way to the normal equipment. The bus fleet was steadily augmented with new vehicles.

Although there were still difficulties of various kinds, the war was now past and Edinburgh Corporation Transport had come through well. The tram and bus fleet had been maintained to more or less the usual standards. Contrary to what has sometimes been suggested, the permanent way had been adequately maintained too and was still sound, while the overhead equipment was perhaps in better shape than ever. Junction renewal was still being done in daytime, but on 23 August 1945 there was an unfortunate slight "misfit" at the east end of George Street and for some hours the incoming service 24 cars had to proceed by Frederick Street and Princes Street, an unusual sight. To assist in loading and despatching cars in Waterloo Place a second crossover was laid in about this time. A change was also made at London Road junction, the island on the down line at the junction, and at which London Road cars did not stop, being removed and replaced by a new one opposite Gayfield Square. There was already one in London Road.

A bus service was run from the Corstorphine tram terminus to Turnhouse for an air display on 15 September 1945 and this became a regular procedure on such occasions. Some bus service alterations were made on 21 October 1945. Service 4 was terminated regularly at Holyrood; Service 16 was terminated at Ardmillan Terrace, while service 5 was extended to Sighthill. Part day service 5 buses turned at Ardmillan Terrace as before and were numbered 25. The tours were restarted, on a limited scale, at Easter 1946. Bus service 18 was now run between Goldenacre and Drylaw Mains, while its alternate journeys to Comely Bank were taken over by a new service, No.17, between Randolph Place and Muirhouse. A part-day tram service between North Junction Street and Stenhouse via George Street introduced in October 1946 was numbered 22 with blue colours and blue side window boards the part-day service to Musselburgh with this number having been withdrawn. The all-night bus services were resumed for the winter in 1946 being now numbered 28 and 29. Additional rolling-stock was required quickly and so eleven secondhand trams were bought from Manchester Corporation, the first arriving in November 1946.

Bus services 4 and 5 were extended out to Calder Crescent in February 1947 as the housing scheme extended ever outwards. From June 1947 tram service 18 was extended to Liberton terminus during part of the evening. The Mound to the Castle summer bus service was restarted on 2 August 1947, and a special service provided under contract to British European Airways between their George Street office and Turnhouse airport. For the winter of 1947-8 the all-night bus service was recast on a wider scale, an hourly service being run on five routes as follows :—

1 Craigmillar to Crewe Road North via Bridges, Princes Street, and Stockbridge.
2 Bath Street, Portobello, to Firhill via Princes Street and Gilmore Place.
3 Bonnington Terrace to Manse Road, Corstorphine, via Goldenacre, Broughton Street, and Princes Street.
4 Waverley to Sighthill.
5 Foot of Leith Walk to Morningside Station via Princes Street.

A flat fare of 6d. applied on each route, but ordinary fares were charged after 3.20 a.m. for the benefit of early workers. The foregoing separate series of numbers was adopted and the terminal stances indicated by black plates lettered in white. These services gained considerable popularity and were now continued all the year round.

New passenger islands were erected on the incoming side at Waverley Steps and at the foot of North Bridge, and the stopping place for cars proceeding to Leith Street at the Register cut out, so that passengers had to guess from which direction the first car would come and proceed to that island.

Post-war industrial unrest came to the undertaking in April 1948 when there was a strike of the body shop staff.

Accommodation now had to be found quickly for the expanding bus fleet, and this at a time when building was very difficult. Vehicles were already being parked overnight in the forecourt of Central Garage. The piece of vacant ground across the railway line from Dryden Street, entering from McDonald Road was therefore adopted as an open-air bus park, a heating system being provided for the radiators.

Indicative of the trend, the island at Hayweights was now being run into so often by vehicles being driven around the corner at an uncontrollable speed, in spite of warning signs, that it was deemed advisable to resite it in Bridge Street. Bus service 17 was now extended down to Granton Square and bus service 18 extended to Davidson's Mains. From July 1949 a summer Saturday and Sunday afternoon bus service was put on between Parkhead Drive, Sighthill, and Cramond, running via Corstorphine High Street, Drum Brae and Barnton. It was numbered 20 and a flat fare of 3d. was charged. Bus service 18 was also extended at weekends to Silverknowes Promenade to which the new access road had been completed.

The manager, Mr. McLeod died while on holiday in September 1948, and was succeeded by the deputy manager Mr. W. M. Little. The latter had served in the undertaking till 1941 when he went to the managership at St. Helens, and later Reading, before returning to his native city as deputy manager in 1946. His appointment was a popular one, — but so far as the public were concerned it was soon to wane. It will nevertheless be appreciated that in modern times at least, there must be very few transport managers who do not have to suffer a disgruntled public. The Report for the year ended 28 May 1949 intimated deficiencies in both the tram and bus accounts and no contributions could be made towards the renewals or reserve funds.

An interesting alteration to the tram services was the extension of services 7, 11, and 28 from Stanley Road down the hill to the foot of Craighall Road. This commenced on 17 October 1949 and provided service on Craighall Road after an interval of more than thirty years. A crossover wire was erected at the new terminus and the old trolley reverser removed at Stanley Road. To meet rapid housing development in the respective areas two new bus services were started on 24 October 1949. No. 24 ran from St. Andrew Square to Bingham Avenue, while No. 25 gave a shuttle service from Liberton tram terminus to Burdiehouse. Next however, Mr. Little proposed to abandon the number 18 tram service, which was a poor paying one, and replace it with a double-deck bus service between Burdiehouse and Davidson's Mains via Newington, Melville Drive, West End, and Queensferry Road. This new bus service took the number 18 and started on 26

March 1950. The shuttle service No. 25 from Liberton terminus was of course withdrawn, and the existing bus service 18 was renumbered 28.

Soon afterwards the Davidson's Mains bus terminus was moved to Quality Street and a cut constructed through the old grass triangle at the cross roads to make a turning-circle for the buses terminating there. From 7 May 1950 bus service 13 ceased to meander through the streets and crescents of the west end, being diverted via Atholl Place and Palmerston Place. The first passenger shelters had recently been erected, the simple "inverted L" type at Waverley Bridge and Nicolson Square, and later, one of the "tunnel" type at Fillyside Road. These were a great boon and their provision was gradually widely extended. A passenger island was provided at Waterloo Place, the original west-most crossover being removed. Other crossovers were removed at the top of Broughton Street and at the east end of George Street.

It was clear something would have to be done about revenue, and an increase in fares was discussed by the council during most of 1950, though it was not until 4 February 1951 that a new scale came into operation. With this the penny fare disappeared. 1½d., 2½d. and 3d. fares covering three, five, or over five stages respectively applied on all services, the fare to Juniper Green remaining at 3½d. Much time had been lost however and with the deficits still mounting a further increase was already called for. This next increase took place on 2 December 1951, when the maximum fare became 5d. and the children's fare 1½d.

The abandonment of the tramway system was by now being whispered, and in June 1950 the manager put forward a report which recommended no extension of the system, and that 25% of the rolling-stock and a corresponding proportion of the existing system be scrapped. Also that only motor buses be used in replacement. The Transport sub-committee, of which Councillor Harkess was convener, and the Civic Amenities committee endorsed this recommendation, but the council remitted it back at the end of July. Much correspondence ensued in the press. In September the committee returned with the same recommendation, and a special meeting of the council was held on 12 October to discuss it. It was now quite evident Mr. Little envisaged an early end to the tramway system and its replacement by motor buses, though a section of the council seemed loth to commit the city to such a drastic change. Nevertheless at their meeting on 2 November the committee's recommendation was approved by 41 votes to 17. After a further spate of "letters to the editor" there was then a lull till the following autumn when the actual replacement proposals were brought up.

Meantime, while the older cars were scrapped, track main- tenance deteriorated to the point of comment. Some junctions, e.g. Theatre Royal, and Leith Depot, were repaved in concrete but this was not satisfactory. The facing junction at Waterloo Place, never in ordinary use, was removed in October 1950. That at the top of Granton Road for the Crewe Toll extension was removed for the second time without ever being used, at the end of 1950. The poles were removed from this partially constructed extension in March 1951 and the rails in October 1953. The junction in Great Junction Street leading across to Duke Street was taken out in January 1951 and crossovers in London Road and at Corstorphine Station Road removed later in that year.

On the other hand the resurfacing of Princes Street had to be started and as complete abandonment of the tramway system was as yet unaccepted, the tracks between Castle Street and the West End were relaid in concrete with an asphalt surface. The passenger islands in Princes Street were also resited and enlarged in the summer of 1951 being provided with modern lighting and adequately illuminated "pawl-posts", though as the latter were by no means robust, the term was now a misnomer. Automatic point controllers were provided at the Hanover Street and Mound junctions, while that at Frederick Street was arranged to be set for the Comely Bank cars by manual operation of a switch on the adjacent centre-pole by the drivers, in each case being reset for the main line by overhead skate. The Post Office junctions con- tinued to be operated from the pavement box but this was now enclosed in a kiosk. Several bus stops were now indicated by con- crete poles incorporating a light in the head.

The Electricity Board having intimated that they wished to cease the D.C. traction supply in Portobello, the Transport Depart- ment installed their own mercury-arc rectifier equipment at the back of Portobello depot, and brought this into use on 4 March 1951.

Staffing was giving rise to difficulty and on Saturdays and Sundays the Corporation had many buses to spare, which the S.M.T. were glad to hire to augment their fleet in the busy summers of 1951 and 1952. More accommodation for buses was still required, and another open-air bus park was formed on ground adjoining the back of Gorgie depot where simple workshop facilities could be available. This was brought into use on 3 June 1951 and the buses on services 1, 2, 4, 5, 18, and 21 were then garaged there. The tram rails outside were removed.

On September 18 1951 the routes proposed for withdrawal under the 25% scheme were disclosed. These were Comely Bank, Slateford, and Stenhouse. There was another spate of press "correspondence" and much argument in the council and elsewhere. This scheme was however approved on 27 September, though it was some time before it could be put into effect. Meantime changes in bus services took place. Service 18 was shortened at Blackhall from 30 December 1951. More comprehensive alterations applied from 17 February 1952. Service 2 was extended to Newcraighall, the double-deckers turning just short of the village as they could not go under the railway bridge, and service 7 was withdrawn. Service 2 was also extended via Stevenson Drive into the new Broomhouse housing scheme, being further extended to Bankhead Broadway at factory hours for the benefit of the Sighthill Industrial Estate. Service 5 was re-routed via Gorgie Road to the Sighthill terminus. In the evenings and on Saturday afternoons and Sundays this service also then cut direct from Junction Street across the Foot of Leith walk to Lochend Road eliminating that portion of the route round through Bernard Street. The Corporation intended also to withdraw service 6, a move which Councillor Harkess found difficulty in explaining since the part of the route between the Saughtonhall area and Haymarket via Roseburn, run only at "rush" hours was well patronised and Saughtonhall would have been left without any service. The residents argued their case before the Traffic Commissioners, and kept their service. With the demolition of the railway bridge at Davidson's Mains double-deck buses were put on service 11 from 31 March 1952, but the service was also reduced to a twenty-minutes frequency. Some journeys on service 21 were diverted to the Princess Margaret Rose hospital on Saturday and Sunday afternoons from 12 April 1952.

The revenue situation was very difficult and in order to secure every potential a contract was arranged with an advertising contractor to use the upper deck side panels of trams and buses. Many people expressed misgivings at this "degrading" practice. Nevertheless it brought in several thousand pounds a year. The advertisements began to appear at the beginning of 1952. Buses were now used on occasions to augment tramway services, should there be a shortage of cars, or a breakdown. The electric heaters were removed from the trams : after all the buses did not have such amenities. The passenger islands at the Waverley Bridge were removed in January 1952.

By the end of 1951 the citizens were getting properly interested in the future of their transport system, and many ward meetings were held at which the convener or other councillors were invariably left in no doubt as to the ratepayers desire to retain the tramway system. The council were apparently still divided and unfortunately, as is so often the case, the question became largely a political one. Certain of the so-called Progressive councillors blossomed into special propagandists for tram scrapping. On the other hand a few of the better informed refused to agree right to the end. Some of the arguments brought forward by the scrapping propagandists were quite fanciful and repeatedly shot down. Figures, "facts", and costs were quoted in confusion. One or two meetings ended in near disorder. The Corporation were asked to accept a loan of a modern tramcar to let the public see what could be done. An independent inquiry was sought, — and a plebiscite, — but to all these quite reasonable requests the council steadfastly refused.

In places the track was now in a deplorable condition and the council sought from the Ministry of Transport, power to borrow £250,000 for renewals. This the Ministry refused as nearly half of the work proposed should have been provided for out of revenue. They were however prepared to sanction £150,000 for certain stretches of route which Brigadier Langley came to inspect. At the 1952 elections, the Dalry ward was fought on the transport issue and the tram-scrapping councillor lost his seat.

The first of the tram routes to be withdrawn was Comely Bank which was replaced by a service of new single-deck buses on 1 June 1952, starting from South St. David Street and carrying the service number 29. The terminus at Comely Bank was moved out to Craigleith Hill Crescent. The junction at Frederick Street was taken out immediately. The single-deck buses did not continue for long however, being replaced by double-deckers on 7 July.

It was now evident that the ruling body in the council were determined to get rid of the trams. Any criticism of the idea was resented. A prominent member said they should not pay attention to newspaper correspondence. So the expected recommendation to scrap the tramways entirely was made public on 15 July 1952. The controversy of course grew fiercer than ever, both inside and outside the council. Few issues can have attracted so much interest over so long a period. The question came before the council finally on 25 September 1952, the decision to scrap the system within three years or as soon thereafter as possible, and replace it with motor buses, being reached by 31 votes to 21. But before the minutes were confirmed at the next council meeting on 6 November a public meeting was held in the Central Halls three days before. Some 400 persons attended and unanimously resolved that the council rescind its decision. Strangely Councillor Harkess was present but didn't oppose the motion! Of course the council paid no attention to this or to the protests and representations received from several local organisations, though in fact 20% of the councillors now refrained from voting. Even an awkward question which the Edinburgh and District Trades Council had in the interval raised with the Town Clerk made no difference. They asked how it was that figures that had been quoted to the Traffic Commissioners by the City Chamberlain in support of recent applications for fares increases, and apparently also used in preparing "the case" for motor buses, differed very greatly from those in the official accounts. The City Chamberlain had stated that from May 1945 to May, 1951 the trams lost £452,240 and the buses lost £84,053, while the accounts showed the former to have in fact a surplus of £70,218 and the latter to have lost £757,804. In a most remarkable reply that "both sets of figures were quite correct" (!) the City Chamberlain admitted that in the figures advanced by him he had deducted £615,836 from the tramways surplus and paid in income tax, while £720,000 spent on purchasing new buses was "not included" in the bus deficit!

Councillor Harkess, the convener of the Transport committee resigned in April 1953, and when his successor in office came to seek re-election in Craigentinny ward in May 1955, the electors expressed their continuing disatisfaction by preferring his opponent.

All this time the finances were going from bad to worse and another increase in fares was called for, involving a Ministry of Transport Order since the statutory maximum was now exceeded. This took effect on 7 December 1952, and the minimum fare became 2d. The early morning return tickets now cost 6d.

It was alleged the Nos. 25 and 26 tram services terminus just west of Drum Brae constituted a danger and to obviate it the former service was extended to the Maybury while the latter was shortened at the Zoo. This alteration was made on 24 August 1952. A week earlier double-deckers had been introduced on bus service 12 consequent on a slight lowering at the railway bridge at Lady Road, and single line traffic with signals through the skew arch at Portobello station. Crossovers were removed at Iona Street and in Ferry Road at Goldenacre and east of Bonnington Terrace. A crossover wire was erected at Saughtonhall Drive for "rush-hour" cars.

On 14 December 1952 tram service 2 between Stenhouse and Granton via George Street, and also the Saturday part route service 22, — was replaced by a double-deck bus service numbered 22. The buses of course could not cut direct between Hope Street and Shandwick Place as the trams had done, and instead proceeded via Queensferry Street, Melville Street and Manor Place. Going towards York Place they also departed from the former tram route by using North St. David Street. It was not till March 1953 however that the overhead equipment on the George Street and Comely Bank routes was cut down, and rail lifting proceeded on the latter. New bus stop poles surmounted by a vertical tubular shaped lantern appeared in the central parts of the city. The "flags" were now aranged to show the service numbers to which they applied, these being displayed in the bottom section of the frame by small number plates which could be readily altered as required.

Bus services 4 and 5 were reorganised on 1 March 1953 so that double-deckers could be used on both the new services which were re-numbered 34 and 35. The arrangement was that from Sighthill terminus service 34 followed the old service 5 route through Gorgie, Fountainbridge, West End, Stockbridge, Leith and Lochend to London Road but then continued via Leith Street and Post Office to Tron Church where it took up the old No. 4 route via Fountainbridge, Slateford, and Longstone back to Sighthill. Service 35 followed this long circuit in the opposite direction.

The Stenhouse tram route closed down finally on 28 March 1953 when service 3 between there and Newington station was replaced the following day by a double-deck bus service of the same number which was extended from Newington to Greenend. At the same time the route was also covered by another bus service numbered 33 which continued from Newington by Lady Road and Old Dalkeith Road to a terminus at the new Inch housing scheme. The passenger islands in Dalry Road at Haymarket were removed a few days before the number 3 service was withdrawn. Bus service 3 was renumbered 43. The tram line out as far as Gorgie depot continued in use for access to the depot for another five weeks until service 4 was withdrawn on 2 May 1953. The No. 4 double-deck bus service which replaced it on the following day was much longer, being extended at the one end from Northfield Broadway to Bingham Road, service 24 being concurrently withdrawn, and at the other end via Craiglockhart Avenue and Firhill to Oxgangs Terrace in the Colinton Mains housing scheme. Thus did a route to town from this area envisaged by the old Colinton Tramways Company forty years earlier come to fruition. St. Andrew Street was used coming up from York Place only, buses in the other direction using St. David Street as was now the usual practice. The pits in Gorgie depot were now filled and the premises converted to a bus garage, the service 1 trams which had used it being transferred to Tollcross depot. Cutting down the overhead and track lifting commenced soon after. With the reduction in tram service one of each "twin" passenger island in Princes Street was removed on the south side, and all the north side islands removed and replaced by single temporary wooden ones so that they could be cleared away for the occasion of a state visit in June 1953.

Sixty cars were sold to a scrap merchant, Jas. N. Connell Ltd. of Coatbridge for £90 each complete, and the method of transporting them was interesting. The cars were driven under their own power to the Corstorphine terminus at the Maybury where they were winched up ramp rails from the track on to Messrs. Connell's special low-loading articulated lorry. Additional garage accommodation was acquired in January 1954 by purchase of premises in East London Street adjoining Central Garage.

The original 25% reduction in the tramway system was now accomplished but of course by this time complete abandonment was authorised and plans were proceeding as quickly as possible. Delivery of the requisite double-deck buses and training tram drivers in bus driving limited progress however and so there was a lull before the next conversion. Meantime some tram service alterations were effected on 31 January 1954 as follows : Service 10 was diverted via Junction Street and Ferry Road to Granton, while service 16 was diverted from this route to Bernard Street in place of service 10, but became a part-day service only. Service 20 was operated during "rush-hours" only and service 27 was withdrawn in the evenings and on Sundays. Service 15 was shortened at the Braids and service 28 withdrawn. Complaint from Fairmilehead however succeeded in restoring the 15 and 28 cuts on 10 May. Bus service 4 was also extended from Oxgangs Terrace to Fairmilehead on 7 March 1954, service 21 being withdrawn.

The next tramway conversion was the well-known No. 1 service between Corstorphine and Liberton, which buses replaced on 28 March 1954, carrying the number 31, and extended from Liberton via Lasswade Road as far as Captain's Road pending completion of suitable road access into the new Hyvot's Bank housing scheme, which was reached on 8 May. A temporary shuttle bus service, numbered 25 had covered the route beyond the tram terminus since 25 January 1954. As now became the usual practice the bus service had many fewer stopping places than the trams had had. The remaining Corstorphine tram services 12, 25, and 26, were replaced on 11 July 1954 by buses, all of which made their terminus in Meadow Place at Drum Brae crossroads, and which they approached via Featherhall Crescent North, returning via the main road. Only service 25 followed the same route east of Princes Street, and it of course used St. David Street going eastwards. Service 12 left its old tram route at Fillyside Road and traversed the Craigentinny housing scheme to Inchview Terrace on the Portobello road proceeding on to Portobello Town Hall. Service 26 was run from Princes Street across to Waterloo Place and via Regent Road to Piershill, being extended a short distance to Restalrig Avenue. The old bus service 12 was renumbered 42.

During the following week some trams were run over the line to be loaded on to Connell's lorry at the Maybury as before, but at the next weekend the overhead was cut down between the section-insulators at Wester Coates and Belmont, as track lifting with

236

urgent roadway reconstruction between Roseburn and Saughton-hall had to be started immediately. This work entailed traffic diversion through minor residential streets, a practice which now became very prevalent. Messrs. Connell thereafter loaded up their cars in North Junction Street where track and overhead were still "in situ" though carrying no tram service.

In the summer of 1954 bus service 4 was extended to Hillend Park on Saturdays and Sundays. Tram service 27 was shortened to Craiglockhart Station on 6 June 1954, the indication Polwarth being shown on the screens. It was however extended again as far as Happy Valley on 17 October 1954. Bus services 9 and 11 were diverted from South Charlotte Street to Castle Street and George Street on their way to and from Charlotte Square from 9 August 1954.

An overall picture of the traffic situation and requirements at any moment, particularly useful on special occasions such as an important football match, became possible in 1954 with the provision of radio communication between a control room set up at the Head Office and a number of patrol vans, breakdown lorry and tower-wagon.

The time was now approaching when the Musselburgh tram service would be withdrawn, and as this was of course outwith the city boundaries, beyond which the Corporation had no power to run buses, a question of policy had to be decided. Any application for the necessary powers would have been opposed by Scottish Omnibuses Ltd. as the Scottish Motor Traction Company had become, and a new agreement with that concern was in any case now necessary in view of the expansion of the city. This new agreement in lieu of the existing one which was fundamentally that of 1920, provided that the Company "will not operate any route wholly within the city boundaries and the Corporation will not operate any route outwith the city boundaries". The protective fare within the city boundary was modified as follows : On Corporation fares up to 4d. the Company to charge 1½d. more, and on 5d. fares 1d. more. Fares over 5d. were to be co-ordinated. The agreement was completed on 1 July 1954 but did not take full effect till varying later dates as noted. The defined spheres of operation were logical and meant that the Corporation could now provide the long sought service to Gilmerton, at the expense of abandoning Musselburgh, whose residents were at first disappointed. The new protective fare arrangements on the other hand were clearly advantageous to the Company and to suburban passengers.

Tram service 15 between Fairmilehead and Kings Road via London Road was replaced on 19 September 1954 by buses following the same route, though eastwards via St. David Street, and extended to a new terminus at Morton Street near Joppa. The old bus service 15 was renumbered 45. This was followed by the replacement of tram service 5 from Morningside Station to Piershill via Salisbury Place and London Road by buses with the same number and same route, though extended slightly at the Piershill end to Restalrig Avenue, on 31 October 1954. Then the tram route between Waterloo Place and Levenhall with services 20 and 21 was abandoned without any replacement service as such after the last car on 13 November 1954. On this date bus service 26 was extended from Piershill to a new terminus at Seaview Terrace, beyond Joppa, and described as Eastfield, thus covering the whole of the tram route from Waterloo Place to that point. On this date also service 25 was likewise extended from Kings Road to Seaview Terrace, and service 12 was extended from Portobello Town Hall to Niddrie Road at Mountcastle Drive South. Service between Portobello and Musselburgh was now catered for by a new Scottish Omnibuses route traversing Portobello as from the same date and to which the new protective fare agreement applied. Over most other routes this agreement did not come into operation until 5 December when some further re-arrangement of Corporation services took place, and in the case of Corstorphine not until 9 December.

The rearrangement of services from 5 December 1954 included the withdrawal of bus services 8, 14, 16, and 45 which were all operated by single-deckers by reason of the low railway bridges at Abbeymount and at Stoneyport beyond Slateford. The road had however been lowered at the latter so that double-deckers were run on the main new service. This was number 44 and ran from East-field via Milton Road and London Road to Princes Street then covering the old service 8 to Juniper Green. The other new services were still single-deck services at infrequent intervals between Portobello Town Hall and Juniper Green via Duddingston Road, Willowbrae Road, Royal Park Terrace, Abbeymount, Canongate, and High Street, whence those numbered 45 followed the old route of that number via Tollcross and Colinton Road, and those numbered 46 followed the old 14 route via Fountainbridge and Slateford. The time-table for service 45 was arranged to provide connections with the Scottish Omnibuses Balerno via Slateford service and the latter's Balerno via Colinton service was considerably reduced. Another extension at the same date was 33 to Fernieside Drive at the one end and to Saughton Road at the other.

When the Portobello tram route was withdrawn the overhead equipment in Waterloo Place and Regent Road was promptly cut down. The junction in Leith Walk at London Road had already been taken out. Then when the cars left in Portobello depot were to be taken away it was found that their escape route by Seafield was cut, some track having been lifted for road repairs. So the cars had to be towed up via Regent Road by motor lorry. The Portobello depot was not converted to a bus garage as the small site was awkward and restricted.

Such was the need of additional revenue that fares were raised again on 17 October 1954 when only two stages were given for 2d. The early morning 6d. return fare was also withdrawn, but to ease the lot of travellers to and from the outlying housing schemes, the maximum fare was reduced to 4d. Less than two months afterwards another wage award upset calculations again, and from 27 February 1955, threepence carried the passenger only four stages instead of six. From 9 January 1955 bus service 3 was also extended to Saughton Road and at the other end to Moredun Park Grove, while a week later bus service 9 was extended to Silverknowes Roundabout. Operation of so many buses in busy streets such as Princes Street now began to show difficulties, and it became necessary to spread out the stopping places so that different groups of services stopped at different points, which generally were sited well away from the intersections of the side streets, and were thus less convenient than the tram stopping places.

The next tram conversion was on 3 April 1955 when service 8 gave way to double-deck buses, also numbered 8, and with the route extended from Granton into the Muirhouse housing scheme, and at the other end out to Gilmerton Station Road thus providing the first Corporation service through the old village. This was followed by service 27 on 7 August 1955, the replacing double-deck bus service 27 being extended to Oxgangs Terrace at the one end and to Crewe Toll at the other instead of the tram terminus at Granton Road Station. A small bus park for reversing and loading was constructed on the north side of Ferry Road immediately east of the "double bridges" which had insufficient headroom for double-deckers, though this didn't preclude drivers from having a go on occasions! The Colinton tram route then closed down with the conversion of services 9 and 10 to double-deck buses on 23 October 1955. Both were extended at the Colinton end only, viz. — service 9 via Woodhall Road to Bonaly Road, and service 10 to Westgarth Avenue. Soon afterwards on 25 December 1955, the latter was altered to proceed to the terminus outwards via Redford Drive, while the former was further extended to Torphin Road from 29 January 1956. The old bus services numbered 9 and 10 were renumbered 39 and 40. Concurrently with the Colinton conversion bus service 19 was altered to a circular route, extending from its former Randolph Place to Pilton route by Boswall Parkway, Wardie Crescent, Granton Road, Goldenacre, Canonmills, Broughton Street, York Place, George Street, Charlotte Square, and Queensferry Street. Previously, on 19 June 1955, service 26 was extended up Drum Brae to Drum Brae Drive, to which the indication Clermiston was applied from April 1956. Service 22 was extended on 17 July 1955 from Granton via Muirhouse, Pennywell Road, Groathill Road, and Telford Road to the service 18 terminus at the Whitehill Garage Blackhall. On this date too, a new double-deck bus service, number 47 was started between Randolph Place and Drylaw Circus via Orchard Brae, Blackhall, Telford Road, and Groathill Road. On 4 December 1955 however the service was altered to run via Orchard Brae, Crewe Toll, Telford Road, and Groathill Road and was extended to Muirhouse.

Two interesting temporary "express" services were run to the "Highland" Show held in June 1955 near the Maybury. One, number 49, ran from Waverley Bridge via Frederick Street, Comely Bank, Blackhall, Barnton, and Maybury Road; the other, number 50, from Atholl Crescent direct via Corstorphine Road. The former had one or two picking up points. Double-deckers were used. The Corporation took over the service to Turnhouse Airport under their own licence from the beginning of 1956 instead of running under contract to British European Airways. The night bus services were augmented, a new route, numbered 6, from Gilmerton to Blackhall starting on 5 December 1955, though it had been operated during the 1955 Festival period, and over a slightly longer route extending to Groathill Road North. Night service 1 was also extended to Oxgangs Terrace, and later, on 26 December 1955, night service 4 was extended to Hay Drive.

The converted Gorgie depot and its adjoining bus park were not entirely suitable as such and incapable of extension, so a site for a completely new bus garage to serve the western side of the city was acquired at Longstone. This was erected complete with all offices and staff amenities and brought into use on 23 October 1955. Later, in 1957, the Gorgie premises were closed and sold.

The sixth increase in fares in less than five years took effect on 29 January 1956 when the fivepenny fare was reintroduced and the child's fare became 2d.

So the last year of tramway operation had arrived and we may look at the situation as it then was. Fairmilehead, Liberton, Grange, Marchmont, Melville Drive, Mound, Hanover Street, Seafield, Junction Street, Ferry Road, Stanley Road, and the Granton Circle were still in operation with services 6, 7, 11, 13, 14, 16, 17, 19, 23 and 28. The tracks and overhead had already been removed from George Street, Charlotte Square, Hope Street, and Shandwick Place out to Corstorphine, Stenhouse, and Slateford; also Comely Bank, Leith Walk to Abbeyhill, Craigentinny Avenue to Kings Road, and most of the Waterloo Place to Joppa and Eastfield section. Gorgie and Portobello depots were closed and the substations at Robertson Avenue, Turnhouse Road, Pennywell, Portobello, and Musselburgh no longer produced traction current. On most of the main roads complete reconstruction was carried out, and the cost of these works was assuming alarming proportions. Princes Street itself, except for the portion between Charlotte Street and Castle Street done in 1951, was now in an almost impossible condition despite repeated extensive patching and it was clear reconstruction could be delayed no longer. So in March 1956 all eastgoing traffic except the trams was diverted into George Street and a gyratory scheme operated in Charlotte Square and St. Andrew Square, the latter necessitating the service 16 trams being diverted to Leith Street. To compensate for lack of bus transport eastwards in Princes Street extra trams were run on the outer circle of service 6. The work was pushed ahead rapidly, the tram tracks being left as they were meantime, and thus for the most part slightly below the adjoining finished surfaces. Light collapsible barriers were placed where the discrepancy in level might be dangerous.

Meantime on 11 March 1956 service 7 was taken over by buses, and tram service 17 withdrawn. The latter gave rise to complaint by dockers and others, so a rush-hour" service was operated over the route between Post Office and Granton via Bernard Street. This ran without service number and white front window boards lettered Leith Docks were carried. On 1 April 1956 bus service 18 was extended from Blackhall to Parkgrove Street, Barnton, running via Strachan Road and Craigcrook Road, and re-joining Queensferry Road at Davidson's Mains crossroads. This diversion was an endeavour to serve the Craigcrook area but was not universally popular.

Leith tram depot was closed on 5 May 1956 and conversion for use as a bus garage commenced. Trams on services 13 and 14 found a temporary home at Shrubhill depot until 27 May when buses replaced services 6 and 19. Withdrawal of these trams from Tollcross depot then enabled those on services 13 and 14 to be housed there. The old bus service 6 was renumbered 36 while the buses replacing tram service 19 carried number 49. Traffic on Princes Street had just been restored to normal on completion of the carriageway resurfacing, except for the West End, the Mound, and east of St. Andrew Street, but to enable work to continue on the latter part towards the Post Office, the remaining Princes Sreet services 11, 13, 14, and 28 were diverted to the York Place route along with service 16. This change was made on 1 June and the track and overhead removed between Post Office and St. Andrew Street. Then on 16 June the Granton Circle trams 13 and 14 made their last journeys and the track lifting already effected from Liberton in to Salisbury Place continued on to the Post Office. In replacement a new bus service numbered 14 started the following day between Newington Station and Muirhouse via Post Office, Pilrig Street, Ferry Road, Goldenacre, and Granton, while tram service 16 was extended from Bernard Street to Granton and became an all-day service. The Post Office to Granton via Bernard Street "rush hour" trams were also taken off. Cowgate and Causewayside substations shut down their traction supply, and the lines as far as the foot of the Mound were fed from McDonald Road and Dewar Place substations respectively. On the same date bus service 7 was extended from Liberton terminus to Kaimes, Captains Road, Lasswade Road, and Kirkgate back to Liberton. Those running in the other direction round this circle at the Liberton end were numbered 37. Service 33 was diverted to East Preston Street and Old Dalkeith Road instead of Lady Road, and service 18 was extended to Maybury Road at Barnton. A new style of uniform was issued to inspectors in the summer of 1956.

The end of the trams was now near. On Wednesday 12 September 1956 services 11 and 16 were replaced by buses, the old bus service 11 being renumbered 41. The buses ran via Leith Street instead of York Place as the trams had been doing. Also in order to get rid of the slightly sunken track in Princes Street as far as possible, tram service 28 was diverted to the Mound route between Princes Street and Tollcross. Track lifting then went ahead between the Mound, West End, and Tollcross. The withdrawal of trams from this route and the regular running of buses over Bernard Street bridge made it necessary to resurface the bridge temporarily as its carriageway was unsuitable for heavy vehicular traffic. It may be recalled that it belonged to the Dock Commission but negotiations had been in train for some time for the Corporation to take it over, with a view to its replacement by a modern bridge. Since April 1955 it had no longer been openable to shipping. Leith substation and its Wardie satelite now ceased traction supply, McDonald Road substation taking over the lines right to Stanley Road and to Granton Road Station. So now only two tram services remained, number 23 Morningside Station and Granton Road Station via Mound and Hanover Street, and number 28 Braids and Stanley Road via Mound, York Place, and Pilrig Street. Most of the overhead and much of the track on the abandoned routes had already been removed, though an unusual example could be seen northwards of Granton Road Station where the overhead line remained "in situ" though track lifting was complete. Poles which carried lighting brackets were taken over by the Lighting Department; the others were removed.

The date fixed for the last trams to run was Friday 16 November 1956, but a week or two beforehand the "Suez crisis" blew up. Tramway abandonment in Glasgow and elsewhere was temporarily deferred and it was proposed that Edinburgh do likewise. But the appeals were rejected and there was no reprieve. During the last week of operation the weather was fortunately fine and an enormous amount of film, still and cine, must have been expended by the public on momentoes of their trams. Very young children had to be photographed on the platform, so they would know when they grew up they had been on a tram. Ticket rolls of yellow paper with "Last Tram Week" printed on the back were used. A decorated tram toured the remaining remnant of the system, illuminated at night. The service cars flew pennants on the trolley ropes.

Then on the final day the restored horse bus appeared on the streets pulled by a pair of horses supplied by St. Cuthbert's Co-operative Association, and with a crew in period uniform. A timetabled tour of the city and inner suburbs was made and naturally attracted much attention. Meanwhile services 23 and 28 continued, coping with the tea-time rush as usual. It was difficult to realise there would be no trams tomorrow.

Bus service 23 was commenced from Granton Road Station at 6.8 p.m. but trams continued to run too until 7.29 p.m. this last running to the foot of the Mound and then to Shrubhill depot, while the previous two had gone as far as Tollcross before proceeding to Shrubhill. From 7.5 p.m. four cars from Morningside ran to Hanover Street and back to Tollcross before going to Shrubhill, while the next four made their last journey right through. Service 28 being a part-day one was not replaced by buses till the following day. The last through journey from Stanley Road was at 6.57 p.m. preceded by the decorated car, thereafter two cars to Tollcross and three to St. Andrew Street before turning for Shrubhill. This last left Stanley Road at 7.44 p.m. The last three from Braids ran to Shrubhill. Spare trams at Tollcross and also the "grinder" were run down to Shrubhill early, but ten trams went up to the Braids, there to form a convoy of service 28 "last trams" to Shrubhill filled with those who had obtained numbered permits for the journey. The normal fare was charged. The last of these, car No. 88 was preceeded at 7.40 p.m. by the decorated car, and was followed from Morningside Station at 7.45 p.m. by No. 217, the actual last car, carrying the town councillors and their invited guests.

Great crowds lined the route all the way, and long before their arrival at the foot of the Mound shortly after 8.00 p.m., the pavements in that area and in Princes Street and the foot of Hanover Street were packed with people who had come from far and near for the occasion. The buses had to be diverted via Market Street, Waverley Bridge, and George Street. On reaching the foot of the Mound these last three cars were halted and joined by the horse bus now "powered" by two white horses. There in a blaze of temporary floodlights, and with the B.B.C. in attendance, their drivers, James Pryde on 88, William Moffat on the decorated car, and James Kay on 217, received inscribed controller keys from the Lady Provost who also handed over a suitably inscribed gold watch to James Kay and wallets to the other two. It should also be recorded that Andrew Birrel was conductor on 217. The preceding ten cars proceeded with their loads to Shrubhill gate and then entered via Pilrig Street and Dryden Street.

The short ceremony over, the three cars, preceded by the horse bus, made their way along Princes Street and into St. Andrew Square where the horse bus fell out and made its own time to Shrubhill. The three cars proceeded through a blare of horns from the buses in St. Andrew Square, and midst large crowds all the way to the depot. They entered by the Leith Walk gates, to where the temporary floodlights had been rushed. The gates closed behind them. It was a good ending, and the public generally had been well behaved, though the last car was de-wired once or twice on the last lap. Souvenir stripping by the few who gained access to the depot was very limited. But many coins were flattened on the rails that evening, and much rhyme and reminiscence appeared in the press. "The Scotsman" wondered if electric traction might not return again in time.

And so an era ended. The traction current was shut down finally at 9.40 p.m., and that same night the overhead was cut down in Princes Street, and the remaining islands removed. No. 217 was away on the scrap merchant's lorry early the following morning. Loading was now done inside Shrubhill depot, and other cars there followed daily. Fortunately however, one, No. 35, was kept for the Department's museum. A tractor was used for moving cars in the depot preparatory to loading, though an attempt was made to use a 460 volt D.C. supply from the workshops.

Before we close this chapter at the end of 1956, a few subsequent developments should be mentioned. The new No. 28 bus service reverted to the original route via West End and Leith Street, while the old service 28 was renumbered 48. Service 26 was extended to Clermiston Gardens on 9 December. The "Suez Affair" now brought fuel rationing and bus services had to be cut. From 17 December services 9, 14, 15, 17, 28, 45, 46, and 48 became part-day only and not at all on Sundays. This also applied to service 12 between Portobello and Niddrie. To compensate somewhat, service 10 was run to Torphin, service 47 to Granton, and service 44 was diverted via Duddingston Road and Mountcastle Drive South to Milton Road. The Ministry of Transport's emergency legislation for temporary fares increase was applied from 23 December, the minimum fare becoming 3d. covering four stages, while the maximum became 6d. The old fares were duly restored later, and also the service cuts, but it was not long before a permanent increase to 3d. minimum and 6d. maximum came into force. All the overhead was cut down before Christmas, the last piece being that through Churchhill, though many poles and rosettes remained to be dealt with. Track lifting and road reconstruction proceeded more gradually, being limited by available funds. It seemed strange to find paving repairs still being carried out on tracks no longer in use, but this was of course necessary where lifting could not be undertaken for some time. The Shrubhill depot had also to be made suitable for buses.

Lastly, the Department's Head Office should be mentioned. The office at St. James' Square, though conveniently situated, was cramped and in many ways unsuitable. There had been a suggestion at the end of the war to take over premises at the east end of George Street, but this did not materialise. Now however a building at 14 Queen Street had been acquired and was being transformed into a Head Office worthy of the undertaking. Every reasonable amenity was provided, and the radio control centre and lost property office were transferred there too. The public date of occupation was 13 January 1957. For Edinburgh Corporation Transport a new era had begun.

The Rolling Stock :—Tramcars

The new top deck covers which the Corporation ordered from Hurst Nelson & Co. for the cable cars were slightly longer than the lower saloons and had four windows each side and a more curved roof, the balcony canopies being of full width symmetrical shape supported by a single stanchion on the centre line. As the bulkhead doors were centrally placed, new stairs with a semi-circular turn had to be provided, but these remained unenclosed by the driver's canopy and balcony panelling. The weight of the cars so reconstructed became 8t. 16c. and their numbers were : 3, 4, 16, 20, 31, 33, 58, 101, 116, 117, 118, 147, 154, 155, 156, 158, 159, 160, 163, 168, 174, 182, 183, 192, 193, 194, 198, 201, 207 and 208.

Mr. Pilcher was planning to use as many as possible of the cable cars for conversion to electric cars and in 1921 a start was made with Nos. 36, 115, 178 and 185 which were reconstructed with new Hurst Nelson top covers and also lengthened platforms with glass vestibules and balcony panels enclosing the stairs. Cushion seats were provided in the lower saloon. No. 36 had a single window on the corners of the platform vestibules, the others had two narrower ones. These cars were put to work on the Leith electric system which, of course, had become part of the Edinburgh undertaking on the amalgamation of Leith and Edinburgh in November 1920. They were at first painted in the Leith style with small size numerals on the dash. No. 36, and also perhaps No. 185, ran on old cable car bogies to which 27 h.p. electric motors and new disc wheels had been fitted. No. 115 was provided with a new type of Brill truck and No. 178 with a Peckham truck, with 32 h.p. motors.

The initial electric car stock thus comprised the thirty-eight former Leith Corporation cars, the four old Slateford cars, and the aforementioned four converted cars. To avoid duplication of numbers the Leith cars were renumbered by increasing the numbers by 230 except in the case of the grinding car No. 60 which was renumbered 1. It seems to have been intended to have a separate set of numbers for such vehicles. The four Slateford cars were removed from their old maximum traction bogies and provided with new trucks, one a Peckham like No. 178, one a Brill type similar to those on the Leith cars, and two got new Brush trucks with 7ft. 6in. wheelbase. The one with the Peckham truck was also reconstructed like a Leith open-top car, — without platform vestibules and re-numbered 229. It was however very soon provided with platform vestibules like the other converted cable cars though it retained its open upper deck. Cushion seats were fitted in the lower saloon. The other three Slateford cars were renumbered 230, 268, and 269 and were also reconstructed in this form though at a later date and without the cushion seats.

E.O.C.

CONVERTED CABLE CAR ON EXPERIMENTAL ELECTRIFIED BOGIES AT STANLEY ROAD
Note the front exit doors opened, the single wider window on the corners of the platforms, and the number, 36 in small Leith style figures.

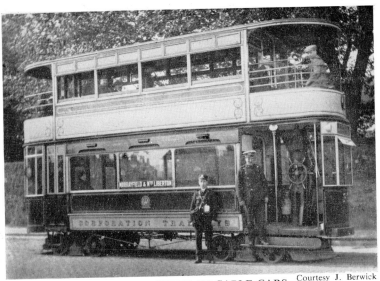

THE LAST WORD IN CABLE CARS Courtesy J. Berwick

No. 33 rebuilt with new closed top, vestibuled Platforms etc. 1922. Compare
with illustration of electric car No. 36. This car had the corner windows on
the platforms like No. 36, as also had No. 192

Having tried all these Peckham, Brill, and Brush trucks and
the converted cable bogies, — which though lighter and faster
were found to be rather heavier on current and somewhat noisy, —
Mr. Pilcher suggested that thirty-seven more cars be fitted up with
bogies for use on the hillier routes; the rest to have single trucks.
It was felt however that standardisation held greater benefits, and
therefore the idea of a number of bogie cars was ruled out. The
Peckham type truck was chosen as standard, and the converted
cable bogies soon discarded, though the Brill and Brush trucks
remained in use. The Peckham type trucks as supplied by Hurst
Nelson & Co. and the Brush Electric Co. had wheels 26in. dia.
or in some cases 27in. dia., the latter size eventually becoming
standard. The wheelbase was 8ft. 6in. and two 40 h.p. motors of
Metropolitan-Vickers type MV101 were fitted. These were of the
normal nose-suspended semi-sprung arrangement. The axleboxes
rode on the patent Peckham pendulum links which gave a steady
motion. Magnetic track brake shoes energised from the rotating
motors through the controller connections were fitted in the
middle of the wheelbase, though it should be mentioned that the
first such truck on No. 178 did not have these shoes, its electric
brake being a plain rheostatic, i.e. the rotating motors dissipated
their generated current in resistances. In many of the later trucks
the motors were MV101B type of 50 h.p. A number of these 50 h.p.
motors were fitted with roller bearings making them type

MV101BR. The motors on No. 115's Brill truck and those on the converted cable bogies were of G.E.C. make.

Returning now to the cable car conversions: Early in 1922 twenty of the thirty cable cars which had originally been fitted with the new Hurst Nelson top-covers were dealt with in the same way as Nos. 36, 115, 178 and 185, but until the first stage of electrification was ready for them in June these were put out on cable bogies and ran as cable cars for a few months. Then they were quickly put on standard Peckham trucks, fitted with controllers and trolley etc. and transferred to the Liberton and Churchhill electrified routes. These twenty cars were Nos. 3, 4, 20, 31, 33, 116, 117, 118, 147, 155, 168, 174, 182, 183, 192, 194, 198, 201, 207 and 208. The remainder of the standard cable cars, — except No. 43, — were all similarly reconstructed and converted to electric cars on standard Peckham trucks, though the provision of cushion seats was soon dropped. The reconstructed cars were 27ft. 8in. overall and they seated 20 passengers in the lower saloon and 36 upstairs. New top deck covers were provided by various builders, but some of the Brown-Marshall built cars were not fitted with top covers at all, retaining an open upper deck with 40 seats and a central trolley mast. The Dick-Kerr and Shrubhill built cars were the last to be dealt with having latterly been used on the Portobello route. Among the latter, Nos. 54, 59, 66, and 72

E.O.C.

STANDARD NEW ELECTRIC CAR ON THE NEW BRIDGE
ON THE EXTENSION FROM GORGIE TO STENHOUSE

retained their unusual feature of a shallow step up into the lower saloon from the platform; which was to prove awkward in the war-time blackout. One of the former type was however exceptionally dealt with earlier. This was No. 222 and in this case the original top cover of 1907 was retained. The bulkheads were removed and new vestibuled ends built on to it enclosing the stairs also. This thus became an all-enclosed car but should not be confused with the rather similar "Crystal Palace" cable car No. 37 which in due course was converted in the normal way with a new top. No. 222 seated 42 on the top deck and was erroneously indicated as seating 22 in the lower saloon which had cushion seats.

By June 1922 some half-dozen of an order for sixteen new cars had been delivered and until that time had been at work on the Leith system. These new standard cars were rather longer than the converted cable cars and had four windows aside in the lower saloon which matched the length and width of the top saloons. They thus seated 22 in the lower saloon, on wooden seats, and the usual 36 upstairs. Their length overall was 29ft. 9in. and weight

D.L.G.H.

CONVERTED CABLE CAR OF E. & D.T.Co. BUILD, WITH LATER ENCLOSED BALCONIES, ALSO WAR-TIME HEADLAMP AND WHITE FENDER, AT SHRUBHILL DEPOT GATE
This is one of the four cars with a step up into the saloon and this can be seen painted white also.

9t. 9c. The stairs turned only through 90° to meet a small landing at the top. Otherwise they were similar to the converted cable cars and had the same folding steps to the platforms. Numbered 121-136 the lower decks were built locally by Messrs. McHardy & Elliott Ltd., and new top covers from the Hurst Nelson order were fitted to them. They ran on standard Peckham trucks.

Substantial orders for further standard cars were then placed with other firms and these began to appear in the summer of 1923, while following the completion of the work of converting cable cars early in 1924, the Shrubhill works proceeded to turn out similar new cars also.

All the standard cars and converted cable cars were equipped with a narrow pair of doors beneath the stairs which could be opened by a small handle convenient to the driver, which movement also folded down a small step outside. This was intended for use as an additional exit from the lower saloon at busy stopping places, but its utility was limited and they soon dropped out of use. One of the new cars from Shrubhill, No. 53, was fitted with rather similar doors to the main entrance on the platform, but these proved inconvenient and were soon removed.

The new cars and the rebuilt cable cars were fitted with roller blind destination screens built in above the driver's window, and also carried the usual board inside the side windows. A new feature was a lantern fixed under the balcony roof above the top of the stairs, showing to the front and side two coloured glasses, one below the other. The coloured glasses were changed according to the service number, which at first was displayed on a coloured oval board the same as on the cable cars. Late in 1922 however an extension was added below the lanterns with a sloping mirror behind, and the service number was then displayed there by a stencil. Open-top electric cars had the lantern mounted on a standard at the top of the stairs, and the number stencil, when added was put on top of the coloured glasses. The former Leith cars were of course also provided with these lanterns.

The cars were painted in much the same livery as before. The waist panels on both decks and the dash panels, also the panel above the side windows on the converted cable cars, were madder,* with gold lining, ornamented in the corners, and bordered by a thin white line. The other panels were white with brown lining bordered by a thin red line, the lining forming scrolls at the ends of the panels on the top deck. Window pillars were white with a thin red or black line, though in some cases parts of the lower saloon corner pillars were madder. The roof was black, and at first the edge was painted white. The rocker panel was lettered Corporation Tramways in gilt lettering with red shading, the num-

* Otherwise known as maroon

ber on the dash panels being similar. The railings etc. on the balconies were red, and the trucks were red picked out with black, and lined white. The interiors were finished in the usual varnished wood. It may be remarked that the white paintwork sometimes aged to quite a yellow tint.

An exception to the foregoing was the grinder car No. 1 which was painted green with white lining and gilt lettering shaded in blue as in Leith days.

The controllers provided were either B.T.H. or Dick-Kerr make, the former predominating, though there were two exceptions with Metropolitan-Vickers controllers, viz. Nos. 9, and 172. Control was the normal series-parallel arrangement with clock-wise movement of the controller handle, while movement in the other direction provided braking notches for the magnetic track brake shoes. All cars were of course equipped with the usual hand brake handle, sand pedal, gong pedal, and standard life-guard equipment. The resistance boxes were accommodated close under the stairs and the circuit-breakers mounted on the lower saloon bulkheads. Contrary to normal practice, headlamps were not fitted, but a small lamp was provided alongside the destination screen. When this was at the back of the car a red spectacle glass inside the casing was swung over it. On new cars built in 1924 and after, this lamp was put above the outer of the two platform corner windows, and the earlier cars were subsequently altered likewise, though this alteration was not done on any of the converted cable cars. The interior lamps were provided with bell-shaped glass shades with a waved edge. Electric bell pushes were fitted con-venient for the conductor's use. The driver was provided with an inside mirror and an outside one giving him a view of the step, both adjustable. A small outside mirror was also fitted at the middle of the top deck for the conductor, but these were soon discarded.

A few odd cars have now to be considered. These comprise four of the earliest Northern section cable cars, three of the con-verted horse cars, Nos. 15, 17, and 19, and the prototype cable car No. 112. Two of the old Northern cars were Nos. 123 and 125 and these two and another, — number unknown, — were re-pillared to make three windows aside. The fourth one, also number unknown, — retained its six windows aside, and as their numbers had been used for the new standard cars they were renumbered respectively 75, 76, 84, and 86. Apart from the re-pillaring mentioned, none of the eight cars were materially altered and were thus very distinctive compared to the new and converted standard cable cars. All were put on Peckham trucks, No. 75 getting the one without track brake shoes from No. 178. This car also had its

251

stairs and seats removed and watering tanks installed, but these were transferred to No. 17 when it was ready. Nos. 15 and 19, and subsequently No. 75 were fitted with track salting chutes and hoppers and brackets for snow ploughs. The other four, Nos. 76, 84, 86, and 112 were used for passenger traffic for a few years, mainly as football extras. Eventually, about 1926, all eight were stripped of their top deck fittings, stairs, etc., provided with platform screens and painted madder overall without any lining. The four which had seen passenger service were fitted with track salting gear. The old Leith grinder car No. 1 had been fitted with platform screens too, but these did not extend round the sides at all. It also got a Peckham truck, while No. 19 got an old Leith Brill truck. Grinding blocks were fitted to No. 17.

In the summer of 1923 No. 177 was the subject of an interesting experiment, suggested by Councillor Mancor, namely the insertion of a rubber ring in the wheels. Unfortunately this attempt at resilience and quietness was apparently not very successful at that time. No. 49 was for a time fitted with a roller blind destination screen in the middle side window, while an advertising route indicator was tried in No. 117. No. 225 ran without track brake shoes for a while, and No. 47 got the new Brill truck from No. 115. Two sets of roller-bearing axle-boxes were tried, an "SKF" set on No. 105 and for a time on No. 208, and a "Hoffman" set on No. 27 briefly, and then on No. 45 till 1930, and finally, from 1933, on No. 89.

In 1924-5 all the Leith top-covered cars were rebuilt and fitted with platform screens, but not the exit doors under the stairs. Those which already had platform screens got new ones and new ordinary metal dash plates. The opening roofs on Nos. 261-3 disappeared. The trucks had their wheelbase lengthened to 7ft. 6in. and some cars got new electrical equipment as well. No. 247 was provided with a new Peckham type truck with a shorter wheelbase. The first car to be dealt with, No. 262, lost its headlights, but these were retained on all the others. All were painted in the standard style with the normal larger red-shaded numerals on the dash. Only a few of the Leith open-top cars were painted thus and none was reconstructed in any way.

About this time the "Milne" reversible cushion seat was devised. When the seat back was thrown over for use in the other direction, linkage moved the seat itself in the opposite direction, thus giving a more comfortable seat and saving space. These were fitted in the top saloons of all new cars from 1925 and subsequently into all the earlier standard cars and most of the converted cable cars too.

It will be remembered that air-operated track brakes were called for on the Comely Bank, Mound, and Hanover Street routes.

The first sets were by G. D. Peters & Co. Ltd. and were fitted to the Dick-Kerr converted cable cars, except No. 222, and also on Nos. 37, 46, 48, 53, and 192. Later sets went to 143-4 and 332-41. The compressor and reservoir were placed under the lower saloon seats, and the driver's valve conveniently fixed between the controller and brake handle. As the hand brake handle would not be used for service stops, cars so fitted were provided with a seat for the driver, carried on folding brackets attached near the controller. In 1925 similar airbrake sets to operate the brake shoes on the wheels were introduced. The cars so fitted are shown in the list. The G. D. Peters group of companies provided sixty sets and the Westinghouse Company thirty-seven sets.

In 1926 further new standard cars were being turned out of Shrubhill works and the numbers reached to 353 with all the old blank numbers used. The earliest of the converted cable cars were now being broken up however, though in the case of the top-covered cars the top deck saloons were fit for further use. So for the next two years no additions to stock were made, the new cars which continued to be built at Shrubhill replacing converted cable cars, taking the same numbers, and using the old top saloons where available. No. 36 was the first replacement and with it the design was slightly modified. The extra exit under the stairs had a step down to a deep well inside instead of an outside folding step, and the doors extended to cover it. A more important innovation was transverse cushion seats, "Milne" type, in the lower saloon. These were arranged in four rows of double seats on one side and single seats on the other with ordinary fixed cushion seats for two over the sandboxes in the corners, the total thus being 20. The conductor's bell-pushes were moved from the window rail to the ceiling. The next three cars, Nos. 33, 185, and 208, were similar but did not have the new seating though they were very soon altered to that form. Subsequent cars all had the transverse seats but the well inside the extra exit was made shallower and the outside folding step reappeared. Cars built after 1927 were slightly wider and had a small radius turning under the lower panel. Most of the new cars were fitted with air-brakes for the wheels, though in some cases they first ran without this refinement for a month or so. The transverse seating arrangement was very popular and the older standard cars were duly altered accordingly. In a few cases an end window on one or both sides of the lower saloon was made openable. The dark green which had hitherto been used for cushion seats gave way to a dull blue colour. On No. 36 the gear ratio was altered to give a higher speed, and this alteration was subsequently effected on several other cars also. These cars carried the letters HS stencilled inside the dash plates for a few years.

By 1929 the few remaining open-top cars were being used only at times of pressure, but traffic was still increasing, so in

1929-30 the fleet was strengthened by an additional seventeen cars, while cars for replacement continued to be built as well. Nos. 354-366 were of standard pattern, except that on Nos. 357, 358, and 360-6 the extra exit feature under the stairs was omitted entirely, and this also applied to replacement cars Nos. 79, 101, and 198. Later a few of the earlier cars were similarly treated. Some of the new cars had white panelled ceilings in the top or both saloons, but in most cases these were eventually replaced by the usual brown. No. 367 was another innovation however, and the remainder Nos. 368-370 were similar to it. In these the top deck was a totally enclosed saloon without bulkheads, the top of the stairs being divided off by a partition and sliding door. A full drop window was provided in each end. Tubular electric heaters were provided, and there were seats for 38. The service number was displayed on a roller blind above two concentric discs with coloured glasses, mounted in a box over the stairs. On No. 367 the number was at first alongside the colour discs, and on this car the lining out was also simplified, the fancy scrollwork being omitted. On the other three all the window pillars were left a dark varnished brown and this became standard for all further new cars. As the top deck panels were now continuous in effect round the car, the lining was done likewise, and the scrolls and also the thin red line omitted. All had a single wider window on the platform corners like old No. 36 had, and this also became standard practice. Red material now began to appear for the seating, and there was also a brown set. The top and bottom decks did not always have the same colour.

Further cars replacing converted cable cars and utilising their old top deck saloons appeared in the old form but the open balcony ends were enclosed. As the old saloon bulkheads remained the stairs were not partitioned off, but the new box containing service number screen and colour discs was fitted in the corner window above them. The full drop window was provided in each end and was useful for dealing with refractory trolley-heads. Opening it in other circumstances incurred the displeasure of the driver on account of the down draught created. Tubular electric heaters were fitted in the top saloon and the seating capacity remained unchanged. The top deck window pillars were brown. The old exit feature under the stairs was omitted. No. 70 was the first to be turned out in this form, followed by another seven, after which the new lower saloons had the same modifications as Nos. 368-370. Further new cars replacing open-top cable cars were of course similar to Nos. 368-370 throughout. Two of these however replaced Leith cars Nos. 264 and 266 though the latter is interesting in that it was originally numbered 371. It also had moquette seating with a floral design, and Metropolitan-Vickers controllers. The earlier standard cars now began to have their ends enclosed and the exit under the stairs removed like No. 70, and where they did not already have transverse seating in the lower saloon this was also fitted.

The body of old No. 177 was adapted to carry a welding set for track repairs, the middle section on each side being taken out, and the platforms shortened. This was put on an old Leith truck and numbered 2. To assist with the nightly rail grinding programme, open-top car No. 230 had its track-brake shoes replaced by grinding blocks in 1931. Not being provided with water tanks it was used following behind the regular grinder cars. Shortly afterwards No. 269 replaced it on this duty, till 1934 after which time only the regular grinders were used, the outlying parts of the system being done during daytime. Latterly No. 269 was stripped of its top deck and stairs, but it was never repainted as a "works" car.

This was a period of many interesting innovations and experiments. First, painting : No. 131 appeared in November 1930 with the colours of the top deck panels transposed. No. 222 was similarly treated in June 1931, but in the meantime No. 270, and new cars Nos. 119 and 161 had appeared similarly but with the upper panel of the top deck painted brown without lining. In the case of No. 270 the lining on the top deck madder panel was red, while in the case of No. 161 the lower saloon rocker panel was painted madder in addition. These were followed in July 1931 by No. 264, a new car, in which both top deck panels were painted aluminium. The rather bare effect was relieved by red lining added to both the panels a few weeks afterwards. Of these various liveries only the first had any merit. No. 161 looked particularly dull. None of them however, was perpetuated. In June 1931 too, the lettering Corporation Transport which had superseded Corporation Tramways on the rocker panels, gave way to Edinburgh Corporation painted in small black unshaded letters in the bottom left hand corner of the panel. Only eight cars, Nos. 106, 161, 200, 264, 291, 308, 310 and 316, were so treated before the wording was altered to City and Royal Burgh of Edinburgh.

In August 1931 75 h.p. motors were fitted to No. 162. These were subsequently on No. 317, and later on the new car No. 261, the cars concerned having a fine turn of speed, — well over 30 m.p.h. No. 162 also had two pairs of track-brake shoes for a time. Some other ideas tried were a motor field-shunt to give increased speed; divided motor armatures; hollow axles and special wheel centres; lighter trolley-booms and different tension springs for them. The "anti-galloping bars" were removed from the ends of the trucks of many cars, and in the case of the first dozen to be done, additional small coil springs were fitted instead.

No. 177 appeared new in June 1931 with a number of new features, and on a new type of truck. Instead of side window

255

boards a roller blind screen was provided in place of the top-light adjacent to the platform entrance. "Numa" air bells replaced the conductor's electric bells, and "Ashanco" ventilators were fitted in the lower saloon. The lighting circuits were arranged with fifteen 40 volt lamps in series, the holders being fitted with a "bridging" device which came into action in the event of a lamp failure. This arrangement allowed of additional lamps, one of which was located at the top of each stair. In the saloons the lamps were enclosed in rectangular globe fittings. This "long-series" system was later applied to quite a number of other cars from time to time, the two additional lamps on the lower deck circuit being located on the saloon ceiling panels, these only being of the enclosed type. On No. 177 bright metal work, such as handrails, controller-top, etc., hitherto brass, was chromium-plated, and this later became standard for all cars.

No. 177's new truck was the first of three supplied by the E.M.B. Co. Ltd. The second was used on No. 371, while the third, which was a Peckham P35 type truck, went to No. 177 again which had meantime lost its first truck to another new car. The first two were known as "Flexible Axle" trucks, but it was the second one, on No. 371, which was un-conventional. In this truck the side members were swept up over the axleboxes which were located only by the heavy underslung springs and not guided by hornways. 75 h.p. "MV107" type fully-sprung motors drove the axles by means of a worm and quill drive, and internal expanding shoes worked on brake drums fixed inside the wheels. This arrangement gave a quieter and smoother ride, but there were maintenance problems, and after a few months the motors, drive, and brake-drums were replaced by orthodox equipment. This truck finished its useful life with some months service on No. 110 in 1934. All three E.M.B. trucks had "SKF" roller-bearings and two pairs of track-brake shoes, though the normal single pair was later provided in the first and third examples. An awkward point was that the outside ground clearance of the first two was inadequate for the centre guard strip on Bernard Street bridge, and they had to be kept off that route.

The air-brake system on these three trucks was also different, and of E.M.B. design. The controller shaft was extended through a valve box mounted on the controller top, and the first notch on the "brake" side of the controller applied air to the track brake shoes. Further movement in that direction energised the track-brake shoe magnets in the normal way. The air was applied to the wheel-brakes by a lever protruding from the right hand side of the valve box, but this brake was automatically released should the controller handle be moved either way from the "off" position. Further, the wheel-brake lever could only be applied against a heavy spring if the controller was not in the "off" position. The risk of skidding the wheels by applying the wheel-brake and track-brake at the same time was thereby avoided. There was also a separate air cock giving a direct track-brake application for emergency use on either platform. Three pressure gauges were provided in a neat metal frame behind the hand brake handle.

Earlier, No. 367 when new, had been provided with a similar E.M.B. brake, but in that case there was no air operation of the track-brake shoes, and of course only two pressure gauges. This had been shortly followed by a Maley & Taunton air brake for wheels and track shoes, on No. 168, the principles of which were the same as the E.M.B. brakes. In the M. & T. layout however the wheel brake was not operated from the valve box on the controller top but by a small detachable lever on a further separate small valve box to the right of the controller. This M. & T. brake was chosen as standard, and within about three years from 1930 all service cars had been fitted with it, the older types of air brake and the E.M.B. brakes being scrapped. When these new air brakes were fitted the old pattern of collapsible driver's seat was discarded, and instead a one-legged stool was provided which was pushed into a socket in the floor. On the earlier sets of M. & T. air brakes the track shoes were operated by a common transverse cylinder, but subsequently separate cylinders were used. A few of the old open balcony converted cable cars survived to get the standard M. & T. brake, as shown in the list, but most of the bodies were then too weak and from these the air brakes were removed again.

The aforementioned E.M.B. trucks, the last two of which were painted red without any lining out, which style now became standard, were followed by a Maley & Taunton "Swing-link" truck on No. 264. This had "Hoffman" roller-bearings and G.E.C. motors. Three pairs of G.E.C. controllers were also obtained, one pair being used on this car, and the others on Nos. 16 and 109. There had also been a new Peckham truck by the Brush Company which differed from the usual ones in having under-slung springs. This was used on No. 151.

The most important development however, was the proposal that Edinburgh should now have a completely new and modern design of tram. Accordingly the council authorised an expenditure of £4000 for one such car. The new car body was built in the Shrubhill works, and had an alloy frame with timber filling and metal panelling. The frame members were continuous from the bottom floor to the roof, the sides being straight and the lower saloon having five windows each side. The upper deck was one long saloon, access being by a staircase partitioned off from the platform and with a sliding door at the bottom. The platform entrance was inset from the saloon corner pillars, so that the folding step when lowered, did not project. The platform corner windows had curved glass. The lower saloon had transverse seats for two, staggered on both sides of the gangway, the sandbox seats at the ends correspondingly seating two and three, a total of 26. The usual arrangement applied on the upper deck except that the centre pair of seats were single ones and two "Doverite" covered grab poles from floor to roof were provided alongside. Similar single seats were provided opposite the top of the stairs, the upper deck total being 38. All the seats were of a wider and deeper type, blue leather in the lower saloon and red in the upper, the side panelling and pillars in rexine to match, and the ceilings panelled in white. Lighting was in enclosed fittings and "Ashanco" ventilators and "Numa" air bells were provided, and tubular electric heaters in both saloons. There was also a headlamp with dimming device, a brake-stop-light, and an air operated screen wiper for the driver. The car was put on the first E.M.B. truck, taken from No. 177, with E.M.B. air-brake, and Metropolitan-Vickers controllers. Its weight complete was 13 tons. Perhaps the most striking feature was its livery, a bright red with the window pillars grey, and a silver line edged with blue below the windows of each deck. Such a departure from normal naturally attracted much attention, and earned the car the nickname "Red Biddy". The car was numbered 180 and entered on service 12 on Sunday 3 April 1932. After a few days work however, the M. & T. truck and air-brake from No. 264 replaced the E.M.B. equipment, which then found its way to No. 197. The red livery was retained till 1935.

Arc type screen wipers, with a drop window, were henceforth gradually fitted on all the standard cars. No. 180's original wiper was a parallel action model. The top of the driver's window was already rather low and this alteration made it more so. The new cars built in 1933 and onwards, except Nos. 6, 34, 81 and 206, therefore had the destination screen box set higher up, projecting slightly above the upper deck floor, to compensate for this.

In 1932 three Brill trucks all differing slightly from one another, were obtained second-hand from Ayr Corporation, after that system closed down, and were put on Nos. 25, 27 and 50. Air brakes were not fitted. All these Brill trucks were however discarded in 1934. Later in 1932 the salt cars gave up their Peckham trucks and were put on old Leith trucks instead. Nine Leith cars, Nos. 232-238, 243 and 247 then received Peckham trucks while No. 248 received the special one formerly on the latter car. Many of the Leith cars, and most of the open-top cars, including all the Leith ones, had now been scrapped, and Shrubhill was busy with new cars of the old standard design as replacements. Nevertheless to keep pace with requirements orders had to be placed outside too.

First, at the end of 1932, came ten cars, Nos. 250-259, from R.Y. Pickering & Co. Ltd., Wishaw, of wood construction and generally to the standard design but fitted with air bells, screen wipers, brake-stop-lights, and headlamps, though the first few ran for a week or two without the latter. Maley & Taunton trucks were provided for these cars, except No. 256 which had another new type of truck, an English Electric FL32 type, with English Electric motors and "Hoffman" roller-bearings. These were quickly followed by two cars, Nos. 260 and 265, generally similar to No. 180 but of all-metal construction, from Messrs. Metropolitan-Cammel. These had flat corner panels on the platforms, and M. & T. trucks, and were painted the usual madder except for the window pillars which were white. The lining was similar to that on No. 180. Later, No. 260 had the lower half of the top deck panel painted white also, while on No. 265 the upper half and all above became white and the lower deck window pillars brown. The roofs of the all-metal cars were provided with duckboards for the use of depot staff, but to deal with possible trolley difficulty in service, they were each equipped with a bamboo pole carried on hooks under the edge of the body.

All the standard cars having been equipped with transverse seating and enclosed balconies, the same and the fitting of screen wipers was now in hand on the converted cable cars of Dick-Kerr and Shrubhill construction. None of the older converted cable cars was so dealt with, nor were they fitted with driver's drop windows and screen wipers. The lining out on the remaining older cars was also now much simplified. No. 222, always with its fully enclosed top deck, had the seating improved along with transverse seating in the lower saloon. In October 1933 brown was adopted for the lower deck window pillars of all cars.

Early in 1933 reconstruction of the Peckham trucks with cross-tying of the motors on the Maley & Taunton system to assist in steadying the running was commenced. The "anti-galloping bars" and tie-bars were removed, a guard bar being fitted in place of the latter, though the first few cars ran without this for a time. As this involved trucks not remaining with the same car body, the trucks as they were rebuilt received a "Rebuilt Truck Number" which was shown, with the date, on a metal plate fixed to the **inside** of one side frame. No. 1, dated 11/2/33, appeared on car No. 328.

The regenerative system of control was tried in 1933, with Metropolitan-Vickers controllers on No. 203. The arrangement is for the motors to act as generators when running downhill or stopping, the energy being returned to the overhead line and easing the load on the power station as well as saving wear on brake gear. There were however difficulties when the line is fed by rectifiers, and the only route supplied throughout by rotary machines was that to Levenhall. So, although deficient in hills from which more advantage could have been gained, No. 203 was put to work on service 21. After a year economies were such that a further eleven cars were altered to this system for that route. Occasionally lack of other cars nearby to absorb the current would produce a rise in voltage too great for the lamps if at night. The transition to and from regeneration often produced a considerable jerk in running which gave rise to strong complaint from one or two of the regular passengers who campaigned for "better cars". Eventually, early in 1939 the regenerative cars were withdrawn from the route and altered to normal, the "Pickering" cars being transferred to Portobello depot in their place.

While still continuing to turn out the older type of car, another car of a new design was built at Shrubhill in 1933. This was No. 261, and was generally similar to the "Pickering" cars except that the lower saloon was straight-sided and thus accommodated double seats on both sides. The City crest on the side panels had a red diamond-shaped background. It was then decided that the older type incorporating top deck saloons from converted cable cars be no longer built and designs were settled for a new standard type.

E.O.C.

SPECIAL CAR No. 180. As originally turned out in 1932 on
E.M.B. truck, at Granton.

METROPOLITAN-CAMMEL ALL-STEEL CAR OF 1934
No. 249 with platform doors. At North Gyle terminus Corstorphine

Meantime twelve more all-metal cars were ordered, six from Messrs. Metropolitan-Cammell, and three each from Messrs. Hurst Nelson, of Motherwell, and the English Electric Company. The "Met-Cams" were similar to the earlier two but much improved by having a domed roof. They were also fitted with turntable type seats of a particularly comfortable design in both saloons. One, No. 249, had folding doors on the platform entrance, for use at the driver's end, but these were later removed. The Hurst Nelson cars also had domed roofs, but the ends of the car were rounded like No. 180, and the seating was also similar to it. The three English Electric cars resembled in general the Hurst Nelsons, but the ends were distinctly sloped back in a sort of "streamline" effort, resulting in a foreshortened upper saloon and hence two seats less. The dome of the roof curved down over the ends so that the end windows were smaller, and the service number box was therefore put behind the main panel below, on the front instead of the corner, with the service colours to the off side of it. One of the English Electric cars, No.267, was put on the English Electric truck from No. 256, while M. & T. trucks were obtained for the others. The City crest was again enclosed in a "diamond" lined on the ordinary colour, and all the window pillars were white. On all the new types of car the destination screens were set up a little

261

into the panel above, and in the case of these Hurst Nelson and English Electric cars, and also No. 261, the lines of the upper deck paintwork were curved up over this. The last of the old type of car to be built, No. 191, was painted similarly. The "Met-Cam" cars and the earlier "Pickering" ones, also Nos. 180, 231, and 261 originally had the circuit-breakers mounted on the platform screen to the right of the driver, but later these were all removed to the orthodox position on the saloon bulkhead. Later, a new position, under the stairs, with a kind of "Bowden-wire" control, was tried on No. 157.

On some of the older cars the top saloon full drop side windows were now replaced by metal-framed half-drop windows. There were many variations including quarter-drops and winding types and sometimes only certain windows were altered, others becoming fixed, while many cars were never done at all.

On 24/3/34 the practice was started of stencilling on the back of the stair the date of the overhaul of the truck, normally a week's work for which the body was lifted off. The inscribing of the date ceased at the end of October 1937.

The last of the open-top cars was scrapped in 1934, and just at the end of the year the first of the new standard Shrubhill-built cars appeared. These were of composite construction, and generally similar in design and appearance to the aforementioned Hurst Nelson cars, though perhaps rather neater. The lower saloon seated the usual 24 and the upper saloon 38. Some of them had the old narrow type of seats in the upper saloon, and No. 88 had these throughout. Nos. 56 and 150 had turntable seats in the lower saloon. The former were of "Nesta" type, the latter of "Peters" type in moquette. The "popularity" of No. 150 was such that it was kept on the Marchmont Circle. Ordinary electric bells were fitted, and except on the first few, the headlamps had a plain yellow glass only. Rebuilt "Peckham" trucks were provided. With these cars there was a further change in painting, the madder part of the upper deck panel being brought down to a point over the destination screen at each end, and the gold line on the lower deck sweeping to a point under the headlamps, and also curving down on the side at the platform end. All the window pillars were brown. Soon however the point of the madder panel gave way to a wider sweep extending over the length of the destination screen, while the line sweeping under the headlamps was instead, broken at each side of the car number. A little later the white and madder portions of the upper deck panel were reversed, and this style of painting remained standard thereafter, all cars of all types being gradually repainted in this manner, except for the few remaining open-balcony converted cable cars and old Leith cars which finally disappeared early in 1936.

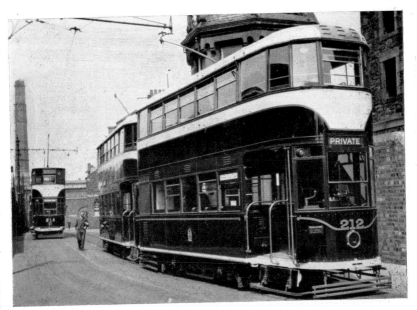

STANDARD 1934 DESIGN SHRUBHILL BUILT CAR;
SHOWING THE UNSHADED NUMERALS USED FOR A TIME

A problem with the straight-sided cars and their enclosed
staircases was the draught which they created down the driver's
back when in motion, due to the air current being trapped behind
him. The answer was found by providing a hinged door which the
driver could draw across the middle of the platform, the air current
dissipating itself behind it.

A further twenty new cars were provided by outside builders
in 1935, eight by Hurst Nelson and six each by English Electric
and Metropolitan-Cammel. These were of the so-called "streamline" design like the earlier three from the English Electric Company. Apart from other minor differences in detail, these cars had
moquette turntable seats in the lower saloon, the "Met-Cams."
having their own make and the others the "Nesta" type. Some
five years later however they were all replaced by the ordinary
"Milne" type seats, though with moquette upholstery in most cases.
The "Met-Cams.", which at first ran from Portobello depot, also
had the service number screens on the near side corner instead of
the front. They ran also, on M. & T. trucks in which rubber
blocks replaced the small coil springs, while the others ran on
rebuilt "Peckham" trucks, though Nos. 21-24 later received
M. & T. trucks of a modified design.

263

"STREAMLINE" TYPE ALL STEEL CAR
No. 12 Hurst-Nelson built, at Stanley Road

These new cars were numbered 11 to 30 and in order to achieve this remaining cars with numbers between 3 and 30 were renumbered. The old Leith grinder car No. 1 and the welding car No. 2 retained their numbers and the "works" cars were renumbered 3 to 10. The details of this tidying up were :—

Old Nos.	3	5	6	7	13	15	16	17	18	19	20	23	24
New Nos.	75	76	84	86	169	4	61	3	182	5	184	41	78

Old Nos.	25	26	27	28	29	75	76	84	86	112
New Nos.	172	112	73	151	138	6	7	8	9	10

By 1939 the fleet had become very standardised. All the odd trucks had been discarded, except the one on No. 197 which lasted a little longer, leaving only "Peckhams" and M. & T.s, and the old Leith trucks on the "works" cars. All service cars were totally enclosed and equipped with transverse seating, screen-wipers, electric heaters on the upper deck, and lower saloon too on straight-sided cars, and the M. & T. air-brake. The "Numa" air bells were being discarded. No. 158 however had continuous bell strips in the saloons instead of bell pushes. A set of trafficator arms had been tried for a while on No. 82, and a lap valve for the air-wheel brakes on No. 88, while during 1935-6-7 No. 81 was the subject of much experimental work on regeneration. This was under the auspices of Maley & Taunton, and the equipment finally ran in service on No. 162 for a short time in 1938 before being abandoned.

On some of the older type of cars the waist panel and rocker panel were replaced by a flush panel with a flat strip beading along the middle and formed into a diamond around the City crest. The whole panel was painted madder with lining similar to that on straight-sided cars but without the curve down at the platforms. On most of these cars a plain unshaded form of numeral was used for the car number on the dash plates. This alteration was applied to various cars from 1938 onwards, the diamond beading being omitted in some later cases, and the beading omitted altogether after the war. The plain unshaded numerals were also used spasmodically on several cars until after the war.

By the end of 1937 forty-six of the new standard cars had been built at Shrubhill. Material was then ordered for a further thirty-eight to replace the remaining converted cable cars. These differed only in details and the use of brown seating and side panelling in the upper saloon and moquette seating in the lower saloon. Construction continued slowly during the war, at least one being turned out each year except 1944, and the last six were completed in 1950.

Some of the old salt cars were scrapped during the war, but the now disused welding car was fitted up for salt duties, and another was built from the remains of old No. 51. Some had their old trolley masts removed. After the war their use was abandoned, and all except the new one were scrapped. This car then replaced the old grinder No. 3, taking its number. Both it and the old Leith grinder were then fitted with illuminated signs worded "Trackwork."

With the universal fitting of headlights during the war, the then obsolete bullseye lights on the corner of the platforms began to be removed, as were also the brake-stop lights. After the war, from 1946, the rocker panels of all the old type cars were painted madder and lined the same as those on which the panels had been altered.

At this time there was a need for additional cars, and new vehicles being difficult to obtain quickly, eleven cars were accepted second-hand from Manchester Corporation. These arrived complete with trucks in 1946, mostly in a sorry state. The Manchester and Edinburgh numbers were :—

| Edinburgh : | 401 | 402 | 403 | 404 | 405 | 406 | 407 | 408 | 409 | 410 | 411 |
| Manchester : | 173 | 676 | 196 | 125 | 558 | 217 | 389 | 231 | 242 | 349 | 381 |

INTERIOR OF UPPER SALOON OF STANDARD 1934
DESIGN OF SHRUBHILL BUILT CAR. CAR No. 220

They were thoroughly rehabilitated and turned out on "Peckham" trucks complete with M. & T. air-brakes and the normal Edinburgh fittings. In appearance they resembled the new standard cars but were slightly longer and for that reason were restricted to the relatively straight Levenhall route in ordinary service. They did not have an enclosed staircase nor a partition and door at the top. Instead there was a trap-door in the floor which was let down over the top of the stairs at the driver's end.

The electric heaters fell out of use with the 1947 power shortage, and afterwards were gradually removed from the cars. No. 11, 12, and 16 got M. & T. trucks in 1948.

It was now time for the oldest of the early standard cars to be scrapped, and No. 122 went first in 1949. In view of the forthcoming change in policy no replacements were made. The first two dozen or so cars to be scrapped were broken up at Shrubhill, but from 1953 the cars withdrawn from service were sold complete to Messrs. Connell of Coatbridge for scrapping.

Meantime in the summer of 1949 six sets of "Timken" roller bearings were obtained followed by twenty-five sets of "Hoffman" make. Six "S.K.F." sets arrived in 1950, and a further twenty-five "Timkens" in 1951-2. These were fitted to "Peckham" trucks. Soon afterwards all the M. & T. trucks were withdrawn and "Peckham" trucks, both "rebuilt" and otherwise, and with ordinary or roller bearings, were used indiscriminately for all types of car and changed fairly frequently. The odd "Met.-Vick." and G.E.C. controllers and most other non-standard items also disappeared. By 1951 no major repairs were being carried out and cars were being withdrawn accordingly. Repainting ceased too. And thus we come to the end, but finally the various decorated cars have to be recorded.

The first was at Christmas and New Year 1933, when No. 74 was fitted up with some 2500 lamps forming outlines and slogans which were varied from seasonal greetings to travel and parcel service enjoinders over the three weeks use. The first week in October 1934 was "Telephone Week", and No. 58 was similarly equipped for Post Office advertising. Meantime during the Royal visit in the second week in July 1934, No. 50 had inevitably been dealt with differently, viz. with some 7500 sprays of artificial flowers forming regal designs on a "grass" background.

D.L.G.H.

INTERIOR OF LOWER SALOON OF STANDARD 1934 DESIGN
OF SHRUBHILL BUILT CAR WITH MOQUETTE SEATING
CAR No. 218

Next there was a more ambitious venture for the Coronation in May 1937. No. 40, preparatory to scrapping, was stripped down to lower saloon waist level and a large representation of a crown mounted there. New dash plates were provided and the whole finished in gold with appropriate blue lettering. Following this, No. 221 when withdrawn from service in February 1939, was painted aluminium with a blue design advertising an "R.A.F. Exhibition". The advertising panels were floodlit by concealed lamps. During the following two months the wording was altered in favour of "National Service". After a period of inactivity, the car appeared once more in June 1940 for "Savings Week", now painted in a gold design and with the floodlighting of course removed.

Finally for the "Last Tram Week" in November 1956, No. 172 was painted white with the City crest on one end and the old Edinburgh and District Tramways Company crest on the other, together with suitable wording and floodlighting.

Fortunately an Edinburgh electric car can still be seen for No. 35 is preserved in the Transport Department's museum.

Edinburgh Corporation Tramcar Fleet List

Code of Symbols on pages 270 to 278

A Converted Cable Car built Brown-Marshall; new top by
    1 McHardy & Elliot
    2 Hurst-Nelson
    3 Cravens

B Converted Cable Car built Brown-Marshall; open top.

C Converted Cable Car Northern section types, open top.

D Converted Cable Car built Milnes; new top as for 'A'.

E Converted Cable Car built Milnes; open top, ex-Slateford line.

F Converted Cable Car built E. & D. T. Co.; new top by
    McHardy & Elliot.

G Converted Cable Car built Dick Kerr & Co.; new top by
    McHardy & Elliot (exc. No. 222)

H Standard Car built by
    1 McHardy & Elliot with Hurst Nelson top.
    2 Leeds Forge Co. at Bristol.
    3 English Electric Co.
    4 E.C.T. at Shrubhill.
    5 E.C.T. at Shrubhill with enclosed balconies when new.

J Standard Car built by Pickering; with no top saloon bulkheads.

K Standard Car built by E.C.T. Shrubhill; with no top saloon bulkheads.

L ex-Leith Car built by B.T.H. Co. with
  1 Brush Electric Co. top.
  2 B.T.H. Co. top.

M ex-Leith Car built by Brush Electric Co. with Brush Electric Co. top.

N ex-Leith Car built by Brush Electric Co. open top.

P Odd Cars built by E.C.T. at Shrubhill, 1932-3.

Q Steel Cars built by
  1 Metropolitan-Cammel
  2 Metropolitan-Cammel, domed roof.
  3 Hurst Nelson, domed roof.

R Standard Cars from 1934 built by E.C.T. at Shrubhill.

S Steel Cars, sloping ends, built by
  1 Hurst Nelson.
  2 English Electric Co.
  3 Metropolitan-Cammel.

T Second-hand Cars ex-Manchester Corporation.

----

a These cars had the earlier type of air-brakes for track shoes.

b These cars had the earlier type of air-brakes for wheels.

c These cars, in addition to all of types F-K and P-T, got M & T air-brakes.

d There was a fourth No. 3, viz. ex-Salt Car 10 converted to Grinder, and 'e'.

e Still in stock on 16-11-56.

f See specific mention in text, (maybe more than once).

No.	YEAR NEW	TYPE	NOTES	YEAR SCRAP	YEAR NEW	TYPE	NOTES	YEAR SCRAP	YEAR NEW	TYPE	NOTES	YEAR SCRAP	DEPOT IN 30 45
1	'23	D1	c	'35	'31	H4	Grinder Car ex-Leith	?	'35	S1	Grinder Car ex-Nº17 d.	?	X / —
2	"	A1		?	'27		Welding Car (ex-Nº177). Re-Nod 75	?					L / —
3	'22	A2	c	?			b	'41					L / —
4	"	"		'35	'33	H5	Salt Car ex-Nº15. Re-Nod 19	?	'35	S1	Salt Car ex-Nº 75	?	L / —
5	'23	F	Re-Nod 76	'31			Salt Car ex-Nº19	'43					L / —
6	"	A1					f Re-Nod 84	?					X / —
7	'24	H4	Re-Nod 86	'35			Salt Car ex-Nº 76	?					L / —
8	'23	A1	b				Salt Car ex-Nº 84	'42					X / —
9	'22	A3	"		'35	S1	Salt Car ex-Nº 86	'56	'35	S2	Salt Car (ex-Nº51). Re-Nod 3	'56	G / —
10	'23	A1	f	'34	"	"	Salt Car ex-Nº 112	"					P / —
11	"	"		'35	"	"	f	"					P / —
12	"	"			"	"	f	"					—
13	"	F	Re-Nod 169	'35									—
14	'22	A1	Salt Car. f										L / —
15	'23	A2	Re-Nod 4		'32	H5	f Re-Nod 61		'35	S1	f	'56	—
16	'22	"	Grinder Car. f		'35	S1		'56					L / —
17	'23	B	Re-Nod 3	?	'28	H4	b Re-Nod 182	'56	'35	S1		'56	—
18	'22	"	Salt Car. f	?	'35	S2							L / —
19	"	"	Re-Nod 5		'28	H4	b Re-Nod 184	'56	'35	S2	f	'56	—
20	"	A2		?	'35	S2	b	"					S / —
21	'23	A1		'35			f						X / —
22	'22	A3		'29		D1	f						L / —
23	'23	A1		?	'28	H4	ex Nº268. c Re-Nod 41	'56	'35	S2	f	'56	— / —
24	"	B	f Re-Nod 172		'35	S3	b Re-Nod 78		"	"	f	"	—
25	"	F	c Re-Nod 112		"	"							S / —
26	"	D1	f Re-Nod 73		"	"							X / —
27	'24	F	b Re-Nod 151										L / —
28	"	H4	(										—
29	'23	A1	c	'33	'33	H5	Re-Nod 138	'56	'35	S3		'56	S / —
30	"	"		'35	'35	S3							—

No.	YEAR NEW	TYPE	NOTES	YEAR SCRAP	YEAR NEW	TYPE	NOTES	YEAR SCRAP	YEAR NEW	TYPE	NOTES	YEAR SCRAP	DEPOT IN '30	DEPOT IN '56
31	'22	A2		?	'30	H5		'55					X	X
32	'23	A1		'34	'35	R		'56					X	S
33	'22	A2		?	'27	H4		'54					L	L
34	"	A3	f	'31	'33	H5		'55					X	S
35	'23	F		'47	'48	R	b f	e					L	S
36	'22	A2		?	'26	H4	f	'50					L	S
37	'24	F	f	'47	'49	R	b f	e					L	G
38	"	H4	a	'55				'56					P	X
39	'23	D1	b	'37	'38	R		"					L	L
40	"	D1	c f	'36	'37	D1	ex-Nº23. c	'36	'36	R		'56	P	S
41	'22	A3	c f	'35	'28	H4	b	'54					L	X
42	"	B	b	?									G	S
43	'24	H4		'53	'32	H5		'55					P	X
44	'22	A1	c f	'36	'36	R		e					L	S
45	'23	D1	a f	?	'32	H5		'55					L	X
46	"	F	f	'42	'46	R		e					L	P
47	"	"	f	'47	'50	"		e					L	P
48	'24	"	f	"	"	"		e					P	P
49	'23	"		"	"	"		e					P	X
50	"	"		Became Salt Car Nº10 in	"	"		e					G	P
51	"	H4	a f	'42	'45	R		'56					G	P
52	'24	F	f	'39	'39	"	f	"					L	X
53	'23	D1		'54	'40	R		'55					G	P
54	"	A1		'40	'35	"	b	"					L	L
55	'22	B		'35	"	H4	b	e					P	P
56	"	A2		?	'28	"	b	'55					L	L
57	"	F	f	?										
58	'23	B		'43	'47	R		e						
59	'22	"		?	'29	H4	b	'55						
60														

271

No.	YEAR NEW	TYPE	NOTES	YEAR SCRAP	TYPE	YEAR NEW	NOTES	YEAR SCRAP	YEAR NEW	TYPE	NOTES	YEAR SCRAP	DEPOT IN 30	45
61	'23	A1		'35	H5	'35	ex-N°16.	'55					L	L
62	"	DI		"	R	'38		'56					X	X
63	'24	H4		'37	"	'53		"					G	S
64	'24	DI		'53	H5	'32		'55					P	P
65	'23	F	c	?	"	'46		e					G	P
66	"	DI	b	'42	H5	'35		'55					G	P
67	"	"	f	'35	"	'32	b f						L	S
68	"	B		'34	R	'34		'56					G	I
69	'22	A3		?	H5	'29		'55					L	X
70	'23	A1		'35	"	'35		'56					L	P
71	"	F	f	'40	F	'41		e					X	L
72	'24	DI		'35	"		ex-N°27.	'45	'47	R			P	L
73	'22	H4	b	'53	H4	'28	ex-N°3.	'55					L	L
74	"	C	f		F		ex-N°5.	'38	'38	R			X	I
75	'23		f	'35	H4	'30	b	'54					X	L
76	"	B		?	"	'33	ex-N°24	"					L	L
77	"	A1		'35	"		f	'55					P	L
78	'22	DI		'33	H5	'37	f	"					L	I
79	'23	A3		'32	R	'35	f	'56					G	L
80	"	DI		'36	"		Salt Car (ex-N°146). Re-N°8	e					L	L
81	"		c	'34	H5	'28	ex-N°7.	'55					X	I
82	"	C	f	'28	H4	'32	f	'53					L	L
83	"	A1	f	?	R			e	H5	ex-N°6		'54	X	X
84	"	C		'53	"	'35		'55					L	P
85	"	H2		'34	H5	'33							X	P
86	"	B		'32									L	L
87	"	A1		'54									X	X
88	"	H2											L	P
89													X	P
90													P	X

272

No.	YEAR NEW	TYPE	NOTES	YEAR SCRAP	YEAR NEW	TYPE	NOTES	YEAR SCRAP	YEAR NEW	TYPE	NOTES	YEAR SCRAP IN 45	DEPOT IN 30	45
91	'23	A1	c	'36	'37	R		'56					X	P
92	"	H2	b	'53									X	X
93	"	·		'54									X	X
94	"	D1		'33	'34	H5		'55					X	L
95	"	H2		'54									X	X
96	"			"									X	P
97	"			"									X	P
98	"			'53	'33	H5		'53					X	X
99	"			'33	'30	H4	b f	'55					X	X
100	'22	A3		?									X	L
101	"	A2		'53	'35	R		'56					I	L
102	'23	H2		'35	'30	H5		'55					X	X
103	"	D1		?	'35	R	b	'56					S	G
104	"	"		'35	'28	H4	b f	'55					S	G
105	"	"	f	"				'56					G	P
106	'22	B		"	'30	K	b							G
107	"	"		'54			b							G
108	'23	H2		?	'32	H5	f	'55					P	L
109	"	A1	f	'53									P	L
110	"	H2		'35	'35	R		'56	'35	R		'56	S	L
111	'22	C	f	'53		D1	ex-N°26. c	'35					P	P
112	"	H4	b	?	'27	H4	b	'54					S	P
113	'24	A1	Re·N°410	?	'28	"	b	"						P
114	'22	A2		?	'30	H5		'55					X	P
115	"	"		?	'27	H4	b						I	L
116	"			?	'31	H5		'53					L	X
117	"			?				'55					L	X
118	"			?	"	K		'56					I	X
119	"	B		?	'36	R	f						G	P
120	'23	A1		'35									S	P

273

No.	YEAR NEW	TYPE	NOTES	YEAR SCRAP	YEAR NEW	TYPE	NOTES	YEAR SCRAP	YEAR NEW	TYPE	NOTES	YEAR SCRAP	DEPOT IN 45	
121	'22	HI		'50									G	L
122	"	"		'49									L	L
123	"	"		'50									L	L
124	"	"		'51									L	L
125	"	"		'50									L	L
126	"	"		"									L	S
127	"	"		'51									L	L
128	"	"		'50									L	L
129	"	"		'49									L	L
130	"	"		'50									L	L
131	"	"		'49									L	L
132	"	"		'51									L	L
133	"	"		"									L	L
134	"	"		'52									L	L
135	"	"		'51									L	L
136	"	"		'49									X	L
137	'23	AI		'35	'35	R						'56	L	X
138	'24	H4		"		H5	ex·Nº29					"	X	X
139	"	"		'53									X	X
140	"	"		'55									G	X
141	"	"		'53									G	G
142	'25	"		'50									L	G
143	"	"		'53									X	X
144	'22	B		'34		R	b					'56	G	P
145	'23	"	Became Salt Con	'29	'29	H4	b					'54	G	P
146	'22	A2		'33	'27	"	b						L	L
147		AI		?	'34	H5						'55	G	S
148		A3		'33	'31	"							G	P
149		AI		?	'35	R	f					'56	S	P
150		AI		'35									P	L

No	YEAR NEW	TYPE	NOTES	YEAR SCRAP	YEAR NEW	TYPE	NOTES	YEAR SCRAP	YEAR NEW	TYPE	NOTES	YEAR SCRAP	DEPOT IN 30	45
151	22	A1	f	'35	'35	H4	ex-N°28	'53					P	G
152	"	"		'33	'34	H5		'56					P	L
153	"	B		?	'28	H4	b	'53					P	X
154	"	A2		?	'30	"	b	'55					L	X
155	"	"		?	'30	H5	b						=	G
156	"	"		'35	'31	"		'56					=	G
157	"	A3		?	'35	R	f						L	G
158	"	A2		'33	'31	H5	f	'55					L	L
159	23	"		'35	'34	"		'56					L	G
160	22	B		?	'35	K		'55					=	P
161	"	A2		?	'31	"	f	"					=	P
162	"	A3		?	'30	H5	f	'56	'50	R		e	=	G
163	23	A1		?	'35	R	b						=	P
164	"	B		'35	"	K		'55					P	P
165	22	A2		?	'31	"		'55	'50	R	f	e	=	P
166	"	A3		?	'30	H5	f						=	P
167	23	H2		'35		F	ex-N°13	'47					L	X
168	22	A3		'54	'36	F	ex-N°25	'47					X	X
169	"	"		'55	'28	R		'56					S	L
170	"	A2		'35	'34	H4	b	'55					S	P
171	"	A3		"	'28	H5		'54					P	S
172	23	B		'33	'31	K	f	'56					=	P
173	"	"	Became Welding Car N°2 in	?	'27	H4	b	'54					S	L
174	22	A2	f	'31	'28	H4	b	'53					=	G
175	"	B	f	?	'32	P	f	'e					=	L

Table of tramcar fleet details (rotated page). Best-effort reading.

No	YEAR NEW	TYPE	NOTES	YEAR SCRAP	YEAR NEW	TYPE	NOTES	YEAR SCRAP	DEPOT IN 30/45
181	'23	B		?	29	H4	b	'55	L/L
182	'22	A2		'35	"	"	ex-N°18	'54	L/G
183		"			'27	"	ex-N°20	'55	G/G
184		A3		'35	'27	H5	b	=	S/S
185	'23	A2		'33	'33	H4	f	'54	L/L
186	'22	A1		?	'27	"	b	=	S/P
187	'23	A3		'35	'28	R	b	'55	L/L
188	'22	B		'34	'35			'56	S/S
189	'23	A3		'33	'34	H5	f	'55	L/L
190	'22	B	a		'27	H5	b	'54	S/S
191	'23	A2	f	'33	'33	H4	b	'55	S/P
192					'28	H5	f	'56	G/G
193				'33	'36	H4	b		P/P
194					'28	R	f	'55	S/S
195		A1		'35	'30	H4	b	'56	
196		B		?	'35	H5		e	G/G
197		A1		'33	'33	R		'54	X/X
198		A2		'35	'35	R	b	'56	L/L
199		A3		?	'28	H4	f	'53	G/G
200		B		'34	'30	H5		'55	S/S
201		A2		'31	'35	R			L/L
202	'23	A1		'34	'33	R	b	'54	P/P
203	'22	A3			'35	H4	f		P/P
204	"	B		'32	'28	H5			X/X
205	'23	A1		?	'33		b		L/L
206	'22	A2			'31	H4	f	'54	L/X
207	"		d	'41	'27	R		e	P/P
208	'23	G	d	'44	'43	"		e	G/L
209	"	"			'47				
210									

No	YEAR NEW	TYPE	NOTES	YEAR SCRAP	YEAR NEW	TYPE	NOTES	YEAR SCRAP	DEPOT IN 30/45
211	'24+	G	a	'40	'41	R		e	L/L
212	'23	"	a	'39	'40	"		e	X/L
213		"	a	'41	'42	"		e	X/L
214		"	a	'39	'40	"		'56	X/L
215		"	a		'39	"		e	X/L
216	'24	"	a	'44		"		e	X/L
217		"	a	'37	'47	"		e	X/L
218	'23	"	a	'47	'38	"		'56	X/L
219	'24	"	a	'39	'48	"		e	X/L
220	'23	"	a	'43	'39	"		'54	X/L
221	'24	"	a	'38		"		e	X/X
222	'22	"	b·f	'39		"		e	X/X
223	'23	"	a	'47		"		e	S/S
224		"	a		'47	"		e	X/S
225		"	a	'38	'50	"		e	X/X
226		"	a·b	'39	'38	"		'56	S/S
227		"	a	'47	'39	Q3			L/L
228		"	b·f	'34	'48	R			L/L
229	SLATE	E	a·f		'35	"			L/L
230	FORD	LI	f			"			L/L
231			f	'33	'34	"			P/D
232	L E I T H		f	'36	'36	"			P/D
233			f			"			
234	C A R S		f			"			
235			f			"			
236			f			"			
237			f		'37	Q3			
238				'33	'34	"			
239						"			
240									

Fleet roster table — **LEITH CARS** (cars 241–330)

Column groups (repeated for each number block): No | YEAR NEW | TYPE | NOTES | YEAR SCRAP | YEAR NEW | TYPE | NOTES | YEAR SCRAP | DEPOT IN 30 / 45

Cars 241–270

No	Y.NEW	TYPE	NOTES	Y.SCRAP	Y.NEW	TYPE	NOTES	Y.SCRAP	30	45
241		L1		33	'34	Q2		'52	L	P
242		"	f					'55	L	P
243		"		36	'37	R		'56	L	L
244		M		33	'34	Q2		'52	L	L
245		"		32			f	'50	L	L
246		"		33				'52	L	P
247		"		36	'37	R		'56	L	L
248		N								
249		"	+	33	'34	Q2	f	'52	L	L
250		"	+	31	'32	J		'56	L	L
251		"								
252					'33			'55	L	L
253					'32			'56	L	L
254								'52	L	L
255					'33			'56	L	L
256					'32			'55	L	L
257			f					'53	L	L
258								'55	L	L
259								'56	L	L
260		L2	+	32	'33	Q1	+	'55	L	L
261		"	f	33	'34	P	+	'56	L	L
262				31		S2	+	'55	L	L
263		M		32	'33	K	ex N°371. f		L	L
264		"		31	'31	Q1	f	'56	L	L
265		"		33	'33	K		'54	L	L
266		"	+	32	'34	S2		'55	L	X
267	SLATE E		+	29	'29	H4			L	L
268			+	35	'35	R		'56	L	L
269	-FORD		f	53					S	G
270	'23	H2							X	X

Cars 271–300

No	Y.NEW	TYPE	NOTES	Y.SCRAP	30	45
271	'23	H2		'52	P	L
272	"	"		'55	P	L
273	"	"		'56	L	L
274	"	"		'52	L	L
275	"	"		'50	L	L
276	"	"		'52	L	L
277	"	"		'56	P	L
278	"	"			L	L
279	"	"		'52	L	L
280	"	"		'56	L	L
281	"	"			L	L
282	"	"		'55	L	L
283	"	"		'56	L	L
284	"	"		'52	L	L
285	"	"		'56	L	L
286	"	"		'55	L	L
287	"	"		'53	L	L
288	"	"		'55	L	L
289	"	"		'56	L	L
290	"	"		'55	L	L
291	"	"		'56	L	L
292	"	"		'55	L	L
293	"	"		'56	L	L
294	"	"		'55	L	L
295	"	"			L	L
296	"	"		'56	L	X
297	"	"		'54	L	L
298	"	"		'55	L	L
299	"	"		'56	S	G
300	"	"			X	X

Cars 301–330

No	Y.NEW	TYPE	NOTES	Y.SCRAP	30	45
301	'23	H2		'54	X	G
302	"	"			X	G
303	"	"		'53	X	G
304	"	"		'54	X	G
305	"	"		'53	G	X
306	"	"			P	X
307	"	"	f	'54	X	X
308	"	"		'55	G	L
309	"	"			X	G
310	"	"	f	'54	P	X
311	"	"	f	'53	X	L
312	'24	H3	f	'54	X	G
313	"	"	f	'55	G	L
314	"	"	f	'53	S	G
315	"	"	f	'54	S	L
316	"	"	f	'55	S	L
317	"	"	f	'53	S	L
318	"	"			S	G
319	"	"			L	X
320	"	"		'55	L	X
321	"	"		'54	G	X
322	"	"		'55	G	L
323	"	"		'52	S	G
324	"	"		'53	S	G
325	"	"		'55	G	G
326	"	"	f	'53	G	S
327	"	"	f	'55	S	S
328	"	"		'53	S	S
329	"	"			S	G
330	"	"		'54	S	S

277

Nº	YEAR NEW	TYPE	NOTES	YEAR SCRAP	DEPOT IN '30	'45
331	'24	H3	b	'53	S	G
332	'25	H4	d	'54	X	G
333	"	"	d	'55	X	L
334	"	"	d		X	G
335	"	"	d	'53	X	G
336	"	"	d		X	G
337	"	"	d		X	G
338	"	"	d	'54	X	G
339	"	"	d	'53	X	G
340	"	"	d		X	G
341	"	"	d	'55	L	G
342	'26	"	d	'53	L	L
343	"	"	b		L	L
344	"	"	d		L	L
345	"	"	b		L	L
346	"	"	b	'55	S	G
347	"	"	b	'53	S	G
348	"	"	b		S	G
349	'27	"	b	'49	S	L
350	"	"	b	'54		L
351	'26	"	b	'53		L
352	"	"	b			L
353	"	"	b	'55		L
354	'29	"	b	'54		L
355	"	"	b	'55		L
356	"	"	b f	'56		L
357	"	"	b f	'55		L
358	"	"	b f			L
359	"	"		'56		L
360	"	"		'55		D

Nº	YEAR NEW	TYPE	NOTES	YEAR SCRAP	DEPOT IN '30	'45
361	'29	H4	b f	'55	—	D
362	"	"	b f		—	D
363	"	"	b f		—	D
364	"	"	b f	'56	—	D
365	"	"	b f	'55	—	D
366	"	"	b f		—	D
367	"	"	b f		—	D
368	"	K	b f		—	D
369	"	"	b f	'56	—	D
370	'30	"	b	'55	X	D
371	"	"	f Re Nº 266		—	D
372	"	"			—	NEVER USED
373	"	"			—	
374	"	"			—	
375	"	"			—	
376	"	"			—	
377	"	"			—	
378	"	"			—	
379	"	"			—	
380	"	"			—	
381	"	"			—	
382	"	"			—	
383	"	"			—	
384	"	"			—	
385	"	"			—	
386	"	"			—	
387	"	"			—	
388	"	"			—	
389	"	"			—	
390	"	"			—	

Nº	YEAR NEW	TYPE	NOTES	YEAR SCRAP
391	'47	T	NEVER USED	'54
392	"	"		"
393	"	"		"
394	"	"		"
395	"	"		"
396	"	"		"
397	"	"		"
398	"	"		"
399	"	"		"
400	"	"		"
401	"	"		"
402	"	"		"
403	"	"		"
404	"	"		
405	'48	"		
406	"	"		
407	"	"		
408	"	"		
409	'49	"		
410	"	"		
411	"	"		

LEYLAND BUS WITH CENTRE ENTRANCE 1920

The Rolling-Stock :— Buses

In the spring of 1919 three charabancs and twelve buses of 35/40 h.p. were ordered from the Leyland Company. The charabancs were orthodox 27 seaters and were painted grey, the Edinburgh licence numbers 1, 2, and 3 being used for fleet numbers, and the registrations respectively B8725, and S9257-8. The buses were Nos. 4 to 15, S9309-20 and were longer with rather box like bodies with a flat roof and a narrow entrance near the rear. A seat was arranged along the back, the off-side, and, — facing backwards, —on a partition just ahead of the entrance, this rear part forming the smoking compartment. The driver had a partition behind him and an off-side door. On his near-side there was a hinged seat for two passengers which could also be reached by a hinged near-side door. The 31 seats had green leather cushions. All windows had top-lights, the near-side ones over the windscreen and the two-windowed back containing roller-blind destination screens. Electric bell pushes were fitted. The livery was the standard madder with white window pillars.

Six more Leyland charabancs were ordered later in 1919, Nos. 16-21 respectively SG53, 1196, 1299, 1300, 1524-5. Soon afterwards it was decided to order six bus bodies for these for winter use. These were built by Cowieson's to the Corporation's own design and had a wide entrance at the centre of the body, forward of which the seats were arranged longitudinally. There was the same arrangement of smoking compartment at the back but no near-side door at the front. In all other features they conformed to the pattern of the preceding bus bodies, and seated 32. They were given different numbers, viz. 150-5. After only one or two season's use they were laid aside to re-appear later as will be told in due course.

Early in 1920 a further thirty Leyland buses were ordered with the standard pattern body, the numbers and bodybuilders being as follows :—

Leyland : Nos. 22-33 : SG1649-53, 2133-6, 2801-3 respectively.

Cowieson : Nos. 40-50 and 150 : SG1654, 2142, 2138, 2137, 2273-6, 2805-8 respectively.

Lincoln Lorries : Nos. 34-9 : SG2139-41, 2277-8, 2804 respectively.

A further thirty buses were also ordered for the steep Northern routes and these necessarily required more power and additional braking, so A.E.C. "Y" type with 40/45 h.p. Tyler engines were chosen. The bodies were of the standard pattern and built by E. & H. Hora of London. They were numbered 157-185, respectively SG2008-15, 2221-6, 2267-72, 2325-30 and 2809-11. The last one was presumably 186, SG2812 and is thought to have been burnt out, the chassis SG2812 appearing in the Department's lorry fleet.

E.O.C.

A.E.C. BUS OF 1921 CONVERTED TO PNEUMATIC TYRES

LONDON TYPE OPEN-TOP DOUBLE-DECK BUS No. 192, 1922

Six more Leyland charabancs were ordered for 1921. These were longer with an additional row, thus seating 33. They were Nos. 186-191, SG2813-5/7/6/8. There was also an additional Leyland SG2819 which may have replaced the destroyed A.E.C. This got one of the centre entrance bodies and was numbered 151, but for some unknown reason disappeared very quickly. An unusual new bus appeared at this time too, an A.E.C. "S" type with single-deck body. The driver was in the forward-control position beside the engine but protected only by a metal dash plate and a light windscreen. The entrance was near the front, there being one window ahead of it and four behind. This bus was No. 192, SG4869, and was painted red. A standard red London open-top double-decker of the A.E.C. "S" type was also sent up on a demonstration and this was retained, as No. 193, N05027. No. 192 was thereupon fitted with an almost identical double-deck body built by Fry, also red, retaining the number 192.

It was four years before any more new buses were ordered and it will be convenient to refer meantime to some alterations made to the existing fleet. The provision of an "ear" on the near-side of the roof to show the service number has already been mentioned. The narrowness of the entrances gave rise to inconvenience and by early in 1921 these were widened on Nos. 7-9, 11, 14, 15, 25, and 29, and possibly two others. On the other hand Nos. 4, 22, 28, 37, 40, and 46 were altered for one-man operation by making the entrance at the front alongside the driver. The original rear entrance was removed but an emergency door and folding step provided in its place, with a lift-up seat inside. The seating capacity was thereby reduced to 30. Later, in 1929, six A.E.C.s were similarly altered, viz. Nos. 158, 161-2, 168-170, and all but the last two were fitted with folding doors. Shortly before this Nos. 32 and 38 exchanged bodies, and the six centre entrance Cowieson bodies were fitted to Nos. 13, 33, 42, 48, 49, and 50, though No. 49 got a Cowieson front entrance body subsequently. The others, except No. 42, then had the smoking compartment seats rearranged to mostly face forward. The off-side drivers' doors were blocked up at an early date in most cases and several buses then had a hole in the panel alongside for the petrol-tank filler.

There was an important experiment early in 1922 when No. 24 was fitted with "Michelin" beaded-edge pneumatic tyres. Afterwards these were put on No. 40 for a short time, while straight-sided pneumatic tyres were fitted to Nos. 6, 7, 8, 23, and 24. These proved successful and after a time all the Leyland buses and charabancs were so fitted. Some of the latter had the front and rear wheels fitted at different times. Most of the A.E.C.s were subsequently fitted too but Nos. 157/9/63-5/72/4-5/8/82/4 were withdrawn in 1927 while still on solid tyres.

About 1928 the service number "ear" on the roof was removed and a roller-blind number put in the top-light over the driver's windscreen. Earlier, a few buses had the front destination screen arranged centrally across the two top-lights. These were Nos. 4, 13, 46, 168, 169, 170, and 181. A little later surviving buses had the waist band and the inside of the roof painted white, but withdrawal was then in full swing and only Nos. 5, 8, 9, 11-13, 29, 31-4, 37-8, 42, 45-6, 48-50, 150, 158, 161-2, 167-8, 170-1, 177, and 179-81 lasted to receive it. At the end of 1930 charabancs Nos. 1-3, and 16-8 were converted to lorries as had been several of the buses withdrawn earlier, both Leyland and A.E.C. The remaining charabancs were then painted a bright red with a darker red band along the top. Two buses were renumbered in 1930, No. 11 becoming No. 31, and No. 38 becoming No. 8.

By the time the next new vehicles came in 1926 design had of course changed. First there were three neat Dennis 14 seater charabancs by Vickers, Nos. 501-3, SF6028-30, and painted grey. Much more striking were eight Leyland Lions PLSC1 model with 29 seat Leyland bodies. To Edinburgh eyes at the time these looked very strange machines, for the only half-cab types seen so far had been the two London type double-deckers, the short-lived No. 192 as a single decker and two new Albions for the S.M.T.Co. The new Lions had a cut-away rear entrance, forward of which was a partition. Between the partition and the entrance was a longitudinal seat for two on each side, then a forward facing seat for two on the off-side and a seat for four across the back, these forming the smoking compartment. There was also an entrance at the front with a hinged door at the top of the steps, while a seat against the front bulkhead held three. All windows had top-lights except the back in which there were two windows with a destination screen centrally above. The roof was well domed, and the white ceiling gave them a light appearance inside. A destination screen-box was mounted above the front of the roof and the service number "ear" to the near-side as usual. The driver's cab was of course completely enclosed. They were robust and lively buses and numbered 504-11, SF6258-61, 6330-1, 6470-1. There were also four more A.E.C. double-deckers with bodies by the Brush Electric Company generally similar to the existing two but with enclosed cab for the driver. These were however painted in the Corporation's standard colours. They were Nos. 153-6, SF6521-4, and ran on solid tyres at first though the now universal pneumatic tyres were fitted later to the front wheels, and afterwards to the rear wheels as well. Destination screen-boxes were fitted to them early in 1931, by which time the original two double-deckers had been scrapped.

LEYLAND LION PLSC/1 TYPE OF 1926

The 1927 additions consisted of fourteen more Leyland Lions, this time PLSC3 with 32 seat bodies of the same design by Croall and by Hall-Lewis. There was a seat for one beside the front entrance and an additional forward facing seat opposite. The seat between the partition and rear entrance was arranged to face backwards on the near-side. The numbers were 512-7, SF8495-8500 with Croall bodies, and 518-25, SF8989-96 with Hall-Lewis bodies, except No.521 which was by Croall. Another novelty was six Karrier six-wheelers WL6/1 with similar Hall-Lewis bodies seating 39. The seating layout followed the plan of the PLSC1s with longer seats over the wheel-arches. The dash panel was also higher and provided with louvred ventilators. These were Nos. 526-31, SF8997-9 and SF9002-4.

In 1928 there were four more Leyland Lion PLSC3, eight more Karrier six-wheelers, and another innovation destined to be the precursor of a long sequence, namely eight Daimlers. The latter were A.D.C. 423 models. All the bodies were by Croall and similar to the preceding ones though there were some variations in the seating on the Daimlers and the dash panels on the Karriers were lower. The service "ears" were not provided on these buses however. Instead a service number screen was incorporated in the near-side end of the destination screen-box and the whole box set into the front of the roof instead of mounted above it. All the earlier buses were subsequently altered likewise. There were also three more Dennis with 14 seat open coach bodies. There was a seat for three between the wheel arches and two double seats on the off-side and three singles on the near-side, all reached from a door at the front, while another door at the rear served the back seat for four. The Dennis were grey, to which a yellow waist panel was added early in 1930. Licence numbers from old buses were now used up again as the following list shows :—

Leyland : Nos. 10, 26 (soon re-num'd 24), 151-2; SC1126-9 respectively.

Daimler : Nos. 157/9-60, 47, 163-6; SC1130-7 respectively.

Karrier : Nos. 172/4-5, 532, 178/82, 533, 184; SC1138-45 respectively.

Dennis : Nos. 14 (soon re-num'd 26), 35/9; SC1146-8 respectively.

No. 172 was destroyed by fire when quite new and replaced by another one registration SC2216.

The last Leylands, PLSC3, for many years were added in 1929. These were Nos. 30, 6, 194-7, 183, 200, 198-9, respectively SC3401-10 with bodies by Cowieson, and Nos. 535, 772-3, 771, 770 respectively SC3411-5 with bodies by Croall. There was a solitary Daimler, a CF/6 with Croall body, No. 534, SC3416, and fourteen of a new type, the A.E.C. Reliance, also with Croall bodies, Nos. 774-87, SC3417-30. The only difference from the preceding bodies was the adoption of one large oval window in the back. The A.E.C.s had "Holt" heaters.

Another new make appeared in 1930 in the form of four Morris Viceroy 20 seater coaches of orthodox design painted red, followed at the end of the year by three Morris Dictators with generally similar though larger 24 seat bodies by Mitchell. These were also red and carried a destination board above the windscreen illuminated by cowled lamps. The former were Nos. 581-4, SC7281-4, and the latter Nos. 48-50, SC8747-9. The standard livery was subsequently applied. The 1930 buses were all Daimlers, CF/6, with Cowieson bodies as before but without top-lights to the windows, and brown leather for the seats. The rear registration number was transferred to an illuminated panel at the bottom of the back. These were Nos. 4, 5, 7, 9, 11, 12, 13, 170, 15, 22, 23, 25, 27, 28, 33, 36, 37, 38, 40, 41, 42, 43, 44, 46, 167, 171, 14, 173, 176, 177, 179, 180, 181, 185, 192, 193, respectively SC7285-7320. In a few cases the old buses with these numbers continued in traffic as well as the new ones so there was a duplication of certain numbers for a month or two, e.g. Nos. 5, 13, 33, 37. Near the end of the year a further Daimler appeared, a CH/6 with fluid flywheel, and similar body by Hume. This was No. 169, SC8791 and seated only 29, there being a single inward facing seat each side immediately in front of the partition.

In 1931 the old licensing system came to an end and the new Traffic Commissioners' small oval white enamelled number plates were fixed to the back of all vehicles. For the next few years these numbers with their M prefix were used as fleet numbers. As with the tramcars the old form of lettering was also discarded in favour of the small City and Royal Burgh of Edinburgh at the bottom of the body on the near-side only towards the front. Both lots of Dennis and the remaining old charabancs were now also painted red in line with the later coaches. Of the pre-1926 fleet only six buses and nine charabancs survived into the new scheme as will be seen from the list on page 295. The Karriers had not been entirely successful and some of them had already been scrapped too. The remainder together with the double-deckers and the pre-1926 vehicles disappeared at the end of 1931, and the Dennises the following year.

E.O.C.

DAIMLER OF 1929-30

The 1931 buses comprised a Crossley, registered SC9901, an Albion Viking, SC9902, a Daimler CG/6, SC9903, fourteen Daimler CF/6, SC9904-17, and three Morris Dictators SC9918-20. All the 31 seat bodies were built locally by Alexander Motors to the same pattern as the preceding ones, but the partition was now omitted. All seats faced forwards except those over the wheel arches and against the front bulkhead, though there were some variations, the rows being staggered on the CF/6s. Other new features were enclosed lighting fittings and air bells for the conductor.

By 1932 the new Ministry of Transport requirements regarding exits etc. rendered necessary a change in the design of body used over the preceding six years. So the nine Daimlers CH/6, registered FS2159-67 had 32 seat Cowieson bodies generally similar to the Alexander Motors ones of 1931 but there was no entrance at the front. There was however, an emergency door on the off-side at the front. There were two similar Morris Dictators FS2157-8, but the body of the latter was of all-metal construction by Metro-politan-Cammel and had a flatter roof. Another six Morris Dictator 24 seat coaches were also added, FS2151-6. Their Alexander Motors bodies had an emergency door between two windows in the back, mcquette seating, and a higher roof with an opening portion, a dual destination screen being incorporated in the front. Air bells were fitted and they were painted in the red coach livery. Later the coach door was replaced by an orthodox bus entrance at the front and the standard bus livery applied.

Over the next two years only a few odd buses were purchased, but much experimental work was being carried out. Leyland SC3407, A.E.C. SC3423 and Daimler SC9903 were adapted to run on tar oil for a period but this was not continued. Another A.E.C., SC3430 received a Beardmore oil engine in August 1933, for which the bonnet had to be slightly extended. Two Morris Dictators with 34 seat front entrance all-metal Metropolitan-Cammel bodies arrived in the early part of 1933. These were FS4422 and FS5936. The emergency exit was in the back and they had rather flat roofs and no service number was provided for. The latter had its destination screen rebuilt in the usual form incorporating this later, while the former was eventually fitted with a separate number box under the canopy. There were also destination screens in the window beside the entrance.

The Corporation's first closed-top double-decker appeared in July 1933 in the form of a Morris Imperial with Park-Royal low-bridge type body seating 50. The platform was enclosed and a service number screen provided back and front with destination screen below at the front only, and above the platform entrance. This was registered FS6340, while another registered FS9611 followed about a year after. The latter seated one less on each deck and the body, this time by Metropolitan-Cammel, showed other minor differences such as the lack of a waist panel. Meanwhile there were four more single-deckers, all different. FS7032 was a Morris Dictator and FS7033 a Daimler CP/6 both with English Electric 34 seat bodies similar to the 1933 ones with the service number beside the destination screen as normally. FS7036 was a Daimler COG5 with a similar Weyman body of more massive appearance. This bus had a Gardner oil engine, while WS637 another Daimler with a rather similar 32 seat body by Roberts, had a Tangye oil engine. On the latter a separate service number box was provided under the canopy and the seating was in red leather. Finally in October 1934 came an A.E.C. "Q" bus with the standard 39 seat Weyman body with entrance near the front and emergency door in the off-side. It carried no service number screen till modified in the usual way later, and was registered WS1508. The A.E.C. Riccardo oil engine was fitted. The window pillars were experimentally painted brown on SC7287 in 1933 but this was not perpetuated.

Further oil engines were also obtained, all the A.E.C. Reliances except the one with the Beardmore engine being fitted with A.E.C. four cylinder oil engines in 1934, while during 1934-5, Gardner five cylinder oil engines were fitted in all the 1932 batch of Daimler and Morris buses, to the Albion, and to SC8791 and FS7033. WS637 received one also in 1936 as did the Morris Imperials. The Crossley was fitted with an oil engine of that make in 1934 and another new one to be tried was a Thornycroft in one of the 1930 Daimlers viz. SC7301. The latter required its bonnet extended and in 1935 received a larger Daimler radiator. This was changed for a neater Thornycroft radiator the following year but in 1937 reverted to its original form with petrol engine.

The Daimler-Gardner combination with Metropolitan-Cammel all-metal body was then standardised, five cylinder engines for single-deckers and six cylinder engines for double -deckers. So in 1935 there were sixteen 54 seat high-bridge type double-deckers otherwise generally similar to FS9611 but with a waist panel registered WS6371-86, 1936 saw single-deckers WS9502-21 with 36 seat bodies with cut-away pattern rear entrance, emergency door on the off-side at the front, and rectangular window in the back. There were the usual front screens and also a destination screen over the entrance and a service number screen to the back beside the step.

By now however the necessity of a better means of identification of vehicles than by the Traffic Commissioners' "M" number was apparent and a new fleet list was drawn up, the different types being separately numbered with a different prefix letter as follows :

A   Daimler single-deckers with oil engines.

B   A.E.C.

D   Daimler single-deckers with petrol engines.

G   Daimler double-deckers, (and later other makes as well).

L   Leyland.

M   Morris. (all types).

X   Other makes not covered by the foregoing.

Each set of numbers started at eleven, the intention being that in due course renewals would take the old numbers, and if the first (say) ten buses were perchance replaced by (say) fifteen new ones there would be a margin of numbers available for them. The aforementioned double-deckers WS6371-86 were accordingly numbered G11-26. The single-deckers WS9502-21 took the numbers A24-43, the numbers A11-23 being allocated to the older vehicles in

STANDARD DAIMLER COG5 TYPE SINGLE-DECKER
OF 1936-9 AT HAY DRIVE

this category. The numbers were painted in fairly small characters on the dash and on the back under the waist panel to the near-side. The numbers were gradually painted on the older vehicles, and the list on page 295 will enable the numbers to be traced through. The issue of "M" number plates ceased in 1939.

A44-53 and G27-41 followed in 1937 being the same as their respective predecessors but with moquette seating, while more arrived in 1938 in two lots each, viz. A54-68 and 69-88; G42-51 and 52-61. The 1937 and 1938 double-deckers seated one or two less and the last lot had a ventilator in the top of the top deck front window.

There were no new vehicles in 1939 and the next to be recorded are the mixed handful received through the Ministry of Supply at the end of 1941. These and the other vehicles acquired during the war are given in the list on page 297. The double-deckers were all more or less of the austerity pattern except for the Bristol which had rounded lines. This and the A.E.C.s had the top deck waist panel of white curved down to the top of the destination screen as on the tramcars. Of the single-deckers, the Tilling-Stevens and the Bristol had a front entrance though the latter was eventually altered to the usual cut-away pattern of rear entrance. In all cases destination and service number screens were arranged on the standard Edinburgh layout, except for the Tilling-Stevens which had a separate service number box below the canopy. The Bedfords were the standard utility models and those up to No. X17 were originally in the production colour. Nos. G62 and G63 also ran in plain grey for their first few months. It will be noticed that the original plan of reserving numbers 1 to 10 had now been abandoned and these were used up before adding higher numbers.

A number of the standard "A" class buses and all the Morris coaches were taken by the W.D. and other services at the beginning of the war, while G44 and G46 were lent to London at the critical period in 1941. All except the Morris coaches duly returned, and in addition two Daimler single-deckers formerly owned by Dundee Corporation and badly damaged in W.D. service were on offer. These were promptly snapped up and completely rebuilt at Shrubhill to almost the Edinburgh standard pattern. They were turned out in a pleasing grey fully lined and varnished and numbered A23, (the previous A23 having been withdrawn in April 1940), and A10. This grey livery was thereafter applied to all the Bedfords, to Nos. G4, 5, 6, and 63, and also to one pre-war bus viz. A51. As the war wore on there was of course increasing difficulty in keeping the older vehicles going. The A.E.C.s were then the oldest vehicles in the fleet and they survived till 1943 while the 1930 series of Daimlers whose sleeve-valve engines were specially difficult for

D.L.G.H.

STANDARD DAIMLER COG6 DOUBLE-DECKER of 1935
OUTSIDE CENTRAL GARAGE
Note the Garage doors have been enlarged

spares also finally petered out at the end of that year when they could be induced to run no longer. Many makeshifts had to be adopted, and No. D55 for example had a second-hand Albion engine. The producer-gas fuel running has already been mentioned.

After the war new Northern Counties bodies were provided for Nos. G1-6 in 1948, while the bodies from Nos. G1, 3, 4, and 5 replaced those on Nos. G64-5, 63, and 66 respectively. New Duple coach bodies were also provided in 1949 for some of the Bedfords while new seating etc. was provided in the remainder, and the standard colour scheme restored, in some cases with a down-swept waist panel. The few other grey buses were also soon restored to standard colours. No. G71 was wrecked in 1945 and subsequently fitted with a reconstructed single-deck body with a front entrance which is believed to have originally belonged to No.M11. Being now a single-decker it was renumbered A11, the original A11 by then having been scrapped. No. A12 was reconstructed as a 26 seater and with additional decorative external mouldings in 1947 for the airport service. No. A14 had been withdrawn in 1944 but the others of that lot, viz. Nos. A13 and A15-9 and also No. A47 were fitted in 1949 with new 36 seat bodies by Alexander's of Stirling. They were generally similar to the immediate pre-war standard pattern but had a larger service number screen at the front, while that on the back was placed centrally. No. A20 was also badly smashed in 1948 and thereafter fitted with a reconstructed body believed to have come off the Crossley, scrapped some years earlier. During 1949-50 several of the Daimler single-deckers were rebuilt similar to the Alexander bodied ones, some having a new curved dash panel as well.

The first post-war deliveries were twenty-seven Guy double-deckers with Gardner engines, Nos. G79-105, in 1945-6. Those with Northern Counties bodies had a high domed roof and, except for Nos. G81-7, had ventilators in the top deck front windows. The service number screens were larger than hitherto and these larger screens were at this time fitted to several older double-deckers. On Nos. G93-105 however, a new arrangement of destination screen with two larger screens above it was adopted. The service number was shown in the one to the off-side and two of the principal points on the route in the other. The earlier double-deckers were duly altered to conform to this pattern, as were also the few surviving pre-war ones. These were followed by twelve Daimler CVD6 double-deckers and fifteen CVG6s. Of the former Nos. G106-12 had Northern Counties bodies as on the Guys and appeared in 1947-8, while Nos. G113-7 with Metropolitan-Cammel bodies of neater design with deeper top-deck windows and no ventilators in front, did not arrive till 1949. The CVG6s all had the Metropolitan-Cammel body and followed in 1949 as Nos. G123-37, the Nos. G118-22 being allocated to a further five CVD6s with Metropolitan-Cammel bodies which arrived towards the end of the same year.

The first new single-deckers were ten Guy Arabs in 1948. These had 35 seat Metropolitan-Cammel bodies generally similar to the reconstructed pre-war Daimlers. They were followed at the end of the year by ten Daimler CVG5s with similar bodies, Nos. A89-98. There was then a gap in the numbers, the Guys being Nos. A131-40. Four Crossley single-deckers were also acquired at this time and numbered A1-4. They had been destined for another operator and had Roe 34 seat front entrance bodies. The emergency door was in the back, and they were turned out painted chocolate colour without any white relieving, but were re-painted in the standard style in 1950. About the end of 1949 fifteen Bristol L6B single-deckers appeared with Brockhouse bodies similar to the Daimlers. These were numbered A162-76, while the old Bristol No. X15 was renumbered A161. Seven Bedfords with standard Duple coach bodies also came in 1949. These were numbered X2, 9, 18, and 22-5, the older ones bearing these numbers being renumbered X32-8.

Forty-seven more Daimler CVG6 with Metropolitan-Cammel double-deck bodies arrived about the end of 1949, numbered G138-84. The Metropolitan-Cammel bodies had ventilators in the panel over the lower saloon windows but commencing with No.G154 these were omitted and they were subsequently removed from all the earlier ones. Fifteen Guy double-deckers with Northern Counties bodies were also added in 1949. These bodies were more like the Metropolitan-Cammel ones, but had the top deck front ventilators and also top-lights to the lower saloon windows and a curved valance to the near-side front wing. They were Nos. G200-14. The next new buses were seventeen A.E.C. double-deckers with Brockhouse bodies very similar to the Daimlers, and these were Nos. G221-37.

By now the numbering system was getting out of hand and a straightforward scheme of numbers without prefixes was adopted in May 1951. The new numbers were painted in larger characters on both sides just behind the cab or bonnet below the waist panel and in the same position as before on the back. The scheme of renumbering was also simple. Those in the "G" series retained their numbers while those in the "A" series had six hundred added.

The Bedford coaches were however excluded from the scheme and kept their old "X" numbers and small characters. A list of numbers under the new scheme is given on pages 297 and 298 and details of registration numbers etc. of the foregoing and subsequent buses will be found therein.

From 1952 onwards increasingly large orders were placed to cover requirements for tramway conversion. Some vehicles call for mention here. There was LRW377, a Daimler G6H/S with Duple rear entrance "Transit" type body which ran in service about the end of 1951 for a month or two. This was painted in Edinburgh colours and numbered 800. Subsequent buses on loan for trial purposes, of which there were several from time to time, were not usually numbered. Nos. 801 and 802, respectively 31 and 32 seats, differed from one another, and from Nos. 803-18 which had 40 seats. These all had cut-away rear entrances, but Nos. 801 and 802 were rebuilt in 1955 as front entrance coaches though still differing from one another, and then respectively 37 and 36 seats. As coaches their livery was white relieved with black, and Nos. 819-21 were also in this style, their front entrance bodies having very flowing lines, and 41 seats.

No. 185 was an orthodox double-decker acquired from Birmingham Corporation in 1953 and had a Comet engine. Double-deckers of 1952 and subsequently were eight feet wide vehicles. Nos. 301-60 were former London Transport buses with re-built chassis and new full-fronted double-deck body seating 55. The Alexander bodies shown for Nos. 62-70/2-8 were fitted in 1954 and were also of full-fronted type, seating 58. On these the service number screen was to the near-side of the other screen, while on the 401 series and all subsequent double-deckers the "route" screen was directly above the destination screen and the service number screen symmetrically to the near-side of both. On these too the destination screen above the platform entrance was moved to over the last saloon window, its place being taken by a service number screen which was now omitted from the back. This latter point gave rise to much complaint. The Alexander and Duple full-fronted bodies differed in detail from the MCW ones and the different lots of the latter had a varying arrangement of ventilator windows, and seating either 60 or 63. Of all the full-fronted bodies only Nos. 301-60 had waist panels and the white panel over the lower saloon windows. No. 575 was turned out unpainted aluminium but soon received a madder band between the decks. Later Nos. 791-800 were turned out similarly. The single-deckers in the 700s were correspondingly renumbered in the 800s in 1956. Nos. 642 and 645 had their waist band painted over madder about 1953, and the 1949 Bedfords received Perkins P6 diesel engines in 1952.

LEYLAND PD/2 TYPE No. 451
in Charlotte Square

D.L.G.H.

EDINBURGH CORPORATION WAR-TIME GUY DOUBLE-DECKER
No. G84
Photographed on hire to S.O.L. summer 1951 at Rosewell.

294

Edinburgh Corporation Motor Bus Fleet List 1931-1939

Reg.	Old	'M'	New	Reg.	Old	'M'	New
S9316	31	388	—	SC1134	163	308	D16
SG1300	19	396	—	SC1135	164	309	D17
SG1524	20	263	—	SC1136	165	310	D18
SG1525	21	264	—	SC1137	166	311	D19
SG2135	29	389	—	SC1140	175	312	—
SG2139	34	391	—	SC1142	178	313	—
SG2274	45	393	—	SC1143	182	314	—
SG2278	8	392	—	SC1144	533	315	—
SG2802	32	390	—	SC1146	26	316	—
SG2813	186	265	—	SC1147	35	317	—
SG2814	187	266	—	SC1148	39	318	—
SG2815	188	267	—	SC3401	30	319	L27
SG2816	190	268	—	SC3402	6	320	L28
SG2817	189	269	—	SC3403	194	321	L29
SG2818	191	270	—	SC3404	195	322	L30
SF6028	501	271	—	SC3405	196	323	L31
SF6029	502	272	—	SC3406	197	324	L32
SF6030	503	273	—	SC3407	183	325	L33
SF6258	504	274	—	SC3408	200	326	L34
SF6259	505	275	—	SC3409	198	327	L35
SF6260	506	276	—	SC3410	199	328	L36
SF6261	507	277	—	SC3411	535	329	L37
SF6330	508	278	—	SC3412	772	330	L38
SF6331	509	279	—	SC3413	773	331	L39
SF6470	510	280	—	SC3414	771	394	L41
SF6471	511	281	—	SC3415	770	332	L40
SF6521	153	282	—	SC3416	534	333	D20
SF6522	154	283	—	SC3417	774	334	B11
SF6523	155	284	—	SC3418	775	335	B12
SF6524	156	285	—	SC3419	776	336	B13
SF8495	512	286	—	SC3420	777	337	B14
SF8496	513	287	L11	SC3421	778	338	B15
SF8497	514	288	L12	SC3422	779	339	B16
SF8498	515	289	L13	SC3423	780	340	B17
SF8499	516	290	L14	SC3424	781	341	B18
SF8500	517	291	L15	SC3425	782	393	B19
SF8989	518	292	L16	SC3426	783	343	B20
SF8990	519	293	L17	SC3427	784	401	B24
SF8991	520	294	L18	SC3428	785	344	B21
SF8992	521	295	L19	SC3429	786	345	B22
SF8993	522	296	L20	SC3430	787	400	B23
SF8994	523	395	L42	SC7281	581	346	M28
SF8995	524	297	L21	SC7282	582	347	M29
SF8996	525	298	L22	SC7283	583	348	M30
SF8999	528	397	—	SC7284	584	349	M31
SF9002	529	299	—	SC7285	4	350	D21
SC1126	10	300	L23	SC7286	5	351	D22
SC1127	24	301	L24	SC7287	7	352	D23
SC1128	151	302	L25	SC7288	9	353	D24
SC1129	152	303	L26	SC7289	11	354	D25
SC1130	157	304	D12	SC7290	12	355	D26
SC1131	159	305	D13	SC7291	13	399	D55
SC1132	160	306	D14	SC7292	170	356	D27
SC1133	47	307	D15	SC7293	15	357	D28

Reg.	Old	'M'	New	Reg.	Old	'M'	New
SC7294	22	358	D29	FS2158	—	313	M12
SC7295	23	359	D30	FS2159	—	263	A11
SC7296	25	398	D54	FS2160	—	264	A12
SC7297	27	360	D31	FS2161	—	266	A13
SC7298	28	361	D32	FS2162	—	267	A14
SC7299	33	362	D33	FS2163	—	285	A15
SC7300	36	363	D34	FS2164	—	299	A16
SC7301	37	364	D11	FS2165	—	282	A17
SC7302	38	365	D35	FS2166	—	268	A18
SC7303	40	366	D36	FS2167	—	283	A19
SC7304	41	367	D37	FS4422	—	4321	M16
SC7305	42	368	D38	FS5936	—	2115	M17
SC7306	43	369	D39	FS6340	—	4706	M33
SC7307	44	370	D40	FS7032	—	4964	M18
SC7308	46	371	D41	FS7033	—	4970	A21
SC7309	167	372	D42	FS7036	—	396	A22
SC7310	171	373	D43	FS9611	—	943	M32
SC7311	14	374	D44	WS637	—	1675	A20
SC7312	173	375	D45	WS1508	—	2434	B25
SC7313	176	376	D46	WS6371	—	2723	G11
SC7314	177	377	D47	WS6372	—	2725	G12
SC7315	179	378	D48	WS6373	—	2727	G13
SC7316	180	379	D49	WS6374	—	2736	G14
SC7317	181	380	D50	WS6375	—	2739	G15
SC7318	185	381	D51	WS6376	—	2753	G16
SC7319	192	382	D52	WS6377	—	2754	G17
SC7320	193	383	D53	WS6378	—	2757	G18
SC8747	48	384	M25	WS6379	—	2760	G19
SC8748	49	385	M26	WS6380	—	2763	G20
SC8749	50	386	M27	WS6381	—	2765	G21
SC8791	169	387	A23	WS6382	—	2766	G22
SC9901	—	2895	X11	WS6383	—	2770	G23
SC9902	—	2938	X12	WS6384	—	2773	G24
SC9903	—	2896	D70	WS6385	—	2778	G25
SC9904	—	1445	D56	WS6386	—	2779	G26
SC9905	—	1485	D57	WS9502	—	5302	A24
SC9906	—	1486	D58	to	—	to	to
SC9907	—	1487	D59	WS9520	—	5320	A42
SC9908	—	1903	D61	WS9521	—	5301	A43
SC9909	—	1902	D60	ASC301	—	5321	A44
SC9910	—	2044	D65	to	—	to	to
SC9911	—	2043	D64	ASC310	—	5330	A53
SC9912	—	2042	D63	ASC311	—	5331	G27
SC9913	—	2041	D62	to	—	to	to
SC9914	—	2176	D66	ASC325	—	5345	G41
SC9915	—	2177	D67	BSC15	—	5761	A54
SC9916	—	2545	D68	to	—	to	to
SC9917	—	2546	D69	BSC29	—	5775	A68
SC9918	—	2897	M13	BSC77	—	5776	G42
SC9919	—	2898	M14	to	—	to	to
SC9920	—	2899	M15	BSC86	—	5785	G51
FS2151	—	265	M19	BWS203	—	6293	A69
FS2152	—	269	M20	to	—	to	to
FS2153	—	270	M21	BWS223	—	6312	A88
FS2154	—	312	M22	BWS224	—	6313	G52
FS2155	—	314	M23	to	—	to	to
FS2156	—	2317	M24	BWS233	—	6322	G61
FS2157	—	284	M11				

Edinburgh Corporation Motor Bus Fleet List, War-Time Additions

No.	Reg.	Make	Body	By
G 9	DSF 983	A.E.C. Regent	H56R	a
G 10	DSF 984	A.E.C. Regent	H56R	a
X 13	DSF 985	Tilling Stevens	B30OF	b
X 14	DSF 986	Tilling Stevens	B3OF	b
X 15	DSF 987	Bristol LG5	B34F	c
G 8	DSF 988	Leyland TD7	H56R	d
G 7	DSG 228	Bristol KG5	H56R	e
X 7	DSG 750	Bedford OB	B32F	f
X 8	DSG 751	Bedford OB	B32F	f x
X 9	DSG 752	Bedford OB	B32F	f x
X 10	DSG 753	Bedford OB	B32F	f x
A 23	DSG 837	Daimler COG5	B36R	g
A 10	DSG 965	Daimler COG5	B36R	g
G 62	DWS 82	Daimler CWG5	H56R	h
G 63	DWS 83	Daimler CWG5	H56R	h y
G 4	DWS 126	Guy (AEC)	H56R	d y
G 5	DWS 127	Guy (AEC)	H56R	d y
G 6	DWS 128	Guy (AEC)	H56R	d y
X 6	DWS 130	Bedford OB	B32F	f x
X 5	DWS 131	Bedford OB	B32F	f
X 4	DWS 132	Bedford OB	B32F	f
X 3	DWS 133	Bedford OB	B32F	f x
X 2	DWS 232	Bedford OB	B32F	f
X 1	DWS 233	Bedford OB	B32F	f
X 16	DWS 234	Bedford OB	B32F	f
X 17	DWS 235	Bedford OB	B32F	f

No.	Reg.	Make	Body	By
G 3	DWS 312	Guy (A.E.C.)	H56R	h y
G 2	DWS 313	Guy (A.E.C.)	H56R	h y
X 18	DWS 373	Bedford OB	B32F	f x
X 19	DWS 374	Bedford OB	B32F	f x
X 20	DWS 375	Bedford OB	B32F	f x
X 21	DWS 376	Bedford OB	B32F	f
X 22	DWS 377	Bedford OB	B32F	f
X 23	DWS 378	Bedford OB	B32F	f
X 24	DWS 379	Bedford OB	B32F	f
X 25	DWS 380	Bedford OB	B32F	f
G 1	DWS 415	Guy (A.E.C.)	H56R	d y
G 64	DWS 420	Daimler CWA6	H56R	h y
G 65	DWS 421	Daimler CWA6	H56R	h y
G 66	DWS 422	Daimler CWA6	H56R	h y
G 67	DWS 544	Daimler CWA6	H56R	e
G 68	DWS 545	Daimler CWA6	H56R	e
G 69	DWS 546	Daimler CWA6	H56R	e
G 70	DWS 547	Daimler CWA6	H56R	e
G 71	DWS 928	Daimler CWA6	H56R	j
G 72	DWS 929	Daimler CWA6	H56R	j z
G 73	EFS 128	Daimler CWA6	H56R	j
G 74	EFS 129	Daimler CWA6	H56R	j
G 75	EFS 130	Daimler CWA6	H56R	j
G 76	EFS 131	Daimler CWA6	H56R	j
G 77	EFS 132	Daimler CWA6	H56R	j
G 78	EFS 133	Daimler CWA6	H56R	j

a—Park-Royal
b—Willowbrook.
c—Bristol.
d—Pickering.
e—Northern-Counties.
f—S.M.T. Co.

g—Edinburgh Corporation Transport.
h—Massey.
j—Brush.
x—New Duple C29F body later.
y—Change of body later — see text.
z—Became single-decker No. All later — see text.

Edinburgh Corporation Motor Bus Fleet List May 1951 — December 1956

No	Reg.	Year New	Make	Body
1	DWS 415	43	Guy (A.E.C.)	N. Counties
2	DWS 313	43	Guy (A.E.C.)	N. Counties
3	DWS 312	43	Guy (A.E.C.)	N. Counties
4	DWS 126	43	Guy (A.E.C.)	N. Counties
to				
6	DWS 128	43	Guy (A.E.C.)	N. Counties
27	ASC 311	37	Daimler COG6	Met. Cam.
to				
31	ASC 315	37	Daimler COG6	Met. Cam.
33	ASC 317	37	Daimler COG6	Met. Cam.
34	ASC 318	37	Daimler COG6	Met. Cam.
36	ASC 320	37	Daimler COG6	Met. Cam.
to				
38	ASC 322	37	Daimler COG6	Met. Cam.
40	ASC 324	37	Daimler COG6	Met. Cam.
42	BSC 77	38	Daimler COG6	Met. Cam.
43	BSC 78	38	Daimler COG6	Met. Cam.
45	BSC 80	38	Daimler COG6	Met. Cam.
48	BSC 83	38	Daimler COG6	Met. Cam.
to				
51	BSC 86	38	Daimler COG6	Met. Cam.
52	BWS 224	38	Daimler COG6	Met. Cam.
to				
61	BWS 233	38	Daimler COG6	Met. Cam.
62	DWS 82	43	Daimler CWG5	Alexander
63	DWS 83	43	Daimler CWG5	Alexander
64	DWS 420	43	Daimler CWA6	Alexander
to				
66	DWS 422	43	Daimler CWA6	Alexander
67	DWS 544	44	Daimler CWA6	Alexander
to				
70	DWS 547	44	Daimler CWA6	Alexander
72	DWS 929	44	Daimler CWA6	Alexander
73	EFS 128	45	Daimler CWA6	Alexander
to				
78	EFS 133	45	Daimler CWA6	Alexander
79	EFS 554	45	Guy 6LW	N. Counties
to				
81	EFS 556	45	Guy 6LW	N. Counties
82	ESC 131	46	Guy 6LW	N. Counties
to				
85	ESC 134	46	Guy 6LW	N. Counties
86	ESC 728	46	Guy 6LW	N. Counties
87	ESC 729	45	Guy 6LW	N. Counties
88	EFS 914	45	Guy 6LW	Met. Cam.
to				
90	EFS 916	45	Guy 6LW	Met. Cam.
91	ESC 207	46	Guy 6LW	Met. Cam.
92	ESC 208	46	Guy 6LW	Met. Cam.
93	ESC 920	46	Guy 6LW	N. Counties
to				
105	ESC 932*	46	Guy 6LW	N. Counties
106	FSC 983	47	Daimler CVD6	N. Counties
to				
110	FSC 987	47	Daimler CVD6	N. Counties
111	FSF 901	48	Daimler CVD6	N. Counties
112	FSF 902	48	Daimler CVD6	N. Counties

* The registration numbers of 102-3 were transposed.

Left table

No	Reg	Year New	Make	Body
113 to 117	FSC 165 to 169	49	Daimler CVD6	Met. Cam.
118	GSF 821	49	Daimler CVD6	Met. Cam.
122	GSF 825	49	Daimler CVD6	Met. Cam.
123 to 137	FSC 170 to 184	49	Daimler CVG6	Met. Cam.
138	GSF 969	49	Daimler CVG6	Met. Cam.
168	GSF 999	49	Daimler CVG6	Met. Cam.
169 to 184	GSG 1 to 16	50	Daimler CVG6	Met. Cam.
185	FOF 298	50	Leyland TD6	Leyland
200	GSG 445	49	Guy Arab 6LW	N. Counties
214 to 221	GSG 459 / HSG 171	49 / 51	Guy Arab 6LW / A.E.C. MkIII	N. Counties / Brockhouse
237	HSG 187	51	A.E.C. MkIII	Brockhouse
240	JSF 655	51 / 52	Leyland PD2/12	Leyland
246	JSF 661	52	Leyland PD2/12	Leyland
247	JWS 67	52	Leyland PD2/12	Leyland
250	JWS 70	52	Leyland PD2/12	Leyland
251	KSF 942	52	Leyland PD2/12	Leyland
260	KSF 951	52	Leyland PD2/12	Leyland

Right table

No	Reg	Year New	Make	Body
301 to 360	JWS 581 to 640	53	Guy Arab 5LW	Duple
401	JWS 640	53	Guy Arab 5LW	Duple
401	LFS 401	54	Leyland PD2/20	M.C.W.
500 to 501	LFS 500 / LWS 501	54 / 55	Leyland PD2/20	M.C.W.
600	LWS 600	55	Leyland PD2/20	M.C.W.
601	GSF 334	48	Crossley SD42	Roe
604 to 610	GSF 337 / DSG 965	48 / 44	Crossley SD42 / Daimler COG5	Roe / E.C.T.
611	DWS 928	44	Daimler CWA6	Cowieson
612 to 613	FS 2160 / FS 2161	32	Daimler CH/6:G	Cowieson / Alexander
615 to 619	FS 2163 to 2167	32	Daimler CH/6:G	Alexander
620	WS 637	34	Daimler CP/6:G	Alexander
621	FS 7033	33	Daimler CP/6:G	Eng. Elec.
622	FS 7036	34	Daimler COG5	Weyman
623	DSG 837	36	Daimler COG5	E.C.T.
624 to 643	WS 9502 to 9521	36	Daimler COG5	Met. Cam.
644	ASC 301	37	Daimler COG5	Met. Cam.
646 to 647	ASC 303 / ASC 304	37	Daimler COG5	Met. Cam. / Alexander

No	Reg.	Year New	Make	Body
648	ASC 305	37	Daimler COG5	Met. Cam.
to	to			
653	ASC 310	37	Daimler COG5	Met. Cam.
654	BSC 15	38	Daimler COG5	Met. Cam.
668	BSC 29	38	Daimler COG5	Met. Cam.
to				
669	BWS 203	38	Daimler COG5	Met. Cam.
688	BWS 223	38	Daimler COG5	Met. Cam.
to				
689	FSC 155	48	Daimler CVG5	Met. Cam.
698	FSC 164	48	Daimler CVG5	Met. Cam.
to				
701	NSF 701	56	Leyland PD2/20	M.C.W.
760	NSF 760	56	Leyland PD2/20	M.C.W.
to				
761	OFS 761	56-7	Leyland PD2/20	M.C.W.
800	OFS 800	56-7	Leyland PD2/20	M.C.W
801	JFS 524	51	Leyland Ryl. Tig.	Alexander
802	JFS 525	51	Leyland Olympic	Met. Cam.
803	HWS 768	52	Leyland Ryl. Tig.	Leyland
818	HWS 783	52	Leyland Ryl. Tig.	Leyland
to				
819	NFS 748	55	Leyland Tig. Cub	Alexander
820	NFS 749	55	Leyland Tig. Cub	Alexander
to				
821	NFS 941	55	Leyland Tig. Cub	Alexander

No	Reg.	Year New	Make	Body
831	ESG 644	48	Guy Arab 5LW	Met. Cam.
to	to			
840	ESG 653	48	Guy Arab 5LW	Met. Cam.
862	FWS 155	49	Bristol L6B	Brockhouse
to	to			
876	FWS 169	49	Bristol L6B	Brockhouse
901	NSF 901	56	Guy Arab IV	Alexander
to	to			
950	NSF 950	56	Guy Arab IV	Alexander
951	OFS 951	56	Guy Arab IV	Alexander
to	to			
970	OFS 970	56	Guy Arab IV	Alexander
X2	GWS 463	49	Bedford OB	Duple
X4	DWS 132	43	Bedford OB	Duple
X6	DWS 130	43	Bedford OB	Duple
X7	DSG 750	42	Bedford OB	Duple
X8	DSG 751	42	Bedford OB	Duple
X9	GWS 464	49	Bedford OB	Duple
X10	DSG 753	42	Bedford OB	Duple
X18	DSG 465	49	Bedford OB	Duple
X19	DWS 374	43	Bedford OB	Duple
to	to			
X21	DWS 376	43	Bedford OB	Duple
X22	GWS 466	49	Bedford OB	Duple
to	to			
X25	GWS 469	49	Bedford OB	Duple

The following were withdrawn as shown : In 1952—36, 38, 57, 59, 61, 610, 620-3; In 1953—29, 31, 48-9, 52, 54, 56, 611-2, 625-6, 629, 631-3, 637, 639, 641, 646, 649, 653-4, 657-60, 667, 671, 673-4, 676-7, 679, 685, 687-8; in 1954—42, 51, 53, 55, 58, 60, 88-92; In 1955—185.

The Corporation's lorry fleet is not within this story, but the tramway tower-wagons and breakdown wagons might well be mentioned. Up till November 1940 these were numbered among the lorry fleet, but a separate list, Nos. 1 to 7 then came into use as shown.

Old No.	New No.	Reg. No.	Year New	Make	Type	Year Scrapped	Notes
1	–	WS 194	14	Halley	Tower	29	
1	1	SC 5273	29	A.E.C.	Tower	45	
4	4	SG 5431	22	A.E.C.	Breakdown	45	
5	–	SG 5077	22	Tilling Stevens	Tower	38	
5	5	SC 3405		Leyland Lion	Tower		ex-bus and old tower '39
17	–	SG 7411	22	Tilling Stevens	Tower	39	
18	2	SF 899	23	Thornycroft	Tower	44	
–	7	SG 2012		A.E.C.	Breakdown	45	ex-bus '32
37	3	AWS 682	37	A.E.C.	Tower		
–	6	SC 3430		A.E.C. (Beardmore)	Breakdown		ex-bus '40; Leyland eng. '43
–	2	DWS 528	44	Austin	Tower		
–	4		45	E.R.F.	Breakdown		(Trade Plates)
–	1	EFS 743	46	Austin	Tower		
–	5	FSF 747	48	Austin	Tower		

The Edinburgh & District Tramways Company, for the Slateford electric line, had a tower (believed to be that subsequently on SG5077) which was mounted on a small Albion lorry when required. WS 194 was of course the Leith Corporation tower wagon. The normal "on call" wagon was SG7411. then AWS 682, and latterly one of the Austins. The two Tilling-Stevens were petrol-electrics,

Passengers carried by Edinburgh Corporation Transport :

Year ended May 1922 :	Cable :	67,986,467	
	Leith :	12,632,560	
	Buses :	20,407,736	
			101,026,763
May 1930 :	Trams :	134,964,188	
	Buses :	29,437,803	
			164,401,991
May 1939 :	Trams :	145,972,840	
	Buses :	60,306,416	
			206,279,256
May 1947 :	Trams :	192,892,899*	
	Buses :	83,487,790	
			276,380,689
May 1950 :	Trams :	186,005,463	
	Buses :	100,611,294	
			286,616,757†
May 1956 :	Trams :	49,144,513	
	Buses :	202,258,656	
			251,403,169

* max. year for trams.

† max. year total.

VIII

SCOTTISH MOTOR TRACTION

By 1905 it was becoming clear that the horse-bus could not meet the demand for local transport much longer. On the other hand the motor bus was still in its teething stages. Could a really reliable vehicle be obtained and a dependable regular service be established? One group of Edinburgh men determined to try, and on 14 June 1905 registered the Scottish Motor Traction Company Limited with an authorised capital of £50,000 though only £15,000 was raised for some years. The Chairman was the Master of Polwarth. George Oliver acted as secretary from an office in Queen Street, and the other directors were R. C. Cowan, J. A. Hood, F. B. Lea, A. B. Patterson, and F. McDougal Wallis. The routes originally proposed were to Queensferry, Eskbank, Loanhead, Lasswade, Penicuik via Morningside, Juniper Green via Fountainbridge, and Kirkliston.

The new company however, wisely decided not to start public services until they were satisfied they had vehicles and experience enough to carry them through. They therefore embarked on a series of trials of various makes of vehicle, including a steam-propelled one. This is said to have been a Lifu with a body by Morton of Wishaw. It may have been the machine subsequently operated by the Lanarkshire Motor Omnibus Company. Many of the trial runs are said to have been made in West Lothian, perhaps to be less in the public eye. W. J. Thomson, later to become Lord Provost of Edinburgh and receive a knighthood, was appointed engineer and manager, Hailing from Caithness he had been trained in the Arrol Johnston motor works and brought good experience with him. The various weaknesses of the trial machines were soon uncovered, and a specification for a vehicle to meet the requirements which the company found necessary was drawn up. A speed of 12 m.p.h. on level and 3 m.p.h. on a 1 in 6 gradient when loaded, was called for. Premises in Lauriston Street, latterly a cinema, were bought for a garage to hold twenty vehicles.

In July 1905 five double-deck Dorkup buses were ordered from the Motor Car Emporium, London, at £885 each. When the first of these arrived on 7 October however it failed in its hill-climbing performance, so the company repudiated the contract and placed an order with the Maudslay Motor Company for five buses. The suppliers of the Dorkup raised an action which resulted in the company agreeing to retain the one Dorkup only at a reduced price of £810. It seems hardly ever to have been used.

On 23 December the first Maudslays began to arrive and fortunately these were satisfactory, so the first public service between the Mound and Corstorphine was started on 1 January 1906. An hourly service was provided, taking half an hour each way, so only one bus was required. The fare was 3d. The press took no interest in the event, but of course Mr. Thomson was there in person, and although we do not know who the driver was, the conductor was Benjamin Thomson well known in more recent years as Inspector "Wee Ben". Ben had come from the horse-buses of the now dissolved Edinburgh Street Tramways Company. He has related how the Master of Polwarth insisted on getting the first ticket from him though he had been instructed not to take his fare.

The company used the Edinburgh licence number as their fleet number, and these first five Maudslays were thus Nos. 51-55, with registration numbers S543-7. They were of orthodox pattern for the period, seating 16 inside on longitudinal cane seats, and 19 on "garden" seats upstairs. A curved hinged door was provided to the saloon. The engine was rated at 30/40 h.p. with chain drive to the artillery type wheels. A "sprag" brake could be dropped on the ground under the middle of the bus to prevent a run-back downhill should the vehicle stall. The colour scheme was green with cream panels and the company's title was shown in full on the sides. Destination was shown on a small board hung from the driver's canopy, and on a route board below the side windows. Acetylene lighting was fitted. With these vehicles the company was able to maintain its service satisfactorily, and looking to developments, immediately ordered five more Maudslays.

In June 1906 a bus was put on between the Mound and Cramond, providing a service every hour and a half, though a much increased service was run at weekends. Another service was run to South Queensferry at 10 a.m., 12.0, 2.0, 4.0, and 6.0 p.m. at a fare of 1/- with a late trip on Wednesdays at 10.30 p.m. for which 1/3 was charged. For this route two Rykneild "toast-rack" charabancs with a wooden roof were used. They were later supplemented by another two. The Corstorphine service was now run half-hourly and started from Waverley Steps. A time-table and fares leaflet was issued regularly.

The second lot of Maudslay double-deckers arrived about October 1906, and these had rather wider bodies, being fitted with transverse seats in the lower saloon and a sliding door. Yet a further order had already been placed and there were eventually sixteen Maudslays. Known registration numbers are S548-51, 781, 839, 1378-9, 1391. Some of the Maudslays exchanged bodies with Rykneilds, and for a time there were thus some Maudslay charabancs and conversely some Rykneild buses. The latter had the reputation of being quite fast, but weak on hills.

The additional vehicles were used on new services from Waverley Steps to Loanhead, with a few journeys terminating at Liberton, and to Dalkeith via Gilmerton, with additional journeys to the latter point only. In October too, the Corstorphine service reverted to hourly for the winter. The Queensferry and Cramond routes were suspended from December 1906 and the Corstorphine bus was extended right out to Uphall, though of course doing only four trips in day. In December there was also a short-lived service at twelve minute intervals between Waverley Steps and Colinton Road.

With further buses being delivered, services were started about the New Year of 1907 to Penicuik, to Bonnyrigg, to Gorebridge, and to Pathead. A service to Kirkliston was started on 2 February and on 1 March it was extended to Winchburgh. This was not successful however, and was dropped altogether after a few more weeks. Against this the other services were immediately popular and were soon augmented. In April 1907 the Forth Bridge and Queensferry route was restarted, but the Pathead route was

S.M.T. Co's. ORIGINAL MAUDSLAY DOUBLE-DECKERS
S546 & 7 at the Mound for Cramond and Forth Bridge respectively, in 1906-7

dropped. The Cramond service was also restarted for the summer on 4 May, while from 3 August till the end of September a charabanc circular tour via Roslin and Penicuik to Carlops returning via Flotterstane was run twice daily. A Sundays only service to West Calder commenced on 6 October 1907, with three trips, while the Cramond service ceased, and the Forth Bridge service was run on Sundays only for another month before suspension for the winter.

One of the earliest accidents occurred on Saturday afternoon 5 October 1907. The bus from Loanhead shed a wheel nearing the foot of Liberton Brae, and toppling over, scattered its complement of top-deck passengers. Five were detained in the Infirmary.

In March 1908 the time-table appeared in a railway-like tabular form, the fares being given on the back. On Sundays slightly higher fares were charged and short distance fares were not offered. From 1 March the Bonnyrigg route was extended to Rosewell, and an additional service run to Gorebridge via the Old Dalkeith Road, described as via Little France. The Forth Bridge service restarted on 9 April, and the Carlops tour on 8 June, though, of course, both were suspended again after the season. The service to Cramond was not revived.

By now the company had established its position on these routes to the surrounding country, — mainly where the railway services were less convenient or more circuitous. The service frequencies were being gradually augmented. Passengers carried in one week in July 1908 were as follows :—Queensferry 2400, Loanhead 3500, Penicuik 2700, Rosewell 3180, Gorebridge 5250, Uphall 3500, West Calder 350, Carlops 250. Ordinarily two vehicles were used for the Queensferry route, two for Loanhead and Penicuik, four for Gorebridge and Rosewell, and two or three for Uphall. With one more on the Carlops tour or West Calder this left two or three out of the then total of about fourteen, to cover maintenance, breakdown, or the occasional accident. Although there were mishaps from time to time, which were liable to be exaggerated in some quarters, no serious accident seems to have been recorded.

The Forth Bridge and Carlops routes were again operated for the summer season in 1909, and in June 1909 a connecting service from Eskbank to Pathead and Blackshiels was shown in the time-tables. The West Calder Sunday service ceased after September but from 5 February 1910 the route was partly covered by a new daily service to Mid Calder and Pumpherston, and the Sunday journeys to West Calder were restarted too on 6 March. In May 1910, and until October, two of the Blackshiels connections continued over Soutra hill, (1200ft.) to Lauder on Saturdays, Sundays, and Mondays, and this was repeated during subsequent summers till about 1914, though latterly only on Sundays. The seasonal Forth Bridge and Carlops routes were again run in 1910. For the November 1910 time-table a re-assessment of running times was made and nearly all were adjusted by a few minutes, — some lengthened, and some cut.

A parcels service had been set up early in 1908 with agents in the various towns and villages, and with the Edinburgh & District Tramways Co's. parcel service co-operating in the city. One of the minor problems was that some of the surrounding towns being Royal Burghs, continued to exercise their ancient rights to levy petty customs. These were however generally resolved by payment of a small annual sum, and after about 1930 the practice was dropped altogether. Private hire work was of course also undertaken from the beginning. Another activity that should be mentioned was a contract to carry the Post Office mails to and from various places, and in this connection some Albion vans in G.P.O. red livery were run nightly to and from Glasgow via Bathgate, Coatbridge, Motherwell and Hamilton, from 1 December 1909. Later, larger Star vans were used for Post Office work. In some cases however, the service buses were used, and from June 1911 the following interesting note appears against the 5.45 a.m. buses to Penicuik and to Rosewell: "Passengers are only carried on the top of the 5.45 a.m. bus to . . . . . , the inside being reserved for mails". It must have been a cold journey in winter if the rule was enforced. From October these two journeys are shown as starting from the G.P.O.

In the summer of 1911 larger premises in East Fountainbridge were taken for occupation by the buses, and the Lauriston Street garage was then mainly used for the mail vans. The Forth Bridge and Carlops routes ran for the season as usual.

On 1 May 1912 the Pumpherston route was extended to join the Uphall route, making a circular service both ways, at a round fare of 2/- from any point, (2/3 on Sundays). Late services, outwards from the city up to 11.0 p.m. were being given on most routes, and at this time it was arranged for the returning buses to run direct to the garage via Nicolson Street and Lauriston Place from the south, or via Lothian Road from the west instead of going right in to the Waverley Steps. A change was made on 1 July 1912 when the starting point was moved from the latter to the top of the Waverley Bridge. A glazed frame remained fixed to the railings at the top of the Waverley Steps however, until the mid-twenties, in which the company displayed their time-table sheets, — later expanded to two sheets. The Forth Bridge and Carlops routes were again run for the season and their starting point remained at the Mound. Two new circular tours were run in August and September

1912. The first was an all-day trip on Mondays, Wednesdays, and Fridays, via Portobello, Haddington, Dunbar, North Berwick, Aberlady, Haddington, and back to town via Newcraighall, with halts at Haddington, Dunbar, and North Berwick. The town council were invited to an inaugural trip. The other ran twice a day on Tuesdays, Thursdays, and Saturdays, via Queensferry, and Hopetoun to Linlithgow, returning via Winchburgh and Kirkliston. On both these tours however, intermediate point to point fares were available. In November 1912 some return fares were offered on the Pumpherston and West Calder routes, and also to the Forth Bridge in the 1913 season. Earlier in 1912 tickets to the value of 10/- were offered at 12½% discount. It may also be noted that children under 12 were allowed half fare but were required to give up their seat to a full fare passenger. Dogs were charged at one-third of the full fare.

On 11 December 1912 there was a strike of the bus crews over some dismissals. There was an attempt to run a few buses by some of the maintenance men, but then they came "out" too, and all services came virtually to a standstill. Earlier in the year the men had joined a trade union and they claimed the dismissed men, as active participants, were being victimised. There was much industrial unrest at the time. As Christmas approached, the Post Office had to make alternative arrangements for mails for these runs had stopped too, but on Christmas Eve the men went back to work on undisclosed terms. It may be mentioned that the company ran a bonus scheme, and many employees were shareholders.

From February 1913 to about 1916 some of the Blackshiels connections were extended to Humbie, and from 2 March the Sunday service to West Calder was diverted to Whitburn instead. The 1913 summer services followed the same pattern as the previous years, the tours starting in June, and "Special Evening Drives" to various destinations were run. On 1 November 1913 some of the Uphall buses were extended to Bangour.

Perhaps the most important event in 1913 however, was the appearance of a new bus, designed and built by the company themselves. A great deal of thought had been given to this vehicle which was undoubtedly far ahead of its time. A novelty which did not become general practice elsewhere until many years later was the location of the driver alongside the engine thus enabling a 32 seat saloon body to be accommodated on a vehicle only 23ft. long. There was a seat facing backwards against the front bulkhead, and the saloon was partitioned into two parts, the rear for smokers, the front for non-smokers. The off-side rear corner was curved and the rear seat curved round inside it. There was a "cut-away" rear entrance with a short screen to the saloon, in the little corner outside of which the conductor could stand on the top step. The

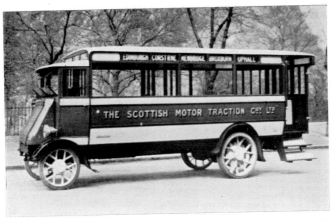

S.M.T. Co.s ORIGINAL "LOTHIAN" BUS S3057 OF 1913

body was built with a full width front, only the plain radiator projecting through, though on the first example built, the radiator was replaced by a slightly sloping cowl, and the roof of the driver's portion was lower than that of the saloon. These two features were however later altered, and while the roof of this first body was always fairly flat, later examples had a more curved roof which gently swept down over the driver's portion. No use was made of the near side half of the driver's cab except sometimes to carry parcels. All windows had top-lights of ground glass on which were painted the places on the route to which the bus was allocated, the termini being also shown on the two above the windscreen, and on the back. After the war the ground glass and painted names were abandoned and paper bills stuck on inside, enabling buses to be changed about when necessary. The earlier bodies had sliding windows in the saloon, but these tended to rattle and were later made fixed and an additional pillar introduced. After the war a clock was provided on the saloon bulkhead. Green leather cushion seats with spring backs were provided, and the conductor's bell was a straightforward pull-cord. The buses were of course fitted with electric light. Later examples had a much more highly curved roof.

A 38 h.p. Minerva Silent Knight engine was fitted driving a four-speed chain-driven gearbox and worm-driven rear axle. Some were fitted with a Tyler engine after the war. Solid tyres were of course fitted but the vehicle was well-sprung. The company aptly called their protegé the "Lothian" but this name did not appear on the machines. The first bus appeared in April 1913, as No.95, S3057, and was put on the Uphall route. It proved very successful being decidedly faster, smoother, and quieter than any of its con-

309

temporaries. The first body had been built by G. Hall & Co. of Pitt Street, but the company then acquired another workshop in Valleyfield Street and commenced body building themselves. The company's full title was now dropped from the sides of the vehicles and only the initials were used. As more Lothians appeared the old Maudslays and Rykneilds were withdrawn, having served the company well. Two of the Maudslays had for a time been fitted with a larger type of radiator designed by Mr. Thomson. Details of the fleet of Lothians will be found in the rolling-stock section, but it may here be remarked that at least one was supplied to an operator in Fife, and a number as goods lorries.

The full range of services applied again in the summer of 1914. In September the Loanhead route was extended to Lasswade, and an interesting variation was the running of the 1.0 p.m. outward journey via Captains Road and thence direct via Edge. A new longer all-day tour to the Border country was run, and called for new charabancs, so five 29 seat Albions were obtained. One was No. 81. When the war broke out it had little immediate effect, but after a few months the War Department commandeered the new Albions. As has been mentioned in another chapter Edinburgh Corporation sold their three Tilling-Stevens buses to the S.M.T.Co. in December 1914, and it is said these were fitted with charabanc bodies, — possibly from the Albions, — but not proving suitable for the S.M.T.'s routes they were re-sold to the Birmingham & Midland Motor Omnibus Co. who used that make.

A 31 seat charabanc body for the Lothian was produced in 1915. In the first one the radiator was sunk in flush with the front of the bodywork, but subsequently this was altered to a projecting radiator, the same as the buses. The first one was also painted green, but afterwards pale yellow was adopted for the charabancs. These new charabancs enabled the summer tours to be continued till September 1916.

For a short time early in 1915 the Bangour service was apparently given on Saturdays and Sundays only, and from April some of the Penicuik buses were diverted through Roslin. The Queensferry service had also been reduced, but in the summer of 1916 some circular trips were run via Barnton, Queensferry, Kirkliston, and Turnhouse, and vice-versa. Then, with so many naval personnel accumulating at Queensferry this route became heavily loaded and the service was substantially increased to a half-hourly one, and continued through the winter too. As the vicinity of the Forth Bridge was under guard, the road between the top of the Hawes Brae and the east end of the town of Queensferry was closed, and the buses proceeded via Dalmeny station and Hopetoun crossroads to enter the town from the west end. The Mid Calder half of the Pumpherston circular route was withdrawn after August 1916.

Jordan's service from Broxburn and his Halley vehicles were taken over in February 1917, and it was proposed to buy up the Edinburgh & District Motor Company too, but this was deferred on account of the already difficult petrol situation.

Soon petrol supplies became even more difficult and further steps had to be taken to maintain services. The answer was found in fitting up all the vehicles to run on coal-gas. A shallow open box was built on the roof of the buses, and a similar box supported on stanchions, fixed over the charabancs, and into this box was lashed a large baloon which was charged with gas in Market Street, and also at the outer termini in some cases. The gas was fed to the back of the engine casing by a tube of thin rubber, and on the charabancs this presented an attraction to schoolboys to try, unsuccessfully, to bring the vehicle to a halt by squeezing it. When returning with a diminished supply, the sagging gas-bag adopted a sort of wave motion from front to back as the vehicle ran through the breeze. There were occasional cases of gas-bags breaking loose altogether. The gas-bags were said to cost £50 each. Wear and tear was heavy and averaged 1¼d. per mile, and with gas at 2.17d. per mile, the total cost amounted to 3½d. per mile. The system served its purpose remarkably well with the fleet of about 35 vehicles, nearly all Lothians, and was indeed slightly cheaper than running on petrol at its then price. It was alleged the buses ran better to Penicuik than back after re-filling there.

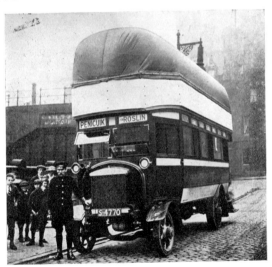

Courtesy "The Rolling Road"

S.M.T. Co's'. STANDARD 'LOTHIAN' BUS
Running on coal gas 1917-8 at Waverley Bridge

311

In 1917 a few of the Penicuik journeys were diverted through Loanhead, including one which already went via Roslin, and the Whitburn route was suspended at the end of the year. The Pumpherston route was also suspended in May 1918 but restarted in April 1919. The charabancs of the Edinburgh & District Motor Co. were eventually acquired, in September 1918 but although roof boxes were partially built on them the job was not completed, and the vehicles soon disappeared. These vehicles are said to have been Commers and Albions. There was also a large W.D. type Maudslay charabanc with a wooden roof running on the Queensferry route shortly after the war, painted grey. The gas-bags were discarded as soon as possible, but some of the boxes remained for a time until there was an opportunity to remove them.

At this period traffic was brisk, and the Queensferry route especially so. The last bus would stand at the Mound long before starting time completely packed, — and no duplicate available. There was no limit and conductors did their best, sometimes squeezing half a dozen passengers onto the steps alone, and hanging on themselves outside of that! Fares would then be collected on alighting. In those days a full load was indicated by repeating the starting signal, i.e. four bells. The now usual "three bells" came into fashion first on the Corporation vehicles with electric bells on which separate rings were less easily given. The charabancs were used on the Queensferry route in the summer and they would be equally crammed with sailors sitting along both sides. The conductor collected his fares and punched tickets hanging on the footboard outside while the vehicle careered along, and clambered along from row to row to do so, with a stride over the rear wheel arch. Today the whole procedure seems very precarious though of course speeds were not so high and the roads quieter. S.M.T. conductors as well as drivers normally wore leggings, and very few women were employed during the war. Uniforms had green piping. Williamson's ticket punches were used and the tickets were printed with all the stage names in full, both sides being used. The colours were: 1d. white; 1½d. mauve; 2d. blue; 3d. green; 4d. brown; 5d. yellow; 6d. brown; 7d. green; 8d. white with blue stripe; 9d. white with green stripe; 10d. white with blue stripe; 11d. white with yellow stripe; 1/- white with red stripe. Higher values cannot now be recorded. No separate series was used for children etc., but two different sets were required for the lower values to cover respectively the south, and west groups of routes. The special Sunday fares had been given up. Return tickets were now issued for the higher fares and were surrendered for an Exchange Ticket of no face value, white with a red number overprinted sideways. Season tickets could also be obtained. Some one-way 1d., 1½d., and 2d. fares were also in vogue here and there, the uphill journey being a halfpenny dearer than downhill, or being offered inwards only within the city. These were printed right across the top of the ticket. Although there were no fixed stopping places drivers were loth to stop on an up grade. The tickets were sometimes carried in a simple holder with two rows foot to foot and also back to back, giving sixteen positions; but often they were just made up into two or three bundles. The crews generally remained on the same route and became well-known to their passengers. At Christmas time many a conductor decorated the inside of his bus with holly and coloured paper streamers.

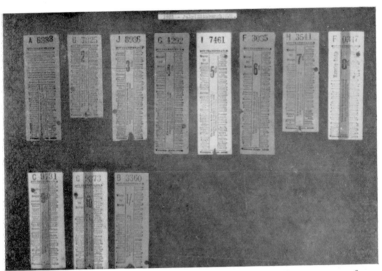

Some S.M.T. Co. Tickets. Colours as in text. Note the one way fares across the top of the 1½d. ticket.

Time-tables were now issued monthly, free, in pocket size booklet form arranged alphabetically, and although the display sheet was still issued to parcel agents etc. for some years, it was abandoned about 1929 by which time three or four sheets had been required to cover all the expanding services. In July 1919 the Carlops, Dunbar and Melrose tours were restarted for the first season after the war, while on 3 October 1919 a service to Winchburgh was started. This had been shown in the time-tables since June with a note that "Due notice will be given when the above service will commence". The highway authority objected to the buses and appealed to the Ministry of Transport who eventually decreed the company to pay one penny per mile run towards the maintenance of the road. The Roads Act of 1920 of course cancelled this. The Queensferry service now ran every fifteen minutes in summer and twenty minutes in winter.

E.O.C.

THE MOUND STANCE 1921. S.M.T. Thornycroft charabanc SG1637 for Forth Bridge, and Lothians and Thornycrofts on various tours White's Halley on left and Clyde in centre. Corporation charabanc in background and Leyland bus "To and from Blackhall Davidson's Mains, Barnton and Cramond" approaching.

The Whitburn route was restarted in March 1920 on Sundays only, but a daily service was given as far as Mid Calder, and from May Whitburn was served daily too. Two new tours were added that summer, one to St. Mary's Loch and Selkirk, the other via Stirling to Alloa from where the passengers sailed down the Forth to Queensferry in the company's motor yacht.

The company's authorised capital was increased to £250,000 in 1919.

The company's position was strengthened by the agreement concluded with Edinburgh Corporation on 12 May 1920, already referred to in another chapter. A year afterwards the company threatened to interdict the Corporation for undertaking private hire work beyond the city. However the Corporation desisted. Although not part of this story it might be mentioned that in July 1920 the company secured a foothold in Dundee by acquiring the Dundee Mechanical Transport Company, and developed some services from that city too. Four vehicles were thereby added to the fleet.

Lothians were still being built of course, and it was the practice for bus and charabanc bodies to be exchanged each season in many cases. More vehicles were required quickly however, and a large number of "J" type Thornycrofts, mostly charabancs, appeared. It is no disparagement to say these did not compare favourably with the Lothians. At first they seemed somewhat unreliable, and a trip to Queensferry was liable to be punctuated by several involuntary stoppages while the driver did a little tinkering with the engine. However these troubles seemed soon to be overcome and they did useful work. Details of these vehicles are given in the rolling-stock section. The Thornycroft buses ran the Whitburn route, and were later much used in the Bathgate district.

At this period International Rugby matches were played at Inverleith, and on these occasions the S.M.T. ran a frequent service to the field from George Street, competing with the Corporation. Similarly charabancs were run to Musselburgh Races at a fare of 1/6. On 24 October 1920 the Bangour route was extended to Bathgate. New ground was broken on 4 December 1920 with a service from Waverley Bridge to Musselburgh and Tranent, running via Milton Road. On Saturdays a frequent service was given and some journeys on Saturdays and Sundays continued on to Haddington. The Haddington extension became daily from 2 May 1921, but reverted to Saturdays and Sundays only during the following winter.

On 8 January 1921 the Winchburgh route was extended to Linlithgow. Later, from 26 October 1922, through tickets were issued to Falkirk by the Scottish General Omnibus Co's. service connecting at Linlithgow. An alternative route to Penicuik via Lothianburn was started later in 1921, and in the following summer charabancs also ran to Roslin via Lothianburn. A new circular route both ways, via Gilmerton, Dalkeith, Wallyford, Musselburgh, and back to Edinburgh was started towards the end of 1921, but the district between Dalkeith and Musselburgh could not yet offer much traffic and the service was taken off again in February 1922, though six journeys continued to be given via Musselburgh to Wallyford. In April these were reduced to Saturdays and Sundays only, and cancelled altogether in June. A route via Tranent to Ormiston commenced in December 1921. The starting point for these east going services to Musselburgh, Tranent, Wallyford, Ormiston, and Haddington was transferred from the Waverley Bridge to the top of Waterloo Place on 1 April 1922. In November 1921 the Eskbank firm of Adam Young who were running the connecting services to Blackshiels was bought up. There was a general reduction of fares on 19 December 1921.

A new type of vehicle appeared in 1921, namely a 14 seat Fiat charabanc for the longer day tours. These were painted brown without lettering, and hence known as "Brownies," and ran on pneumatic tyres. A bus version was built soon afterwards for use on some of the longer routes to be mentioned and also in the Bathgate district where competition developed. Details are given in the rolling-stock section. These were normally operated without a conductor.

Most of the services were gradually being considerably increased in frequency. The Bathgate route was cut at Uphall on 1 March 1922, a connecting service being run between Broxburn and Bathgate by William Young & Co. of the latter town. Passengers changed at Broxburn on the outward journey though, coming back, Uphall was the advertised changing point. This applied in the case of Pumpherston too from October, and the Broxburn-Pumpherston service was extended to Mid Calder and West Calder, with connections from Edinburgh at Mid Calder. Through running to Bathgate was recommenced however with the acquisition on 1 January 1923 of William Young & Co.'s services between Broxburn and Bathgate, and between Bathgate, Armadale and Linlithgow. William Young & Co. continued to operate their other routes in the Bathgate district till 1 April 1923, when these too were taken over by the S.M.T. Co. Most of William Young & Company's vehicles had been destroyed in a fire at their garage. A new garage was built in Bathgate by the S.M.T. Co. later in the year. In the summer the company's two new motor yachts "Auld Reekie" and Cramond Brig", (each carrying 120 passengers), gave pleasure cruises from Hawes Pier at the Forth Bridge, as had also been available before the war. Summer weekend traffic to Queensferry was very heavy and the company were proud to advertise themselves as "The company which can and does run a three minute service to the Forth Bridge". It was an achievement, requiring about thirty vehicles, but the local passengers were not forgotten and some vehicles were regularly turned at Blackhall or Barnton to cater for them. There was no Telford Road then and the Blackhall turning point was at Forthview Terrace. When the touring charabancs returned in the early evening from their day's trips, they would be sent hurrying out to Queensferry to help bring in the crowds, usually without conductors. Driver's hours were of course not so rigidly controlled in those days. As already mentioned elsewhere, the tours stance was removed from the Mound to St. Andrew Square in 1922, and the S.M.T.Co. occupied the west side.

A new route was started from Waverley Bridge via Slateford and Juniper Green to Balerno on 15 July 1922. Another from Waterloo Place to North Berwick via Longniddry, Aberlady, and Gullane, at 9.30 and at two-hourly intervals till 5.30 started on 6 May 1923. This was run on Sundays only at first, and the first bus proceeded from Fountainbridge via Haymarket to Waterloo Place. It was a popular route and was augmented from 19 August, later becoming daily. A further route leaving the Gorebridge route at Newtonloan proceeded to North Middleton, and was started on 1 June 1923. A through service to West Calder was put on in November 1923, but was later withdrawn. There was another general reduction in fares in November 1923. In the summer of 1924 the Broxburn-West Calder route was temporarily cut at Mid Calder while the Almond bridge was closed for repair.

One of the few accidents in the company's earlier history occurred on 19 September 1924 when the steering gear failed, due to a metallurgical flaw, on a Lothian bus as it rounded the curve at Balerno railway station on its outward journey. Some of the railway passengers leaving the station were caught and two girls were killed and three other persons injured.

Production of the Lothian ceased after 1924, about one hundred having been built. Manufacturers were now improving their designs and equally suitable large vehicles were becoming available. The company however continued to build many of their bodies. Pneumatic tyres were fitted to the Lothians, and most of the Thornycrofts too, and nearly all the former remained in service until 1929 or 1930. Two or three survived as salvage wagons for some years more. The clearance for the front wheels had to be raised to suit the pneumatic tyres in the case of the Lothians, and this presented a curious effect in the case of a few bodies on which this was done before pneumatic tyred wheels were fitted. The

Lothians were heavy to handle when on pneumatic tyres as the steering-wheel was very small by later-day standards. Two Lothians were fitted with six-cylinder Minerva engines and on these, being longer, the body had to be mounted a few inches further back, with a short aluminium cowl between it and the radiator. The rear mudguards were thus not concentric with the rear wheels. These were SG4580 and SG4581.

A firm in the Bathgate area named Scott, was taken over in 1924. In January 1925 the Dean Motor Transport Company's service to Boness was taken over, and from 1 July the ordinary Queensferry route from the Mound was followed. After the summer the Fiat buses replaced the former operator's charabancs. Henderson's Central Motor Service of Boness was bought up in March 1925.

At this time the legal speed of buses was still 12 m.p.h., but the 14-seaters, weighing less than two tons, were allowed the then general 20 m.p.h. speed limit, so now most of the time-tables were speeded up to an average to suit the 20 m.p.h. limit and a note added "As the above service is made out for small buses, the intermediate times, also arrival times at the destinations, may be somewhat later should large buses be run"'. As the 12 m.p.h. speed limit had long become a dead-letter, it made no difference in practice.

The practice of printing the stage names on the tickets had now become impracticable on such a growing network, and stage numbers appeared instead. The General Strike of 1926 resulted in the complete suspension of S.M.T. services from 4 May till 11 May, no attempt being made to run services with voluntary labour. Some of the independent operators attempted spasmodic journeys over some S.M.T. routes however. An enquiry and booking-office in Princes Street near the Waverley Bridge was opened in June 1926.

A variation of the North Berwick route, namely via Drem, commenced on 1 September 1926, but about 1929 this was altered to turn northwards at Ballencrieff cross roads to join the usual route at Aberlady. Meantime on 1 June 1927 a 'limited-stop'' service to North Berwick was tried, but was withdrawn again a few months later. Stops were made only at Musselburgh Town Hall, Longniddry, Aberlady and Gullane, and point-to-point passengers were not carried.

The R. T. Motor Services route to Peebles was taken over in June 1926, though the old stance at St. David Street continued to be used for a few years. In April 1926 the border firm of Brook & Amos was bought up, followed by the Selkirk Motor Company in October 1926. A direct service between Edinburgh and Galashiels and Selkirk was not commenced till 1 August 1927 however, when another route from Edinburgh direct to Lauder, Earlston, and Jedburgh was also started. Some journeys ran via the village of Oxton. In October 1926 two or three operators in West Lothian and Lanarkshire were acquired and their routes linked up into a through service between Edinburgh and Glasgow. For a few years a "limited-stop" service officially taking two and a quarter hours was given in addition to the ordinary service, the buses used carrying a large inscribed board mounted on top of the front of the roof. A small light shone on this at night. Allen & Kennedy of Broxburn were acquired in November 1926 but continued to run between Livingstone Station and Edinburgh under their old name for some time. Two S.M.T. buses, (see list), ran carrying Allen & Kennedy's name during 1928 and 1929. The service to Livingstone Station was transferred to Waverley Bridge in 1930 and became Saturdays only in 1931. A daily service was provided from Bathgate in 1933.

Another new route was to Ratho village started about 1927, and proceeding via the Calder Road and Dalmahoy. In 1928 this service was altered to reach Ratho via the Glasgow Road and Ratho Station, but in 1930 it was again changed and given from Chambers Street, routed via Gogar station and Ratho Park to Ratho, from where it was extended down to the Glasgow Road at Ratho Station, and continued to Pumpherston, in place of the direct service there which had been transferred to the Chambers Street stance the previous year. By the next year the service was once more altered when the direct Pumpherston service from Chambers Street was restored, and the Ratho service terminated at Ratho Station, running from Waverley Bridge. The starting point of the Pumpherston service was removed to Waverley Bridge also three or four years afterwards. In subsequent years two odd journeys were run between St. Andrew Square and Dalmahoy Gate via Glasgow Road, Gogar station and Ratho Park in the summer.

The Border Motor Transport Company was acquired in September 1927, followed by Ramsay of Peebles in October, and Turnbull of Kelso in December.

A rather alarming accident occurred on 8 October 1927 when a 14-seater bus (SF 2061) got out of control on the steep hill into Boness and overturned, injuring eleven passengers.

A route to Gifford via Ormiston and Pencaitland was started in February 1928 and the service continued on into Haddington to link these two places. A few of these buses made a diversion through West Salton, and there were some journeys to Pencaitland only which ran via Winton. The Haddington route was extended to Dunbar on 1 March 1928 under an arrangement with Stark's

Motor Service, mentioned in the next chapter. Berwick could be reached through the border network but the Dunbar route was also extended there on 6 April 1928. Newcastle was first reached via Jedburgh in June 1928, and in October the alternative route via Dunbar and Berwick was established jointly with United Automobile Services Ltd. of Darlington consequent on the joint acquisition of the business of Amos Proud and Sons who had started the service in 1927. About 1927 certain Peebles journeys were diverted from Penicuik to run by Auchendinny and Howgate to Leadburn, and the route was also extended in 1928 to Innerleithen and Walkerburn. Likewise some Blackshiels journeys were run via Edgehead. A few buses to and from Lasswade took the direct road either via Kirk Brae or via Captains Road. Philpstoun, and also Blackness, could be reached by connecting services from Linlithgow. Then from 1 August 1928 the services using the Waterloo Place stance were transferred to the north side of St. Andrew Square, and proceeded via York Place and London Road. Some fare cutting was necessary to meet the "White Line" competition on the North Berwick route.

Now of course, the S.M.T. was becoming much more than a local company serving the district around Edinburgh, with which our story is concerned. It is not appropriate therefore to record in detail the development of the longer distance services and those in other areas, though, for the sake of continuity, mention of the more important of the former may perhaps be permitted.

With so much expansion additional garage and workshop accommodation was required and a large new garage was built on a site at New Street with a new head-office building above. This was completed in November 1928. Buses entered down a slope from a point opposite Market Street, and the exit was direct from the garage floor level to a point lower down New Street. The touring coaches continued to be garaged at Fountainbridge, but in October 1936 an extension on two floors was added to the north end of the New Street garage, the lower floor being entered from Low Calton Road. The workshops were also then transferred to New Street and Fountainbridge and Valleyfield Street were given up by the buses.

In February 1929 the company arranged to take a controlling interest in the business of Walter Alexander & Sons, Ltd., Falkirk, and also the Midland Bus Company, Airdrie. Then on 15 August 1929 the company was itself reconstructed with a capital of £1,800,000, the L.M.S. and L.N.E. Railway companies holding a half share between them, in accordance with their policy of investing in established road transport undertakings, arising from their new powers to engage in road transport services, granted by the Railway Road Powers Acts of 1928. This major financial

(Sir) W. J. THOMSON
Manager and later chairman of the S.M.T. Co. Ltd. 1905 - 1949

development did not produce any evident change in the company's operations, and little or no integration between the road and railway services except for interavailability of ordinary rail and bus tickets which was introduced on many routes soon afterwards. A return bus ticket used for return by rail usually incurred a supplementary payment however.

At this milestone let us take a look at the annual mileage run by the company's vehicles, to see how they have grown :—

1906	161,200
1914	728,000
1918	1,040,000
1928	10,500,000

The Whitburn route was extended through to Glasgow via Shotts and Hamilton on 8 December 1928. Carlisle was reached through the borders in April 1929, and then Stirling, under Alexander's guise as related in the next chapter, in July 1929. The latter was extended to Callander and Crieff by the next year, but after 1931 the services running through beyond Linlithgow were transferred to Alexander's auspices though S.M.T. vehicles were sometimes used for duplication. For a period in the early part of 1930 the services on the Linlithgow road were diverted at the Drum Brae via Craigs Road to regain the main road near Turnhouse. The little extra traffic gathered was however not worth the inconvenience of following this narrow hilly road. The last of the opposition on the Broxburn route was removed when West Lothian Motor Services were taken over on 6 September 1929. Oakbank was served on Saturdays and Sundays only by this time, and by 1932 could also be reached daily from Broxburn.

In the earlier days the fare for dogs was one-third of the ordinary fare, but now it had been reduced to one-sixth.

White's service from Chambers Street to Balerno was taken over on 20 February 1930, while a new circular service from Dalkeith via Newtongrange, Mossend, and Dewartown was given on Saturdays only in 1930. Services from Peebles were also developed, extending to Moffat via Abington, and then in 1930 a through service from Edinburgh to Dumfries via Leadburn and Tweedsmuir was started jointly with the Caledonian Omnibus Company of Dumfries. Summer services to Blackpool, Liverpool, and Manchester were run jointly with Ribble Motor Services of Preston from June 1930, and a one-day service to London operated in April 1930 with the acquisition of Thomson's Tours.

A charge of one penny was now made for the pocket timetables, while a comprehensive volume covering all the "group" companies was also issued at twopence.

The long-standing green and cream colour scheme of the company underwent a major change in the spring of 1930 when it gave place to blue. Waistbands painted cream which had been dropped a year before, reappeared with it. After another nineteen years, green and cream came back again in June 1949, but during the intervening years several variations in colour were applied to specific small groups of vehicles. Details will be found in the rolling-stock section.

Several small local operators in West Lothian were taken over in 1931, viz. Dewar, Beuken, McDowal, Brodie, and Masson; followed by Lamond, Rendall, and Anderson, in March and April 1932, when the network absorbed local services between Broxburn and Queensferry via Newbridge and via Niddrie; and Broxburn and Winchburgh. Broxburn to Boness, with a workers' bus continuing to Grangemouth, was started the following year.

On the other side of the city, Bowen's route from Chambers Street to Tranent via Niddrie Mill, Newcraighall, Musselburgh, Smeaton, and Elphinstone, with a local service also between Wallyford and Niddrie Mill, was taken over on 11 June 1931. This was followed on 24 February 1932 by Dunn's services between Chambers Street and Cousland via Niddrie Mill, Millerhill, Musselburgh, and Smeaton; and between Cousland and Portobello where the terminus was at Brighton Crescent, via Smeaton, Dalkeith, and Niddrie Mill; also between Penicuik and Musselburgh via Roslin, Loanhead, Lasswade, Bonnyrigg, Dalkeith and Millerhill. Soon after the Chambers Street-Cousland service was terminated at Smeaton except on Saturdays and Sundays, and later withdrawn altogether beyond Whitecraigs.

A useful book of "Instructions to Drivers and Conductors of Public Service Vehicles" compiled by W. T. Wells was issued to the staff in 1932. Another change about this time was the introduction of the "Setright" ticket machine, and so the old type of tickets disappeared after 1934. Just before this a kind of universal single/return blue and white ticket had been tried.

A rather circuitous route to Lanark commenced on 12 September 1932 running via Lothianburn, Penicuik, Carlops, West Linton, Dolphinton, Dunsyre, and Carstairs, with a view to serving the district deprived of its railway service on the L.M.S. Dolphinton branch from Carstairs. The Walkerburn service was extended to Galashiels. A special return journey for hospital visitors was made on Sundays to East Fortune Sanatorium. In 1933 a summer service was run on Saturdays and Sundays from Gorebridge to Port Seton. The Glasgow and the Dunbar routes were also linked up in the summer so that passengers did not require to change in Edinburgh, but this arrangement was abandoned about 1937.

There was also a summer service to Inverness. A few Blackshiels journeys were again extended to Humbie. Local services in Peebleshire were acquired from the Caledonian Omnibus Company in August 1933. Some of the Gorebridge buses were diverted to serve Easthouses instead of Eskbank on their way between Dalkeith and Newtongrange in 1933, and in April 1935 some of these Gorebridge journeys were extended to the new housing scheme at Birkenside. Afterwards the local Middleton service was given as an extension of this route. In March 1935 some of the Lasswade buses were extended to Polton Road-end. In May 1935 many of the Queensferry journeys were extended out to Hopetoun crossroads where housing development was taking place on the western outskirts of the town, and two months later several journeys were diverted through Dalmeny village before descending the Hawes Brae. A direct service to the growing Wallyford village and variation of the routes to Haddington by running a few journeys via Pencaitland and then direct to Haddington instead of via Gifford also came about this time.

The advent of the Road Traffic Act in April 1931 had precipitated the new numbering scheme for the vehicles, which is detailed in the rolling-stock section. The Traffic Commissioners were also anxious that all bus services should be numbered. This was of course an undertaking of considerable magnitude. A scheme was however devised for routes radiating from Edinburgh, starting with No. 30 so as to avoid confliction with the numbers of the Corporation services. Services wholly in the outlying areas used separate series of numbers with a prefix, e.g. border area B; West Lothian etc. C; Dalkeith, Musselburgh etc. D, though the local routes from Broxburn and Linlithgow were numbered merely 1 to 25. New vehicles were now usually equipped with roller-blind destination screens and a number-screen, surmounted by a small panel lettered SMT, on the front only, supplemented by the time-honoured paper bills on which the letters were now printed in blue instead of black. Existing vehicles continued to depend on these, and bore no service numbers. These service numbers were given in the time-tables and displayed on the vehicles where so equipped from 1934. The system was however so complex and so many buses could not show the numbers that it is doubtful if they served any useful purpose to the public, and the same is probably true today. The list was as follows :—

1	Broxburn	—	Hardale
2	Broxburn	—	Oakbank
3	Broxburn	—	Pumpherston
4	Broxburn	—	Winchburgh
5	Broxburn	—	S. Queensferry via Winchburgh
6	Broxburn	—	S. Queensferry via Newbridge
7	Broxburn	—	Boness via Bridgend & Borrowstoun
8	Broxburn	—	Boness via Philpstoun & Borrowstoun

9	Broxburn	—	Grangemouth via Bridgend & Borrowstoun
10	Broxburn	—	Boness via Philpstoun & Castleloan
11	Broxburn	—	Threemiletown
12	Broxburn	—	Linlithgow via Uphall & Bridgend
13	Linlithgow	—	Boness via Champany
14	Linlithgow	—	Boness via Borrowstoun & Castleloan
15	Linlithgow	—	Boness via Lochmill, Borrowstoun & Newton
16	Blackness	—	Boness
17	Linlithgow	—	Avonbridge via Standburn
18	Linlithgow	—	Standburn
19	Linlithgow	—	Blackness via Champany
20	Blackness	—	Avonbridge
21	Linlithgow	—	Bathgate via Armadale
22	Linlithgow	—	Philpstoun via Gateside
23	Linlithgow	—	Winchburgh
24	Broxburn	—	West Calder
25	Broxburn	—	Mid Calder
30	St. Andrew Sq.	—	North Berwick, direct
31	St. Andrew Sq.	—	North Berwick via Ballencrieff
32	St. Andrew Sq.	—	Haddington via E. Salton & W. Salton
33	St. Andrew Sq.	—	Dunbar
34	St. Andrew Sq.	—	Pathead via Ormiston
35	St. Andrew Sq.	—	Ormiston
36	St. Andrew Sq.	—	Tranent, direct
37	St. Andrew Sq.	—	East Fortune
38	St. Andrew Sq.	—	Pencaitland via Winton
39	St. Andrew Sq.	—	Haddington via E. Salton
41	St. Andrew Sq.	—	Haddington direct
42	St. Andrew Sq.	—	Gifford via Ormiston & Pencaitland
43	St. Andrew Sq.	—	Pencaitland via Ormiston
44	St. Andrew Sq.	—	Cockburnspath
45	St. Andrew Sq.	—	Musselburgh Races
46	Chambers St.	—	Elphinstone via Woolmet
47	St. Andrew Sq.	—	Haddington via Winton, Pencaitland & Samuelston
48	St. Andrew Sq.	—	Haddington via Ormiston, Pencaitland & Samuelston
50	Waverley Bridge	—	Gorebridge via Little France
51	Waverley Bridge	—	Rosewell via Little France
53	Waverley Bridge	—	Pathead via Little France & Edgehead
60	Chambers St.	—	Tranent via Newcraighall & Elphinstone
61	Chambers St.	—	Smeaton via Woolmet
62	Chambers St.	—	Cousland via Millerhill
70	Waverley Bridge	—	Gorebridge via Gilmerton & Eskbank
71	Waverley Bridge	—	Rosewell via Gilmerton & Eskbank
72	Waverley Bridge	—	Middleton via Gilmerton
73	Waverley Bridge	—	Middleton via Little France
74	Waverley Bridge	—	Blackshiels via Gilmerton & Edgehead
75	Waverley Bridge	—	Bonnyrigg via Gilmerton
76	Waverley Bridge	—	Gilmerton
77	Waverley Bridge	—	Eskbank via Gilmerton
78	Waverley Bridge	—	Pathead via Gilmerton
79	Waverley Bridge	—	Pathhead via Gilmerton & Edgehead
80	Waverley Bridge	—	Newtongrange via Gilmerton
81	Waverley Bridge	—	Edmonstone Road

82	Waverley Bridge	—	Blackshiels via Gilmerton
83	Waverley Bridge	—	Humbie via Gilmerton
84	Waverley Bridge	—	Gorebridge via Gilmerton & Easthouses
85	Waverley Bridge	—	Birkenside via Gilmerton
86	Waverley Bridge	—	Birkenside via Little France
87	Waverley Bridge	—	Dalkeith via Gilmerton
90	Waverley Bridge	—	Lasswade via Liberton & Loanhead
91	Waverley Bridge	—	Lasswade via Captains Road
92	Waverley Bridge	—	Penicuik via Liberton & Loanhead
93	Waverley Bridge	—	Lasswade via Kirk Brae
94	Waverley Bridge	—	Penicuik via Liberton & Roslin
95	Waverley Bridge	—	Penicuik via Captains Road
96	Waverley Bridge	—	Penicuik via Liberton, Loanhead & Roslin
97	Waverley Bridge	—	Penicuik via Liberton
98	Waverley Bridge	—	Straiton via Liberton
99	Waverley Bridge	—	West End Cottages via Liberton
100	Waverley Bridge	—	Loanhead via Liberton
101	Waverley Bridge	—	Roslin via Liberton & Loanhead
102	Waverley Bridge	—	Roslin via Liberton
103	Waverley Bridge	—	Polton Mill Road End via Liberton
104	Waverley Bridge	—	Polton Mill Road End via Captains Road
105	Waverley Bridge	—	West End Cottages via Captains Road
110	Waverley Bridge	—	Ratho Station Road via Ratho
111	Waverley Bridge	—	Ratho
112	Waverley Bridge	—	Livingstone
113	Waverley Bridge	—	Bathgate, direct
114	Waverley Bridge	—	Uphall
115	Waverley Bridge	—	Broxburn
116	Waverley Bridge	—	Pumpherston via Ratho
117	Waverley Bridge	—	Pumpherston direct
118	Waverley Bridge	—	Armadale
119	Waverley Bridge	—	Dalmahoy via Ratho
120	Waverley Bridge	—	Kirkliston
121	Waverley Bridge	—	Winchburgh
122	Waverley Bridge	—	Linlithgow via Gorgie
130	Chambers St.	—	Balerno via Colinton
131	St. Andrew Sq.	—	Balerno via Slateford
140	Waverley Bridge	—	Oakbank
141	Waverley Bridge	—	Midcalder
142	Waverley Bridge	—	Bathgate via Midcalder & Uphall
143	Waverley Bridge	—	Pumpherston via Midcalder
150	Waverley Bridge	—	Penicuik via Lothianburn
151	Waverley Bridge	—	Roslin via Lothianburn
160	Mound	—	S. Queensferry
161	Mound	—	Boness, direct
162	Mound	—	Boness, via Miller's Pit
163	Mound	—	Cramond Brig
230	St. Andrew Sq.	—	Newcastle via Grantshouse & Berwick
231	St. Andrew Sq.	—	Newcastle via Coldingham & Berwick
232	St. Andrew Sq.	—	Berwick via Coldingham
250	Waverley Bridge	—	Glasgow via Shotts
260	Waverley Bridge	—	Hawick via Little France
261	Waverley Bridge	—	Carlisle via Little France
262	Waverley Bridge	—	Galashiels via Little France
263	Waverley Bridge	—	Selkirk via Little France

270	Chambers St.	— Newcastle via Little France & Jedburgh
271	Chambers St.	— Jedburgh via Little France
272	Chambers St.	— Kelso via Little France
273	Chambers St.	— Newcastle via Little France & Kelso
274	Chambers St.	— Kelso via Little France & Edgehead
290	Waverley Bridge	— Galashiels via Howgate & Peebles
291	Waverley Bridge	— Galashiels via Penicuik & Peebles
292	Waverley Bridge	— Walkerburn via Howgate & Peebles
293	Waverley Bridge	— Peebles via Roslin & Penicuik
294	Waverley Bridge	— Walkerburn via Penicuik & Peebles
295	Waverley Bridge	— Peebles via Penicuik
296	Waverley Bridge	- - Lanark
297	Chambers St	— Dumfries
298	Waverley Bridge	— Peebles via Howgate
310	Waverley Bridge	— Glasgow via Bathgate
314	Glasgow	— Dunbar, direct
321	Waverley Bridge	— Callander
322	Waverley Bridge	— Crieff
323	Waverley Bridge	— Stirling

Numbers for the longer distance services have been omitted, but it will be seen that provision was made for a good variety of possible short-workings. Some, such as 122, were workers' buses.

In the early summer of 1935 nearly all the tours operators in Edinburgh were taken over, as mentioned in the next chapter : Only Cruikshanks held out till 1938.

Congestion at the Waverley Bridge was now becoming acute. Buses arriving from the west proceeded via the Mound and Market Street, which was used as a "park" for buses before proceeding to their stance. So arrangements were made for the starting point of all S.M.T. services to be concentrated in St. Andrew Square. This took effect on 1 June 1936. The services to the east continued to use the north side of the square, those to the south took the south side, those to the west the east side, except Balerno and the Queensferry road buses which were at the north-west corner. The south-west corner was used for tours and specials, though extended tours and the London service remained at the Mound. Buses from south and west entered via St. David Street, those leaving the west proceeding via George Street and Castle Street. The Queensferry road buses used George Street and Charlotte Square in both directions. The stances were of course on the gardens side. The old uniform with leggings gave way to the cooler trousers in the summer of 1936. At the end of December 1936 the lone little outpost of the British Electric Traction group, the "Coast Line" service of the Musselburgh & District Electric Light & Traction Co. Ltd., between Waterloo Place and Port Seton was transferred to S.M.T. ownership. The starting point was also transferred to St. Andrew Square, but the old route via Kings Road and Baileyfield Road continued to be followed.

The growing village of Gowkshill, up the hill from Newton-grange, was given a service in 1938. A Sunday journey was now run to East Fortune from Dalkeith also, and similar journeys from Dalkeith and from Newtongrange to Newbattle.

The Balerno via Colinton route was also linked to the Port Seton route on Saturdays and Sundays, the buses proceeding right through and being further extended to the caravan site at Seton Dene. In the summer this service continued right through to North Berwick.

So by the summer of 1939 we find the S.M.T. providing a very complete network all around Edinburgh: Almost every village was served. Basically the services to Balerno and to Port Seton ran every ten minutes, while Gilmerton was similar on average. Queensferry had a bus every fifteen minutes. Tranent, and Penicuik's average interval was similar, while Broxburn, and Dalkeith were served even more frequently. A half-hourly service was run to North Berwick, and to Linlithgow. Fares were kept at a very reasonable level, and the following examples may be quoted: Barnton 3d., Juniper Green 3d., Gilmerton 4d. or 6d. return, Musselburgh 5d. or 8d. return; Kirkliston, Balerno, Loanhead, and Dalkeith were 6d. with a return fare of 11d. in the case of the latter two. Queensferry, Port Seton, and Tranent were 9d. and 1/4d. return. Broxburn, and Penicuik were 10d., the former being 1/3d. return and the latter 1/6d. return. Linlithgow was 1/- and there was no reduced return fare offered. The inconsistency of the return fares seems to have arisen with the piecemeal expansion of services under varying conditions. Double-deck buses were normally used for Penicuik, Lasswade, Rosewell, Gorebridge, etc. and Balerno via Slateford routes. They were used on other routes on occasion too, but some places, e.g. Linlithgow, were barred to them by low bridges.

Then came war. Outwardly there was little sign of any preparations by the S.M.T.; but they were ready, and immediately, sufficient buses were fitted up with complete "black-out" curtains to keep services running, and the rest rapidly followed. This lighting policy,—quite different to that of Edinburgh Corporation, — enabled the normal lighting to be used in the vehicles and was no doubt of advantage to the longer distance passengers. On the other hand passengers could not tell where they were and reliance had to be placed on the conductor or conductress, who was often equally "lost" with the inevitable unfortunate result on occasion. The older double-deckers with open platforms had to have a little screening fitted on the back. Headlights, of course, had to conform to regulations and the company intimated that the various running times were applicable to the hours of daylight only. Early in the war some buses were taken for ambulance duties, and these were followed by some forty or so, requisitioned by the military authorities. The usual annual replacements were on order however, and duly received in 1940. Four double-deckers were lent to London later in the year.

At the end of the 1939 season the tours, summer services, and long-distance services ceased, though the London service was continued for a few months more. Special routes such as that to East Fortune were no longer required. On the other hand a new service via Gullane was given to West Fenton air-station. One of these journeys ran via Port Seton. The caravan site at Seton Dene became a regular dormitory, and two Port Seton journeys were extended there Monday to Friday. The accent was on essential traffic. Gradually the services had to be cut somewhat to meet the call of fuel rationing. The times of the last buses were brought forward in some cases, and Sunday services were more sparse. Duplication had to be virtually eliminated, and loadings were thus generally heavy. Nevertheless a remarkably good service was provided throughout the war.

Sixty Bedford utility buses were obtained, and the bodies for these, and many more besides including the Edinburgh Corporation ones, were built by the S.M.T. at Marine Gardens. The Ministry of Supply were also able to provide a number of double-deckers, and further double-deck bodies were obtained and fitted to former coaches. An early experiment was made, in March 1940, with a gas-producer fixed to the back of an AEC bus, No.B3, while later a number of AEC and Leyland vehicles were adapted for the standard producer-gas trailers and run on the fairly flat North Berwick route. A few buses on busy short distance routes were fitted with longitudinal seats to give increased standing capacity in 1942.

Season tickets for adults were withdrawn about July 1941 but weekly tickets available for one, or alternatively for two, daily return journeys, excluding Sundays, were made available at appropriate rates. The charge for dogs was increased to one-quarter fare. To assist in loadings at rush-hours some buses were run non-stop to outlying towns, such as Bathgate, in 1941. Then, in 1943, to discourage the long distance traveller who had alternative rail service, some of the remaining long routes were cut, e.g. Edinburgh-Newcastle cut at Berwick, so that there was no effective through service. However a new service to be recorded was one on Saturdays and Sundays only to Kirknewton which started in February 1943. The road through Turnhouse was closed because of the aerodrome and continued so for some time after the war, necessitating a diversion via Gogar.

When the war ended the vehicle "black-out" equipment was speedily removed, though the restoration of headlights to a satisfactory condition took much longer. There had been little change in the local routes being run, but some districts were growing rapidly and commanded a much increased service, e.g. Birkenside and Easthouses. An effort was made to provide improved services as soon as possible but the effects of continued fuel rationing made this a slow process. Nevertheless the long-distance services were restarted on a restricted scale in the summer of 1946. In 1947 the suburban services to Gilmerton, and nearby Danderhall were increasing with the growing population. Port Seton buses continued on to Seton Sands for the summer, while the Cousland-Portobello service was suspended during the winter. Some buses on the Millerhill route proceeded via Danderhall, and the Kirknewton route was continued on to Mid Calder. There were two buses on Saturdays to Glenkinchie road-end in East Lothian. Various useful school or workers services, usually once in in the morning and out in the evening, appeared in the time-tables such as Cousland to St. Andrew Square, Wallyford to St. Andrew Square via Inveresk, Danderhall to Dalkeith via Millerhill. Other workers' journeys were run direct to and from such places as the North British Rubber Works, and other factories in Edinburgh and Leith, being operated to Dalkeith, Linlithgow, Bathgate, etc. All of these were not advertised however.

A local acquisition in December 1947 was the Dalkeith—Bonny-rigg—Cockpen—Newtongrange — Easthouses — Dalkeith circular service, and the Wednesdays, Saturdays and Sundays service from Dalkeith to Carrington and Toxside hitherto run by Cockburn of Dalkeith. Local services in Musselburgh grew, including new ones to Stoneybank, to Ashgrove, to Edenhall hospital, and to Preston, i.e. near Prestonpans station, — the latter extended to and from St. Andrew Square via Kings Road on Sunday evenings, still with its Dalkeith area service number D92.

A list of the numbers allocated to new services since 1934 should now be given :

40   West Fenton via Kings Road and Port Seton
43   Glenkinchie road-end
49   Wallyford via Willowbrae
50   route extended to Birkenside
52   Humbie via Little France and Edgehead
54   Pathead via Little France
55   Blackshiels via Little France and Edgehead
56   Humbie via Little France
57   Eskbank via Little France
58 Gilmerton (previously 76)
68   Bonnyrigg via Gilmerton (previously 75)
69   Gorebridge via Gilmerton and Gowkshill
75   Middleton via Little France & Easthouses
80   Birkenside via Gilmerton and Gowshill
82   altered to via Little France
84   route extended to Birkenside
86   Middleton via Gilmerton and Easthouses

88   Dalkeith via Little France
89   Birkenside via Gilmerton, Easthouses, and Gowkshill
123   Linlithgow
124   Linlithgow Bridge
135   North Berwick via Kings Road and Port Seton
142   Bathgate via Livingstone station
144   Kirknewton
164   Hopetoun crossroads
165   Hopetoun crossroads via Dalmeny
166   South Queensferry via Dalmeny
167   Boness via Mannerston
170   Musselburgh via Kings Road
171   Seton Dene via Kings Road
172   Port Seton via Kings Road
249   Glasgow via Bellshill

It is noteworthy that the company had managed to keep its same scale of fares despite the war. About the only increase was a half-penny on the fare to Juniper Green. On the other hand there were one or two instances of small reductions.

The company had turned over much of its resources to war work, and had equipped a large building at Portobello, the old "Marine Gardens", — where military and other vehicles were assembled. After the war this was turned into a modern body-building works for the company's needs, being opened as such in July 1948.

With such large scale activities the company's vehicles inevitably met with accidents from time to time, but while some of these were no doubt alarming, very few resulted in serious casualties to passengers. Two in the Edinburgh area may be mentioned. After a sidelong collision on the Glasgow road near Ingliston on 6 June 1934 a westgoing bus crashed into a tree and one passenger was killed while twenty four others and the crew were injured.

On 20 June 1941 a bus from Port Seton travelling westwards at speed up Portobello Road got out of control and crashed head-on into a tramcar killing five bus passengers and injuring thirty-three.

Another major change in the company's constitution was now impending. Early in 1948 the new British Transport Commission cast their eye towards the well integrated bus industry in Scotland, and arrangements were made for the Commission to investigate the company's finances with a view to nationalisation. The result was the approval at a special general meeting of the company on 8 April 1949, of the sale of the company's bus undertaking to the British Transport Commission with effect from 1 April 1948. The finances of the preceeding year were duly sorted out and a new company, Scottish Omnibuses Limited registered on 8 April 1949. The Scottish Motor Traction Co. Ltd. then devoted itself to its other interests, but by agreement, the fleet name S.M.T. was continued on the buses and coaches of S.O.L. The change to the green livery in June 1949 has already been mentioned, and it is said that this was quite coincidental. Otherwise there was little or no sign of the change of ownership, and the new company continued to operate as of old. At this time, however, Sir William Thomson, as he had now become, retired, whereupon Mr. James Amos, who had come along with Brook & Amos in 1926, became chairman of the new company. Mr. Robert Beveridge who had been with the company since 1914 was appointed general manager. "Sandy" Bracken, another of the small staff from the earliest days, and long since chief engineer retired in 1948.

The Caledonian Omnibus Company, — also nationalised, — was disbanded and its services taken over by the "Scottish bus group" in June 1950, S.M.T. then taking the Edinburgh-Dumfries service entirely. The first post-war fares increase took effect in December 1950, and there have been further increases in most years since.

With fuel rationing finished and traffic booming at summer weekends Scottish Omnibuses found they could use many more vehicles than they had available, despite considerable additions to the fleet. Use was made of other vehicles from the "group" or allied companies where opportunity offered, but in addition, in July 1951 and for several summers following, a few dozen buses, both single and double-deck, were hired from Edinburgh Corporation on Saturday afternoons, and used on a wide variety of "S.M.T." services. A new Rule Book was issued to the staff of all the "group" companies in May 1951, while a well-produced monthly staff magazine, "The Scottish Omnibus" made its debut in February 1955.

An interesting extension of route commenced on 10 September 1951 arising from the withdrawal of the passenger train service from Polton, when it was agreed to run five journeys, including some from Dalkeith, down the very steep hill into the little village, so that in the absence of trains a walk to Polton road-end was avoided. On 18 August 1952 the long distance services were transferred to a new stance at the east end of Queen Street, thus easing the position at St. Andrew Square, which was becoming chaotic on summer Saturdays. The Dumfries service was also transferred there from Castle Terrace, and in April 1954 the Queen Street stances were equipped with stance poles of the latest type being used by the Corporation.

As mentioned in the previous chapter, a new agreement was concluded with the Corporation on 1 July 1954 covering the respective spheres of operation and fares. As a result of this and the withdrawal of the Portobello and Musselburgh tramway service,

S.O.L ST. ANDREW SQUARE BUS STATION
On the opening day 5 April 1957

the S.M.T. service from St. Andrew Square to Port Seton and its variations (Nos. 170-1-2) were diverted to follow the old tram route through Portobello and Joppa, together with a new service to Galt Road, Musselburgh from 14 November 1954. The latter was extended to Wallyford on 6 February 1955. The local journeys to Gilmerton and other points within the city boundary to which the company hitherto ran "duplicates" at busy periods ceased as the Corporation services were augmented, though the Corporation's then circuitous route to Barnton did not satisfy residents there as an effective substitute. A gyratory system for all traffic was put into operation temporarily in St. Andrew Square in the spring of 1956, in connection with the roadway repairs in Princes Street, and this necessitated the stances being changed to the "buildings" sides around the Square.

Early in 1956 Mr. Roderick Mackenzie was appointed general manager in succession to Mr. Beveridge, then due to retire.

A long-standing grievance of the travelling public was the lack of a bus station, for St. Andrew Square provided no shelter whatever for waiting passengers. The company had decided before the war that this amenity would be provided and started purchase of their chosen site. Of course the war halted all progress with the project, and afterwards resumption was delayed by difficulties with planning permission for a reasonably long period. Eventually however the scheme reached fruition with the official opening on 5 April 1957 of the station at Clyde Street with its four platforms with shelters and other amenities. It cost over £250,000, and can handle 120 buses per hour. Even so congestion can arise in the summer peak periods. An exhibition of coaches was held on the opening day, and normal traffic commenced to use it on 6 April, with a gyratory traffic system round St. Andrew Square, St. Andrew Street, and St. David Street. Buses enter the station via York Place and Elder Street except those from the south which proceed from the Post Office via East Register Street. All buses depart into St. Andrew Square. The site is eminently suitable in contrast to the town-planners' proposals for two or more bus stations at points as far removed from one another and from the main railway station as Shrubhill, and Morrison Street.

The Rolling Stock :

The vehicles in use up to the end of the first war period have already been described, and numbers given as far as is known, with the exception of the Lothians, details of which now follow. (For the purposes of this work, numbers shown preceeded by E are Edinburgh licence numbers; by D are Dundee licence numbers; by G are Galashiels fleet numbers; and by B are Bathgate fleet numbers, though these prefixes were not actually used.)

New	Reg. No.		Bodies	Co. Nos.		
1913	S	3057	c/o/c	E95		
	S	3597	c/o	E55?		
	S	3662	c/o/c	E91		
	S	3703	c	E94		
	S	3841	c/o	E93	E893	
	S	4068	c	E96?	D48?	E66
	S	4100	c	E92		
	S	4287	c	E97?	D50?	E78
	S	4288	c	E98	D188	
	S	4399	o/c	E82	D187	
	S	4400	c/o/c	E83	G119	
	S	4543	o/c	E84		
	S	4617	c	E85		
	S	4654	c/o	E88	E889	
	S	4655	c/o	E89	E891	
	S	4716	c/o	E72	E872	
	S	4748	o	E70?	D57?	
	S	4770	c	E75	G133	
	S	4813	o/c/o	E76	E876	
	S	4836	c	E51	G131	
	S	4846	c/o	E52	E852	
	S	4849	c	E73		
	S	4851	c	E53		
	S	4963	c	E74?	D46?	E69
	S	5224	c	E54		
	S	5496	c	E56		
	S	5550	c	E57	G122	
	S	5595	c	E55	G120	
	S	5697	c/o/c	E58		
	S	5862	c	E59		
	S	5916	c	E60?	D58?	E355
	S	6423	c/o/c	E61		
	S	6729	c/o/c	E62	D186	
	S	6761	c	E63		
	S	7063	c	E66?	D47?	
	S	7322	c	E65?	D58?	E97
	S	7618	c/o/c/o/c	E86		
	S	7715	c/o/c	E90		
	S	8461	c	E71		
	S	8533	c/o	E74	E874	
	S	8594	c	E77		
	S	8668	c/o	E79	E879	
1919	S	9102	c/o/c	E64		
1919	S	9103	c/o	E80	E840	
1920	S	9555	c	E102		
1920	S	9622	c/o/c/o	E103	E843	
1920	S	9707	c/o/c	E104		
1920	S	9728	c/o	E105	E845	
1920	S	9830	c/o	E106	E846	
1921	SG	791	o	E107?	D56?	
1921	SG	792	o/c	E108		
1921	SG	887	c	E109		
1921	SG	888	c/o	E110	E850	
1921	SG	1039	c/o	E111	E851	
1921	SG	1890	c	E70		
1921	SG	2106	c	D49?	E354	
1921	SG	2107	c	E140?	D48?	E356
1921	SG	2128	c	E65	G130	
1921	SG	2129	c/o/c	E67	G134	

335

New	Reg. No.	Bodies	Co. Nos.	
1921	SG 2319	c/o/c	E232	
1921	SG 2755	c/o	E233	
1921	SG 3387	o/c	E107	
1921	SG 3756	c	E99	G132
1921	SG 4580	c	E231	G135
1921	SG 4581	c	E234	
1922	SG 5639	c	E101	G121
1922	SG 7201	c/o	E228	
1922	SG 7202	c/o/c/o/c	E229	
1922	SG 7203	c	E230	
1923	SG 7680	c/o/c	E227	
1923	SG 7681	c	E226	D121
1923	SG 7738	c	E225	
1923	SG 7985	o/c	E224	
1923	SG 7991	o	E223	
1923	SG 8034	o/c/o	E222	
1924	SF 226	o/c/o/c	E215	
1921	SF 227	o/c	E216	
1924	SF 228	o/c/o/c/o/c	E217	
1924	SF 229	o/c	E218	
1924	SF 230	o	E219	
1924	SF 253	o	E242	
1924	SF 254	o	E256	
1924	SF 274	o	E257	
1924	SF 275	o/c	E258	
1924	SF 330	o	E259	
1924	SF 365	o/c/o	E260	
1924	SF 427	c/o/c	E351	
1924	SF 503	c	E353	
1924	SF 504	c/o/c	E352	

Inglis

S.M.T. BUSES AT THE WAVERLEY BRIDGE STANCE, 1921
The third bus is a Thornycroft, the others are Lothians, some still carrying
the box in which the gas bag had been fixed.

The changes of body shown, open or closed, are mainly in respect of the period 1925-1930. Several of the charabanc bodies were without beading and the side panels were formed into a rounded top over the frame. There were also one or two bodies which otherwise differed slightly from the usual patterns described. S4288 had disc wheels in its solid tyre days for a time. SF228 was operated as an Allen & Kennedy vehicle during 1928-9.

Details of the four ex-Dundee Mechanical Transport Co. vehicles are lacking, but Thornycroft TS2989 which received an S.M.T.-built bus body and became E60 was doubtless one of them.

The three charabancs acquired from Adam Young of Eskbank were a Dennis which was soon disposed of and two Thornycrofts. These were probably SY816 and SY901. The first of these was an early model with low-set radiator and was fitted with a wooden roof, becoming E243. The second received an S.M.T.-built bus body and was promptly sold to the G.N.S. Railway Co.

The large batch of "J" type Thornycrofts purchased between 1921 and 1925 were as follows; there being also an earlier one S7075 (o) E136.

SG1259	o	E112			SG1935	o	E137 PT	
SG1260	o	E113			SG1952	o	E138 PT	
SG1261	o	E114			SG1972	o	E139 PT	
SG1359	o	E87			SG2063	?	D48	
SG1360	o	E122 PT	c	in 1927	SG2284	c	E68 PT	
SG1433	o	E124 PT			SG2895	c	D58	
SG1434	o	E125 PT			SG2960	c	E235 PT	o as E337
SG1497	o	D? E214 PT						in 1927
SG1538	o	D? E244?			SG2961	c	E236	
SG1591	o	E116			SG2994	c	E237 PT	
SG1636	o	D? E357 PT			SG3247	o	E140 PT	
SG1637	o	E130 PT			SG3302	?	D?	
SG1664	o	E115? D?			SG3303	o	E118	
SG1675	o	E126 PT			SG3454	o	E123 PT	
SG1721	c	E119 PT			SG3526	o	E81 PT	
SG1722	o	E117? D?			SG3689	o	E100 PT	
SG1723	o	E131 PT			SG3923	?	D53	
SG1724	o	E132 PT			SG8033	o	E221	
SG1725	o	E133 PT			SG8243	c	E212	
SG1824	o	E120			SG8290	c	E213?D49	o as E212
SG1825	o	E127 PT						and PT in 1927
SG1830	o	E128 PT			SG8714	c	E129? D51	
SG1856	o	E121			SF3001	c	E358	o as E220 and
SG1857	o	E134						PT in 1927
SG1858	o	E135 PT			SF3662	c	E361	

There were at least eight different types of charabanc body (o) seating 27, including some similar to both patterns on the Lothians. The bus bodies (c) were also similar to the Lothians. Those vehicles later fitted with pneumatic tyres are marked PT. The last six buses were forward-control models with 32 seats, and there were a few more of these, e.g. E96, though when SG8290 and SF3001 became charabancs in 1927 they were altered to normal control. The last of the Thornycrofts disappeared about 1928.

Next came the Fiats, the first in 1921, the last in 1926, all fourteen seaters on pneumatic tyres :

SG4067	o	E238		SF 32	o	E325	
SG4068	o	E239		SF 33	o	E326	
SG4131	o	E240		SF 34	o	E327	
SG4239	o	E242?		SF1814	c3	E329	
SG4832	o	E241 Conv. to cl		SF1815	c3	E328	D83
SG5545	o	E270 Conv. to cl		SF1984	c3	E331	
SG5818	o	E245		SF2060	c2	E332	D81
SG5819	o	E246		SF2061	c2	E333	
SG5820	o	E247 Conv. to cl		SF2166	c2	E334	
SG5896	o	E248		SF2477	o	E336 Conv. to cl	
SG7793	o	E250 Conv. to cl		SF2478	o	E335	
SG7794	o	E249		SF2542	o	E338	
SG7832	o	E253		SF2543	o	E339	
SG7833	o	E252 Conv. to cl		SF2839	o	E340	
SG7834	o	E251 Conv. to c2		SF2840	o	E341	
SG7920	o	E254		SF2841	o	E342	D75
SG8316	o	E255 Conv. to cl		SF2842	o	E343 Conv. to cl,	
?	o	E301 Conv. to c3					D118
SG9705	o	E300		SF2921	o	E344	D76
SG9706	o	E302		SF2922	o	E345	
SG9707	o	E305 Conv. to c3,		SF2923	o	E346 Conv. to cl	
		D82		SF2997	o	E347	D77
SG9708	o	E307		SF2998	o	E348	
SG9709	o	E303		SF2999	o	E349	
SG9710	o	E304		SF3661	c2	E362	
SG9711	o	E306		SF3663	c2	E363	
SG9712	o	E308 Conv. to c3		SF3753	cl	E364	
SG9744	o	E309		SF3754	c2	E365	
SG9745	o	E310		SF3755	cl	E366	D119
SG9798	o	E313		SF3829	c2	E367	
SG9799	o	E312 Conv. to c2		SF4978	o	E420	
SG9800	o	E311		SF4979	o	E421	
SG9877	o	E316		SF4980	o	E422	
SG9878	o	E314		SF4981	o	E423	
SG9879	o	E315		SF4982	o	E424	
SG9918	o	E317		SF5275	o	E425	
SG9919	o	E318		SF5276	o	E426	
SG9920	o	E319		SF5277	o	E427	
SG9978	o	E321		SF5278	o	E428	
SG9979	o	E322 Conv. to cl		SF5601	o	E429	
SG9980	o	E323		SF5767	o	E436	
SF 31	o	E324					

The buses marked cl had a rather square body with an inset front entrance; those marked c2 had more rounded corners to the body and a flush front entrance. Those marked c3 were similar but had windows aside the rear emergency door, as also had those marked cl. The bus bodies were painted green with black uppers, but in some cases the normal green and cream livery was applied later. The charabancs (o) were brown and bore no lettering.

Five other acquired Fiats were used in Edinburgh. Usually on the Boness route SX2104, E350, was a twelve seat bus with a small neat body though branded as fourteen seats, and probably came from Henderson of Boness. The other four were charabancs with non-standard bodies from unknown sources about 1926-7; — LS1037, E434; LS1241, E435; ES3323, E330; and ES3465, E369. The last of the Fiats disappeared about 1929.

Following the Fiats came nine Beardmore and four International buses in 1925 as under. The Beardmores had fifteen seat bodies similar to the "c3" pattern, while the fourteen seat Internationals were more similar to the "c1" pattern. Painting was as for the Fiats. Both types were mostly used on the North Berwick route, and lasted only till 1929.

SF3797	Beardmore	E370	SF3856	Beardmore	E379
SF3798	Beardmore	E371	SF3857	Beardmore	E380
SF3799	Beardmore	E372	SF3858	International	E369?
SF3800	Beardmore	E373	SF3859	International	E377
SF3823	Beardmore	E374	SF3860	International	E378
SF3824	Beardmore	E375	SF3861	Beardmore	E368
SF3838	International	E376			

It should here be mentioned that during 1924-5 Lothian SG3756 and Thornycroft SG8243 had the lower panel painted green instead of cream, and about the same period a number of vehicles were painted a glossy dark grey all over. These were: Lothian SG2107, Thornycrofts SG1637, SG1935, and TS2989, Fiats SF1814, SF1815, and SF1984.

There is no information available about the few vehicles acquired from William Young, and Scott, but the Dean Motor Transport Co. handed over the following charabancs which were duly painted brown:

?	Rochet-Schneider	14 sts.	E202
?	Rochet-Schneider	14 sts.	E337
WA5080	Crossley	14 sts.	E330
SG 9365	Rochet-Schneider	20 sts.	E200
SF 535	Rochet-Schneider	20 sts.	E291
SF 536	Gotfredson	14 sts.	E293

The first three disappeared in 1926 but the Gotfredson survived as a runabout tender until about 1939.

The fourteen-seat Reo vehicles acquired from the R.T.Co. and re-painted as the Fiats, were:

SG9035	chara.	?	SG9730	chara.	E197	
SG9253	bus	E262	SF2279	chara.	E263	G123
?	bus	E195	SF2280	chara.	E264	G124
SG9613	chara.	E196 G136	SF2628	chara.	E266	G125

S.M.T. Co's. LIGHTWEIGHT MAUDSLAY 32-SEATER OF 1926 WITH
SHORT BROS. BODY

By 1925 production of Lothians had ceased and the company were looking for a substitute. An order was therefore placed for sixty Maudslay forward-control buses. Ten of the earlier ones had S.M.T. bodies similar to the Lothians. For the remainder a lighter type of body was built by Short Bros. and by Vickers. These latter differed from one another in the shape of roof and other details. All had full front cabs and 32 seats. At that time there was a proposal that buses under 3¾ tons weight might be allowed to run up to the then general 20 m.p.h. speed limit. These Maudslays had only single rear tyres, and those with the Short Bros. and Vickers bodies just came within the 3¾ tons weight limit. The proposed change in the law did not materialise however.

It is necessary at this point to refer to the numbering scheme which the company introduced in June 1931 consequent on the cessation of local authority licensing and the Edinburgh fleet numbers hitherto used. The company's 1931 fleet list will require to be given in full, and as all the Maudslays were included in that list they need not be repeated here. Their earlier Edinburgh numbers will be found also in the 1931 list.

Next there are the buses which were acquired with the Tennant, Hendry, and Lawson group. Those which were given Edinburgh licences were :

SX2286	Dennis		E121	VA3875	Leyland	32 sts.	E211
SX2297	Dennis		E120	VA4613	Dennis	28 sts.	E118
SX2345	Halley	24 sts.	999(!)	VA4614	Dennis	28 sts.	E129
SX2358	Halley		E115	VA5103	Gilford	24 sts.	E117
SX2384	Halley		E118	VA5554	Gilford	24 sts.	E116
SX2398	Albion	28 sts.	E96	VA5276	Albion	27 sts.	E113
SX2402	Albion	28 sts.	E87	VA5385	Albion	27 sts.	E112
VA3529	Leyland	32 sts.	E210	VA5603	Albion	26 sts.	E114

340

The 'SX' Dennis were of an older type than the 'VA' ones and were put on the Boness route. Both types had front entrances. Of the Halleys the remarkable number definitely inscribed on SX2345 will be noticed but no explanation can be offered. This bus had a front entrance. SX2384, which soon returned to Bathgate in favour of VA4613, had a double entrance, and there were several others of this model in that district. Some later acquired S.M.T. bodies from the Thornycrofts. SX2358 was a more modern type, also with a double entrance body. It was a fast vehicle and was generally on the Whitburn route. The Leylands were old rear entrance buses and didn't last long. There were several more of them in the west. The Gilfords had front entrances, and VA5103 was operated as an Allen & Kennedy vehicle in 1927-9. The Albions were modern vehicles, normal-control, with Albion bodies of normal lines except VA5603 which was a little different. The 'SX' ones had front entrance, the others rear entrance.

Allen & Kennedy's fleet was a small one. Those in running order when taken over were two 20 seat front entrance Reos SX2263 and SX2313 respectively E400 and E401. Also a modern 24 seat front entrance Albion SX2406, E403.

Information regarding the fleets acquired with the various border firms is scanty, and as the vehicles did not come to Edinburgh, no attempt will be made to list them, except insofar as any survived to be included in the 1931 list. There were Turnbull's vehicles which became A85-8, G60, and K167-8. Of these G60 was a charabanc, A85 and K168 generally similar to the S.M.T. Maudslay coaches about to be mentioned, and the others were of ordinary Albion outline. The four vehicles from Amos Proud should also be mentioned, viz. G61-2 and H49-50. These had standard Leyland bodies. L1, with a substantial looking body came from Ramsay, of Peebles. In 1929 Fairbairn contributed A81, while A32-3 of the then orthodox open coach design had been ordered by that firm and spent their first summer in Fairbairn's deep blue livery. They were then about the last coaches to be painted in the pale yellow livery before the company's colour scheme was changed in May 1930 to blue for all types of vehicle.

Reverting to 1926, the company's next new vehicles, late in the year, came from the Albion factory, and unusually were normal-control buses. It may be they had been ordered by Tennant. They were of typical Albion appearance, and details will be found in the 1931 list. Two more Albions followed, and these again, while being forward-control models, had ordinary "half-cab" Albion bodies, thus departing from S.M.T. practice of full-fronted machines.

A large number of forward-control Albions with full-fronted bodies appeared in 1927. These were quite luxurious for their time,

341

with "armchair" type leather seats. 1927 also saw a new type of vehicle for touring work. These were 26 seat Maudslays with side screens and a folding hood, but were not really charabancs as the seats were reached from a central aisle from a door at the front, there being also another door near the back. Details of all these are given in the 1931 list.

The 1928 additions included more full-fronted Albions and in these and all buses subsequently, top lights to the windows were omitted. The Maudslay buses of that year were similar, and separate waist bands were also omitted on both these and the Albions. The Star coaches were a smaller version of the 1927 Maudslays but the 1928 Maudslay coaches were slightly different, having more robust side screens. There were also the Star buses with rather square bodies there being only minor differences between the two bodybuilder's product. Again details are given in the 1931 list.

1929 saw another change as most of that year's purchases were Leylands, though there were also some Maudslay buses which were generally similar to the 1928 lot, except for the last two which were of a flatter shape. The "Titan" double-deckers were the standard Leyland product, the first twenty-seven having an open staircase, while the last ten were of the improved version with the platform and stair enclosed. Of the original lot, four, viz. SC2923-4 and SC2938-9, respectively E673-4 and 688-9 were sold early in 1931 to the Glasgow Omnibus Co., a subsidiary company, and thus did not reach the 1931 list. The "Lions" had the then standard rear entrance Leyland body except for the first five, the bodies of which

S.M.T. Co's. ALBION No. A19

D.L.G.H.

S.M.T. Co's. LEYLAND 'TITAN' TD1 TYPE No. J21

were however on generally similar lines though with front entrance and of more massive appearance. These five were turned out in the silver-grey livery of the Midland Bus Co. which later formed the nucleus of the Western S.M.T. Co., but were repainted in standard colours about the end of the year. Of the standard bodied lot, those which became G21/8-50/2/8 had "cut-away" pattern entrances, but G21 and G51 subsequently exchanged bodies. The first two "Tigers" had standard Leyland front entrance bodies, the remainder were coaches with a flat roof. Except for these, and the Maudslays, all the 1929 vehicles had destination screen boxes incorporated in the front of the roof, another novelty for the S.M.T.Co., though on the single-deckers the roller blinds were not fitted in them till some years later. The numbers of all these will be found in the 1931 list.

Of the West Lothian Motor Services vehicles, the Albions, Daimlers, and Dennis were taken into S.M.T. stock. The latter were sent to the borders and soon sold but require to be mentioned as the prefix E was allocated for them in the new numbering scheme. The Albion which became A82 was of typical Albion lines and the Daimlers which became D8-9 were rather similar. The others were somewhat different, the Daimler which became D12 being rather ungainly looking with the window line of the driver's cab higher than the rest of the windows. Except for this one and D8 these vehicles remained in their former dark green livery but with S.M.T.Co. lettering for some time.

The Thornycrofts and Daimlers from Thomson's Tours were of orthodox open coach pattern except for the last two Daimlers which were closed coaches of low sleek lines. His Reo and Cottin-Desgoutes charabancs did not survive for the new list and were as follows : Reos, SF1658 E381, SF2145 E383, SF2541 E385: The others were delicensed. The four buses from White's Motor Hiring Co. do not call for special notice, but a Maudslay 50 seat double-decker with open staircase and painted silver and green which ran in trial service with the S.M.T.Co. for a short time in 1929 should be mentioned. This was VC1778 and carried the Edinburgh number 128.

In 1930 the company made another innovation with an A.E.C. "Regal" MY3479 which originally carried the Strachan body with "cut-away" rear entrance later to appear on B2. This had the Edinburgh number 80, but in March 1931 SC9871 appeared with the said Strachan body and numbered 80, while MY3479 re-appeared with its Cowieson body in June as B1, the new numbers having meantime come into use. SC9871 however was of particular note in having an oil engine, and it was not long before the company standardised on this type of power unit for buses. To return to 1930 however, there were also two lots of Leyland "Tiger" coaches for long distance work. The Cowieson ones were of similar appearance to the previous year's ones but with destination screen boxes : The Burlingham ones were more low set, and both were provided with specially comfortable seating. Another new make was a series of eight small Chevrolet open coaches, while a more unusual one still was an S.M.C., otherwise a six-cylinder "Sunbeam", which had a 31 seat "cut-away" pattern rear entrance body by Taylor of Norwich. This was UK9189, receiving Edinburgh number 79, and though the prefix M was allocated in the new list the vehicle was disposed of before the renumbering.

Two other buses which ran on trial in the first few months of 1931 have to be mentioned. The first was a Tilling-Stevens with a 38 seat front entrance body MS9978, and this was followed by an Albion "Valkyrie" with a 32 seat front entrance body GG2513. Both, in turn, carried the Edinburgh number 217.

An important change was made in May 1930 when a blue livery was adopted for all vehicles. Later there were many variations which will be mentioned in due course. Then in 1932 the full spread out lettering gave place to just a closely spaced S.M.T.

The numerical details of the vehicles included in the 1931 list should now be given, and this list is extended to include the additions up to 1956. The basis of the numbering scheme was that each make of chassis was numbered separately with a corresponding prefix letter, and the prefix letter was applied alphabetically to each make in the fleet when the list was drawn up. Leylands were further sub-divided, and the letters then used were A up to P, omitting I and O. E, L, and M dropped out at once and L was then used for a separate series for Stark's buses at Dunbar. The vehicles acquired from the several firms taken over about 1932 required the use of further letters and R, S, T, U, V, and W came into use together with a new E. Of these S, T, U, and V soon disappeared, to be used again, — except U, — for other new types afterwards acquired, followed by a new M and the use of O, also later, X. E was used for a third time during the war and BB for double-deck versions of B. In 1956 double-deck versions of other makes were dealt with similarly so that E became DD as D had then recently been re-used, and J became HH. Several of the second-hand vehicles though listed, were never repainted in S.M.T. colours, while many more were never even included in the fleet list at all. In 1935 S was used for the third time to cover the few odd vehicles of various makes which were subsequently acquired and retained for service.

The fleet numbers were now shown on embossed metal plates fixed on the front of the driver's cab, though later in some cases the numbers were painted on instead, mostly in the case of new vehicles. The garage to which the vehicle was attached was also similarly shown below or alongside, in accordance with the following code :

A—New Street Edinburgh	E—Kelso	I—Broxburn
B—Bathgate	F—Linlithgow	J—Berwick
C—Dundee area	G—Dalkeith	K—Peebles
D—Galashiels and Hawick	H—Airdrie	L—Carlisle

In 1937 Musselburgh was added as WA. L was dropped about this time, but revived in 1957 as a separate code for Hawick. Public Service Vehicle licence plates were of course carried on the back of the vehicle in the usual way, but as these numbers had no significance to the company they need not be quoted.

It would be impractible to describe the many different types of bodywork represented over the next twenty-five years or so, but in order that some indication can be given the following key has been adopted. Additional notes on the more important batches of new vehicles will be mentioned later. Any of the second-hand vehicles of note will be dealt with at the end of each section, as will any other points for individual mention.

345

a	Bus	FC	Full-front
b	Coach	NC	Fully open
c	Bus	FHC	Fixed roof, front entrance
d	Bus	FHC	Fixed roof, rear entrance
e	Bus	NC	Fixed roof, front entrance
f	Bus	NC	Fixed roof, rear entrance
g	Coach	FHC	Fixed roof, hinged door
h	Coach	FHC	Opening roof, hinged door
j	Coach	FHC	Opening roof, sliding door
k	Bus	NC	Opening roof
l	Coach	FHC	No near side canopy
m	Coach	NC	Fixed roof, hinged door
n	Bus	FHC	Double entrance
p	Bus	FHC	Double-deck
q	Coach	NC	Hinged door
r	Coach	NC	Sliding door
s	Bus	FHC	Opening roof, front entrance
t	Bus	FHC	Opening roof, rear entrance
u	Coach	NC	Opening roof, hinged door
v	Bus	NC	Double entrance
w	Coach	FC	Full-front
x	Bus	FHC	as 's' but six-wheeler
y			Under-floor engine types.

A : Albion

No.	Reg. No.		New Body		Seats	Bodybuilder	Former Nos.	Withdrawn
1	SC	205	1927	a	29	Croall	E546	1933–4
2	SC	206	1927	a	29	Croall	E547 D190	1933–4
3	SC	219	1927	a	29	Croall	E548	1933–4
4	SC	220	1927	a	29	Croall	E549	1933–4
5	SC	261	1927	a	29	Croall	E552 D56 E649	1933–4
6	SC	262	1927	a	29	Croall	E553	1933–4
7	SC	263	1927	a	29	Croall	E557	1933–4
8	SC	264	1927	a	29	Croall	E556	1933–4
9	SC	265	1927	a	29	Croall	E555	1933–4
10	SC	266	1927	a	29	Croall	E554	1933–4
11	SC	267	1927	a	29	Croall	E551	1933–4
12	SC	268	1927	a	29	Croall	E550 D46 E646	1933–4
13	SC	568	1928	a	29	Croall	E559 D81	1933–4
14	SC	569	1928	a	29	Croall	E558 D123	1933–4
15	SC	570	1928	a	29	Croall	E560 D82 E547 E560	1933–4
16	SC	2028	1928	a	29	Cowieson	E421 D193	1934–5
17	SC	2029	1928	a	29	Cowieson	E428 D194	1934–5
18	SC	2030	1928	a	29	Cowieson	E434 D185 D195	1934–5
19	SC	2031	1928	a	29	Cowieson	E435	1935–5
20	SC	2032	1928	a	29	Cowieson	E436	1934–5
21	SC	2033	1928	a	29	Cowieson	E439	1934–5
22	SC	2034	1928	a	29	Cowieson	E443 D183	1934–5
23	SC	2035	1928	a	29	Cowieson	E444 D184	1934–5
24	SC	2036	1928	a	29	Cowieson	E445 D185	1934–5
25	SC	2037	1928	a	29	Cowieson	E446	1933–4
26	SC	2038	1928	a	29	Cowieson	E447	1934–5
27	SC	2039	1928	a	29	Cowieson	E448	1934–5

No.	Reg. No.		New Body		Seats	Bodybuilder	Former Nos.	Withdrawn
28	SC	2040	1928	a	29	Cowieson	E449 D83	1934–5
29	SC	2041	1928	a	29	Cowieson	E450 D89 D187	1934–5
30	SC	2042	1928	a	29	Cowieson	E214 E445	1934–5
31	SC	2043	1928	a	29	Cowieson	E537 D196	1934–5
32	SC	4405	1929	q	26	Albion	E355	1938
33	SC	4406	1929	q	26	Albion	E356	1938
34	SF	7010	1926	e	28	Albion	E536	1933
35	SF	7078	1926	f	24	Albion	E244 D18	1933
36	SF	7079	1926	f	24	Albion	E537 D47	1933
37	SF	7146	1926	f	27	Albion	E538	1933
38	SF	7147	1926	f	24	Albion	E539 D49	1933
39	SF	7148	1926	f	24	Albion	E540 D50	1933
40	SF	7149	1926	e	28	Albion	E541	1933
41	SF	7150	1926	f	24	Albion	E542 D57	1933
42	SF	7151	1926	f	29	Albion	E543	1933
43	SF	7152	1926	d	32	Albion	E544	1933
44	SF	7453	1926	d	32	Albion	E545	1933
45	SF	9211	1927	a	29	?	E625 D53	1933–4
46	SF	9212	1927	a	29	?	E626 D53 E648	1933–4
47	SF	9256	1927	a	29	?	E627	1933–4
48	SF	9269	1927	a	29	?	E628	1933–4
49	SF	9270	1927	a	29	?	E629 D78 E636	1933–4
50	SF	9292	1927	a	29	?	E630 D48	1933–4
51	SF	9293	1927	a	29	?	E631 D58 E537	1933–4
52	SF	9302	1927	a	29	?	E632 D52	1933–4
53	SF	9303	1927	a	29	?	E633 D54	1933–4
54	SF	9310	1927	a	29	?	E634	1933–4
55	SF	9354	1927	a	29	?	E635	1933–4
56	SF	9355	1927	a	29	?	E636 D197	1933–4
57	SF	9356	1927	a	29	?	E637	1933–4
58	SF	9357	1927	a	29	?	E638	1933–4
59	SF	9381	1927	a	29	?	E639 D45 E651	1933–4
60	SF	9382	1927	a	29	?	E640	1933–4
61	SF	9522	1927	a	29	?	E641 D45	1933–4
62	SF	9523	1927	a	29	?	E642 D58	1933–4
63	SF	9542	1927	a	29	?	D116	1933–4
64	SF	9543	1927	a	29	?	D117	1933–4
65	SF	9544	1927	a	29	?	E643 D55	1933–4
66	SF	9545	1927	a	29	?	E644	1933–4
67	SF	9546	1927	a	29	?	E645 D51	1933–4
68	SF	9547	1927	a	29	?	E646 D198	1933–4
69	SF	9574	1927	a	29	?	E647	1933–4
70	SF	9575	1927	a	29	?	E648 D191	1933–4
71	SF	9634	1927	a	29	?	E649 D199	1933–4
72	SF	9667	1927	a	29	?	E650	1933–4
73	SF	9668	1927	a	29	?	E651 D192	1933–4
74	SF	9689	1927	a	29	?	E652	1933–4
75	SX	2398	1926	e	28	Albion	E96 E266	1933
76	SX	2402	1926	e	28	Albion	E87 E300	1933
77	SX	2406	1926	e	24	Porteous	E403	1933
78	SX	2784	1928	f	26	?	E765	1933
79	SX	2785	1928	f	26	?	E764	1933
80	SX	2826	1928	f	26	?	E766	1933
81	GE	4562	1929	e	29	?	G138	1933
82	GE	432	1928	e	28	?	E767	1933
83	ES	9308	1926	e	24	?	D180	1933
84	GS	41	1926	e	29	?	D74	1933

No.	Reg. No.	New	Body	Seats	Bodybuilder	Former Nos.	Withdrawn
85	KS 3700	1926	b	28	?	E574	1932
86	KS 3763	1926	c	32	?	E566	1934
87	KS 3820	1927	e	26	?	E713	1934
88	KS 3821	1927	e	26	?	E714	1934
89	RS 8305	1927	c	32	?	D79	1933
90	RS 8306	1927	c	32	?	D80	1933
91	VA 5276	1925	f	27	Albion	E113 E263	1933
92	VA 5385	1925	f	27	Albion	E112 E264	1933
93	VA 5603	1926	f	26	?	E114 D122	1935
94	SC 74	1927	e	28	?	Ex-Bowen	1933
95	SY 3991	1929	e	28	?	Ex-Bowen	1933
96	FS 1114	1931	s	32	Cowieson		1938
97	FS 1115	1931	s	32	Cowieson		1938
98	FS 1116	1931	s	32	Cowieson		1938
99	SX 2302	1925	e	24	?	Ex-Masson	1934
100	SX 2769	1928	e	24	?	Ex-Masson	1934
101	FS 1762	1932	s	32	Alexander		1938
102	HH 5230	1930	n	30	?	Ex-Hudson	1935
103	HH 3318	1926	e	20	?	Ex-Hudson	1933
104	HH 4185	1928	v	25	Albion	Ex-Hudson	1934
105	SY 4169	1930	e	28	Mitchell	Ex-Sword	1935
106	FS 6540	1933	k	20	Cowieson	Ex-Bell	1940
107	KS 4336	1928	u	26	?	Ex-Graham	1938
108	KS 4738	1929	u	26	?	Ex-Graham	1938
109	GS 1189	1929	e	26	?	Ex-Lowson	1936
110	NL 7458	1924	e	20	?	Ex-Lowson	1935
111	SY 2692	1925	q	20	Roberts	Ex-Bowen	1936
112	SY 3308	1928	q	20	?	Ex-Bowen	1936
113	SY 1855	1923	b	14	Alex. Motors	Ex-Bowen	1935
114	US 9608	1935	j	32	Duple	Ex-Dick	1948
115	SF 4942	1925	q	14	?	Ex-Sword	1935
116	RR 8219	1927	c	32	?	Ex-Browning	1936
117	GD 9724	1928	d	30	?	Ex-Browning	1935
118	WS 5569	1935	t	34	Cowieson		1948
119	VA 7075	1927	e	26	?	Ex-Irvine	1941
120	VA 9990	1930	e	30	?	Ex-Irvine	1941
121	US 9605	1935	j	26	?	Ex-Irvine	1941
122	VD 6298	1936	j	32	?	Ex-Irvine	1941
123	VD 7969	1937	j	32	?	Ex-Irvine	1941
124	VD 9383	1938	x	39	?	Ex-Irvine	1941

Notes : A92 bore the Edinburgh number 262 for a time before correction to 264, the former number belonging to one of Bowen's vehicles. A93 was rebodied with an 'e' type body in 1933. A94-5, 102-5, 116-7 were of typical Albion outline, and A107-8, 111-2, 115 were of orthodox appearance. The other second-hand vehicles were rather different though several such as A100, 106, 109, 110 were very neat. A114 was an up-to-date coach with a well curved roof back and front. A32-3 were "Vikings," A96-8/124 were "Valkyries", A101/14/8 were "Valiants", and A106/21-3 were "Victors".

A : (Second) ; Austin

No.	Reg. No.	New	Body	Seats	Bodybuilder	Withdrawn
1	JSF 409	1952	w	32	Kenex	1952

A : (Third) ; Bristol

No.	Reg. No.		New	Body	Seats	Bodybuilder	Withdrawn
1	LSC	61	1954	y	38	East. Counties	
to	to						
30	LSC	90	1954	y	38	East. Counties	
31	NSG	793	1956	y	38	East. Counties	
to	to						
45	NSG	807	1956	y	38	East. Counties	

AA : Bristol

No.	Reg. No.		New	Body	Seats	Bodybuilder	Withdrawn
1	NSG	778	1956	p	60	East. Counties	
to	to						
15	NSG	792	1956	p	60	East. Counties	

B : A.E.C.

No.	Reg. No.		New	Body	Seats	Bodybuilder	Withdrawn
1	MY	3479	1930	h	28	Cowieson	1938
2	SC	9871	1931	d	30	Strachan	1938
3	FS	248	1931	h	28	Cowieson	1940
to	to						to
13	FS	258	1931	h	28	Cowieson	1943
14	FS	2251	1932	t	34	Alexander	
to	to						
73	FS	2310	1932	t	34	Alexander	
74	FS	5561	1933	j	28	Burlingham	1940
to	to						
79	FS	5566	1933	j	28	Burlingham	1940
80	KW	9396	1930	g	30	Burlingham	(1) 1937
81	FS	8541	1934	j	32	Burlingham	1942
to	to						
92	FS	8552	1934	j	32	Burlingham	1942
93	FS	8553	1934	t	34	Burlingham	
to	to						
122	FS	8582	1934	t	34	Burlingham	
123	FS	8583	1934	t	34	Cowieson	1938
124	FS	8584	1934	t	34	Cowieson	
125	FS	8585	1934	t	34	Cowieson	
126	JR	468	1933	g	30	Weyman	(2) 1941
—	TY	9607	1932	g	28	Strachan	(2) 1935
—	TY	7081	1930	g	26	?	(2) 1935
127	SY	4512	1931	u	24	Duple	(3) 1945
128	SY	3943	1929	l	30	Vickers	(3) 1937
129	WS	636	1934	r	26	Burlingham	(4) 1940
130	WS	4478	1935	s	32	Alexander	
to	to						
154	WS	4502	1935	s	32	Alexander	
155	WS	4503	1935	t	34	Cowieson	
to	to						
168	WS	4516	1935	t	34	Cowieson	
169	WS	4517	1936	s	38	Alexander	
170	VD	1286	1932	c	32	Cowieson	(5) 1945
to	to						to
175	VD	1291	1932	c	32	Cowieson	(5) 1947
176	GX	2742	1932	h	32	Duple	(6) 1940
177	GF	5124	1930	h	31	London Lorries	(6) 1946
178	SX	4031	1935	j	32	Burlingham	(6) 1943

No.	Reg. No.		New	Body	Seats	Bodybuilder	Withdrawn
179	BSC	516	1938	t	34	Alexander	
to	to						
193	BSC	530	1938	t	34	Alexander	
194	MV	346	1931	u	26	Park-Royal	(7) 1940
194	ELY	529	1939	c	36	?	(8)
195	CSF	201	1939	s	35	Alexander	Some
to	to						in
214	CSF	220	1939	s	35	Alexander	1954
215	DSC	302	1940	s	39	Alexander	and
to	to						1955
234	DSC	321	1940	s	39	Alexander	
235	ESC	429	1946	s	35	Duple	
to	to						
284	ESC	478	1946	s	35	Duple	
285	FFS	182	1947	s	35	Alexander	
to	to		to				
344	FFS	241	1948	s	35	Alexander	
345	GSC	233	1948	s	35	Burlingham	
to	to						
363	GSC	251	1948	s	35	Burlingham	
364	GSC	457	1949	w	31	Burlingham	
365	GSC	684	1949	j	35	Burlingham	
to	to						
384	GSC	703	1949	j	35	Burlingham	
385	GSF	704	1949	s	35	Alexander	
to	to						
404	GSF	723	1949	s	35	Alexander	
405	HWS	907	1951	y	30	Alexander	
to	to						
424	HWS	926	1951	y	30	Alexander	
425	LSC	566	1954	y	45	Park-Royal	
to	to						
430	LSC	571	1954	y	45	Park-Royal	
431	LWS	875	1954	y	45	Park-Royal	
to	to						
438	LWS	882	1954	y	45	Park-Royal	
439	HWS	941	1951	y	30	Alexander	
to	to						
444	HWS	946	1951	y	30	Alexander	
445	JSF	145	1952	y	40	Alexander	
to	to						
454	JSF	154	1952	y	40	Alexander	
455	KSC	532	1953	y	30	Alexander	
to	to						
462	KSC	539	1953	y	30	Alexander	
463	KSC	540	1953	y	38	Alexander	
to	to						
479	KSC	556	1953	y	38	Alexander	
480	LWS	883	1955	y	45	Park-Royal	
to	to						
496	LWS	900	1955	y	45	Park-Royal	
497	LWS	901	1955	y	41	Park-Royal	
to	to						
521	LWS	925	1955	y	41	Park-Royal	
522	NSG	813	1956	y	41	Park-Royal	
to	to						
546	NSG	837	1956	y	41	Park-Royal	
547	NSG	543	1956	y		Park-Royal	

Notes : (1) Ex-County; (2) Ex-Orange Bros.; (3) Ex-Dick; (4) Ex-Herd; (5) Ex-Western S.M.T.Co.; (6) Ex-Browning; (7) Ex-Robertson; (8) Ex-Caledonian. Post-war rebodying :— 's' type 35 seat bodies by Alexander were fitted to B15, B17, B23, B25, B29, B31-2, B34-6, B38, B40, B43, B47, B52, B57, B59-61, B67-8, B70, B93, B104, B108-10, B113, B117, B131-40, B142-50, B152, B154-69 in 1946-7-8 and to B197, B201, B203-4 in 1953 and to B194(ii) and B374 in 1955. Slightly different bodies by Burlingham were fitted to B14, B16, B18-22, B24, B27-8, B33, B39, B41-2, B44-6, B48-51, B53, B55-6, B64-6, B69, B71-2 in 1948 and again slightly different bodies by Croft to B30, B54, B58, B62-3, B73 also in 1948. 'w' type 37 seat bodies by Burlingham were fitted to B141, B153, B179, B180, B182-5, B187-8, B199, B207, B209, B226, B230 in 1952 and slightly different 35 seat bodies by Burlingham to B310-29 in 1953 and to B385-404 in 1954. B330-44 were lengthened and reconstructed as 'w' type 35 seat coaches in 1953 by Dickinson's of Dunbar. B26 acquired a 'j' type body in 1946 but an 's' type 35 seat body by S.O.L. was fitted in 1952. Earlier B157, B165 and B166 had been rebodied with bodies of similar but slightly different type to their original ones, and B175 got one of these too.

Of the second-hand vehicles B127 and the first B194 were "Rangers" of rather sleek lines with the window-line slightly stepped down towards the rear. B129 was a "Regent" of straighter lines, while B128 was one of the original "Reliances". B178 had a body with a centre entrance and pleasing line, but none of the others call for comment.

B405-24 B439-79 were "Mark IV", B425-38, B480-521 were "Monocoaches", and B522-47 were "Reliances".

Some premature withdrawals resulting from accidents should be mentioned, viz :— B37 in 1934, B225 in 1943, B223 in 1944, and B296 in 1947.

BB : A.E.C.

No.	Reg. No.		New	Body	Seats	Bodybuilder	Withdrawn
1	DSG	167	1942	p	55	Brush	1955
2	DSG	168	1942	p	55	Brush	1955
3	FS	5561	1944	p	53	Alexander	Some
to	to						from
8	FS	5566	1944	p	53	Alexander	1955
9	FS	8541	1944	p	53	Alexander	on-
to	to						ward
20	FS	8552	1944	p	53	Alexander	
21	FWS	741	1948	p	53	Alexander	
22	ESC	422	1948	p	53	Alexander	
to	to						
28	ESC	428	1948	p	53	Alexander	
29	FFS	150	1948	p	53	Alexander	
to	to						
60	FFS	181	1948	p	53	Alexander	

No.	Reg. No.		New	Body	Seats	Bodybuilder		Withdrawn
61	GSF	644	1949	p	53	Duple		
to	to							
80	GSF	663	1949	p	53	Duple		
81	GSF	664	1950	p	53	Burlingham		
to	to							
100	GSF	683	1950	p	53	Burlingham		

Notes : BB21 had to be re-registered from ESC421 owing to a licensing error. BB71 was destroyed in an accident in 1954 and reconstructed with an S.O.L. body being re-registered LWS218.

C : Bedford, etc.

No.	Reg. No.		New	Body	Seats	Bodybuilder		Withdrawn
1	SC	7511	1930	b	14	Alex. Motors	E422	1934
to	to						to	
8	SC	7518	1930	b	14	Alex. Motors	E429	1934
9	SH	3380	1929	e	20	Alex. Motors		(1) 1932
10	SH	3902	1930	e	14	?		(1) 1932
9	SC	8310	1930	e	14	?		(2) 1934
10	SX	3203	1930	e	14	?		(2) 1934
11	FS	5567	1933	u	20	Burlingham		1940
to	to							
16	FS	5572	1933	u	20	Burlingham		1940
17	SX	3179	1930	e	14	Porteous		(3) 1934
18	FS	8586	1934	u	20	Burlingham		1940
to	to							
29	FS	8597	1934	u	20	Burlingham		1940
30	FS	8598	1934	u	12	S.M.T.Co.		1941
to	to							
32	FS	8600	1934	u	12	S.M.T.Co.		1941
33	FS	8601	1934	u	14	S.M.T.Co.		1940
to	to							
37	FS	8605	1934	u	14	S.M.T.Co.		1940
38	SY	4220	1930	b	11	Alex. Motors		(4) 1936
39	FS	349	1931	u	15	?		(5) 1937
40	FS	2923	1932	u	20	Alex. Motors		(5) 1937
41	SC	7456	1930	b	14	Alex. Motors		(5) 1935
42	WS	4791	1935	r	20	Duple		1941
43	WS	4792	1935	r	26	Duple		1941
44	WS	4793	1935	r	20	Duple		1941
45	WS	4794	1935	r	24	Burlingham		1941
46	WS	8061	1936	r	20	Duple		1941
to	to							
65	WS	8080	1936	r	20	Duple		1941
66	ASF	334	1937	r	20	Duple		1953
to	to							to
90	ASF	358	1937	r	20	Duple		1954
91	ASF	359	1937	r	14	Duple		1953
to	to							to
95	ASF	363	1937	r	14	Duple		1954
96	EFS	151	1944	e	32	S.M.T.Co.		1945
to	to							to
155	EFS	210	1944	e	32	S.M.T.Co.		1949
156	FFS	856	1947	r	29	S.M.T.Co.		
to	to							
168	FFS	868	1947	r	29	S.M.T.Co.		
169	FFS	869	1947	r	25	S.M.T.Co.		
to	to							
187	FFS	887	1947	r	25	S.M.T.Co.		

No.	Reg. No.		New	Body	Seats	Bodybuilder	Former Nos.	Withdrawn
188	JS	7799	1948	r	29	S.M.T.Co.		
189	JSF	814	1952	w	30	Burlingham		
to	to							
208	JSF	833	1952	w	30	Burlingham		

Notes : (1) Ex-Gardner; (2) Ex-Nichol; (3) Ex-McNair; (4) Ex-Bowen; (5) Ex-Herd. Nos. C1-8, the second C9, and both C10s, as well as C17, C38 and C41 were Chevrolets, and the first C9, was a "G M C" C188 was originally numbered C206. C156 to 175 received Burlingham 24 seat 'w' type bodies in 1953.

D : Daimler

No.	Reg. No.		New	Body	Seats	Bodybuilder	Former Nos.	Withdrawn
1	SC	2745	1928	d	30	N. Counties	E434	1931
2	SC	4191	1929	q	26	Cadogan	E386	1935
3	SC	4760	1929	q	26	Cadogan	E382	1935
4	SC	5118	1929	l	26	Buckingham	E578	1934
5	SC	5237	1929	u	28	?	E419	1934
6	SC	5300	1929	m	26	Hoyal	E380	1934
7	SC	5388	1929	m	26	Hoyal	E384	1934
8	SC	5392	1929	c	32	Hall Lewis	E738	1933
9	SC	5431	1929	c	32	Hall Lewis	E739	1933
10	SX	2945	1929	n	32	Strachan	E737	1933
11	SX	2946	1929	n	32	Strachan	E736	1933
12	TS	8168		n	31	N. Counties	E224	1933
13	SY	4142	1930	n	32	N. Counties	(1)	1933
14	SY	4068	1929	e	26	?	(1)	1931
14	TY	7165	1930	e	26	Hall Lewis	(2)	1935
15	SC	4593	1929	m	22	Hoyal	(3)	1936
to	to							
17	SC	4595	1929	m	22	Hoyal	(3)	1936
18	SC	7556	1930	m	24	Hoyal	(3)	1939
19	SC	7557	1930	m	24	Hoyal	(3)	1939
20	SY	3940	1929	q	28	?	(1)	1936
21	SY	3640	1928	q	28	?	(4)	1935
22	WS	1523	1934	j	32	Brush	(4)	1945
23	SY	5035	1934	j	32	Brush	(4)	1943
24	SY	4997	1934	j	31	Eng. Electric	(4)	1943
25	SY	4189	1930	l	32	?	(4)	1935
26	SC	5237	1929	u	28	?	(5)	1935
27	SY	5509	1935	j	32	Roberts	(1)	1945
28	FS	366	1931	u	28	Dickson	(6)	1937
29	FS	3389	1932	h	30	Cowieson	(6)	1939
30	FS	9314	1934	l	32	Harrington	(6)	?
31	FS	9776	1934	l	29	Westwood & Smith	(6)	?
32	WS	3869	1935	l	32	Harrington	(6)	?
33	SC	7889	1930	l	26	Westwood & Smith	(6)	1936
—	FS	6007	1933	f	32	?	(7)	1940

Notes : (1) Ex-Bowen; (2) Ex-Dewar; (3) Ex-Scott; (4) Ex-Bowen; (5) Ex-Sword; (6) Ex-Westwood & Smith; (7) Ex-Irvine. D1, the first D14 and D21 were A.D.C.s. D15-20, D26, were of low sleek line. D22-4 were of straightforward neat appearance, the first two running for some time in Dick's red and white livery with S.M.T. lettering; the former had a Gardner 5-cylinder oil engine. D27 had a well curved roof and ran for a while in Bowen's livery. D30-1-2 were rather elaborate with a stepped-up window line, the last having a particularly raked driver's screen and slightly raked pillars. The remainder do not call for comment.

D : (Second) ; Guy (Second)

No.	Reg. No.		New	Body	Seats	Bodybuilder	Withdrawn
1	LSC	91	1954	s	39	S.O.L.	
to	to						
5	LSC	95	1954	s	39	S.O.L.	

E : A.J.S.

No.	Reg. No.		New	Body	Seats	Bodybuilder		Withdrawn
1	SX	3254	1931	c	32	Roberts	Ex-Rendall	1935
2	SC	4807	1929	q	20	?	Ex-Herd	1936
3	SC	7566	1930	u	20	Haywood	Ex-Herd	1936

E : (Second) Later DD ; Guy

No.	Reg. No.		New	Body	Seats	Bodybuilder	Withdrawn
1	DSG	176	1943	p	55	N. Counties	
2	DSG	177	1943	p	55	N. Counties	
3	DSG	178	1943	p	55	Brush	
4	DSG	179	1943	p	55	Brush	
5	DWS	352	1943	p	55	N. Counties	
6	DWS	353	1943	p	55	N. Counties	
7	DWS	354	1944	p	55	Massey	
8	DWS	355	1944	p	55	Massey	
9	DWS	843	1944	p	55	N. Counties	
10	DWS	844	1944	p	55	N. Counties	
11	DWS	845	1944	p	55	Roe	
12	DWS	846	1944	p	55	Roe	
13	DWS	921	1944	p	55	Roe	
14	DWS	922	1944	p	55	Roe	
15	EFS	350	1945	p	55	Weyman	
to	to						
22	EFS	357	1945	p	55	Weyman	
23	HGC	108		p	56	Park Royal	
24	HGC	113		p	56	Park Royal	
25	HGC	120		p	56	Park Royal	
26	HGC	122		p	56	Park Royal	
27	GYL	350		p	56	Park Royal	
28	HGC	123		p	56	Park Royal	
29	HGC	144		p	56	Massey	
30	HGC	145		p	56	Massey	
31	HGC	188		p	56	Weyman	

Notes : E23-31 were ex-London Transport vehicles in 1952 and were withdrawn in 1953, while a number of the others have been withdrawn subsequently.

F : Gilford (First list)

No.	Reg. No.		New	Body	Seats	Bodybuilder	Former Nos.	Withdrawn
1	SC	160	1927	f	26	?	E547	1931
2	SC	250	1927	f	26	?	E558	1931
3	SC	838	1927	f	26	?	E559	1931
4	FS	1509	1931	f	28	?	Ex-Bowen's SC46 re-registered	

F : Gilford (Second list)

No.	Reg. No.	New	Body	Seats	Bodybuilder		Withdrawn
1	FS 1509	1931	f	26	?	Previously F4	1934
2	SY 3483	1928	e	24	?	Ex-Dunn	1934
3	SY 3498	1928	e	24	?	Ex-Dunn	1934
4	SY 3916	1929	e	20	?	Ex-Dunn	1932
5	SC 4198	1929	t	32	Wycombe	Ex-Bowen	1936
6	UV 5637	1929	u	24	?	Ex-Sword	1936

G : Leyland Lion

No.	Reg. No.	New	Body	Seats	Bodybuilder	Former Nos.	Withdrawn
1 to 5	SC 2941 to 2945	1929	c	31	Midland	E691 E136 to E695 E140	1933
6 to 8	SC 3348 to 3350	1929	d	31	Leyland	E94 to E96	1939
9	SC 3353	1929	d	31	Leyland	E85	1943
10 to 17	SC 3354 to 3361	1929	d	31	Leyland	E86 to E93	1939
18 to 24	SC 4301 to 4307	1929	d	31	Leyland	E97 to E103	1939
25	SC 4308	1929	d	31	Leyland	E104	1945
26 to 32	SC 4309 to 4315	1929	d	31	Leyland	E105 to E111	1939
33	SC 4316	1929	d	31	Leyland	E112 D76	1939
34	SC 4317	1929	d	31	Leyland	E113	1939
35	SC 4318	1929	d	31	Leyland	E114	1939
36	SC 4319	1929	d	31	Leyland	E115	1938
37 to 41	SC 4320 to 4324	1929	d	31	Leyland	E116 to E120	1939
42	SC 4325	1929	d	31	Leyland	E123 D120	1939
43	SC 4326	1929	d	31	Leyland	E122 D119	1948
44	SC 4327	1929	d	31	Leyland	E121 D118	1939
45	SC 4328	1929	d	31	Leyland	E124	1939
46	SC 4329	1929	d	31	Leyland	E125	1939
47	SC 4330	1929	d	31	Leyland	E126 D77	1939
48	SC 4331	1929	d	31	Leyland	E127	1939
49	SC 4332	1929	d	31	Leyland	E128 D121	1945
50	SC 4333	1929	d	31	Leyland	E129	1939
51	SC 4334	1929	d	31	Leyland	E130	1939
52	SC 4335	1929	d	31	Leyland	E131	1945
53	SC 4336	1929	d	31	Leyland	E132	1939
54	SC 4337	1929	d	31	Leyland	E134	1940
55	SC 4338	1929	d	31	Leyland	E135	1939
56	SC 4407	1929	d	31	Leyland	E84	1939
57	SC 4408	1929	d	31	Leyland	E83	1939
58	SC 4409	1929	d	31	Leyland	E82	1939
59	SC 4410	1929	d	31	Leyland	E81 D75	1945
60	KS 3470	1925	q	25	?	E576	1932
61	TY 2423	1926	c	31	?	E703	1933
62	TY 3066	1927	c	31	?	E701	1933
63	SY 3419	1927	c	30	Leyland	(1)	1933
64	VA 4995	1925	e	20	?	(1)	1933
60	FS 3212	1932	t	32	Alexander		1940

No.	Reg. No.		New	Body	Seats	Bodybuilder	Former Nos.	Withdrawn
61	SY	4441	1931	l	28	Roberts		(1) 1940
62	TD	5015	1926	c	31	Leyland		(2) 1936
65	FH	6413	1929	d		Leyland		(3) 1939
66	VA	9505	1929	d	31	Midland		(3) 1938
69	UC	7191	1928	l	34	?		(4) 1935
70	SY	3419	1927	c	29	Leyland		(4) 1935
71	HH	1836	1923	q	25	?		(5) 1936
67	SY	3484	1928	d	31	Leyland		(6) 1937
to	to							
72	SY	3489	1928	d	31	Leyland		(6) 1937
73	SY	3659	1928	d	31	Leyland		(6) 1937
to	to							
76	SY	3662	1928	d	31	Leyland		(6) 1937
77	SY	4125	1930	c	32	Leyland		(6) 1939
78	SY	4126	1930	c	32	Leyland		(6) 1939
79	SY	4127	1930	c	32	Leyland		(6) 1939

Notes : (1) Ex-Bowen; (2) Ex-Lowson; (3) Ex-Western, S.M.T. Co.; (4) Ex-Browning; (5) Ex-Westwood & Smith; (6) Ex-Coast Line. The seemingly inconsistent re-use of numbers above 59 for later vehicles will be noticed. The first G60 and also G71 were older type Leylands, while G64 was a "Leverette" with a body of somewhat dumpy appearance. G63, later to return as G70, also G62(ii) and G67(ii) to G76 had standard Leyland bodies, while G65-6 were generally similar to G6-59. G65 had "Gruss" air-springs.

H : Leyland Tiger

No.	Reg. No.		New	Body	Seats	Bodybuilder	Former Nos.	Withdrawn
1	SC	3351	1929	c	30	Leyland	E210 E800	1954
2	SC	3352	1929	c	30	Leyland	E211 E801	
3	SC	4339	1929	h	29	Cowieson	E802	1954
to	to						to	
30	SC	4376	1929	h	29	Cowieson	E829	1954
31	SC	7531	1930	h	26	Cowieson	E830	1938
to	to						to	
42	SC	7542	1930	h	26	Cowieson	E841	1938
43	SC	7991	1930	h	27	Burlingham	E842	1938
to	to						to	
48	SC	7996	1930	h	27	Burlingham	E847	1938
49	TY	3677	1928	d	31	Leyland	E709	1954
50	TY	3678	1928	d	31	Leyland	E712	1954
51	FS	5573	1933	t	34	Burlingham		
to	to							
84	FS	5606	1933	t	34	Burlingham		
85	FS	5607	1933	t	34	Met.-Cam.		
to	to							
104	FS	5626	1933	t	34	Met.-Cam.		
105	KS	6165	1933	j	32	Duple		(1) 1955
106	WS	4518	1935	t	34	Cowieson		
to	to							
115	WS	4527	1935	t	34	Cowieson		
116	GK	431	1930	d	28	?		(2) 1937
to	to						?	
118	GK	433	1930	d	28	?		(2) 1937
119	GK	437	1930	d	28	?		(2) 1937
120	VD	1432	1932	s	30	Burlingham		(2) 1947

No.	Reg. No.		New	Body	Seats	Bodybuilder	Former Nos.	Withdrawn
121	AG	8268	1932	s	32	Burlingham	(2)	1954
122	AG	8269	1932	s	30	Burlingham	(2)	1940
123	AG	8274	1932	s	30	Pickering	(2)	1940
124	AG	8276	1932	s	30	Pickering	(2)	1950
125	AG	8277	1932	s	30	Pickering	(2)	1948
126	AG	8280	1932	s	30	Pickering	(2)	1940
to	to							
128	AG	8282	1932	s	30	Pickering	(2)	1940
129	AG	8283	1932	s	30	Pickering	(2)	1938
130	AG	8285	1932	s	30	Pickering	(2)	1940
131	AG	8286	1932	s	32	Pickering	(2)	1954
132	VA	8459	1929	c	32	?	(2)	1937
133	VA	8790	1929	c	31	?	(2)	1937
134	VA	8793	1929	c	31	?	(2)	1937
135	VA	8891	1929	d	32	?	(2)	1938
136	VA	8952	1929	c	30	?	(2)	1937
137	VA	8957	1929	d	32	?	(2)	1937
138	WS	8081	1936	w	22	Burlingham		
to	to							
143	WS	8086	1936	w	22	Burlingham		
144	SY	5441	1935	d	32	Brush	(3)	1954
145	SY	5442	1935	d	32	Brush	(3)	1955
146	SY	5443	1935	t	32	Brush	(3)	
147	SY	5444	1935	t	32	Brush	(3)	1955
148	SY	5712	1936	d	32	Brush	(3)	1955
149	SY	5713	1936	t	32	Brush	(3)	1955
150	SY	5714	1936	t	32	Brush	(3)	1955
151	SY	5715	1936	d	32	Brush	(3)	1955
152	ASF	364	1935	t	35	Alexander		
to	to							
181	ASF	393	1937	t	35	Alexander		
182	ASF	394	1937	s	35	Alexander		
to	to							
196	ASF	408	1937	s	35	Alexander		
197	ASF	409	1937	j	30	Duple		1954
to	to							
204	ASF	416	1937	j	30	Duple		1954
205	SY	6020	1937	d	32	Brush		1954
to	to							
207	SY	6022	1937	d	32	Brush		1954
208	SY	6023	1937	t	32	Brush		
209	SY	6024	1937	t	32	Brush		
210	CSF	221	1939	t	35	Alexander		
to	to							
243	CSF	254	1939	t	35	Alexander		1956
244	CWS	165	1939	j	30	Alexander		
245	DSC	281	1940	s	39	Alexander		
to	to							
263	DSC	299	1940	s	39	Alexander		
264	DSC	301	1940	s	39	Alexander		
265	MS	9076	1929	s	32	Alexander	(4)	1940

Notes : (1) Ex-Graham; (2) Ex-Western S.M.T. Co.; (3) Ex-Coast-Line; (4) Ex-Irvine. Rebodying; In 1937-8 new "t" type bodies of the current pattern were provided on H1-10, H12-17, H19, H21-7, H29, H49, H50 while the others up to H48 were withdrawn. H110 got a different "t" body in 1944 but reverted to the orginal type later. Cowieson 34 seat "t" bodies went to H105 and H175 in

1946-7. Except for H59, H98 and H99 which had earlier been destroyed in fires, H51-104 were all rebodied in 1949, those up to H76 with "j" type 35 seat bodies by Burlingham, and H77 upwards with "s" type 35 seat bodies by Alexander. The latter were also put on H146, H208 and H209 in 1954. H138-43 were converted to double-deckers and re-numbered accordingly in 1942, and H106-9, H111-3, H115 and H161-3, H174 similarly in 1945. H114 had been burnt out in 1937. A Dorman-Ricardo oil engine was tried in H16.

The buses transferred from the Western S.M.T. fleet were rather a mixed lot. The bodies of H132, H135, H137 were of Leyland appearance. The others were more rounded but H133-4, H136 had flatter roofs. H116-9 had a large illuminated panel worded "Western" mounted above the front of the roof and they ran in S.M.T. service for a month or so with these in place. H121 and H132 were in the Western white coach livery which they like-wise retained for a time. The others were blue. The Coast-Line buses had high domed roofs and an unusually large destination screen box. H105 from Graham was a neat vehicle of straight-forward lines. Of H152-196, H210-243, H245-264 several were withdrawn from 1953 onwards.

J : Later HH; Leyland Titan

No.	Reg. No.		New	Body	Seats	Bodybuilder	Former Nos.	Withdrawn
1	SC	2921	1929	p	51	Leyland	E671	1947-8
2	SC	2922	1929	p	51	Leyland	E672	1947-8
3	SC	2925	1929	p	51	Leyland	E675	1947-8
to	to						to	
15	SC	2937	1929	p	51	Leyland	E687	
16	SC	2940	1929	p	51	Leyland	E690	1947-8
17	SC	3341	1929	p	51	Leyland	E691	1947-8
to	to						to	
23	SC	3347	1929	p	51	Leyland	E697	1947-8
24	SC	5221	1929	p	48	Leyland	E698	1947-8
to	to						to	
26	SC	5223	1929	p	48	Leyland	E700	1947-8
27	SC	5224	1929	p	48	Leyland	E210	1947-8
to	to						to	
33	SC	5230	1929	p	48	Leyland	E216	1947-8
34	BSC	531	1938	p	53	Leyland		
to	to							
53	BSC	550	1938	p	53	Leyland		
54	CSF	255	1939	p	53	Leyland		
to	to							
59	CSF	260	1939	p	53	Leyland		
60	WS	8081	1942	p	53	Alexander		
to	to							
65	WS	8086	1942	p	53	Alexander		
66	DSG	169	1942	p	53	Leyland		
67	WS	4518	1945	p	53	Alexander		
to	to							
70	WS	4521	1945	p	53	Alexander		
71	WS	4523	1945	p	53	Alexander		
to	to							
73	WS	4525	1945	p	53	Alexander		

No.	Reg. No.		New	Body	Seats	Bodybuilder		Withdrawn
74	WS	4527	1945	p	53	Alexander		
75	ASF	373	1945	p	53	Alexander		
to	to							
77	ASF	375	1945	p	53	Alexander		
78	ASF	386	1945	p	53	Alexander		
79	CK	4150	1929	p	52	Cowieson	Ex-Campbell	1948
80	GE	7260	1930	p	52	Cowieson	Ex-Campbell	1948
81	GG	908	1930	p	52	Cowieson	Ex-Campbell	1948
82	UF	7422	1931	p	52	Short-Bros.	Ex-Campbell	1946

Notes : J81 had the Glasgow Corporation arrangement of destination screen box. Several of J34 to 65 were withdrawn from 1954 onwards.

K : Maudslay

No.	Reg. No.		New	Body	Seats	Bodybuilder	Former Nos.	Withdrawn
1	SC	1159	1928	a	31	Cowieson	E654	1935-6
2	SC	1160	1928	a	31	Cowieson	E653	1935-6
3	SC	1161	1928	a	31	Cowieson	E655	1935-6
to	to						to	
12	SC	1170	1928	a	31	Cowieson	E664	1935-6
13	SC	2044	1928	b	26	Hoyal	E539	1934-6
14	SC	2045	1928	b	26	Hoyal	E540	1934-6
15	SC	2046	1928	b	26	Hoyal	E542	1934-6
16	SC	2047	1928	b	26	Hoyal	E550	1934-6
17	SC	2048	1928	b	26	Hoyal	E552	1934-6
18	SC	2049	1928	b	26	Hoyal	E626	1934-6
19	SC	2050	1928	b	26	Hoyal	E629	1934-6
to	to						to	
23	SC	2054	1928	b	26	Hoyal	E633	1934-6
24	SC	2055	1928	b	26	Hoyal	E639	1934-6
25	SC	2056	1928	b	26	Hoyal	E643	1934-6
26	SC	2057	1928	b	26	Hoyal	E645	1934-6
27	SC	2058	1928	b	26	Hoyal	E665	1934-6
to	to						to	
32	SC	2063	1928	b	26	Hoyal	E670	1934-6
33	SC	2064	1928	a	31	?	E220	1935-6
34	SC	2065	1928	a	31	?	E221	1935-6
35	SC	2066	1928	a	31	?	E235	1935-6
to	to					?	to	
41	SC	2072	1928	a	31	?	E241	1935-6
42	SC	2073	1928	a	31	?	E243	1935-6
to	to					?	to	
44	SC	2075	1928	a	31	?	E245	1935-6
45	SC	2076	1928	a	31	?	E247	1935-6
46	SC	2077	1928	a	31	?	E248	1935-6
47	SC	2078	1928	a	31	?	E250	1935-6
to	to					?	to	
52	SC	2083	1928	a	31	?	E255	1935-6
53	SC	4377	1929	a	32	S.M.T.Co.	E51	1935-6
to	to						to	
78	SC	4402	1929	a	32	S.M.T.Co.	E76	1935-6
79	SC	4403	1929	a	32	Weyman	E77	1935-6
80	SC	4404	1929	a	32	Weyman	E78	1935-6
81	SF	3645	1925	a	32	S.M.T.Co.	E359	1932
82	SF	3646	1925	a	32	S.M.T.Co.	E360	1931
83	SF	4268	1925	a	32	S.M.T.Co.	E201	1932
84	SF	4269	1925	a	32	S.M.T.Co.	E213 E249	1931
85	SF	5599	1926	a	32	S.M.T.Co.	E430	1931

No.	Reg. No.		New	Body	Seats	Bodybuilder	Former Nos.		Withdrawn
86	SF	5600	1926	a	32	S.M.T.Co.	E431		1931
87	SF	5678	1926	a	32	S.M.T.Co.	E433		1931
88	SF	5679	1926	a	32	S.M.T.Co.	E432		1932
89	SF	5680	1926	a	32	Short Bros.	E451		1932
90	SF	5681	1926	a	32	Short Bros.	E452		1932
91	SF	5688	1926	a	32	Short Bros.	E453		1932
92	SF	5689	1926	a	32	Short Bros.	E454		1932
93	SF	5712	1926	a	32	Short Bros.	E459		1932
94	SF	5713	1926	a	32	Short Bros.	E458		1932
95	SF	5714	1926	a	32	Vickers	E476		1932
96	SF	5754	1926	a	32	Short Bros.	E468		1932
97	SF	5768	1926	a	32	Short Bros.	E457		1932
98	SF	5769	1926	a	32	Short Bros.	E455		1932
99	SF	5770	1926	a	32	S.M.T.Co.	E438		1932
100	SF	5771	1926	a	32	S.M.T.Co.	E437		1932
101	SF	5772	1926	a	32	Short Bros.	E456		1932
102	SF	5773	1926	a	32	Short Bros.	E461		1932
103	SF	5787	1926	a	32	Vickers	E477		1932
104	SF	5809	1926	a	32	Short Bros.	E479		1932
105	SF	5810	1926	a	32	Short Bros.	E478		1932
106	SF	5811	1926	a	32	Short Bros.	E460		1932
107	SF	5821	1926	a	32	Short Bros.	E465		1932
108	SF	5822	1926	a	32	Vickers	E481		1932
109	SF	5823	1926	a	32	Short Bros.	E480		1932
110	SF	5911	1926	a	32	Short Bros.	E462		1932
111	SF	5912	1926	a	32	Short Bros.	E464		1932
112	SF	5913	1926	a	32	Short Bros.	E463		1932
113	SF	5948	1926	a	32	Short Bros.	E470		1932
114	SF	5949	1926	a	32	Short Bros.	E469		1932
115	SF	5950	1926	a	32	Vickers	E484	D48	1932
116	SF	5951	1926	a	32	Vickers	E483	D54	1932
117	SF	5997	1926	a	32	Short Bros.	E467		1932
118	SF	6017	1926	a	32	Vickers	E482		1932
119	SF	6018	1926	a	32	Short Bros.	E466		1932
120	SF	6044	1926	a	32	Vickers	E485	D55	1932
121	SF	6045	1926	a	32	Short Bros.	E472		1932
122	SF	6046	1926	a	32	Short Bros.	E471		1932
123	SF	6047	1926	a	32	Vickers	E486	D78	1932
124	SF	6048	1926	a	32	Vickers	E487		1932
to	to						to		
126	SF	6050	1926	a	32	Vickers	E489		1932
127	SF	6120	1926	a	32	Short Bros.	E474		1932
128	SF	6121	1926	a	32	Short Bros.	E473		1931
129	SF	6122	1926	a	32	Vickers	E492		1932
130	SF	6123	1926	a	32	Short Bros.	E475		1932
131	SF	6124	1926	a	32	Vickers	E493		1932
132	SF	6125	1926	a	32	Vickers	E494		1932
133	SF	6185	1926	a	32	Vickers	E491		1932
134	SF	6186	1926	a	32	Vickers	E490		1932
135	SF	6433	1926	a	32	Vickers	E495	D51	1932
136	SF	6434	1926	a	32	Vickers	E496		1932
137	SF	6463	1926	a	32	Vickers	E497		1932
138	SF	6492	1926	a	32	Vickers	E498		1932
139	SF	6557	1926	a	32	Vickers	E499		1932
140	SF	6558	1926	a	32	Vickers	E500		1932
141	SF	9155	1927	b	26	Short Bros.	E600		1934-5
142	SF	9158	1927	b	26	Short Bros.	E601		1934-5
143	SF	9182	1927	b	26	Short Bros.	E602		1934-5
144	SF	9183	1927	b	26	Short Bros.	E603		1934-5

No.	Reg. No.		New	Body	Seats	Bodybuilder	Former Nos.	Withdrawn
145	SF	9221	1927	b	26	Short Bros.	E604	1934-5
146	SF	9222	1927	b	26	Short Bros.	E605	1934-5
147	SF	9235	1927	b	26	Short Bros.	E606	1934-5
148	SF	9236	1927	b	26	Short Bros.	E609	1934-5
149	SF	9237	1927	b	26	Short Bros.	E608	1934-5
150	SF	9238	1927	b	26	Short Bros.	E607	1934-5
151	SF	9275	1927	b	26	Short Bros.	E610	1934-5
152	SF	9286	1927	b	26	Short Bros.	E611	1934-5
153	SF	9287	1927	b	26	Short Bros.	E616	1934-5
154	SF	9288	1927	b	26	Short Bros.	E615	1934-5
155	SF	9289	1927	b	26	Short Bros.	E614	1934-5
156	SF	9290	1927	b	26	Short Bros.	E613	1934-5
157	SF	9291	1927	b	26	Short Bros.	E612	1934-5
158	SF	9308	1927	b	26	Short Bros.	E617	1934-5
159	SF	9309	1927	b	26	Short Bros.	E618	1934--5
160	SF	9336	1927	b	26	Short Bros.	E619	1934-5
to	to						to	
164	SF	9340	1927	b	26	Short Bros.	E623	1934-5
165	SF	9942	1927	a	30	S.M.T.Co.	E624	1936
166	—							
167	KS	3105	1926	e	24	?	E575	1931
168	KS	3701	1927	q	28	?	E580	1933
169	TY	9403	1932	g	26	Strachan	Ex-Orange Bros.	1938

The five with D numbers subsequently regained their previous
E numbers.

L : Reo (First)

No.	Reg. No.		New	Body	Seats	Bodybuilder	Withdrawn
1	DS	1301	1927	e	20	?	1931

Afterwards, the Leyland buses belonging to Stark's of Dunbar
which were painted in S.M.T. livery were given numbers with the
L prefix thus :

L : Leyland (Stark's)

No.	Reg. No.		New	Body	Model	Seats	Bodybuilder	Former Nos.	Withdrawn
1	SS	2786	1928	Lion	c	32	?	E442	?
2	SS	2819	1928	Lion	d	32	?	E440	1934
3	SS	3033	1929	Lion	d	31	Leyland	E441	1940
4	FV	1098	1930	Badger	u	24	Leyland		1940
5	FV	1099	1930	Badger	u	24	Leyland		1940
6	SS	3161	1930	Tiger	d	31	Leyland	E443	1940
7	SS	3472	1932	Tiger	t	32	Alexander		
8	SS	4768	1937	Tiger	s	35	Alexander		
9	SS	6440	1947	Tiger	s	35	Alexander		
10	SS	6609	1947	Tiger	s	35	Alexander		
11	SS	7525	1950	Tiger	s	35	Alexander		

Notes : L1 was rebodied with a "t" type 31 seat body by
Forbes Brebner of Crieff in 1933 and L7 received a new "t" type
Alexander body in 1940. L6's body had a more sloping roof at the
front than the usual bodies of the period. The Alexander
bodies were the same as those supplied to S.M.T. vehicles at the
same dates. L3 and L4 did not carry their numbers, nor were they
lettered S.M.T.

The other Stark's vehicles painted in S.M.T. livery but not numbered were as follows :

Reg. No.	Make	New	Body	Seats	Bodybuilder	
SS 4044	A.E.C. "Q' type	1934	w	35	Weyman	withdrawn 1943
CAG 807	A.E.C. Regal	1948	l	33	Burlingham	Stark's No. A1
SS 9615	A.E.C. Reliance	1955	y	45	Alexander	Stark's No. A4
SS 9616	A.E.C. Reliance	1955	y	45	Alexander	Stark's No. A5

M : Morris (Second)

No.	Reg. No.	New	Body	Seats	Bodybuilder		Withdrawn
1	SY 4242	1930	q	20	Morris	Ex-Bowen	1936
2	SY 4511	1931	u	20	Eastwood & Kenning	Ex-Dick	1937
3	SY 4248	1930	q	20	?	Ex-Dick	1935
4	SY 4930	1932	e	20	London Lorries	Ex-Dick	1937
5	FS 3397	1932	s	30	Park Royal	Ex-Browning	1938
6	XS 2578	1930	q	20	?	Ex-Browning	1935

Notes : M2 and M3 retained Dick's red and white livery with S.M.T. lettering for a time, only the former eventually becoming blue. M5 was a "Dictator" the others were "Viceroys".

N : Star

No.	Reg. No.	New	Body	Seats	Bodybuilder	Former Nos.	Withdrawn
1	SC 2010	1928	b	14	Short Bros.	E301	1935-6
2	SC 2011	1928	b	14	Short Bros.	E304	1935-6
3	SC 2012	1928	b	14	Short Bros.	E305	1935-6
4	SC 2013	1928	b	14	Short Bros.	E308	1935-6
5	SC 2014	1928	b	14	Short Bros.	E309	1935-6
6	SC 2015	1928	b	14	Short Bros.	E311	1935-6
7	SC 2016	1928	b	14	Short Bros.	E312	1935-6
8	SC 2017	1928	b	14	Short Bros.	E315	1935-6
9	SC 2018	1928	b	14	Short Bros.	E317	1935-6
10	SC 2019	1928	b	14	Short Bros.	E318	1935-6
11	SC 2020	1928	b	14	Short Bros.	E320	1935-6
12	SC 2021	1928	b	14	Short Bros.	E322	1935-6
13	SC 2022	1928	b	14	Short Bros.	E328	1935-6
14	SC 2023	1928	b	14	Short Bros.	E329	1935-6
15	SC 2024	1928	b	14	Short Bros.	E330	1935-6
16	SC 2025	1928	b	14	Short Bros.	E331	1935-6
17	SC 2026	1928	b	14	Short Bros.	E332	1935-6
18	SC 2027	1928	b	14	Short Bros.	E333	1935-6
19	SC 2084	1928	e	20	Hall Lewis	E334	1934
20	SC 2085	1928	e	20	Hall Lewis	E336	1934
21	SC 2086	1928	e	20	Hall Lewis	E342	1934
22	SC 2087	1928	e	20	Hall Lewis	E343	1934
23	SC 2088	1928	e	20	Hoyal	E344	1936
24	SC 2089	1928	e	20	Hall Lewis	E346	1934
25	SC 2090	1928	e	20	Hall Lewis	E347	1934
26	SC 2091	1928	e	20	Hall Lewis	E349	1934
27	SC 2092	1928	e	20	Hoyal	E350	1934
28	SC 2093	1928	e	20	Hoyal	E357	1936
29	SC 2094	1928	e	20	Hoyal	E358	1934
30	SC 2095	1928	e	20	Hoyal	E361	1934

No.	Reg. No.		New	Body	Seats	Bodybuilder	Former Nos.	Withdrawn
31	SC	2096	1928	e	20	Hoyal	E362	1932
32	SC	2097	1928	e	20	Hoyal	E363	1936
33	SC	2098	1928	e	20	Hoyal	E364	1934
34	SC	2099	1928	e	20	Hoyal	E365	1936
35	SC	2100	1928	e	20	Hoyal	E366	1936
36	SC	2101	1928	e	20	Hoyal	E367	1934
37	SC	2102	1928	e	20	Hoyal	E369	1934
38	SC	2103	1928	e	20	Hoyal	E379	1934
39	SC	100	1927	q	19	?	Ex-Herd	1935

Notes : The following were rebodied in 1932 with "u" type 18 seat bodies by Alexander Motors Ltd. — N23, N28, N.32 N34 and N35. N27 acquired a destination screenbox on the front.

O : Leyland Lioness

No.	Reg. No.		New	Body	Seats	Bodybuilder	Former Nos.	Withdrawn
1	SY	3929	1929	u	26	?	Ex-Dick	1935
2	SY	338	1927	q	27	?	Ex-Dick	1935
3	TD	9220	1927	k	26	?	Ex-Dick	1935
4	TY	5609	1929	e	26	?	Ex-Dick	1935
5	TE	1140	1927	m	24	?	Ex-Browning	1935
6	GE	1808	1928	q	26	?	Ex-Browning	1935

Note : O3 retained Dick's red and white livery with S.M.T. lettering while it lasted.

P : Thornycroft

No.	Reg. No.		New	Body	Seats	Bodybuilder	Former Nos.	Withdrawn
1	SC	1921	1928	q	20	?	E579	1934
2	SC	7076	1930	q	20	?	E387	1934
3	DS	1128	1925	e	20	?	Ex-Anderson	1934
4	SX	2432	1926	e	20	?	Ex-Rendall	1934
5	SX	2594	1927	e	22	?	Ex-Rendall	1934
6	SX	2625	1927	e	20	?	Ex-Anderson	1934
7	SX	2818	1928	e	20	?	Ex-Anderson	1934
8	SX	3030	1930	e	22	?	Ex-Rendall	1934
9	SC	1069	1928	u	18	?	Ex-West.& Sm.	1936
10	SC	1450	1928	u	18	?	Ex-West.& Sm.	1936
11	SC	3885	1929	q	25	?	Ex-West.& Sm.	1936
12	SC	3997	1929	u	24	?	Ex-West.& Sm.	1936
13	SC	3998	1929	u	24	?	Ex-West.& Sm.	1936
14	FS	5168	1933	q	20	?	Ex-West.& Sm.	1936

Notes : P3 was a rather box-like affair, but most of the others were neat and orthodox. P11 had the later type of plated radiator, while P14 was a "Speedy".

R : Reo (Second)

No.	Reg. No.		New	Body	Seats	Bodybuilder		Withdrawn
1	GE	7415	1930	e	24	Mitchell	Ex-Dunn	1934
2	SY	4279	1930	k	24	Eaton	Ex-Dunn	1934
3	SY	4251	1930	e	20	?	Ex-Dunn	1934
4	SY	4246	1930	e	20	?	Ex-Dunn	1934
5	SY	2808	1926	e	24	?	Ex-Dunn	1934
6	SB	3093	1928	f	20	?	Ex-Lammond	1932
7	SC	7412	1930	u	15	?	Ex-West.& Sm.	1936
8	SC	9981	1931	u	14	?	Ex-West.& Sm.	1936
9	SC	9982	1931	u	14	?	Ex-West.& Sm.	1936

Notes : R1, R2, R8, R9 were more substantial looking models than the others.

S : Ford

No.	Reg. No.		New	Body	Seats	Bodybuilder		Withdrawn
1	SY	3931	1929	e	14	?		
2	SY	4066	1930	e	14	?	Ex-Dunn	1932
3	SC	6721	1930	e	20	?	Ex-Dunn	1932
							Ex-Lammond	1932

S: (Second); Dennis

No.	Reg. No.		New	Body	Seats	Bodybuilder		Withdrawn
1	SX	2775	1928	e	14	?	Ex-McNair	1934

S : (Third); Sundry vehicles

No	Reg. No.		New	Make	Body	Seats	Bodybuilder		Withdrawn
1	FG	6262	1926	Lancia	e	20	?	Ex-Lowson	1936
2	—								
3	SX	3747	1933	Dennis-Lancet	w	30	Dennis	Ex-Browning	1941
4	TS	4937	1925	Lancia	q	20	?	Ex-Robertson	1938
5	TS	7825	1929	Lancia	q	24	?	Ex-Robertson	1938
6	FS	8	1931	Guy	u	20	?	Ex-Cruikshanks	1939
7	SC	7373	1930	Guy	u	20	?	Ex-Cruikshanks	1939
4	VA	9257	1929	Clyde	f	26	?	Ex-Irvine	1940
5	VD	742	1931	Dennis-Arrow	d	32	?	Ex-Irvine	1941
6	DSG	170	1942	Dennis-Lancet II	c	35	Strachan		1953
to	to		to						to
11	DSG	175	1943	Dennis-Lancet II	c	35	Strachan		1954
1	LWS	926	1955	S.M.T.	y	32	S.O.L.		
2	NSG	928	1956	Albion-Nimbus	y	32	?		1956

Notes : The two fresh starts in the series will be noticed. The sloping front, tail, and bulbous roof of S3 made it a somewhat unusual vehicle.

T : Guy

No.	Reg. No.		New	Body	Seats	Bodybuilder		Withdrawn
1	NU	4892	1928	e	20	?		
2	NU	5776	1929	e	20	?	Ex-Sword	1932
–	SM	4387	1931	q	20	?	Ex-Sword	1932
							Ex-Rendall	1934

T : (Second); Leyland Cheetah

No.	Reg. No.		New	Body	Seats	Bodybuilder	Withdrawn
1	WS	8001	1936	a	36	Alexander	1944-6
to	to						
60	WS	8060	1936	a	36	Alexander	1944-6
61	BSC	501	1938	s	35	Alexander	
to	to						
75	BSC	515	1938	s	35	Alexander	

U : De Dion Bouton

No.	Reg. No.		New	Body	Seats	Bodybuilder		Withdrawn
1	SY	2816	1926	e	20	?		
1	SF	5052	1926	b	14	?	Ex-Dunn	1934
3	SF	5053	1926	b	14	?	Ex-Scott	1934
							Ex-Scott	1934

364

V : Morris

No.	Reg. No.		New	Body	Seats	Bodybuilder		Withdrawn
1	FS	334	1931	q	15	Hoyal	Ex-Scott	1934
2	SC	1479	1928	q	15	Hoyal	Ex-Scott	1934
3	SC	1480	1928	q	15	Hoyal	Ex-Scott	1934

V : (Second); Leyland Cub

No.	Reg. No.		New	Body	Seats	Bodybuilder		Withdrawn
1	KS	5732	1933	u	20	Cowieson	Ex-Graham	1940
2	SY	4641	1932	q	20	Duple	Ex-Bowen	1940
3	SY	4642	1932	q	20	Duple	Ex-Bowen	1940
4	SY	4667	1932	q	20	Duple	Ex-Bowen	1940
5	FS	6078	1933	r	20	Duple	Ex-Herd	1940

W : Commer

No.	Reg. No.		New	Body	Seats	Bodybuilder		Withdrawn
1	FS	433	1931	u	14	Hoyal	Ex-Scott	1935-6
2	FS	434	1931	u	14	Hoyal	Ex-Scott	1935-6
3	SY	4442	1931	u	19	Roberts	Ex-Bowen	1936-7
4	SC	4289	1929	q	20	?	Ex-Bowen	1936-7
5	WS	3407	1935	l	24	Duple	Ex-West.& Sm.	1940
6	YJ	3666	1936	w	26	Cadogan	Ex-Robertson	1941
7	YJ	3667	1936	w	26	Cadogan	Ex-Robertson	1941
8	YJ	2241	1935	u	20	Cadogan	Ex-Robertson	1941
9	YJ	1424	1934	u	20	Cadogan	Ex-Robertson	1941
10	YJ	576	1933	u	20	Cadogan	Ex-Robertson	1938
11	YJ	4589	1937	u	20	Cadogan	Ex-Robertson	1941
12	FS	2868	1932	u	20	Waveney	Ex-Cruickshanks	1940
13	FS	9813	1934	u	20	Waveney	Ex-Cruickshanks	1940
14	WS	9743	1936	w	26	Waveney	Ex-Cruickshanks	1941
15	AWS	400	1937	w	20	Waveney	Ex-Cruickshanks	1941
16	BSG	915	1938	w	20	Waveney	Ex-Cruickshanks	1941
17	VD	1418	1932	b	20	?	Ex-Irvine	1940

Notes : W13 had a highly domed roof.

X : Bristol

No.	Reg. No.		New	Body	Seats	Bodybuilder		Withdrawn
1	SY	4506	1931	c	32	?	Ex-Coast-Line	1939
2	SY	4507	1931	c	32	?	Ex-Coast-Line	1939
3	SY	4730	1932	n	30	?	Ex-Coast-Line	1939
4	SY	4731	1932	n	30	?	Ex-Coast-Line	1939

Notes : X3-4 had the more modern radiator.

The following buses were sold to Alexanders with the Dundee area services in 1950 :—H2, H24, H153-60, H165-6, H169, H170, H172, H176-8, H183, H213-5, H220-3, H225-7, H229-35, H239, H240, H242-3, and T61-75.

To continue with some description of the new vehicles year by year; the 1931 purchases comprised only eleven A.E.C. Regals with Cowieson bodies similar to those on the previous year's Leylands, together with three Albion "Valkyries" and an Albion "Valiant", all four with orthodox bodywork.

S.M.T. Co's. A.E.C. REGAL SINGLE DECKER OF 1932
No. B65 at the Mound

In 1932 there appeared a further lot of A.E.C. Regals with bodies for ordinary service. These had a cut-away rear entrance, an opening roof ahead of a solid-sided luggage rack, and large destination screen box with service numbers alongside. This front had a vertical face and was surmounted by a small panel lettered S.M.T. They had moquette upholstery and were very comfortable buses. Most of them were fitted with oil engines later. As indicated in the list five Stars were rebodied, their general lines resembling the foregoing except for the large destination and service number screens. A start had also been made in fitting coachwork over the backs of the Star and Maudslay coaches, thus shortening the folding hoods.

The 1933 buses resembled the previous year's ones but were Leyland Tigers with oil engines. There were also six Bedford coaches, and for the London service six A.E.C. Regals which were provided with lavatory accommodation and also with oil engines. Twelve more similar coaches followed in 1934 but in these the lavatory was omitted. The 1934 service buses were also A.E.C. Regals again but with sloping destination screens and other minor differences. These had four-cylinder oil engines. There was also another series of Bedford coaches of varying sizes.

In 1935 there were Leyland Tigers again, resembling the previous ones and with the now standard oil engine, and also a solitary Albion with similar body and a Gardner six-cylinder oil engine. There was also a batch of A.E.C. Regals with what might now be described as dual-purpose bodies. A vertical fronted combined destination, service number and S.M.T. panel was incorporated in the front of a well domed roof into which a panel over the side windows was also set to display a bus travel

366

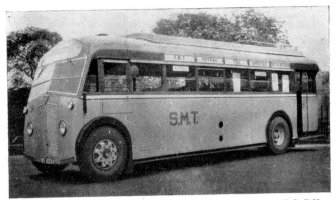

S.M.T. Co's. LEYLAND CHEETAH SINGLE-DECKER
of 1936 No. T34 at the Mound

slogan. The new fashion for a downswept moulding over the rear
wheel was followed in these vehicles and their livery was a darker
blue with the waist and "tail" of a greenish blue colour. The
lettering S.M.T. was also much smaller and enclosed in a diamond
device. This colour scheme and downswept "tail" moulding was
applied to most acquired coaches in 1935 and also to existing
coaches being repainted, though in the earlier examples the
ordinary blue and white colours were used. In the interests of
continuity it should here be mentioned that in 1936 the downswept
"tail" moulding went out of favour except where taken-over
vehicles already had it. From 1937 the greenish blue colour gave
way to white again and between then and 1939 several coaches
reverted right back to straight waist band and ordinary blue and
white livery, though in all cases the small S.M.T. in the diamond
device remained standard for coaches. The small S.M.T. panels
mounted above the roof were removed from most vehicles of all
types around 1936.

The Bedfords of 1936 had a more modern appearance with a
sloping front and back and the last two windows set higher. Both
these and the six London service Leyland Tigers were painted a
very dark navy blue. The latter were not of very attractive
appearance, but bore names on the back, viz.— in order,
Kenilworth, Ivanhoe, Bride of Lammermoor, Lady of the Lake,
Rob Roy, and Heart of Midlothian. For service buses sixty
Leyland Cheetahs were ordered. Their bodies resembled, in
general, the 1935 A.E.C. Regals but had a full front with well raked
windscreens and concealed radiator. The rear entrance was, as
usual, of the cut-away pattern, and the ordinary blue livery was
used.

The 1937 Bedfords had a neater appearance with a uniform window line and a blue livery of a new shade which seemed to have a slight grey tinge. This appeared on a few other coaches too on repainting in 1938-9. The "t" type bodies of the 1937 Leyland Tigers were similar, apart from their fronts, to the previous year's Cheetahs, while the "s" type ones resembled the semi-coaches of 1935 but with a neater back and the omission of the slogan panel. The Duple bodied ones however were different, having a well curved roof and generally of pleasing lines. These last two types introduced a new coach livery to mark the Coronation in that year, namely pale yellow relieved with a red band sweeping down towards the back. This livery was subsequently applied to a few other coaches on repainting.

The 1938 A.E.C. Regals were generally similar to the previous service buses. The double-deckers however differed from the earlier ones in having flatter fronts. Some of these earlier ones were reconstructed about this time and most of these then lost their "piano" front. In some cases the platform and stair was enclosed as well. Another lot of similar double-deckers came in 1939, together with more A.E.C. Regals of semi-coach pattern and in "Coronation" livery, and Leyland Tiger service buses in ordinary blue. On these A.E.C.s the roof luggage rack was omitted in favour of a boot inside at the back, and this became standard practice thereafter. Fortunately the 1940 order, A.E.C. and Leyland, all of the dual-purpose type and generally similar to the previous ones were duly received. On these the pale yellow livery was modified by the relieving panel being blue instead of red.

D.L.G.H.

S.M.T. Co's. A.E.C. 'REGAL' SINGLE-DECKER OF 1939 IN "CORONATION" LIVERY. No. B198 parked in Queen Street

It now became a matter of what could be got through the Ministry of Supply. First, early in 1942, were two A.E.C. Regal double-deckers with austerity lines which ran their first few months in grey paint. These were followed by a Leyland Titan which differed only in detail. The former London service coaches H138-143 also appeared as double-deckers with bodies similar to the aforementioned, and renumbered J60-5. Then the earlier London service A.E.C.s were similarly converted to double-deckers in 1944, B74-9 B81-92 becoming BB3-20, while further Leyland Tigers were similarly dealt with in 1945, viz. H106-9/11-3/5 and H161-3/74 becoming respectively J67-78. These 1944 and 1945 conversions were turned out in grey and retained this colour till after the war. Meantime some Guy Arabs with 6LW engines and double-deck austerity bodies by various builders and hence detail differences, were added over the years 1943-4-5. Of these E15-7 had external roof ribs and these and also E5-6/9-10 had utility wooden seats. E3-10 and E15-7 wore grey livery, retaining it till after the war in most cases, while E11-4 were in a dark blue relieved only by white on the lower saloon window pillars. E9-10 had this livery also for a time later. Restrictions had been eased by the time E18-22 arrived and these had a more shapely roof at the back. The whole lot, and also BB1-2 were reconstructed with minor improvements in the early fifties.

For single-deckers there were sixty of the standard utility Bedfords in 1944-5 which served only till sufficient new buses could be obtained after the war. A few were eventually repainted in the ordinary blue livery, but all had been withdrawn by the end of 1949. The only other war time single-deckers were the six Dennis Lancet II with austerity shape bodies which were also in grey till after the war. It is thought that H120 was the only pre-war vehicle to be painted grey during the war.

The first new vehicles after the war were the Duple bodied A.E.C.s of 1946-7, with a curved roof of pleasing lines and front screen set in a raked and curved shape panel. Those with Alexander bodies which followed in 1947-8 were of straighter lines and had more orthodox screen boxes. Still more with Burlingham bodies were added in 1948, these differing in having a more domed roof with a panel above the side windows and a deeper front screen box. Many bodies of these Alexander and Burlingham types were also provided to rebody the pre-war A.E.C.s and Leyland Tigers as detailed in the list, while the few supplied by Croft's had a flatter roof. All the foregoing with the exception of the Burlingham bodies were in the pale yellow livery with red "flashes" and blue roof, and this livery was applied also to some of the pre-war Bedfords in 1946.

S.M.T. C,'s. POST-WAR A.E.C. 'REGAL' SINGLE-DECKER OF 1946
No. B268 with Duple body at St. Andrew Square

S.M.T. Co,'s. POST-WAR A.E.C. 'REGAL' DOUBLE-DECKER OF 1950
No. BB87 WITH BURLINGHAM BODY

B364 was a somewhat ugly coach in pale yellow with green mouldings, though its appearance was improved a little afterwards. It was however the first of eight foot width and the forerunner of the graceful and well-known "Seagull" model of Burlingham's. As shown in the list many A.E.C.s, both prewar and post-war, subsequently received "Seagull" coach bodies. Meantime there were also the Burlingham semi-coaches of 1949 with a curved roof and door mouldings to match, used both for new A.E.C.s and rebodying pre-war Leylands. The earlier post-war Bedfords had the standard Duple design of body but most of these subsequently received "Seagull" bodies as had the later ones when new. The "Seagull" bodies of different seating capacities showed other minor differences and the 37 seaters had solid cornice panels.

Pre-war vehicles not rebodied were reconstructed with, in most cases, minor modifications, though some were lengthened to thirty feet. The 1948 double-deckers were of plain angular line but the 1949 and 1950 series were of much improved appearance with a more raked front, and the latter had curved frames for the end windows.

In June 1949 the colour scheme reverted to green with "flashes" of a darker shade and all vehicles were thereafter turned out in this livery, except for the Bristol coaches, the Mark IV A.E.C.s with 38 seat bodies, and B364 and B547, for which the pale yellow with green mouldings was retained. The other Mark IV A.E.C.s received this livery too later on. Most of the 1940 bodies were reconstructed with either a narrow straight waist panel painted white, or no panelling in which case the S.M.T. and diamond device was in aluminium flanked by a moulding. A few 1937 "s" type bodies were treated similarly.

The bodies on the Mark IV A.E.C.s were very comfortable though somewhat box-like in appearance, as were the Mono-coaches with their high domed roof. The separate lots of the former had various detail differences. The Bristol coaches and "Lodekas" were the standard product and do not call for description, while the Reliances were modelled on orthodox and neat lines.

It will be appreciated that an enormous number of variations in detail and in painting appeared on individual vehicles over the years, which it would be tedious to record even if space could be found. There were also odd vehicles of various makes which ran on trial service for short periods.

D.L.G.H.

S.O.L. LIGHTWEIGHT 32 SEAT BUS OF 1955. No.S1

One other vehicle has to be mentioned however. The Company desired an economical light weight bus and, as in 1913, set about building it themselves. The resulting vehicle, in 1955, numbered S1, was an all Scottish production with an Albion engine. Several novel features were incorporated such as rubber suspension. 24ft. long by 7ft. 9in. wide and of integral construction, its appearance was rather box-like though somewhat improved later. Nevertheless carrying 32 passengers for its 3½ tons weight it gave a good account of itself. It might have been called a "Lothian", but so far has been anonymous. The Albion Nimbus which followed was a very similar vehicle.

X

SOME OTHER BUS OPERATORS

After the first world war there was, in general, a fresh start to road motor services, aided by the many ex-army chassis which were available fairly cheaply, and followed a few years later by new light vehicles, mainly of American and Continental origin. Many men were attracted to investing their savings in such a venture, passenger or goods or both. In Edinburgh the Scottish Motor Traction Company was of course now well established and scope for competition was therefore limited, so that the new firms in the city mostly concentrated on day and afternoon tours in the surrounding countryside. Although these facilities are hardly a part of this story, it is nevertheless as well to mention the firms concerned as some essayed ordinary bus services as well, and eventually most of the firms passed into the hands of the S.M.T.Co.

It may be mentioned first that during the railway strike in September 1919 a fourteen seat charabanc was run twice a day from the Waverley Steps to Glasgow by the Bathgate Motor Company.

In 1920 Edinburgh Corporation were concerned at the damage caused to their roads by buses and charabancs, and so licences were then being granted subject to a payment to them of one penny per bus-mile run on such roads. (The agreement with the S.M.T.Co. was for a halfpenny.) The practice was of course disallowed by the Roads Act 1920, which provided for all road users contributing to the new Road Fund on a national basis.

One of the best known operators just after the war was White's Motor Hiring Company, of Russell Road, who had been in business at least as far back as 1914, when they owned a Halley charabanc, (S4011). Now there was a Daimler, (148; S9402), a more up-to-date Halley, (SG2109), and a smaller Clyde, (A3402?), followed by two A.E.C.s, (272; SG4036, and 147; SG7347). All ran on solid tyres and were painted dark green. Later in the "twenties" a number of 14-seater pneumatic tyred Lancias were used and a lighter shade of green adopted. These were as follows :

141;	VA 2773	149;	ES 3026	273;	LM 6021	399;	J 3413
142;	LM 6017	268;	LU 4453	398;	XD 7312	406;	SX 2344

The last one was an 18-seater.

At the beginning of October 1927 the firm started a bus service from the foot of Chambers Street to Balerno via Lauriston Place, Bruntsfield and Colinton Road using three new 26-seat rear entrance normal control Gilfords, (561-2-3; SC160, SC250, SC838) and a 30-seat rear entrance half-cab A.D.C., (407; SC2745). The latter was painted blue and white at first. Pre-printed tickets were used, of which the 2d. ones are known to have been red. The half-hourly service was a useful one, and on 20 February 1930 it was acquired, along with the four buses, by the S.M.T.Co.

White's carried on with their tours, but now on a very modest scale, with a new 14-seater Chevrolet, (148; SC7012), and a second-hand Leyland charabanc, (149; FY3017). The Lancias and the others had gone, and a few years afterwards the firm was wound up.

Another operator of the war time period was W. Lawley, of Gayfield Square, who ran a dark green A.E.C. charabanc on the Queensferry road for a short time, and later, about 1923-4, a Berliet charabanc, (265; SG8189), on tours.

In the summer of 1920 Hay and Company, of Port Seton, tried a charabanc between there and Joppa, while the Peebles Motor Company ran a 24-seater charabanc on weekend tours from their garage in Haymarket Terrace. The latter firm was later bought up by the S.M.T. Company. Guy Bros. of Aberlady ran a charabanc between Port Seton and Aberlady on Sundays in the summer of 1921.

James Bowen, of Musselburgh operated a more extensive programme of tours from Edinburgh, with the following charabancs, painted dark green :

Albion;	284;	SY1204	18 seats	A.E.C;	261;	SY1860 27 seats
	283;	SY1855	14 seats		146;	SY1892 27 seats
	285;	SY2307	14 seats		?	SY2270 28 seats
	265;	SY2692	18 seats	G.M.C.;	279;	SY2417 14 seats
	203;	SY3308	18 seats	Morris;	572;	SY3304 15 seats
Dennis;	391;	SY2911	14 seats		573;	SY3305 15 seats
	390;	SY2926	14 seats			

They also operated some service in the Musselburgh — Smeaton district in the early twenties and eventually received some compensation from the Scottish Motor Traction Company when that company entered on that route.

On 22 October 1927 they also started a bus service from the foot of Chambers Street via Dalkeith Road, Newcraighall, Musselburgh, Wallyford and Smeaton to Elphinstone, and for this traffic acquired during the course of the next year or two, the following buses painted red with white uppers :

564;	SY 3419	30 seat front entrance half-cab		Leyland Lion
565;	SC 74	28 seat front entrance normal control		Albion
599;	SY 3459	18 seat front entrance normal control		Dennis
262;	VA 4995	20 seat front entrance normal control		Leyland Leverette
282;	SY 3991	28 seat front entrance normal control		Albion
281;	SY 4068	26 seat front entrance normal control		A.D.C.
561;	SY 4142	32 seat double entrance half-cab		Daimler

The first four, as least, of these carried the firm's fleet numbers 1 to 4. This service was taken over by the S.M.T. Company on 11 June 1931 together with the buses in use.

Bowen continued to run the tours and gradually added the following coaches to his fleet :

Commer;	286; SC4289	20 seats	Leyland Lion;	261;	SY4441
Daimler;	599; SY3940	29 seats	Commer;	—	SY4442 19 seats
Chevrolet;	279; SY4220	14 seats	Leyland Cub	—	SY4641 20 seats
Morris;	402; SY4242	20 seats	Leyland Cub	—	SY4642 20 seats
Gilford;	562; SC 46 (normal control)		Leyland Cub		SY4667 20 seats
Gilford	563; SC4198 (half-cab)		Daimler	—	SY5509 32 seats

D.L.G.H.

BOWEN'S GILFORD COACH after acquisition by the S.M.T. Co. whose No. F5 can be seen.

The Gilfords came from the "White Line" fleet to be mentioned later, and SC46 was later re-registered FS1509. However, in May 1935 that part of the business was also acquired by the S.M.T. Company with the remaining vehicles, which it may be remarked, included the veteran Albion SY1855, — and the firm then concentrated on its motor engineering business in new premises in Pitt Street Edinburgh. After the second world war they sought a licence to operate tours from Musselburgh, but this was refused.

Another of the earliest post-war touring operators was George A. Cruikshanks, and this firm was also the last to be absorbed by the S.M.T. Company shortly before the second world war, namely in October 1938. Cruikshanks' fleet, over the years, comprised the following, painted light grey :

Dennis;	277;	S	9260	27 seats	Reo;	414	SF	9295	14 seats
	276;	SG	100	27 seats	Commer;	—	FS	2868	20 seats
	294;	DS	775	18 seats		—	FS	9813	20 seats
	288;	SF	4841	14 seats		—	WS	9743	26 seats
Guy;	274;	SC	7373	20 seats		—	AWS	400	20 seats
	—	FS	8	20 seats		—	BSG	915	20 seats

Other touring operators of the early "twenties" were :—

Tait, of Duncan Street, Leith, with a light grey 27 seat Thornycroft, (274; SG3394), a dark blue 18 seat Thornycroft, (275; SF4819), and a 1934 Commer, (FS9694).

W. H. Herd with his "Chieftain" line fleet as follows, all painted dark red with a white top band : (WS636 was "The Mountain Chieftain," and WS4794 "The Chieftain of the Isles.")

Crossley;	287;	SG	5854	10 seats	A.J.S.;	293;	SC	4807	20 seats
Cottin-						205;	SC	7566	20 seats
Desgoutes;	292;	ES	5780	14 seats	Leyland Cub	—	FS	6078	20 seats
	290;	ES	7808	18 seats	Bedford	—	FS	349	15 seats
later	291;	ES	7808	18 seats		—	FS	2923	20 seats
Star;	290;	SC	100	20 seats		—	WS	4794	24 seats
Chevrolet;	202;	SC	7456	14 seats	A.E.C.				
					Regent	—	WS	636	26 seats

A. & W. Scott pioneered long-distance tours with the name "Azure Blue" coaches, using a 14 seat Cottin-Desgoutes, (269; SG7126), an 18 and a 14 seat De Dion, (respectively 271; SG5474 and 267; SG9603), two 15 seat Morris, 411/410; SC1479, SC1480), two further 14 seat De Dion, (412-3; SF5052-3). and in 1929-30 five 22/24 seat Daimler saloons, (271/408-9/268/270 SC4593-5, SC7556-7), which were also used on services to London and to Inverness. Later additions were a further Morris, FS334, and two 14 seat Commers, FS433-4. One of the Scott family went off on his own in 1927 with a 20 seat full-fronted Bristol coach, (204; SF7950), styled the "Silver King", and A. & W. Scott became W. Scott & Co. This firm was taken over by the S.M.T. Company in December 1932. Herd was taken over by the S.M.T. Company in May 1935, and Tait and A. Scott went out of business about 1934.

Other small concerns in the "twenties" were the Eagle Touring Co. with a dark red 18 seat Albion, (418; SF4942), and William Kerr & Co. who ran until 1929 with a dark blue 18 seat

Cottin-Desgoutes, (206; SG9388) and a grey Albion, (205; SF8089).
William Sword bought Kerr's Cottin-Desgoutes and the Eagle
Touring Co's Albion, and later a Daimler (SC5237) from the
S.M.T. Company, and a 24 seat Gilford, UV5637). In the spring
of 1935 he too sold out to the S.M.T. Company.

A larger and better known firm was Westwood & Smith with
a garage at Gorgie near Saughton Park where they built their own
distinctive bodies for most of their "Royal Blue" coaches which
were relieved with grey upperwork. Their fleet over the years from
1922 comprised the following :

Guy;	281;	SG5485	14 seats	Reo;	747;	SC 7412	15 seats
later	141;	SG5485	9 seats		—	SC 9981	14 seats
	415;	SF4921	12 seats		—	SC 9982	14 seats
	416;	SF4922	14 seats	Leyland;	—	HH 1836	25 seats
	417;	SF4923	15 seats	Daimler;	148;	SC 7889	26 seats
	571;	SF8095	18 seats		—	FS 366	28 seats
Lancia;	278;	SF 44	18 seats		—	FS 3389	30 seats
Thornycroft;	144;	SC1069	18 seats		—	FS 9314	32 seats
	143;	SC1450	18 seats		—	FS 9776	29 seats
	142;	SC3885	25 seats		—	WS 3869	32 seats
	145;	SC3997	24 seats	Commer;	—	WS 3407	24 seats
	280;	SC3998	24 seats				
	—	FS5168	20 seats				

This firm and their remaining vehicles were also acquired by
the S.M.T. Company in April 1935.

E. Thomson also specialised in long-distance tours and in 1929
started a one-day service to London. His fleet comprised the
following vehicles painted in various colours as shown :

386;	ES5626	14 seat charabanc Cottin-Desgoutes, yellow
382;	ES5677	14 seat charabanc Cottin-Desgoutes, yellow
381;	SF1658	14 seat charabanc Reo, yellow
383;	SF2145	14 seat charabanc Reo, yellow
387;	SF4543	14 seat charabanc Reo, brown
387;	SC1865	20 seat coach Thornycroft, brown
579;	SC1921	20 seat coach Thornycroft brown
386;	SC4191	26 seat coach Daimler normal control, brown
382;	SC4760	26 seat coach Daimler, normal control, brown
578;	SC5118	26 seat coach Daimler, half-cab, brown
419;	SC5237	26 seat coach Daimler, normal control, brown
380;	SC5300	26 seat saloon Daimler, normal control, grey
384;	SC5388	26 seat saloon Daimler, normal control, grey
387;	SC7076	20 seat coach Thornycroft, brown

This concern was absorbed by the S.M.T. Company on 11
April 1930.

We now come to the firms who were primarily bus operators.
On 1 October 1923 a small firm, the Dean Motor Transport
Company, of Belford Road, and managed by a William Thomson,
put on a charabanc service between George Street at Hanover

Street and Boness, running via Stockbridge, Queensferry, and
Newton. The fare was 2/-. Two small Rochet-Schneiders, (202 and
337), were used.

Another firm, R. T. Motor Services Ltd., with a garage at
St. Clair Place and H. M. Drysdale as manager, started services
from the same stance in George Street, to Grangemouth via
Linlithgow and Polmont, and also to Peebles very soon afterwards.
The fare to Grangemouth was 3/- single, 5/6 return, and to Peebles
2/9 single, 5/- return. The return tickets were available for a month
and a 3/6 day return was offered on both routes on Wednesdays
and Saturdays. The Grangemouth route was not successful however, and was withdrawn in June 1924, the company concentrating
on the much more popular Peebles route. They also ran tours.

However in October 1924 the Dean Motor Transport Company,
who now had two more, larger 20 seat Rochet-Schneiders, (200;
SG9365 and 291; SF 535), with a 14 seat Gotfredson, (293; SF536),
and a 14 seat Crossley, (330; WA5080), in addition, tried the R. T.
Company's Grangemouth via Linlithgow and Polmont route, and
also extended some of their Boness journeys to Grangemouth too.
The Dean Motor Transport Company's fare to Grangemouth was
2/6 single, 4/- return. But Grangemouth still did not provide traffic
to and from Edinburgh and the route via Linlithgow and Polmont
was very soon dropped again. In January 1925 when the Company
was taken over by the S.M.T. Company only the Boness route was
being run. Their charabancs were painted pale blue with a white
top band. Soon after passing into the hands of the S.M.T. Company
the Crossley was disposed of to a garage in Queensferry who
secured an Edinburgh licence, 406, for it for a short time.

The R. T. Motor Services continued to operate the Peebles
route till June 1926 when the S.M.T. Company consolidated its
position by taking them over too. Previously, from 1 July 1925,
the starting point had been changed to St. David Street on account
of the opening of the George Street tramway route. The Company's
fleet of 14 seat Reos were painted white some being buses and some
charabancs as follows :

?	SG9035 charabanc	197	SG9730 charabanc
195	? bus	263	SF2279 charabanc
262	SG9253 bus	264	SF2280 charabanc
196	SG9613 charabanc	266	SF 2628 charabanc

In 1925 James Armstrong of Duke Street Leith bought a 14
seat Reo charabanc (209;SF3588) painted dark blue and bearing
the name on the back "Sunny Leith". With this he tried a route
from the foot of Leith Walk to Queensferry via Ferry Road,
whereupon the S.M.T. Company very soon ran him off by putting
on a temporary competitive service. Later, in 1927 he tried a service

from the foot of Leith Walk every two hours to Port Seton via London Road. This was advertised on 27 September as "withdrawn till further notice (bus being overhauled)". Restarting to Port Seton on 27 May 1928 he reverted to the service to Queensferry again, every one and a half hours, from 17 June, but soon afterwards ceased regular operation.

More lasting was the route into Edinburgh started in 1924, at first at weekends only, by Andrew Harper of Peebles. His route however was not from Peebles but from West Linton via Carlops, Flotterstane and Fairmilehead to Castle Terrace. It was soon extended to Biggar and to Broughton, and a connecting service given to Peebles. On such a sparsely populated route his fares were relatively high, but on summer Saturdays and Sundays his resources were fully taxed. Known examples of his tickets are 3d. white, 5d. green, 1/- brown, 1/3 green, 1/6 blue. The firm's services in Peeblesshire gradually expanded and in 1930 absorbed a route between Edinburgh and Dumfries which had been started the previous year by Dickson of Dumfries using two dark red Guys (401; SW1861 and 402; SM4387).

However the Caledonian Omnibus Company Limited, Dumfries, also started on the Edinburgh-Dumfries route in 1930 with two red and white 32 seat front entrance Leyland Lions,

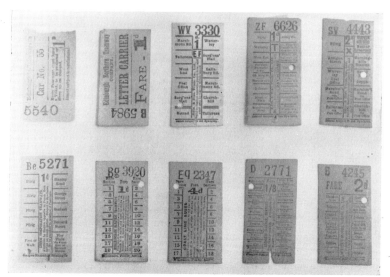

SOME OTHER OPERATOR'S TICKETS
Top row : E.S.T. Co. 1d blue; E.N.T. Co. 1d. special, yellow;
E. & D.T. Co. 1d. white; 1d transfer, blue, 2d. red.
Bottom row : L.C.T. 1d., white; Musselburgh Tramways 1d., white;
Coast Line 4d., green; Harper's' 1/3d., green; White's Motor Service 2d., red

313-4; SM6919 and SM6918, respectively Caledonian Nos. 54 and 53. The latter was soon replaced by SW2551, No. 46. Then early in 1932 Harper's business was acquired by the Caledonian who however transferred the Peebleshire routes to the S.M.T. Company in August 1933 in exchange for certain S.M.T. local services in the Carlisle district. Caledonian however continued to run the Edinburgh-Dumfries service jointly with S.M.T. After the nationalisation of the two companies Scottish Omnibuses Ltd., as the S.M.T. Company had become, took over this service entirely under a rationalisation scheme in June 1950.

Harper's fleet, painted dark blue with cream uppers, was as follows :

Harper No.	Edinr No.	Reg. No.	Body and Make	Cale. No.
1	392	DS1031	14 seat charabanc, Guy	—
2	397	DS1060	14 seat charabanc, Guy (This one was painted yellow)	—
3	396	DS1185	14 seat front entrance bus, Reo	—
4	296	DS1288	14 seat front entrance bus, Reo	—
5	570	DS1303	14 seat front entrance bus, Reo	—
6	395	DS1184	18 seat front entrance bus, Dennis	—
7	289	DS1235	16 seat front entrance bus, Dennis	—
8	569	DS1304	32 seat rear entrance bus, Albion, half-cab	118
9	297	DS1362	32 seat rear entrance bus, Albion, half-cab	121
10	567	DS1403	25 seat coach, Albion, normal-control	122
11	394	DS1092	18 seat front entrance bus, Thornycroft, (later a coach)—	
12	298	DS1128	20 seat front entrance bus, Thornycroft	—
13	295	DS1209	24 seat front entrance bus Thornycroft	—
14	—	DS1302	22 seat front entrance bus Thornycroft	—
15	389	DS1342	20 seat front entrance bus Thornycroft	119
16	568	DS1356	30 seat front entrance bus Thornycroft normal-control	120
17	—	DS1402	20 seat coach, Thornycroft	—
18	289	DS1404	24 seat front entrance bus Thornycroft, (later 24 seat coach)	123
19	388	DS1405	20 seat coach Thornycroft, (later 16 seat f.e. bus)	—
20	395	DS1406	24 seat front entrance bus Thornycroft	124
21	289	DS1421	20 seat coach Thornycroft (later 19 seat f.e. bus)	125
22	299	DS1438	24 seat front entrance bus Thornycroft	126
23	393	DS1474	31 seat rear entrance bus Thornycroft, full front	127
24	396	DS1475	32 seat rear entrance bus Thornycroft, full front	128
25	388	DS1476	31 seat rear entrance bus Albion, full front	129
26	577	DS1477	31 seat rear entrance bus, Leyland Lion, half-cab	130
27	397	DS1521	30 seat rear entrance bus Thornycroft, half-cab	132
28	—	SM4387	20 seat coach, Guy (ex-Dickson)	—
29	296	DS1593	31 seat rear entrance bus Thornycroft, half-cab	133
30	298	DS1594	32 seat rear entrance bus Leyland Lion, half-cab	134
31	207	DS1595	32 seat rear entrance bus Thornycroft, half-cab	135
32	208	DS1596	32 seat rear entrance bus Thornycroft, half-cab	136
12	209	DS1617	32 seat front entrance bus A.E.C. Regal, half-cab	137
17	397	DS1618	30 seat coach Thornycroft, half-cab	138
19	—	OU8891	? Thorncroft half-cab	131
28	—	DS1690	32 seat Leyland Lion half-cab	139
7	—	DS1691	? Albion Valkyrie half-cab	140
6	—	DS1698	? Commer	?

MESSRS. ANDREW HARPER'S THORNYCROFT
BUS No. 23

Some of the vehicles did not get Edinburgh numbers when new but eventually displaced earlier ones, and it will be noted that some were never licensed by Edinburgh. The Caledonian Omnibus Company later used Dennis Lancet buses on the route.

Reverting to 1924, George Deans advertised a bus from Lauder to Edinburgh, George Street, in July 1924, on Tuesdays and Thursdays, but this does not appear to have survived for long.

About 1924 the Broxburn road became the scene of much competition from firms in West Lothian. A strange medley of vehicles from the ubiquitous 14 seat Reos to large Caledons appeared under various fleet names. Some, including "Progressive" soon disappeared from Edinburgh, but Allen & Kennedy, of Broxburn, who ran from Pumpherston and Livingstone Station via Morrison Street, Bread Street, and Lawnmarket (?) to Chambers Street held out for a time, and although bought up by the S.M.T. Company in November 1926, continued to run this service under their own name until about 1929. Their dark blue buses were: 20 seat Reos, 400; SX2263, and 401; SX2313, and a 24 seat Albion, 403; SX2406. There are thought to have been a few earlier vehicles also.

Simpson's also of Broxburn, and also running to the Chambers Street stance, held out too, using a 14 seat Reo, 409; SX2314, and two 20 seat Minervas, 408; SX2363 and 577; SX2421, originally bright red and buff, but later green and cream and boldly

THE UBIQUITOUS REO 14-SEATER OF THE "MID-TWENTIES"
Simpson's Motor Service of Broxburn

GILFORD BUS OF DUNN'S MOTOR SERVICE:
Musselburgh—Smeaton route

lettered S.M.S. In 1929 this firm were reorganised and expanded under the name of the West Lothian Motor Service with a new fleet of dark green vehicles as follows :

769; SX 2775	19 seat front entrance Dennis
768; SX 2776	19 seat front entrance Dennis
765; SX 2784	26 seat rear entrance Albion
764; SX 2785	26 seat rear entrance Albion
766; SX 2826	26 seat rear entrance Albion
767; GE 432	28 seat front entrance Albion
737; SX 2945	32 seat double entrance Daimler, half-cab
736; SX 2946	32 seat double entrance Daimler, half-cab
738; SC 5392	32 seat front entrance Daimler, half-cab
739; SC 5431	32 seat front entrance Daimler, half-cab
224; TS 8168	32 seat double entrance Daimler, half-cab

SC5392 ran painted grey and TS8168 was red, while the two earlier Minervas became respectively 769 (in place of SX2775) and 205. The new regime did not last long however, selling out to the S.M.T. Company on 6 September 1929. Dennis SX2776 was later acquired by Wilkie, of Balerno, who used it for a service from the S.M.T. terminus there to the top of the hill on Saturdays and Sundays. It was a useful help for Pentland Hill walkers and continued for several years before the second world war.

On the other side of the city the Dunn family were running services in the area between Musselburgh and Dalkeith, and in 1929 commenced a service from Cousland via Smeaton, Musselburgh and Millerhill in to Chambers Street using two orange coloured 20 seat front entrance Gilfords, 404-5; SY3483/3916. Dunn's various services were acquired by the S.M.T. Company on 24 February 1932. Other vehicles in the family's fleet were :

De Dion	SY2816 20 seats	Reo	SY2808 24 seats
Gilford	SY3498 20 seats	Reo	SY4246 20 seats
Ford	SY3931 14 seats	Reo	SY4251 20 seats
Ford	SY4066 14 seats	Reo	SY4279 24 seats
		Reo	GE7415 24 seats

The difficulties of the Port Seton tram route have already been mentioned. This was greatly aggravated when John Harris started his "White Line Pullman Cars" from Chambers Street to Port Seton in July 1927. Harris had been refused a licence by the Edinburgh authorities, and eventually defied them. He started his service with a flourish at one o'clock on Friday 8 July, "free to the public both ways". Naturally large crowds took advantage of the free hurl. A twenty minute service at a fare of 8d. single 1/2 return was introduced from the following day. Musselburgh was 5d. single, 9d. return. Harris declared war in his inaugural press advertisement which included this "Notice to the Public": "Many applications have been made to the Magistrates for permission to run this service. To every one we have had a blank refusal, no reason being given. They prefer to maintain the present monopoly.

Such monopolies are not allowed in any other town in Britain. 'White Line Pullman Cars' have therefore no option but to do their best in the face of this monopoly which is maintained by the Edinburgh Magistrates, and with your assistance break it. Monopoly means higher fares for you. Our fares are the lowest in passenger service. Our coaches are the most comfortable and safe on the road. Though we have no permission to run in Edinburgh we have been granted permission and stances in Musselburgh, Prestonpans, Cockenzie, and Port Seton. Support the service that gives you better travelling and lower fares. Ride White Line and ride happy".

Two days later he intimated his regret that he could not reply to the many letters of support he had received, but quoted part of a somewhat colourful one from Port Seton. He faced his first prosecution for running without a licence on 22 July and was fined £2. His advertisement that day was headed "White Line Pullman Cars v. Tramp Cars. Monopoly broken by the straight White Line". He drew attention to his prosecution and to the new cut in tram fares resulting from his competition.

In the middle of August he advertised the Port Seton fare as 9d. single 1/2 return. Appearing in court on 19 August, for the third time he said he would prefer to go to jail. However he didn't and a stated case was again called for. Still his unauthorised service continued to run and after his fifth appearance in court on 14 September he had paid altogether £178 in fines. His unorthodox perseverance however now bore fruit for his continued negotiations with the Magistrates resulted in a licence to run from Calton Steps in Waterloo Place, instead of from Chambers Street, and to proceed via Baileyfield Road and Milton Road instead of through Portobello High Street as he had hitherto run. This took effect from 22 September.

Flushed with apparent success Harris now set about expansion, resulting in the formation on 26 January 1928 of the Edinburgh Omnibus Company (White Line Pullman Cars) Limited with a capital of £145,000 and directors drawn from Glasgow and elsewhere. E. J. Walsh, late of the M. & D. E. L. & T. Co. was connected with the concern, which gave £26,000 for Harris' "White Line Pullman Cars". Little more capital was forthcoming however.

The writing was now on the wall for the Musselburgh and District Electric Light & Traction Company, and we have seen how the following month they replaced their trams with their bright red "Coast Line" buses. For their stance they also used the top of Waterloo Place, and followed the same route as the "White Line" buses. Competition was of course very keen. On 1 August 1928 "White Line" extended their service every forty

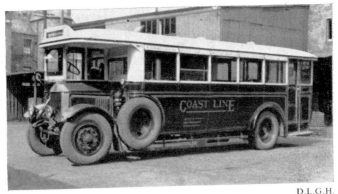

M. & D. E. L. & T. Co. "COAST LINE" ALBION
No. 728.

COAST LINE 'BRISTOL' BUS IN THE OLD TRAM DEPOT.
The rails can still be seen.

minutes through to North Berwick, whereupon "Coast Line" promptly followed suit, running every twenty minutes. To do so they borrowed vehicles from the S.M.T. Company and also arranged interavailability of return tickets with that company. Then, with delivery of additional vehicles, "White Line" immediately stepped up their service to a twenty minutes frequency too. However, the "White Line" fleet of purple and black, — later purple and white, — vehicles was being run very hard. The initial lot of front entrance Reo "Speed Wagons"', 581-6; SF9141-4/ 9554/6 were done after about a year's work. The 28 seat rear entrance Gilfords, 587-92; SC 45-50, and 32 seat half cab Dennis coaches 593-8/760-3; SC1844/6/5/9/7/8/50-3 respectively. struggled on, while the Reos had been replaced in 1929 by 32 seat rear entrance half-cab Gilfords, 581-6; SC4193-8. Quite suddenly later that year the service ceased. It was said there were some difficulties arising from maintenance matters. Few of the vehicles seem to have been a proposition for other operators though SC45-6 and SC4198 were acquired by Bowen. On a petition by creditors the firm went into liquidation in October 1929.

After the demise of the "White Line" service the "Coast Line" extension to North Berwick was taken off and the Musselburgh company settled down to work its expanding local traffic until, in December 1936, the service was taken over by the S.M.T. Company. The "Coast Line" fleet consisted of the following, all except the Albions passing to the S.M.T.Co.

Co. No.	Edinr. No.	Reg. No.	Type and Make
	721-6;	SY3484-9	31 seat rear entrance Leyland Lion
	727-8;	SY3549/64	32 seat rear entrance Albion
	729-32;	SY3659-62	31 seat rear entrance Leyland Lion
	733-5;	SY4125-7	32 seat front entrance Leyland Lion
	590;	SY4240	30 seat rear entrance Albion
	591-2;	SY4238-9	30 seat front entrance Albion
	—	SY4506-7	32 seat front entrance Bristol
	—	SY4730-1	30 seat double entrance Bristol
L01-4		SY5441-4	32 seat rear entrance Leyland Tiger
L05-8		SY5712-5	32 seat rear entrance Leyland Tiger

The rear entrances on the Albions were of the "cut-away" type, while those of the other types were not. On the Bristols a low collapsible gate was fitted across the bottom of the rear steps, this door not being used in winter. These and the Leyland Tigers had high domed roofs, half of each group of the latter having an opening portion. All the buses had roller-blind destination screens on the front only, those of the Leyland Tigers being of a very large size. The original Leylands also carried a board along the sides of the roof inscribed Edinburgh Portobello Musselburgh Prestonpans Port Seton, while on the Albions these names were painted on the tops of the windows. The Leyland Tigers were fitted with oil engines. While delivery of Nos. 590-2 was awaited, the manufacturers lent two demonstration buses GE3516 and OF7099 which ran with the Nos. 590-1 from May to July 1930. Both were rear entrance vehicles, the latter painted blue and cream, and the former with a navy blue fabric skin.

The Coast Line 4d. ticket was green.

Long distance services are not part of this story, but for the sake of completeness it may be mentioned that Amos Proud, of Choppington, Northumberland, ran to Edinburgh Waterloo Place from Newcastle from 8 August 1927, using dark green Leylands with Edinburgh licence numbers 701-12, and were followed by other operators from the same quarter. John Turnbull, of Kelso, started a service in to Chambers Street on 4 June 1927 with blue vehicles, taken over by the S.M.T. Company in December 1927. These were followed by even longer distance services, such as those from Lancashire. The S.M.T. Company in due course acquired or participated jointly in most of these.

Meantime, in 1928, the S.M.T. were running as far as Haddington, when, early in that year, Stark, of Dunbar, started a service in to Edinburgh, using, at first, two 26 seat front entrance Lancias, 440-1; SS2247/ES6831, and two 32 seat Leyland Lions, 442/440; SS2786/2819. Almost immediately however, the S.M.T. Company came to an arrangement with the firm, and from 1 March 1928 Stark's vehicles were repainted in S.M.T. colours. The Lancias soon disappeared and as time went on new vehicles were acquired for the route, but even yet are kept apart from the S.O.L. fleet and registered in East Lothian, though lettered with the S.M.T. insignia.

An interesting episode occurred in 1929 when James Penman, of Bannockburn wished to run in to Edinburgh from Stirling. This time Edinburgh refused licences. The company therefore ran their service through Edinburgh and on to Musselburgh. Only passengers already holding return tickets could therefore be picked up in Edinburgh, but with an attractive cheap retrun

D.L.G.H.

COAST LINE LEYLAND TIGER OIL ENGINE BUS OF 1935
IN THE OLD TRAM DEPOT.

fare to Stirling many found means of meeting this requirement. Others would go to Musselburgh by other means to join the bus there. Nevertheless it is perhaps not surprising that the company and its conductresses were sometimes in court for alleged infringement of the regulations. Conversely, of course, the Falkirk and/or Stirling authorities refused to licence the S.M.T. Company for an extension of their Edinburgh-Linlithgow service with which the Scottish General Omnibus Company's service connected at the latter town. Such artificial restrictions can rarely be made effective however, and as W. Alexander & Sons Ltd. of Falkirk had become a subsidiary of the S.M.T. Company, a number of Alexander's vehicles which were already licensed in Falkirk and Stirling were repainted in S.M.T. colours and took up existing S.M.T. Edinburgh licence numbers. From July 1929 they ran the S.M.T. Edinburgh-Linlithgow service, continuing to Stirling bearing a label "On Hire to W. Alexander & Sons Ltd."! Penman was then absorbed by Alexander's and the Musselburgh scheme ceased. It may be of interest to mention that various local authorities licensing buses in their areas of jurisdiction were wont to stipulate their own regulations which could be awkward, and as an example, buses on the aforementioned route bore a notice inside "No Smoking Allowed while passing through the Burgh of Falkirk". After the introduction of the Road Traffic Act in 1931 this sort of thing, and the necessity of the S.M.T.-Alexander hybrids of course ceased. Penman usually used red Albions on their service. The Alexander vehicles used in S.M.T. livery were as follows :

1929 : 32 seat front entrance Leyland Tigers :—

| 370; MS8838 | 372;   ? | 374; MS8833 | 376;   ? |
| 371; MS8841 | 373; MS8433 | 375; MS8842 | 378; MS8836 |

1930 : 30 seat front entrance Leyland Lions :—

218; MS9033	223; MS9100	227; MS9155	230; MS9191
219; MS9034	225; MS9035	228; MS9157	231; MS9192
222; MS9101	226; MS9154	229; MS9190	232; MS9193

MS9154 had run in 1929 as No. 377. MS9155/7 had 29 seats. Also in 1930, - 31 seat rear entrance Gilfords, 233-4; MS8672 and MS 9302.

A service from Wishaw and Hamilton by Motor Ways Ltd. had also been refused the necessary licence in Edinburgh.

The Road Traffic Act which came into operation in 1931 also made the possibility of new independent operators setting up services remote. The S.M.T. Company gradually acquired the remaining local services in the outlying areas such as Dalkeith and in West Lothian etc., though Cockburn's Dalkeith-Cockpen service did not fall into the net until after the war, and Wiles of Port Seton still runs a service from there to Tranent and to Longniddry and Haddington. One new independent service should be mentioned however. Wilson, of Carnwath, secured a licence for a sparse service in from Carnwath via Tarbrax, the Lanark Road and Fountainbridge to a stance at Castle Terrace. This service started about the end of 1945. Brown front entrance Bedford buses were used.

SOME CONCLUDING NOTES

Much water has flowed under the many bridges over the Water of Leith or should we rather say many wheels have rolled along Princes Street since the days at which our story commenced. What a change has unfolded. From the dark evening when Willie Elliot's Musselburgh coach started off from Waterloo Place without him, coming to a halt at Portobello twelve minutes later, his inside passengers quite unperturbed thought only "Willie was driving unusually fast". Were the raconteurs to be located and an abler pen available another book of reminiscence could doubtless be written.

Nevertheless older readers may well recall when the descent of the Hawes Brae called for bottom gear, and even then some passengers preferred to get out and walk down. Naturally equipment would nowadays seem crude, for example the handlamp standing on the stair that sufficed for a "headlight" in later cable car days. The laborious business of getting the hood up on a charabanc when it came on to rain, (though sometimes the crew would keep on running in the hope the rain would go off!); and starting up the engine before leaving the terminus by swinging the starting-handle.

So many things were so very different in the changing pattern over the years. Until the thirties it was the rule rather than the exception for the conductor to call out the stopping-places, but this useful practice has now gone. A few older hands carried it on till after the war and some readers may recall the embellishments regularly added by a certain worthy on electric tram service 12, "Next stop the Zoo, for the monkeys, the . . .", gave him good scope for his humour and plenty of variation, but he had something to add for most stopping-places.

The complications of the cable system have already been mentioned, but the remark of an old lady watching the driver's manipulations through the saloon window as he left the Post Office expressed it neatly; "What a queer work these men have".

At the present time public transport seems to be on the down grade in face of competition from the private car. In the struggle to make ends meet services have deteriorated and even the standard of comfort is not always what is was, — an aspect more easily lost sight of. Whether this trend can be reversed time will tell : This work is an attempt only to recall the past. Those interested in the daily passenger movements into and out of the city will find a useful survey in the Scottish Geographical Society's Magazine Vol. 69 No. 3 in 1953.

LIST OF SUBSCRIBERS

J. F. D. Aherne, Edinburgh 9.

W. Allan, Edinburgh 7.

C. F. Armstrong, Gt. Missenden, Bucks.

J. Ashworth, Manchester 14.

A. Askew, London N.W.10.

R. Atkinson, Alderley Edge, Ches.

D. M. Bailey, A.C.A., Leicester.

N. Bamforth, Manchester.

E. Ballance, Goole.

T. Barker, B.Sc., Birmingham 32.

G. M. Baxter, Huddersfield.

D. Beath, Edinburgh 5.

G. Beckett, Sidmouth, Devon.

E. Beddard, Rickmansworth, Herts.

P. E. Berry, Southampton.

A. Best, Pembury, Kent.

R. P. S. Bevin, Horley, Surrey.

T. Bingham, Reading.

S. S. Birley, Sheffield.

J. K. D. Blair, C.A. Edinburgh.

J. Breeze Bentley, Guiseley, Yorks.

R. Brook, Huddersfield.

G. A. Booth, Edinburgh 15.

F. D Bottomley, Norwich.

J. P. Bowlas, Stockport.

F. M. Boxall, FSF., AMIEx. London N.8.

Dr. W. H. D. Boyes, Saltcoats, Ayrs.

A. M. Boyne, Edinburgh 15.

K. Bradshaw, Lincoln.

R. W. Brash, Ayr.

R. T. Braun, Richmond Hill, 18,L.I., N.Y., U.S.A.

I. A. Bremner, Newburgh-on-Tay, Fife.

Brighton Hove & District Omnibus Co. Ltd., Hove 3.

N. Brooks, Tottington, Nr. Bury.

S. Broomfield, Blackpool.

W. J. E. Broschart, Rockaway, 11693, N.Y., U.S.A.

A. Brown, Leeds 7.

J. S. Brownlie, Glasgow, E.1.

A. W. Brotchie, Edinburgh 9.

J. F. Bruton, London S.W.6.

H. Brown, Edinburgh 11.

J. T. Buckle, Sidcup, Kent.

H. Butter, Chateau-d'Oex, Switzerland.

I. M. Campbell, Inverbervie, Angus

W. A. Camwell, Birmingham 20.

P. J. Cardno, Huddersfield.

C. Carter, London S.W.12.

K. E. Catford, Edinburgh 4.

R. D. Caton, Birkenhead.

W. Cheyne, Edinburgh 12.

I. M. Church, Leiston, Suffolk.

J. W. Circuitt, Sale.

F. F. Clough, Upper Colwyn Bay.

A. M. Clark, Bristol, 9.

G. B. Claydon, Birmingham 23.

D. G. Coakham, A.R.I.B.A., Bangor Co. Down.

A. J. Cocker, Oldham.

E. B. Coghill, Bearsden, Glasgow

M. G. Collignon, Eastbourne.

392

G. M. Colman, L.R.A.M., A.R.C.M., London N.12.

W. B. Connell, Billericay, Essex.

B. Connelly, Gidea Park, Essex.

B. Cook, Illinois, U.S.A.

I. M. Coonie, Paisley.

Insp. B. O. Cooper, Luanshya, Rhodesia.

J. Copland, Bradford 8.

D. Cormack, Lockerbie, Dumfrieshire.

I. L. Cormack, M.A., Glasgow.

J. E. Cull, Worcester.

D. J. Currie, Burntisland, Fife.

P. Daniels, Chessington, Surrey.

G . H. Davidson, Woolwich, S.E.18.

J. J. Davis, M.Sc. (Eng), A.M.I.Mech.E., London, S.W.16.

Dr. R. P. Doig, Dundee

B. Donald, Leeds 15.

A. J. Douglas, Kilmarnock.

A. Doyle, Edinburgh.

G. Druce, Croydon.

J. E. Dunabin, Warrington.

I. Dunnet, Edinburgh 3.

Eames (Reading) Ltd., Reading.

T. J. Edgington, Rickmansworth, Herts.

D. W. Elliott, Scarborough.

J. A. N. Emslie, Glasgow.

W. T. Evans, Sydney, Australia.

K. A. J. Everett, London E.10.

Edward Exley Ltd., Baslow, Derbys.

J. N. Faill, Newcastle-on-Tyne.

D. F. Felton, Birmingham 25.

G. S. Ferrier, Stornoway.

L. N. Field, Bromley, Kent.

A. G. R. Findlay, Perth.

W. Fisher, Edinburgh 7.

N. N. Forbes, Liverpool 22.

A. R. Forsyth, C.A., Brechin, Angus.

C. Galletly, Glasgow W.3.

Major J. Galletly, T.D. A.R.I.B.A., A.M.T.P.I., F.R.I.A.S., Aberdeen.

P. R. Geissler, Edinburgh 6.

L. A. Gibson, Broadstairs.

D. S. Giles, Wescliff-on-Sea.

D. Gill, Hazel Grove, Cheshire.

I. C. Gillespie, A.M.I.C.E., Greenock.

J. C. Gillham, Ealing W.5.

L. H. Goddard, Worthing.

A. H. Gould, Glasgow, W.1.

E. Gray, B.Sc. (Econ) AD.B., Salford 6.

F. P. Groves, Newton Aycliffe, Co. Durham.

G. L. Gundry, New Malden, Surrey.

A. G. Gunn, A.R.I.C.S., Edinburgh 10.

R. Hadley, Purley, Surey

H. L. Hale, Birmingham 16.

J. J. Halley, Ashford, Middx.

Dr. R. S. B. Hamilton, Southampton.

R. N. Hannay, Wolverhampton.

E. N. C. Haywood, Nottingham.

G. S. Hearse, Corbridge, Northumberland.

W. S. Heaton, Flixton, Lancs.

R. G. Hemsall, Southsea.

Dr. R. P. Hendry, Rugby.

W. Hennigan, Sheffield 5.

Dipl.-Ing M. Heyneck, Saarburger Strabe 27. Germany.

D. D. Higgins, Leeds 8.

B. Hodgkinson, Stansted, Essex.

P. T. Hodgson, Greenford, Middx.

J. K. Holdsworth, Huddersfield.

R. Holroyd, Ilkley.

E. Hudson, Cleethorpes.

H. J. P. Hudson, Huddersfield.

R. H. Hughes, Altrincham.

D. Hunt, Maybole, Ayrs.

M. M. Hunter, Edinburgh 3.

J. T. Inglis, M.A. Edinburgh 10.

A. H. Jacob, Liverpool 13.

R. E. Jack, Edinburgh 10.

A. B. James, Oxford.

D. M. Jepson, Grantham.

H. V. Jinks, Oxford.

N. Johnstone, Victoria, Australia.

A. E. Jones, Chatham, Kent.

Miss W. Jones, F.B.S.C., F.I.P.S.,
Wrexham, Denbighs.

J. W. Jordan, London N.W.6.

J. Joyce, London S.W.20.

D. Kaye, Worthing.

C. Kidd, Manchester 22.

D. M. Kirby, Leicester.

D. P. Kirker, Auckland,
New Zealand.

C. F. Klapper, Bromley, Kent.

G. H. Laird, Glasgow, C.4.

Miss A. M. Lamb, London S.W.11.

G. E. Langmuir, Bearsden, Glasgow.

S. P. Laursen, Randers, Denmark.

C. E. Lee, London W.C.1.

A. A. Leese, Stafford.

Leith Dock Commission,
Edinburgh 6.

C. J. Lent, Essington, Staffs.

R. Lewis, Chilwell, Notts.

G. C. Lewthwaite, Leeds 12.

H. O. Lintern, North Hykeham,

D. Littler, Huyton-with-Roby, Lancs.

F. N. T. Lloyd-Jones, Wigan.

K. A. Lockett, Stockport.

E. S. Lomax, Edinburgh 3.

H. Luff, London S.W.8.

A. Lucking, East Grinstead.
Lincs.

J. W. Lumley, London S.E.25.

L. Mann, Hockley, Essex.

I. McGregor, Glasgow S.1.

Dr. W. H. McKendrick, Blackwood.
Mon.

W. McDonald, Glasgow C.3.

J. I. McIntosh, Edinburgh 5.

H. Mackie, London S.W.12.

N. D. G. MacKenzie, Reading.

J. Mackenzie, London S.E. 15.

R. D. McLeod, Edinburgh 9.

J. G. H. McLoughlin, Edinburgh 4.

W. D. McMillan, Glasgow N.1.

N. S. C. Macmillan, Glasgow.

Dr. W. G. McCutcheon, Morley,
Yorks.

F. McCallum, Aberdeen.

K. P. G. Markland, Kirkuk, Iraq.

E. Manock, Walshaw, Lancs.

F. R. Martin, B.A., Dewsbury.

W. R. Mason, Edinburgh 3.

B. B. Mattews, Manchester 14.

D. J. Mechem, Burgess Hill, Sussex.

A. Meeson-Smith, Southall, Middx.

I. W. M. Menzies, Ontario, Canada.

J. C. Miller, Edinburgh.

R. L. Mitchell, Halifax.

D. J. Mitchell, Halifax.

M. J. Mitchell, Portlethen,
Kincardineshire.

J. B. Morris, Birmingham 12.

H. R. Morton, Southport.

W. Morton, Edinburgh 9.

P. H. Mountford, M.A., Orwell,
Herts.

J. K. Nelon, Ilford, Essex.

G. L. Newcombe, New Barnet,
Herts.

B. R. Newman, London N.22.

R. G. E. Newman, Lancing, Sussex.

L. M. R. Nicholson, Bromley, Kent.

R. T. Ninnis, Epsom, Surrey.

A. C. Noon, Liverpool 17.

H. A. Norris, London S.E.6

J. R. Nuttall, Pool-in-Wharfedale,
Yorks.

J. O'Brien, London S.W.2.

E. Ogden, Lydgate, Lancs.

W. D. Oliphant, North Berwick.

A. D. Packer, Market Drayton, Salop.

F. M. Palmer, Watertown, Mass. U.S.A.

R. B. Parr, Bingley.

E. C. Parsons, Sheffield 3.

G. K. Peacock, Liverpool 12.

H. A. H. Pearmain, Ilford, Essex.

F. K. Pearson, Poulton Le Fylde, Lancs.

D. R. Pease, Ilford.

J. L. Perkins, Edgware, Middx.

J. D. Petty, B.Sc. A.M.I.Mech.E., Middlesborough.

W. S. Philip, Aberdeen.

A. Pickard, Glasgow N.2.

G. R. Pickles, Overstrand, Norfolk.

K. P. Plant, Sheffield 6.

G. H. Platt, Purley, Surrey.

E. R. Pollard, Little Sutton, Wirral.

G. C. Potter, Sale.

D. M. Pratt, Shelton Lock, Derbys.

A. Prentice. Edinburgh 3.

J. H. Price, London S.E.19.

B. J. Prigmore, London, S.W.7.

R. W. Rattray, Keighley.

C. L. Rayner, Southend-on-Sea.

H. M. Rea, Bangor, Co. Down.

Miss E. Read, Cape Town, S. Africa.

Dr. R. A. Read, T.D., Edinburgh 9.

A. Redpath, Edingburgh 12.

J. S. Reeves, Bognor Regis.

"J. J." W. Richards, Birmingham 28.

C. D. Riley, Huddersfield.

I. T. Rix, Norwich.

J. G. Robertson, Leeds 11.

J. Robertson, Edinburgh 7.

M. J. Robertson, Edinburgh 7.

W. G. F. Roberts, Manchester 20.

C. D. Robinson, A.T.D., N.D.D., Durham.

S. G. Robinson, Billingshurst, Sussex.

Joachim von Rohr, Dusseldorf.

C. Romain, Swindon, Wilts.

Lt. D. W. Ronald, R.E.,

D. H. Rowledge, Derby.

H. L. Runnett, Handforth, Cheshire. Urswick, Lancs.

W. D. Ryan, Newcastle-under-Lyme.

G. M. Sawford, London N.22.

D. Scoular, Edinburgh 12.

W. S. Sellar, Edinburgh 10.

B. A. Sharpe, Carshalton Beeches. Surrey.

A. Simpson, Nelson, Lancs.

G. G. Simpson, Windsor, Berks.

D. E. Sinclair, Glasgow W.2.

E R. Smart, B.D.S., North Shields.

T. Smeaton, Derby.

G. Smith, Haverhill, Suffolk.

G. E. Smith, California, U.S.A.

H. F. H. Smith, Bournemouth.

K. H. Smith, Northampton.

N. F. Smith, Norwich.

S. L. Smith, Rotherham.

S. M. Swift, Manchester 13.

W. A. C. Smith, Glasgow S.1.

J. G. Smithson, M.A., A.M.I.E.E. Leicester.

G. Swift, Crowborough, Sussex.

J. Soper, Leeds 7.

H. J. Southall, Kingswinford, Staffs.

S. A. Staddon, Sunderland.

T. K. Stamp, Newcastle-on-Tyne 4.

T. Steele, Wallsend, Northumberland.

J. W. Steel, Guiseley, Yorks.

C. G. Stevens, London E.10.

J. L. Stevenson, Glasgow, S.1.

C. Stringer, Manchester 10.

Dr. G. P. Stilley, M.A., Derby.

A. Stewart, Glasgow, E.2.

E. K. Stretch, Newcastle, Staffs.

W. B. Stocks, Huddersfield.

A. J. Stoyel, Thornton Heath, Surrey.

A. R. Spencer, A.M.I.C.E., Birmingham 23.

D. H. D. Spray, London S.W.16.

K. R. Sutton, Altrincham.

W. F. Sweetman, Southend-on-Sea.

R. V. Taft, Dudley Worcs.

Dr. G. B. Tait, Dewsbury.

H. Taylor, Rochford, Essex.

P. H. Tangye, London S.E.23.

T. Taylor, Manchester.

W. Tennant, Glasgow, N.1.

A. K. Terry, Leeds 8.

W. E. C. Terry, London S.E.22.

J. Thacker, Grantham.

Dr. W. G. Thomas, Manchester.

D. L. Thomson, Glasgow W.2.

J. M. Thompson, Uttoxeter, Staffs.

L. A. Thomson, Iford, Essex.

W. A. Thornton, London S.W.2.

H. E. Tolson, A.A.I., Blackburn.

G. C. Train, Wishaw, Lanarkshire.

E. V. Trigg, Smethwick 41., Staffs.

G. R. Tribe, Hemel Hempstead.

T. L. Underwood, Jr., Washington 18 D.C., U.S.A.

R. Varley, Derby.

R. J. Varley, Manchester 20.

H. S. Waddington, West Hartlepool.

A. Walker, Edinburgh 10.

C. S. N. Walker, Cheltenham.

J. Walter, Hellerup, Danmark.

F. Ward, Ryde, Isle-of-Wight.

F. Ward, Huddersfield.

M. J. Waring, Wimborne, Dorset.

P. M. Warriner, Harrogate.

B. S. Waterson, Dundee, Angus.

A. J. Watkins, Bexley, Kent.

S. J. Watson, Kidderminster.

A. G. Wells, M.P.S., Canterbury.

D. Wheatley, Birmingham 26.

S. N. J. White, Wolverhampton.

W. Wike, Bury.

H. Williams, Manchester 23.

S. Williams, Nottingham.

J. R. Williamson, Edinburgh 4.

M. S. Wilson, Leeds 12.

R. T. Wilson, Walsall, Staffs.

R. J. S. Wiseman, B.A., Mansfield, Notts.

J. L. Wood, Glasgow S.2.

R. S. Wood, Prestwich, Lancs.

B. Woodriff, B.A., Kingston-upon-Thames.

C. A. Woodside, New South Wales, Australia.

C. Wright, Bradford 6.

M. G. C. Wyatt Wheeler, F.S.A., Randwick, Glos.

K. Yates, Birmingham 6.

I. A. Yearsley, London, S.W.15.

G. A. Yeomans, Hilton, Derbys.

W. J. Young, Leeds 16.

F. W. York, Fareham, Hants.

PUBLISHERS NOTE

The Publishers would like to take this opportunity of thanking all subscribers for their interest and subscriptions, without which the production of this valuable addition to historical transport publications would not have been possible.

OUR

OTHER PUBLICATIONS ON TRANSPORT

ARE

PENNINE JOURNEY by W. B. Stocks

THE MANCHESTER TRAM by Ian Yearsley

HUDDERSFIELD TRAMWAYS by Roy Brook

The publishers will gladly furnish particulars of the above books

THE ADVERTISER PRESS LIMITED
Premier Works
Paddock Head, Huddersfield